The Injustice of Place

Also by Kathryn J. Edin and H. Luke Shaefer

$2.00 a Day: Living on Almost Nothing in America

The Injustice of Place

UNCOVERING THE LEGACY OF POVERTY IN AMERICA

Kathryn J. Edin, H. Luke Shaefer,
and Timothy J. Nelson

MARINER BOOKS
New York   Boston

HarperCollins books may be purchased for educational, business, or sales promotional use. For information, please email the Special Markets Department at SPsales@harpercollins.com.

FIRST EDITION

Designed by Chloe Foster

Library of Congress Cataloging-in-Publication Data

Names: Edin, Kathryn, 1962– author. | Shaefer, H. Luke, author. | Nelson, Timothy Jon, author.
Title: The injustice of place : uncovering the legacy of poverty in America / Kathryn J. Edin, H. Luke Shaefer, and Timothy J. Nelson.
Description: First edition. | New York : Mariner Books, [2023] | Includes bibliographical references and index.
Identifiers: LCCN 2023009674 (print) | LCCN 2023009675 (ebook) | ISBN 9780063239494 (hardcover) | ISBN 9780063239524 (paperback) | ISBN 9780063239500 (ebook)
Subjects: LCSH: Poverty—United States. | Rural poor—United States. | Cities and towns—United States. | United States—Economic conditions—Regional disparities.
Classification: LCC HC110.P6 E344 2023 (print) | LCC HC110.P6 (ebook) | DDC 339.4/60973—dc23/eng/20230302
LC record available at https://lccn.loc.gov/2023009674
LC ebook record available at https://lccn.loc.gov/2023009675

23 24 25 26 27 LBC 5 4 3 2 1

We dedicate this book to the scholars who painted indelible portraits of life in America's internal colonies nearly a century ago: Charles S. Johnson, William Boyd "Allison" Davis, Burleigh B. Gardner, Mary R. Gardner, Ida B. Wells, Hortense Powdermaker, John Dollard, Paul S. Taylor, and James S. Brown.

Contents

Introduction   1

1. America's Internal Colonies   19

2. Separate, Unequal   39

3. Nothing to Do Here but Drugs   69

4. A Tradition of Violence   94

5. Little Kingdoms   122

6. The Invisible Hand   147

7. Revolt and Retribution   169

8. The Sins of Our Fathers   198

9. Healing America's Internal Colonies   223

Acknowledgments   245

Appendix A: The History and Theory of Internal Colonies   251

Appendix B: The Index of Deep Disadvantage   261

Notes   275

Credits   327

Index   329

Introduction

IT IS HARD TO SAY exactly when we first noticed the pattern. Just before we hit the outskirts of a Cotton Belt town, the fields would give way to a string of gleaming white antebellum homes with large lawns, old-growth trees, and grand entrances framed by columns reaching two or three stories high. Merging onto the majestic arterial boulevards leading into town, we would see more imposing homes presiding over meticulously manicured grounds.

In Sparta, a rural hamlet near Augusta, Georgia, it appears as though someone has invested millions to restore an elegant Greek Revival home. New windows and shutters gleam. Yet just across the street lies a dilapidated shack, one room deep, with a sagging roof. Over in Demopolis, Alabama, sits the venerable Gaineswood, a massive structure known for its elaborate interior suites, including domed ceilings, remarkable decorative arts, and original antebellum furnishings. Left out of the photos on Gaineswood's website and tourist brochures are the aging wood cottages in varying states of disrepair, the tumbledown trailers, and the sagging modular houses that flank the historic home.

County seats in the region typically feature a leafy square where a courthouse of sometimes massive proportions—and stunning architectural beauty—stands over streets that are hollowed-out carcasses of a more prosperous time. There is often an imposing Confederate monument on the courthouse lawn honoring soldiers of the war waged a century and a half ago. Nearly without fail, there is at least one upscale business—a home goods store, clothing boutique, high-end restaurant, art gallery, or gourmet coffee shop—catering not to the average resident but to the remnants of the white gentry and to tourists who come to see the grand homes.

What becomes abundantly clear as we travel across the country to see America's most deeply disadvantaged places firsthand is that they are often home not only to desperate poverty but also to considerable wealth.

In the fall of 2017, a program officer named Andrea Ducas at the Robert Wood Johnson Foundation wrote to us out of the blue. Two of us (Kathy and Luke) had written a book that combined insights drawn from national poverty data and ethnography to paint a picture of the unseen lives of some of America's poorest *families*—those living on cash incomes of less than $2 per person per day. Would we, she asked, be interested in collaborating on a project to do the same thing for America's poorest *places*?

Immediately, we were intrigued by the idea of studying places instead of people. The social sciences had a rich tradition of community studies from about the turn of the twentieth century onward. Yet broadly speaking, these days the proud tradition of the community study seems a bit out of vogue. More recently, prominent work in the social sciences conducted by towering figures such as William Julius Wilson, who wrote the landmark book *The Truly Disadvantaged*, theorized that place is key to understanding how people's lives unfold. But most of this work has focused on neighborhoods in big cities. Matthew Desmond has made the case that poverty is not just the experience of not having enough, but is the by-product of relationships between the actual people—tenant and landlord, worker and employer—within a place. Following this idea to its logical end means studying the relationships among a whole variety of actors in a given community. We wondered: Why were so few of our colleagues studying whole communities? Why weren't we?

Ducas raised another question: Could we understand poverty

more holistically if we included not only income as a measure but health as well? When President Lyndon B. Johnson declared an "unconditional war on poverty" on January 8, 1964, the nation lacked any method of counting the poor, or even a firm notion of how poverty should be defined. As Johnson led the nation into this "war," his administration scrambled to come up with a measure that could be used to chart progress. The gauge, it was decided, would be the minimum amount needed to put food on the table multiplied by three (at the time, food constituted a third of the average family budget). Ever since, poverty researchers have been locked in endless debate about how poverty should be measured. Nonetheless, in virtually all cases, poverty has continued to be defined as a lack of income.

While there is no doubt that income is a vital indicator of well-being, it had become clear to us that it was just one part of a bigger picture. Thus, we decided to harness the immense growth in the nation's data infrastructure to build a more nuanced way to measure community disadvantage than had ever before been possible.

To assess the level of disadvantage in a community, such as a county or a city, we combined traditional income-based measures with other markers, including health. Especially in the United States, health outcomes vary tremendously by race, ethnicity, and income. In 2008, life expectancy for highly educated white males was eighty years, but only sixty-six for low-educated Black men, whose average life span resembled numbers seen in Pakistan and Mongolia. In 2011, the infant mortality rate for Black mothers in the United States was comparable to that in Grenada and just a bit better than that in Tonga. The rate for non-Hispanic whites was much closer to that in Germany and the Netherlands. Meanwhile, a tidal wave of new research was showing that a person's health is shaped more by their context—their income, family circumstances, and community characteristics, for example—than by their genetic profiles or the medical care they receive.

Ultimately, as the scope of our study of place-based disadvantage grew, we chose to incorporate two well-measured health outcomes, one that captured conditions at the start of life and the other at the end. In a particular community, what were a baby's chances of being born with low birth weight, which is closely associated with infant mortality and other threats to children's health? In that community, how long could the average person expect to live?

We also recognized the importance of measuring whether disadvantage in a particular place persisted for children growing up there. Especially in the American context, it is almost an article of faith that kids should have the opportunity to do better than their parents. Recently, a team of economists employed confidential IRS data to create a measure of intergenerational mobility (the chance that children born low-income could rise up the economic ladder) for every city and county in the nation. These researchers used tax records to follow children born in the 1980s through adulthood to see where they stood on the income ladder compared to their parents. It was already understood that there were big differences in intergenerational mobility by parental income, ethnicity, and race, but the most stunning revelation of this new research was how much variation there was by place. In some communities, a child born into poverty would probably stay low-income as an adult. Yet in others, they had a much better chance of reaching the middle class. It seemed clear to us that to measure the depth of disadvantage in a community, it would be important to include the rate of mobility from one generation to the next.

We chose to bring the term "deep disadvantage" into the conversation about measuring poverty in order to capture the complexity of the problem when a person's life chances are hindered by multiple conditions or circumstances, including by the community in which they live. Given our aims, "disadvantage" is more accurate than simply "poverty" because it implies an injustice. The term is moral. People are being held back—unfairly.

We incorporated our multidimensional measures of well-being into the Index of Deep Disadvantage, which reflects two traditional income poverty indicators (the official poverty rate and the rate of deep poverty, meaning those with incomes below half the poverty line), two markers of health (low birth weight and life expectancy), and the rate of intergenerational mobility for children who grow up low-income. Since there was no obvious way to decide which factor was more important than another, we used a sophisticated machine learning technique called "principal component analysis" to rank the roughly 3,000 counties in the United States along with the 500 most populous cities on a continuum of disadvantage that accounted for income, health, and intergenerational mobility. We were a long way from limited War on Poverty–era metrics.

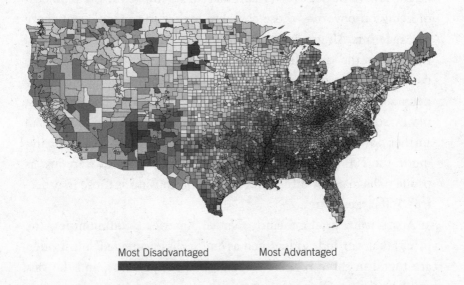

Most Disadvantaged   Most Advantaged

Immediately, we could see from the rankings that the geographical pattern was stark. The first surprise—especially for three professors who had spent our careers studying urban poverty—was that the "most disadvantaged" places on our index were mostly rural. There is considerable poverty in cities like Chicago, Los Angeles, and New York. But in our apples-to-apples comparison, none of those cities ranked even among the 600 most disadvantaged places in the nation. For the most part, the only cities and urban counties to find themselves among the most disadvantaged were a relatively small number of industrial municipalities in the Northeast and Midwest, such as Cleveland, Detroit, and Rochester.

Among the rural counties at the top of the list, what we found didn't fit what most people think of as "rural." While some of these were majority-white, many, indeed most, were communities of Black and Hispanic Americans. We could see, too, that many places with large Native American populations ranked among the most disadvantaged in the nation (19 of the top 200). Beyond these, though, not one community in the western part of the United States registered among the "most disadvantaged" (those in the top fifth). While some might say we ought to have considered the impact of the high cost of living on poverty—those costs are higher in some places—there are trade-offs. Although people pay more for housing in those places, there are at the same time structural advantages in those areas of the country, such as good health care systems, a more generous safety net, public transportation, and higher-quality schools. This, we think, is why some high-cost big cities like San Francisco and Seattle fall further down our index than expected. We also found that those living in the 200 most disadvantaged places on our index were just as prone to have major difficulties paying for housing as those in America's 500 largest cities.

Apart from predominantly Native American communities, the places that our index identified as "most disadvantaged" most often are found in three regions—Appalachia, South Texas, and the vast southern Cotton Belt running across seven states.

To learn more about these places, we sent teams of researchers to specific locales in the summer of 2019. The Mississippi Delta, also known as the Yazoo-Mississippi Delta, is a region that encompasses portions of Mississippi, Louisiana, Arkansas, and Tennessee, including Leflore County, Mississippi. That's where Ryan Parsons was living while conducting his dissertation research when he joined our team. Jasmine Simington and Meg Duffy spent that summer in Marion County, in the Pee Dee region of South Carolina, which switched from cotton to tobacco production in the late nineteenth century. Both communities ranked among the most disadvantaged majority-Black places in the nation. Liv Mann and Emily Miller spent the summer in Clay County, in eastern Kentucky, one of the most disadvantaged majority-white places in the country. Lanora Johnson divided her time between the Pee Dee region and eastern Kentucky. In each location, we engaged ordinary residents and community leaders in lengthy conversations. We participated in community events such as parades, festivals, and fundraisers. We volunteered at local charities. On multiple visits to each of these places, we—Kathy, Luke, and Tim—met with a subset of families and leaders, conducting follow-up interviews to pursue additional themes.

The following fall, Emily and Meg made initial forays into two counties that are among the most disadvantaged majority-Hispanic places in America: Zavala and Brooks Counties, in South Texas. Several months later, we visited the area, striking up impromptu conversations in parking lots and cafés and holding a focus group with community leaders who were gracious enough to show up on a Friday morning at the local parish hall. The plan was to send a team of researchers to these South Texas communities in the summer of 2020.

Then the COVID-19 pandemic intervened, interrupting our ability to travel and to have face-to-face conversations. Locked down in our homes, we turned to history books, government reports, old ethnographic accounts, and first-person narratives—some penned more than a century ago—to learn more. We conducted interviews virtually. As the pandemic ebbed in the early summer of 2021, we, along with researchers Maricruz Moya, Karen Kling, and Christine Jang-Trettien, descended on South Texas.

Throughout, our team met online to exchange stories. We soon learned that every place we were studying was a "first in the nation" or a "capital of the world" of something. Did you know that Marion County's largest city, Mullins, was once known as the "Tobacco

Capital of South Carolina," the very place where the coveted "bright leaf" strain was first introduced to the state, earning some of the planters who grew it—but not their tenant labor—small fortunes? Or that before Kentucky's Clay County had coal mines, it was once the salt-mining epicenter of the eastern United States, its purveyors deploying the labor of enslaved people to generate wealth along its creek beds? Is it news to you that it was in Leflore County, Mississippi, and the surrounding area that the antebellum cotton plantation economy was most faithfully reproduced *after* the Civil War, with vast profits drawn from the labor of Black tenant farmers? Did you know that Brooks County, Texas, once boasted the largest Jersey dairy cattle herd in the world, known far and wide for the delicious butter carrying the county seat's name, Falfurrias? Did you realize that the seat of Zavala County, Crystal City, once laid claim to the title "Spinach Capital of the World"?

The pandemic-inspired immersion in local history was a crucial turning point for our understanding of America's most deeply disadvantaged places. As we pored over our regions' pasts, we began to realize that what they shared in common was a history of intensive resource extraction and profound human exploitation not seen to the same degree elsewhere in the United States. In these places, it was not enough to be comfortably profiting from one's enterprise. The goal of the landowning class was to build vast wealth on the backs of those laboring on the land. In each place, this economic pattern emerged (or, in the case of the Cotton Belt, fully flourished) in the late nineteenth or early twentieth century. In each place, one industry linked to national and global markets came to dominate the economy, a pattern that held, broadly, into the 1960s, when King Cotton, King Coal, and the others would bow to the twin forces of automation and competition from global markets.

When we began sending teams to specific locales, we did not know that these patterns would be shared to such a profound degree. Yet we would have had to be exceedingly dull or stubborn to have missed the fact that these places resembled, well, colonies. Internal colonies within the borders of the United States. Using terminology such as "nation within a nation" or "colony" to describe the exploitation of communities of color within the United States has a long history among Black scholars and activists (notable proponents have included Frederick Douglass, Kenneth Clark, Stokely Carmichael, and Malcolm X), among others. We set out to build on this work.

For the places we identified as the most deeply disadvantaged, as the fallout from systems of historic inequality started to come clear, specific themes began to emerge.

In the antebellum era, Clay County, Kentucky, was home to both the mighty salt barons, whose works lined the banks of the creeks, and a tapestry of subsistence farms. Big Timber and Big Coal took over after the Civil War. Today, the opioid crisis is ravaging the region. Locals lament the decline of the local movie theater—now a Pentecostal church—and the loss of the bowling alley; numerous bars, cafés, and beauty salons; and a park that has been plowed under for a highway construction project. The social infrastructure of a community that draws people together and creates the safety net that, when strong, can catch people when they fall has grown weak. People blame the rise of opioid use on the fact that in this place, there is "nothing to do but drugs."

In South Texas, spinach and onion fields were once so vast they met the sky at the vanishing point in almost every direction, yielding fabulous profits for those who owned the land. In some areas, the fields still stretch to the horizon today. Yet extreme hardship was the lot of the landless laborers who planted and harvested those crops. Forced to migrate to find work the rest of the year, generations of children were robbed of their right to a decent education. Even today, adult illiteracy rates in these South Texas communities are among the highest in the nation. High school graduation rates among the younger generation have soared, but test scores remain abysmal, especially in reading.

Residents of every place we got to know for this book can recount stories of local government corruption: the FBI storming City Hall to arrest nearly every member of city government; local officials imprisoned for buying votes and collaborating with drug dealers; corporations getting sweetheart deals to bring a new factory to town but never delivering. Yet when leaders are asked to name the biggest challenges facing their communities, government corruption rarely comes up. Instead, they usually focus on the flaws of the poor.

People don't need to do more than scan the front page of the *Greenwood Commonwealth*, the newspaper that serves Leflore County, Mississippi, to know that violence is an issue. It is the number one problem facing the community according to Black residents we spoke to, though white folks were largely oblivious to it. As we would soon learn, this county and the larger region it represents—the vast Cotton Belt stretching from the Carolinas to eastern Arkansas and Louisiana—is indeed among the most violent in the nation. Violence has plagued this region for well over a century.

In Marion County, South Carolina, it seemed that every one of our conversations started with a discussion of the flooding that had come in the wake of back-to-back hurricanes. On the white side of the small, hard-hit town of Nichols, spanking-new replacement homes had risen. In contrast, homes in the Black part of town and in Sellers, a nearly all-Black hamlet where the flooding had devastated much of the town, were still moldering. Many houses were rendered uninhabitable, though some people were nonetheless living in them. As we dug deeper we learned that in myriad ways those who already had been struggling before the floods were struggling even more after. Centuries-old racial inequality in the Pee Dee region deepened in the wake of the disasters, due to systemic racism encoded in the very government programs that were supposed to help people recover.

We initially thought that these themes—unequal schooling, the collapse of social infrastructure (the places where people build social bonds), violence, entrenched public corruption, and structural racism embedded in government programs—were at least somewhat unique to each place. Yet what turned out to be most remarkable was the degree to which they were shared.

Soon after we mapped our index for the first time back in 2018, one of our researchers, Ryan Parsons, showed us another map, from 1860, depicting enslavement in the South on the eve of the Civil War. The correspondence between this map and the map of our index showing contemporary regions of deepest disadvantage was chilling. Along with a growing number of scholars of history and race, we began asking this question: Could it be that the social and economic relations in a place a century and a half ago continue to shape conditions in that place today? The message was clear: To understand the challenges facing a place of deep disadvantage, the first step is to learn about its past.

In each of these internal colonies, the past appeared to be prologue to the present. But how? We began by exploring the history of the Cotton Belt. We supplemented the many volumes of systematic, rich description authored by prominent Black sociologist Charles S. Johnson of Fisk University with essays by anti-lynching activist Ida B. Wells. We studied the meticulous ethnographic work of Black anthropologist William Boyd "Allison" Davis and his white coauthors, and that of anthropologist Hortense Powdermaker and psychologist John Dollard, both white scholars hailing from Yale University. Each had studied a portion of the Cotton Belt in the late 1920s and early 1930s when the cotton economy reached its apex. Noted historical works like James C. Cobb's *The Most Southern Place on Earth* also offered valuable insights. There were vital first-person accounts like that of Ned Cobb, a Black Alabama tenant farmer who spent a decade in prison for standing up to a white landlord in support of a neighboring tenant's rights, and whose story is captured in Theodore Rosengarten's award-winning *All God's Dangers*. These and other works chronicled life in the Cotton Belt from the time when the first white settlers arrived. Fortunately, for each of the other regions, there were similar gems. From these texts, we began to stitch together a sense of how the history of these places has shaped the present.

Tribal lands are an essential chapter in the story of America's

Our Map of Deep Disadvantage Compared to a Map of Enslavement from 1860

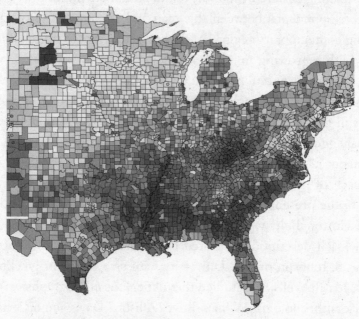

Most Disadvantaged   Most Advantaged

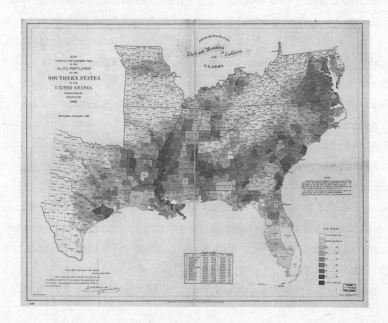

internal colonies. After enslavement and disease had decimated the Native American population, reservations served as the holding ground for a people ruthlessly removed or pushed back to make way for the vast economic and human exploitation that would take place across the Cotton Belt, Appalachia, and South Texas. For this book, we wanted to include one of the Native American tribal lands that appeared high on our index. Building relationships to conduct research on tribal lands, however, takes time. While we tried to make connections with tribal researchers who had the vital expertise and relationships we lacked, the way forward became fraught, to say the least, as the COVID-19 pandemic claimed a disproportionate share of Native lives. Several communities that ranked highest on our index—including number-two-ranked Oglala Lakota County in South Dakota, home to the Pine Ridge reservation—made national news when tribal governments imposed lockdowns and installed checkpoints on state and interstate highways to protect their citizens from outsiders who might be carriers of the disease. Actions such as these sparked a power struggle with South Dakota governor Kristi Noem, who declared the checkpoints illegal. We acknowledge that this critical chapter remains unwritten in this book.

Undoubtedly, if we had chosen different communities within the regions we focus on here, additional themes would have emerged. The insights we share in these pages are just the tip of the iceberg. As much as anything, this book is meant to illustrate an approach: starting with the nation's rich big-data infrastructure to identify pockets of deep disadvantage, listening carefully to community members through ethnographic research in specific locales within these regions, attending carefully to the role of history, and, when possible, returning to big data to test the hypotheses generated on the ground.

After all the interviews had been conducted in each of these regions, after all the histories, ethnographies, government reports, and first-person accounts had been read, an additional step was required. In the summer of 2021, two of us (Kathy and Tim) got into a car and began a fourteen-state road trip. We wanted to visit as many of the top 200 places on the index as we could. We felt that, before characterizing them, it was imperative that we drive around each community, take a walk around the county courthouse, stop at a diner or coffee shop, and strike up informal conversations with locals.

Despite the considerable distances involved, we made it to 132 of the top 200 places of deepest disadvantage. Adding in 23 places that we had been to for other research, we visited a total of 155 locations, more than 75 percent of the top 200. Our objective was to ensure that the index reflected truth on the ground. Were there observable differences between the top 200 and those a little lower down the index? Could we sense a difference once we crossed the county line separating an advantaged from a disadvantaged place? The answer to both questions in nearly all cases was a resounding yes.

But there were exceptions. Our data were drawn from reputable sources, yet errors are always possible. This became clear when we traveled to the town of Radford, Virginia, which purportedly ranked 45th on the index. Instead of the vacant buildings and unkempt lots observed elsewhere on our journey, the place resembled a stage set for Thornton Wilder's play *Our Town*. Digging deeper, we learned that Radford and several other Virginia cities ranking high on the index purportedly had life span averages so short that they were not just implausible but downright unbelievable. We concluded that, due to complex reasons involving administrative jurisdictions in these places, the Centers for Disease Control and Prevention numbers were wrong. We adjusted.

The trip was a safeguard against these errors. Yet an additional benefit of conducting this visual audit was in the stories it revealed. Driving through the countryside in some of these regions, one can be lulled by the beauty of the landscape, as in the rolling hills of Alabama, with their tidy pecan groves, bucolic grazing lands dotted with cattle, and fields rich with soybeans and corn. But in both the outskirts of the cities and their downtowns, blight is prevalent, and the passerby realizes that each is in fact a very disadvantaged place.

In these places, there are ample reminders of the past. In Montgomery, Alabama, for example, which comes in at number 244 on our index, we toured two sites overseen by the Equal Justice Initiative: the Legacy Museum, colloquially known as the "lynching museum," and the National Memorial for Peace and Justice, with its display of eight hundred granite slabs resembling caskets—one for each county where lynching crimes took place between 1877 and 1950. At the memorial, we learned that forty-eight lynchings have been documented in Leflore County, Mississippi, alone.

Next we explored the Mississippi Delta, the portion of the Cotton Belt along the Mississippi River. Traveling south on the Mississippi side, we reached Mound Bayou, in Bolivar County. Established in 1887 by former slaves, the settlement was designed to be a self-reliant community of Black Americans, home to Black-owned farms, businesses, schools, hospitals, and banks. Theodore Roosevelt praised Mound Bayou as "the Jewel of the Delta," while Booker T. Washington called the community a model of "thrift and self-government." For decades it prospered, shielding residents from Jim Crow. But it experienced a decline in the second half of the twentieth century due to market fluctuations, increasing rates of racial integration in other parts of the nation, and the many pernicious forces that have dispossessed the vast majority of Black farm owners across the nation.

Over in central Appalachia, we drove through the remains of company towns, often only one or two streets wide, lining the banks of the creeks in the hollows—narrow valleys that sometimes stretch for miles between the mountains. We traveled through Benham, Kentucky, in Harlan County, a town built by the International Harvester Company, and to the town of Lynch, also company owned. There is still a handsome brick building there bearing a historical marker titled "Lynch Colored School." The school was built for the Black high school students of Benham and Lynch by the US Coal and Coke Company in 1923, and it was said to be the finest Black school around. The building now sits vacant, while the former white school has been converted into a bed-and-breakfast. Also in Lynch, next door to the now defunct Mine Portal 31, are the communal baths the company built for the miners, today adapted for other uses. Across the street is a gourmet coffee shop and bakery.

From these clues, one might think that the mine workers were well cared for, but the former company homes, with their crude cookie-cutter architecture and porches lined with mismatched, worn couches and chairs, tell a different story. Today the houses are generally so cramped (given the large families) that the occupants' possessions spill out onto their lawns, mixing in with the junk cars and broken appliances that are retained for spare parts. Writing in the 1960s, noted local author Harry M. Caudill described how employers like International Harvester anticipated the massive decline in the demand for labor due to impending automation and competition from other fossil fuels. In light of this, the companies were eager to divest from their company-owned homes. Cynically, they offered them for purchase to the miners, ostensibly to improve the workers' morale, luring them with promises that there would be work for them for years to come. Then came the massive layoffs.

As we turned from studying people to studying places, we came to the task equipped with tools our predecessors could only dream of— data that offer a picture of the conditions of America's communities that is more comprehensive than ever before. These tools, combined with on-the-ground ethnography, and historical data, shine a bright light on where people experience the toughest and most intractable problems across the nation. We are now armed with new revelations about poverty and a new understanding of how deeply disadvantage is woven into the history and present-day institutional fabric of particular places. In the final chapter of this book, we turn to the idea that our nation must launch a fresh offensive against poverty with a relentless focus on the country's most deeply disadvantaged regions.

The Injustice of Place tells the stories of America's internal colonies—

where disadvantage has been endemic for generations—and calls us to envision a different future, where no corner of the country is left behind. To quote President Lyndon Johnson, the architect of the War on Poverty, "The Great Society rests on abundance and liberty for all. It demands an end to poverty and racial injustice, to which we are totally committed in our time."

1

America's Internal Colonies

TODAY, THE MOST OBVIOUS VESTIGE of the nation's once vast internal colonies are the myriad symbols that celebrate their past. In Crystal City, Texas, Popeye—with trademark pipe stem clenched in his wide mouth, each forearm the size of a Butterball turkey—stands six feet high on a round pedestal in the middle of downtown. The inscription on the statue's base—"The Spinach Capital of the World"—illuminates why this South Texas city has honored the cartoon character for so many decades.

Crystal City lies in the heart of what is known as the Winter Garden of Texas, a multicounty region roughly ninety miles southwest of San Antonio that was once an agricultural giant in the cultivation of spinach, onions, and other irrigated vegetables. The industry ballooned in the 1920s as new rail lines were laid and the invention of the refrigerated railcar permitted producers to transport onion bulbs and leafy greens across the nation. As the prominent placement of the Popeye statue attests, Crystal City still celebrates this legacy. Each year the city hosts the Crystal City Spinach Festival. Activities include a spinach-eating contest (medical waiver required) and a cook-off. Young women and girls compete to be part of the Spinach Festival Queen's Court. Winners ride on a special float festooned with colorful flower arrangements and balloons as the festival parade winds through town. Spinach green and gold are the high school colors.

As you travel along Mississippi Highway 7, at the Greenwood city line, a large sign welcomes you to "The Cotton Capital of the

World," the calligraphy bracketed by stylized cotton bolls and underlined with the circular logos of the town's civic organizations. In Greenwood, cotton has held pride of place since Reconstruction, despite the threat of the boll weevil and the collapse of the cotton market in the late 1800s and again during the Great Depression. Each year, the Junior Auxiliary of Greenwood hosts the Cotton Ball fundraiser, which, according to the *Greenwood Commonwealth*, "features the crowning of the King and Queen of Cotton. . . . Guests enjoy a variety of activities, including live and silent auctions, a patron's party, presentation of the Cotton Ball maids, and live entertainment."

Almost seven hundred miles east of Greenwood, where the historic Cotton Belt melts into the Tobacco Belt, lies the coastal South Carolina town of Mullins, in the heart of what is known as the Pee Dee. The area is named for the Great Pee Dee River and its many tributaries, which flow south through the region from the North Carolina border before joining the Atlantic Ocean at Winyah Bay. Each fall, Mullins sponsors the Golden Leaf Festival and barbecue cook-off commemorating the strain of tobacco introduced to the Pee Dee in the late 1880s. This "bright leaf" strain smoked so smooth it popularized the cigarette. During the 1880s cotton market slump, Pee Dee planters jilted cotton for this new cash crop. With railroad tracks running right through town, the city was soon home to the largest tobacco market in the state, a position it maintained for much of the early twentieth century, until the industry was restructured during the New Deal and World War II. While Mullins has no "smoke-off" to parallel the spinach cook-off in Crystal City, several of the old tobacco warehouses still stand. Some tobacco conglomerates, including R. J. Reynolds, maintain a presence here. Today, the town's historic train depot—once crucial for getting the crop to market—is home to the South Carolina Tobacco Museum.

In the bituminous coal fields of central Appalachia, there are two coal museums. The one in eastern Kentucky occupies the former company store of US Steel's "model" town of Benham, housed in an imposing four-floor structure complete with a 1950s-era soda fountain and reconstituted diner, though the building is now powered not by coal but by solar panels. A few miles down the road in the former model town of Lynch, built by International Harvester, non-claustrophobic visitors can descend into the Portal 31 exhibition mine. The second museum, in Beckley, West Virginia, features a fully reconstructed coal camp. The website promises that "the Coal Company House, Superintendent's Home, Pemberton Coal Camp Church, and the Helen Coal Camp School, give visitors a true representation of early 20th century coal camp life."

Across rural America, monuments, celebrations, and museums are markers of local pride. Indeed, Crystal City has vigorously defended its claim to the title "Spinach Capital of the World" against upstart Alma, Arkansas—also a former spinach mecca that has erected multiple statues of Popeye. Yet in South Texas, the vast Cotton Belt, central Appalachia, and the Pee Dee region of South Carolina, these symbols celebrate a past that is fraught, to say the least. They commemorate the very industries that, for a century or more, spelled misery and hardship for thousands, if not millions, while profiting only a few. They memorialize the intensive resource extraction and resulting human exploitation that made these places America's internal colonies.

How did the identities of these communities become so bound to the economic legacies of the past? A superficial read of the evidence suggests that geology is destiny. The bituminous coal forming over centuries in the mountains of central Appalachia; the alluvial soil of the Yazoo-Mississippi Delta building through thousands of years of annual flooding; a belt of fertile black earth stretching across Alabama and Georgia and into South Carolina left by the waters of an ancient lake; the artesian aquifers bottled up underground southwest of San Antonio: each feature of geology was like a character in a play, waiting in the wings—sometimes for eons—for its moment on history's stage. But geology is not destiny. Though geological features were certainly necessary, they were not sufficient to produce the vast industries that were built upon them. That process required the acquisition of land, capital, technology, and access to national and global markets. Most important, however, was an ample supply of exploitable people to provide cheap labor.

In each case, there was a moment when it all began, a sudden break between past and future—even if those involved didn't fully realize it at the time. Someone with the right skills, resources, and connections happened to be at the right place at the right time to help solve a perplexing problem. A chance sighting of an inky rock outcropping in the American wilderness remained lodged in the memory of a determined entrepreneur. An experiment born of desperation catalyzed the resurrection of an old industry, but in a new locale. A rancher late in midlife threw caution to the wind to try his luck with onion seeds imported from Bermuda, with immediate and spectacular success. In each instance, the moment was followed by a boom that transformed an entire region's economic and social life within a few short years.

THE MOMENT COMES TO THE COTTON BELT OF THE DEEP SOUTH

As motorists travel down I-95, crossing through the Carolinas and Georgia en route to Walt Disney World and other Florida attractions, most have no idea, as they whiz by Savannah, that they are traveling within a mile or so of the spot where one of the most consequential events in American history took place. A neglected historic marker just north of the city on Georgia State Route 21 commemorates the event, though the sign is dwarfed by an IKEA distribution warehouse and an office park. During the colonial era, this was Mulberry Grove, a silk and rice plantation on the Savannah River owned by a British loyalist who forfeited the property to the US government after the Revolutionary War. The new government gave the land to General Nathanael Greene as a reward for his heroic military service (deemed so notable that more than a dozen US counties are named for him). After his death in 1786, Greene's widow, Catherine, inherited the plantation and experimented with planting short-staple cotton.

In the spring of 1793, a recent Yale graduate with a gift for tinkering left New England for the South to assume a tutoring post. On the way, the young man, Eli Whitney, learned that the job would pay only half the salary he had anticipated. Fellow traveler Phineas Miller invited Whitney to come work at Mulberry Grove, which he managed for Catherine Greene. She asked Whitney if he could find a way to solve the aggravating problem of separating the cotton fibers from the seeds.

Whitney had never laid eyes on a cotton boll in his life. Yet in a short time, according to one version of the story, he had devised a simple machine featuring a rotating drum with wire teeth that pulled the fibers away from the seeds. According to the National Archives, however, others deserve at least as much credit for the invention, including Catherine Greene herself and several of the plantation's enslaved people, whose names are not known.

Realizing that the cotton "gin" (short for "engine") could generate a fortune, Whitney and Miller raced to Philadelphia, then the nation's capital, to patent the device with Secretary of State Thomas Jefferson. They never saw a profit; despite the patent, bootlegged models spread across the country like wildfire. Yet the gin changed the course of history by doubling the market value of the crop. The great cotton rush was on.

By 1800, the United States was producing 36.5 million pounds of cotton—two-thirds of it grown in South Carolina and Georgia. Over the next two decades, the output grew more than 450 percent. By that time, cotton cultivation had moved westward, as the greedy crop depleted centuries' worth of nutrients from the soil. For planters thirsty for fresh acreage, the federal government proved to be an indispensable ally, acquiring vast tracts from foreign powers via the Louisiana Purchase and through forced concessions from Native American tribes, and in turn opening millions of acres across the Deep South and the Delta to cotton cultivation. As cotton plantations spread like a rash across the South, so did slavery. According to historian Sven Beckert, "All the way to the Civil War, cotton and slavery would expand in lockstep, as Great Britain and the United States had become the twin hubs of the emerging empire of cotton."

Mississippi became the nation's twentieth state in 1817. At that time, much of the land was still in the possession of the Choctaw and Chickasaw Nations, and only became US territory after the 1830 Treaty of Dancing Rabbit Creek. The leader of the Choctaw who signed the treaty was a young man of mixed French Canadian and Native heritage named Greenwood LeFlore. LeFlore stayed on after the Choctaw were forcibly removed to Oklahoma and became one of the largest landowners in the state. Just east of where Greenwood, Mississippi, now stands, LeFlore built the palatial mansion he christened "Malmaison" in homage to his hero, Napoléon Bonaparte, where he lived in splendor in the midst of imported French furnishings while four hundred enslaved people toiled on his 15,000 acres planted in cotton. Much of the land to the west of his plantation, referred to simply as "the Wilderness," was empty of people, "a wild territory where panthers, bears, and snakes lived in the dense cane jungle." This land—soon to be known as the Delta—"was destined from the beginning to be the domain of substantial planters . . . who possessed both the financial resources and the slaves required to clear and drain the land and take full advantage of its exceptional fertility," writes historian James C. Cobb. Yet it wasn't until after the Civil War that the alluvial soil would be fully exploited.

If it could be said that there is a place where human destiny unfolded from the very earth, that place would be the Mississippi Delta. Within its bounds lie almost 7,000 square miles of the richest and deepest topsoil ever cultivated. According to historian John Willis, "With each spring thaw for thousands of years, the Mississippi River carried off the rich topsoil of the Midwest. Then, just south of Memphis, the river predictably bulged over its banks . . . deposit[ing] a thick, rock-free and fecund soil upon the Yazoo-Mississippi Delta—conditions fit for a king. King Cotton that is."

On the eve of the Civil War, "as many as sixty thousand Delta slaves produced a staggering 66 million pounds of cotton" per year, transforming the Delta into the most important producer of the world's most important commodity. In this region, cotton absorbed everything—the land, the capital, the labor. To secure property, clear it for planting, acquire seed and fertilizer, and—in the antebellum period—ensure a sufficient supply of enslaved people all required substantial capital, which planters sought from the Northeast and abroad. After the Civil War, the Cotton Belt's dependence on outside capital only increased.

As the industrial revolution dawned, cotton fever was so pervasive in the South that the massive industrialization gripping the rest of the nation barely registered there. Economist Jay Mandle notes that of the 5.6 million manufacturing jobs created between 1890 and 1910 across the United States, fewer than 400,000 of them were in the six states where cotton was most dominant. In 1910, Ulrich Phillips, a celebrated southern historian of the early twentieth century, condemned the Cotton Belt as "decadent," responsible for stymieing all diversification by "[keeping] the whole community in a state of commercial dependence upon the North and Europe."

The rapid expansion of cotton wealth across the South is exemplified by the story of Greenwood, Mississippi. By the early twentieth century, Greenwood was linked to the intercontinental railroad system, which could transport its only commodity to lucrative markets unreachable before. The sudden rise in the price of cotton at that time prompted planters to clear more of the Delta backcountry to cultivate the "white gold." In the blink of an eye, the rise birthed a regional elite that flourished, in stunning contrast to the legions of impoverished laborers in its midst. Writing in 1935, Delta native David Cohn hyperbolized, "Cotton is more than a crop in the Delta. It is a form of mysticism. It is a religion and a way of life."

Nowhere else reaped the benefits of this boom more than Greenwood. In 1892, the Sanborn Fire Insurance Company's map of the city shows a small settlement with two sawmills, a cotton warehouse, and a few square blocks of modest homes. Its 1905 corollary identifies a dozen or so churches, two schools (one white and one "colored"), the Delta Hotel, the Elks Lodge, and even an opera house. In 1906, a handsome new courthouse was built, one of the largest in the state. The following year, the city erected the castle-like Jefferson Davis School, serving white children in grades one through twelve. Large Queen Anne and Classical Revival mansions sprang up on West Washington Avenue during this time. Soon after the turn of the century, Greenwood became the symbolic center of the entire Delta region.

The Works Progress Administration's 1938 *Travel Guide to the Magnolia State* describes (with a whiff of condescension) how thoroughly cotton and its attendant wealth permeated the life of the city, which was "completely surrounded by cotton fields and centered about its gins, compresses and warehouses. . . . Cotton built the gins and compresses and the pretentious mansions on the Boulevard." But while some planters acquired fortunes, the majority labored under crushing debt. In 1936, Thomas J. Woofter published the results of a study of 646 cotton plantations across the cotton-growing states, showing that landowners' debts had almost quadrupled between 1910 and 1928. At the end of the period, more than half of these landowners' debts totaled more than 40 percent of the appraised value of their land and its attendant buildings, animals, and machinery. The author offered this diagnosis: "These areas are utterly subject to King Cotton, booming when the King is prosperous and slumping when the King is sick."

It is hard for the modern reader to grasp what conditions in this region were like fully seventy years after emancipation. As psychologist John Dollard, studying one Delta county around that time, observes, "One sees flat cotton fields, an occasional puff of woodland against the horizon, rain-blackened Negro cabins in great numbers along the road and, in the fields, the cotton crop in some state of its growth or decay . . . and here and there, but less frequently than the sentimental northerner would imagine, a plantation mansion."

The prominent Fisk University sociologist Charles S. Johnson, who conducted hundreds of interviews with tenant farmers in the Cotton Belt in the late 1920s and early 1930s, describes how the "hard white highways of Alabama [have] drawn a ring as distinct as the color line around . . . decaying plantations—each with its little settlement of black peasantry."

If plantation life among Black people before the Civil War can rightly be described as an unending forced labor camp, tenancy after freedom was a perpetual, inescapable form of indentured servitude. In 1930, roughly six in ten Black Americans were tenant farmers, and another three in ten were farm laborers. Landlords often shortchanged their tenants when it came to "settling up" time. They also did everything in their power to block tenants' access to government relief, no matter how lean the year, on the assumption that it might discourage these laborers from toiling for survival in their fields. These laborers included women and even very young children.

Meanwhile, tenancy ensured material deprivation on an almost unimaginable scale. Any profits doled out at financial settlement time, generally in early December, when crops were sold and debts subtracted from the proceeds, rarely lasted much past Christmas. Yet the "furnish system," where landlords furnished seed, fertilizer, implements, and other basic provisions on credit, did not operate during the months between settlement and the beginning of planting season, typically in late March or early April. This guaranteed virtual starvation during a significant portion of the year unless seasonal employment could be secured off the farm. Not only was there insufficient food, but diets were deficient in many vitamins and nutrients. Based on his research with tenant farmers, Johnson reported, "The consequences of this were severe, the most direct and spectacular being the wide prevalence of pellagra," an affliction known to cause mental confusion, diarrhea, abdominal pain, and scaly skin sores. To examine causes of death among Blacks, Johnson obtained data from the health department of Macon County, in the heart of the Alabama Cotton Belt, and found that "heart disease, stillbirths, tuberculosis, influenza, nephritis, cancer, pellagra, and malaria" were among the most common killers, though he cautions that, due to a lack of access to doctors, many of these records relied on folk diagnoses. Nonetheless, he concludes that "the figures for mortality, morbidity . . . , poverty, insufficiency of food and clothing, are barren records for an understanding of the human struggle behind them."

BOOM IN THE PEE DEE

On a cotton farm near the Atlantic coast, Frank Mandeville Rogers was experimenting with something new. In the late 1870s, Rogers had purchased about fifteen hundred acres of prime farmland near the town of Florence, South Carolina. By the mid-1880s, cotton prices had collapsed, often yielding so little that production costs nearly canceled profits. By chance, Rogers encountered a visiting clergyman who suggested growing bright leaf tobacco instead. Bright leaf, developed in the "Old Belt" tobacco-growing region of North Carolina and Virginia in 1839, was the first American strain smooth enough to allow cigarette smokers to inhale and enjoy the experience—and the nicotine rush that came with it.

Intrigued by the clergyman's suggestion, Rogers sent inquiries to growers in that region, at first meeting with sharp skepticism that the crop could be grown that far south. Undeterred, he planted the first few acres of bright leaf in South Carolina in 1885. Cigarettes had recently become a craze thanks not only to the smoothness of the bright leaf strain but also to the invention of the cigarette-rolling machine, favorable tax policies, and an economic upturn that put a 5-cent pack of cigarettes within the reach of the masses. Rogers built a curing barn, while gathering advice from experienced tobacco hands recruited from the Old Belt. In 1887, he and a business partner sold a twenty-acre crop for $4,611, earning a net profit of $2,930—a phenomenal $146 per tilled acre, about ten times the yield per acre of cotton in those years.

Rogers became an evangelist for bright leaf. A master proselytizer, he earned the backing of the publisher of Charleston's leading newspaper, the *News and Courier,* and the state agricultural commission. One scholar writes that, by the first decade of the twentieth century, "the Pee Dee landscape was literally transformed. Thousands of curing barns, their furnaces winking in the black August night, bore witness to the change, as did scores of warehouses, a dozen new banks, hundreds of new stores and homes, and thousands of new jobs in the fields and towns of the region." While the population of South Carolina grew by 13 percent between 1900 and 1910, several tobacco towns in the Pee Dee region, including Mullins and nearby Marion, swelled by more than 200 percent. In the Pee Dee, King Cotton had been dethroned.

Much less has been written about the tobacco economy of the Pee Dee than about that of the cotton-rich Delta, but what evidence we have suggests that the patterns of exploding growth and near-complete market domination seen there were repeated in the Pee Dee. During the 1890s alone, the state's tobacco production increased one hundred–fold. The expansion of bright leaf in the vicinity of Marion County was nothing short of phenomenal, a 688-fold increase between 1890 and 1899. Though Pee Dee planters hailed bright leaf tobacco as their savior from the market swings of King Cotton, they soon found themselves subject to a new tyrant: Big Tobacco. As it turned out, the tobacco companies that controlled the industry were no less rapacious than their cotton counterparts, and the crop required close attention throughout the year, with virtually no lay-by period, deepening planters' dependence on tenant labor.

THE WINTER GARDEN OF SOUTH TEXAS

The moment came to South Texas under the aegis of Thomas Carter (T. C.) Nye, who would become known as "the father of Texas onions." Nye had had a hard-knock start in life. When he was orphaned as an infant, the county tried to sell him at auction, but there were no takers. He was placed with an elderly spinster who raised him at the county's expense. Just sixteen when the Civil War broke out, Nye joined the Confederate army and was captured twice. After the war, he spent three decades on a cattle ranch near Cotulla, in South Texas. Then, in the late 1890s, at the ripe old age of sixty-four, he decided to try something different. With what could only be described as wild success, Nye produced a bumper crop of onions on the US-Mexico border near Laredo. Grown from seed imported from Bermuda, they netted a profit of $200 an acre.

Publicity soon followed, and the notion that South Texas was ideal for irrigated farming began to take hold. By the early 1900s, the Winter Garden, as the area north of Laredo would later be called, became known for its rich soil, mild temperatures (by Texas standards), and copious water supply, plus a proven crop with potentially enormous profits. Thus, "the stage was set for the beginning of a series of some of the greatest land-colonization schemes in South Texas history," according to historian James Tiller. Inspired by Nye's success, cattle ranchers with massive landholdings—outraged by the cartel-like practices of the meatpacking industry—began feverishly subdividing ranchland into farm plots. They formed land agencies that advertised in newspapers up north during the winter, luring chilly Midwesterners with the promise of abundant land and sunshine, and offering would-be home seekers (or "home suckers," as the Texans sometimes derided them) special rail excursion fares to inspect the plots. Migrants also came from Virginia, the Carolinas, and Georgia, fleeing spent plantation land to the east.

In Zavala County, home to Crystal City, a legendary "cattle raiser" from the days of the open range, Colonel Ike T. Pryor, subdivided his 100,000-acre 77 Ranch in the early 1900s. The owners of the Cross-S Ranch, also in Zavala County and one of the largest in the United States, did likewise. In the decades between 1900 and 1930, new towns boomed in quick succession alongside the plots, not only in the Winter Garden but across South Texas.

Anglo ownership of the land had been impossible before the United States negotiated the Treaty of Guadalupe Hidalgo in 1848.

That year, the area north of the Rio Grande came under American rule, allowing vast tracts that had been granted by the Spanish and Mexican governments to Mexican families who had lived on the land for generations to be subdivided and sold. Anglo ranchers quickly began amassing large parcels, including the 77 and Cross-S Ranches in the Winter Garden and the mighty King Ranch in the Trans-Nueces region, the largest in the country, spanning 1.25 *million* acres. By one estimate, more than 80 percent of all the land in South Texas changed hands in the decades after 1848, with some acquiring their property through deception or violence.

This remote landscape had begun to connect to global markets after the Civil War, when cattle ranching became big business. Capital from British and eastern US sources funded much of the development at the time. In the Trans-Nueces region, beginning roughly sixty miles north of McAllen, cattleman Ed Lasater was bankrolled by English and Scottish financiers. This relationship "typified the manner in which large quantities of foreign money were channeled into Texas between 1880 and 1920 to finance ambitious undertakings," notes Dale Lasater, the speculator's grandson. It was a harbinger of things to come.

With a foreign taste for investment already in place, T. C. Nye's bumper crops spurred a rush to convert ranchland to irrigated vegetable farms. The speed of the transformation was breathtaking. In the 1920s alone, the number of acres farmed in Zavala County grew twentyfold. The population increased by more than 300 percent as laborers from Mexico arrived in large numbers to work the ever-expanding harvests of spinach, onions, and other kitchen staples. Agricultural economist Paul S. Taylor toured the region at that time and observed that the move from ranching to farming in neighboring Dimmit County was similarly dramatic: "From a sparsely settled cattle and sheep range of the southwestern frontier, it has been passing to an irrigated district which watches intently the daily fluctuations in the market price of Bermuda onions in New York."

Beyond the railroads and the region's natural artesian wells, the single most important resource South Texas offered was a nearly inexhaustible labor supply just across the border, with workers who could be lured by very meager wages. Right at the time labor demand boomed, the Mexican Revolution—an extended period of regional conflicts between 1910 and 1920 that has been called the "defining event of modern Mexican history"—displaced thousands. This confluence of events fundamentally changed the social order of the region. By 1930, Zavala County was home to 7,660 Mexican-origin people, nearly three-quarters of the population, up from just 239 in 1910. Of South Texas's fourteen counties, only four had a majority-white population by 1930. While relations between owners and ranch hands had been long-standing and governed by paternalism, "the modern society was characterized by wage laborers, impersonal contracts, and a rational market orientation," according to sociologist David Montejano. Laborers were typically paid $1 a day, a wage one Anglo farmer defended this way: "What a Mexican should be paid is just enough to live on, with maybe a dollar or two to spend. That's all he deserves. If he is paid any more he won't work so much or when we need him; he's able to wait around until we have to raise the [pay]."

With the arrival of laborers in such large numbers, white landowners began instituting laws and adopting practices that mirrored those used to control Black labor in the Cotton Belt. To ensure that workers would be available for planting and harvest, Anglos relied not only on minimal wages but also, as Montejano notes, on a "web of labor controls," including "horsewhipping, chains, armed guards, near-starvation diets . . . , vagrancy laws, local pass systems and labor taxes." Meanwhile, Anglos propagated bigoted beliefs about "dirty" Mexicans' inherent inferiority. As a numerical minority, Anglos were especially fearful of labor revolts, a paranoia fueled by lurid stories, such as that of the fate of Texas rebels at the hands of the Mexican army at the Alamo, as taught in schools.

The physical appearance of the neighborhoods in towns reflected the social hierarchy: sturdy wood-frame houses, paved streets, and enclosed sewers in the white neighborhoods; shacks, dirt roads, and privies in the Mexican part of town. These shacks were not meant to be year-round dwellings. White landowners increasingly eschewed sharecropping for wage labor as the region developed, employing workers only during peak harvest and planting time—a few weeks or months out of the year. Thus, Mexican-origin families were forced to migrate to find year-round employment, from the cotton fields of Texas's Coastal Bend to the sugar beet fields of Minnesota and the Great Plains, and on to the cucumber fields of Wisconsin and the fruit orchards of Michigan. By 1941, fully 96 percent of the 5,500 Mexican Americans in Crystal City were migrant workers, a somewhat higher percentage than in neighboring counties.

Meanwhile, Anglos sought to dominate the landless laboring majority even further, including denying them the vote through poll taxes, the white primary (in which only Anglos were allowed to vote), and other nefarious means. Due to the connivance of local capitalists and complicit politicians, the labor laws that governed the rest of the nation, such as the minimum wage, simply didn't apply. Unemployment insurance or welfare? These laborers were deemed ineligible. In sum, the laboring class in South Texas was exploited and subjugated to an extreme degree.

BIG COAL COMES TO CENTRAL APPALACHIA

Fifty-four years after Eli Whitney first ventured south to take up teaching, another Yankee, nineteen-year-old Jedediah Hotchkiss, left his small village near the foothills of the Catskill Mountains to embark on a walking tour through Appalachia. Ambling into the Shenandoah Valley, Hotchkiss ended up in Staunton, Virginia, nestled between the Blue Ridge and Allegheny Mountains. He became one of the area's leading educators and founded several schools. Hotchkiss also earned such a reputation as a skilled mapmaker and expert on the landscape of western Virginia that during the Civil War, General Robert E. Lee chose him as his topographical engineer.

While on assignment one day during the war, Hotchkiss spied several large coal outcroppings along the eastern base of Virginia's Flat Top Mountain, far from the established anthracite coal fields of Pennsylvania, Ohio, and Indiana. Though fully occupied with the war, he made note of the sighting.

After the war, Hotchkiss took a teaching post at Washington University (later known as Washington and Lee) in Lexington, Virginia, under the presidency of Lee. Upon Lee's death in 1870, Hotchkiss returned to Staunton, where he mounted a campaign to convince financiers that the coal outcroppings he had seen could be the foundation of an industry to replace the slave-based agricultural economy destroyed by the war. Hotchkiss hired prospector Isaiah Welch to investigate the claims of a Tazewell County blacksmith that he was mining all the coal for his shop from his own property. What Welch discovered on the blacksmith's land was a coal seam thirteen feet high—twice that of any then known in the United States. Though it would take another decade—after a depression and the construction of the Norfolk and Western Railway—the Flat Top–Pocahontas Coalfield was finally developed, turning the little town of Big Lick, Virginia, into the booming city of Roanoke almost overnight. Almost twenty-five years after first noting those outcroppings, Hotchkiss helped usher in the industrial age in western Virginia. It was only a matter of time before coal mining would spread across central Appalachia.

First, however, control over the land had to be wrested from the Native people living there. Daniel Boone had led the first white families through the Cumberland Gap and into Kentucky in 1773, a trek that violated King George III's promise to Indigenous peoples that Europeans wouldn't settle beyond the mountains. Thus provoked, the Cherokee attacked, and six members of the band—including Boone's eldest son—were killed. Within two years, Boone was back in Kentucky working for the Transylvania Company, a private firm formed for the purpose of securing Cherokee land for white settlement—an action promptly condemned by the governors of both Virginia and North Carolina for its illegality. Undeterred, the company met with Cherokee leaders in 1775. The firm walked away from the meeting with roughly half of present-day Kentucky.

Settlement of the mountains was slow, and most of the population growth over the early years was from natural increase, with subsistence farm families moving farther up the creeks and valleys as they sought more-arable land. The discovery of salt springs in 1800 in Clay County drew the attention of several prominent Virginia businessmen. The resulting salt mines became a crucial Kentucky industry linking the region to the national economy, a story we tell in more detail in chapter 5.

From the early 1800s onward, Clay County exhibited extreme economic inequality—a characteristic of all our internal colonies. By 1816, just thirty-two residents owned more than three-quarters of the land. In his study of the Beech Creek farming settlement in Clay County, which lies a few miles from the present-day town of Oneida, ethnographer James S. Brown noted that in the 1860s, the territory was "largely owned by a few men." This situation of the landed few and the landless many would have important repercussions as the region began to industrialize at century's end.

It was then that agents of big corporations descended on rural settlements throughout Appalachia, scouting for timber and coal. After arriving at a farm on horseback, these "mineral men," as they became known, would accept an invitation to the family table. Following the meal, the agent would "casually produce a bag of coins and offer to purchase a tract of 'unused ridge land' which he had noticed on his journeys or the mineral rights to the property." It was hard for a cash-poor farmer to resist. What these mountain farmers didn't realize—until after the coal companies arrived, in some cases years later—was that they had signed notorious "broad form deeds," which transferred to the coal companies not only the mineral wealth but also the right to remove it, "by whatever means" the companies deemed necessary. These means would come to include strip mining and even mountaintop removal. With thousands of strokes of individual pens, from western Virginia to West Virginia to Kentucky, the fate of Appalachia was sealed.

It wasn't just mineral rights that were bought and sold. By 1892, out-of-state corporations had developed "a virtual land monopoly" in eastern Kentucky, holding deeds to more than 80 percent of assessed land in Bell County, which adjoins Clay County on its southern border, and fully 60 percent in other nearby counties. In the period between 1890 and 1930, central Appalachia transitioned from subsistence agriculture to extractive industry, as railroads penetrated ever farther into the region, spurring the clear-cutting of vast stands of timber and the extraction of large seams of coal. In both industries, the prior generation of Appalachian salt capitalists greased the skids for the new investors.

It was during this period of industrialization that images of the mountain residents as "hillbillies" began to form in the popular imagination. From 1886, when an Appalachian travelogue was published in *Harper's Magazine*, through the 1901 release of novelist John Fox Jr.'s *Blue-Grass and Rhododendron*, the idea that "a separate and inferior people had settled Appalachia," throwbacks to more primitive and even "barbarian" humans, was entrenched. In an 1899 *Atlantic Monthly* article titled "Our Contemporary Ancestors in the Southern Mountains," Berea College president William Goodell Frost declared, "It is a longer journey from northern Ohio to eastern Kentucky than from America to Europe; for one day's ride brings us into the eighteenth century!" The idea that mountain whites were of substandard racial stock was particularly in vogue in the eugenics-infused social sciences of the 1920s and carried over into the "culture of poverty" analyses of Appalachia that followed. Indeed, the discounting of the laboring class as of substandard racial stock was part and parcel of—and a necessary precondition for—the pattern of extraction practiced in each of the internal colonies.

As central Appalachian coal mining took off, the companies' need for labor expanded dramatically. Accordingly, within a year after major industrialization, a county's population typically doubled. Yet the sharp rise in demand did not lead to an increase in wages, as simple economic theory would suggest, because operators could draw on immigrants from eastern Europe and discouraged sharecroppers from the Deep South, along with those most readily at hand: native Appalachian subsistence farmers.

When investigating the living conditions of miners and their families in the region in the mid-1920s, the US Coal Commission found that roughly 80 percent were living in company-controlled towns, a story we tell in chapter 3. Even more concerning to the commission was the lack of legal protection for those living in a company-owned house. The moment a miner lost his job—for any reason—the family could be evicted. "The knowledge that the two precious eggs—the job and the family shelter—are in one basket and that at any hour of the day the husband might come back with both broken is a constant and grim companion [which] the mine-worker's wife is powerless to forestall," the report read. Yet owners' control of the people who labored in the mines didn't stop there. One West Virginia attorney general reported that "to 'maintain their feudal proprietorship' the operators resorted freely to the use of armed mine guards, blacklists, and martial law, as well as their domination of county governments and courts, and an 'elaborate espionage and spy system.'" Coal companies controlled not just their towns and the families who lived there, but politics as well: miners regularly received "silent instructions" about how to vote.

Meanwhile, the danger to miners was unvarying. "Falls of coal and rock from the roof, gas and dust explosions, unsafe haulage systems, electrical shock, and other job-related dangers daily exposed the mine worker to the risk of death or disability," wrote one observer. Accordingly, between 1906 and 1935, nearly 50,000 mine workers lost their lives. One person who grew up in the Blue Diamond mining camp during the 1920s later recalled that "the worst thing about living in the mining camp, one was always in constant dread. . . . Many a time I'd go to bed and I'd lay and worry whether Dad would come back alive or not. . . . Sometimes great tragedies came upon whole families [where several family members were] caught in one section, killed."

THE LIVING LEGACY OF AMERICA'S
INTERNAL COLONIES

Read one way, the stories of America's internal colonies are ones of American innovation, ingenuity, and entrepreneurship. Great wealth was extracted from these regions in the form of raw materials that fueled not only national but global markets. Yet from the start, these were also the places in the nation with the most inequality, severe poverty, ill health, and limited mobility. They remain so today.

Although each of these places has unique features and the level of exploitation varies, the parallels between America's internal colonies are inescapable. Rather than trying to retain laborers through competitive wages, the capitalist class strove to close off any competition; consistent with elite interests, very little new industry, if any, came into these regions. The dominance of labor-intensive industries with their rock-bottom pay schemes meant that these areas had employment structures akin to feudal systems: very few, and sometimes non-resident, owners who often relied on a small cadre of managers to oversee the impoverished many. Owners saw to it that taxes stayed low by denying the laboring class the franchise or, when that failed, by stripping them of suffrage via literacy tests, poll taxes, the white primary, and rampant vote buying, thereby undermining investment in schools and other civic infrastructure.

In the chapters that follow, we illuminate exactly how, in each region, these patterns have yielded a powerful living legacy today. We document the extraordinary manifestations of this legacy: separate and highly unequal schooling; crumbling social infrastructure; violence; generations of entrenched public corruption; systemic racism; elite backlash to civil rights; and the reproduction of highly exploitative economic and social relations into the present day. Each of these themes is richly illustrated in the portraits of the places we paint in the pages of this book.

Separate, Unequal

ON FEBRUARY 13, 1968, Senator Robert F. Kennedy and his automobile entourage pulled up outside a one-room structure in Barwick, Kentucky, home to a bleak coal camp nearly swallowed up by the surrounding hills. As a legion of politicians, aides, and reporters piled out of the cars and crowded inside the school, the kids were scared—some too afraid even to look at the great man. Kennedy quickly read the room. Rather than delivering his prepared remarks, he moved quietly up and down the rows of desks arranged around a potbelly stove—solemnly shaking a hand, murmuring a reassurance. In one photo, he is smiling as he bends down to greet two little girls.

Kennedy had come to coal country to learn about poverty, but through images like these, the nation, too, would catch a glimpse of the deplorable condition of many of eastern Kentucky's schools. Absentee timber and coal executives could safely ignore them. Their own children needn't attend, and there were few middle-class constituents to please in towns like Barwick. Many of eastern Kentucky's schools were one-room affairs like the one Kennedy visited that day, serving students from kindergarten to third grade. Dropout rates were appalling. Our analysis of census data from 1950 indicates that across the nation that year, roughly a third of adults had completed high school. The same was true of only about 14 percent in eastern Kentucky.

Rates of high school completion in the Cotton Belt regions of Alabama and Mississippi were a bit better, though still well below the national average. Student dropout tended to occur in much earlier grades in the Cotton Belt. In the Winter Garden, less than half of adults had completed middle school.

In eastern Kentucky as elsewhere in the internal colonies, the main problem was a failure to invest in the enterprise of education: coal demanded strong backs, not keen minds. While the state had long underinvested in its schools, devoting about a quarter of the national average to educational funding in the 1960s, spending varied dramatically from school to school. The *Washington Post* reported that in the late 1980s, while one school district in suburban Louisville spent $3,186 in local revenue per pupil, another, in eastern Kentucky, spent only $118. In 1989, the Kentucky Supreme Court deemed Kentucky schools unconstitutional. Ordering the creation of an entirely new system, the court demanded that "the children of the poor and the children of the rich . . . must be given the same opportunity and access to an adequate education." Yet still today, high school graduation and college completion rates in Appalachian Kentucky fall far behind comparable figures for the rest of the state.

Meanwhile, in the Cotton Belt and South Texas, school inequality has taken an even more pernicious form: a legacy of separate and highly unequal schools, first by law before the passage of *Brown v. Board of Education* (1954) and then by other machinations since. Between 1964 and 1975, many Cotton Belt whites effectively upended *Brown* by standing up all-white, private "segregation academies," egged on and financially supported by Citizens' Councils formed for the explicit purpose of maintaining segregated schools. Though many of these would eventually close, those that remained would subsequently provide their communities a vehicle to accomplish an almost complete resegregation of schools.

In South Texas, Anglo elites responded to *Brown* by pretending to comply. Whites retained control of the school board, students were mostly separated by ethnicity in the lower grades, and the practice of dividing students into "ability" groups—a process that never placed Hispanic children in the top tracks or white kids in the bottom tracks—and establishing other informal quotas ensured that Anglo students would continue to claim most of the perks, including the coveted spots on cheerleading squads.

To fully understand the power of this mechanism of suppression, it's important to comprehend the system of education that prevailed in both the Cotton Belt and South Texas in the years before *Brown:* namely, separate and highly unequal schools, sanctioned by law in all fourteen southern states including Kentucky and West Virginia. We chose as our starting point the 1930s, an era when these regions were fully constituted as internal colonies.

BEFORE *BROWN* IN THE COTTON BELT

The insidious scheme of separate and drastically unequal was deployed in an especially dramatic way in Cotton Belt counties where Black Americans made up large majorities: the funding earmarked for Black schools was diverted to white schools. This diversion was, according to sociologist Allison Davis and colleagues in the classic work *Deep South*, "highly profitable to the white schools. In 'white' counties, on the other hand, colored people constitute so small a part of the total population that the diversion of funds to white schools would be of little or no value to improving those schools."

Another key difference, one not captured in per-pupil spending, was that county governments paid for the construction and maintenance of white schools, while it was up to Black parents to provide spaces—often in churches—for Black students to learn. Stoves, blackboards, and teaching materials were standard issue in white but not Black schools. Black teachers' salaries were a fraction of those earned by their white counterparts, as was the length and quality of their training. Finally, while buses carried white rural children to and from school, Black children had to walk.

Even so, according to anthropologist Hortense Powdermaker, the most consequential factor in lower academic achievement among Black students was the short length of the school year. School terms for Black children in the Cotton Belt lasted only a few months, depending on the need for cotton pickers and the whim of the white school boards, which decided whether to keep children in school in the face of that demand. In her 1939 book *After Freedom*, Powdermaker noted that although Black students were in school for approximately half as much time as white students, "both have the same grade system." Thus, she wrote, Black children "must be rushed through their work at an excessive pace. It is not possible to give two years to each grade, both because these children least of all could afford so long a course, and because parents, teachers, and pupils feel that a promotion must occur at the end of each year, even though the school year is only four and a half months long. Consequently there are children in the fifth grade of country schools who cannot read."

White attitudes about the education of Black children were rooted in the belief that educated Black people "were less amenable to the caste sanctions, less deferential, submissive, and dependent, and therefore a danger to the efficient working of the caste system," observed Allison Davis and colleagues. In *Caste and Class in a Southern Town*, published in 1937, John Dollard wrote that whites were opposed to educating Black people in other than vocational fields because "they tend to become better competitors with middle- and upper-class white people and this potentiality of competition sharpens caste antagonism." In Sunflower County, Mississippi, for example, Dollard reported "there is a colored high school in the town, not at all a common thing, which offers a three, instead of a four, year course; this means that the graduates from it cannot go directly to college but must spend a pre-college year away from home. For the Negroes who are demonstrably least well-endowed economically, this is a heavy handicap to the educational and status advancement of their children." Meanwhile, white high schools offered a four-year course, which was required for college admission.

The circumstances of Cotton Belt Black children struggling to learn in separate and highly unequal schools may be familiar to many readers. Perhaps less familiar are the conditions that prevailed in South Texas, which one Mexican American civic leader decried as

"Jim Crow in a Sombrero Hat." These conditions should come as no surprise: Some of the white ranchers and farmers who settled South Texas in the early twentieth century had left depleted Cotton Belt plantations. They applied lessons from their experiences exploiting and repressing Black people back east.

While we don't have the same level of documentation on the educational experiences of students in South Texas as we do for the Cotton Belt, an extensive report published in 1929 by the Social Science Research Council used Zavala County's neighbor Dimmit County as a case study for the Winter Garden region. The report found that "probably at no time during the school year" are more than 25 percent of the seven- to seventeen-year-olds in school. Weak state compulsory education laws and the fact that many Mexican Americans were exempt due to their rural locations meant that "we don't enforce the attendance law," one school authority told the report's author, regional economist Paul S. Taylor. Mexican American children were in fact diligently included in the school census, although, as was true in the Cotton Belt, the per-pupil allocation of funding went disproportionately to the white schools.

Until the 1954–55 school year, some districts in Dimmit County had only one K–12 "American" school, which Mexican American children were not usually allowed to attend. Those Mexican American students who did advance through the segregated lower grades were almost never promoted to the English-speaking high schools. Officially, segregation in the lower grades was justified by language differences. The unofficial reason was no doubt more potent: segregation would prevent "race mixing." According to one Anglo farmer, "A man would rather his daughter was dead than that she should marry a Mexican." As in the Cotton Belt, segregation in schools was crucial to maintaining a strict division by ethnicity.

Meanwhile, the schools were utterly inadequate to the task: there were no maps, only old books left over from the white school, and no running water. As another Anglo farmer told Taylor, "Some of the people here say, 'what do you want to educate an old *pelado* for? He will want 12 cents a row transplanting onions [instead of 10].'" Another offered a slightly more nuanced view: "They should be taught something, yes. But the more ignorant they are the better laborers they are. . . . If these [local Mexicans] get educated, we'll have to get more from Mexico."

Most Hispanic families in South Texas were not tenant farmers, as in the Cotton Belt, but migrant workers who had to travel hundreds or even thousands of miles to find work in the late spring, summer, and fall before coming back to the Winter Garden to harvest in the fall. Almost all the Hispanic adults we interviewed in the South Texas counties of Brooks and Zavala recalled working in the fields and the journey to the upper Midwest for sugar beet season, then across to Michigan for cherries, a migratory cycle that persisted even into the early 2000s for some. Kids in these families were lucky if they got back to Crystal City in time to start school a half month late, only to leave again before the school year ended. The conditions of work varied in South Texas and the Cotton Belt, but the result was the same: the school year for these children was drastically shortened.

As was common for schools across Dimmit County, Crystal City High, the so-called American school, graduated any number of white students each year, but precious few Mexican American kids completed even the elementary grades. In fact, in the early 1940s, one government study found that the average Hispanic eighteen-year-old in Crystal City had completed only 2.6 years of school. One in five had never finished first grade. These conditions persisted for many years and profoundly shaped the educational trajectories of the grandparents (and some of the parents) of the current school-age population.

THE RISE OF SEGREGATION ACADEMIES

On our 2021 road trip, which began in the Pee Dee region of coastal South Carolina, we passed Pee Dee Academy, established in Marion County in 1965. In neighboring Williamsburg County, we encountered Williamsburg Academy, founded in 1969. To the west, in Barn-well County, we found Jefferson Davis Academy, established in 1965. In Lee County, Robert E. Lee Academy opened its doors the same year. Over in Hancock County, Georgia, we discovered John Han-cock Academy, founded in 1966. As we drove west through Dougherty County, we noticed Deerfield-Windsor School, founded in 1964, and in Early County, we noted that Southwest Georgia Academy first welcomed students in 1970. Clearly, we were looking at a pattern.

In Alabama, there were many more instances of that pattern: John T. Morgan Academy, Lowndes Academy, Macon East Acad-emy, and Wilcox Academy, to name just a few. All were founded between 1964 and 1975. Entering Mississippi and traveling over to the Delta, we encountered dozens of private academies established in these same years. Sometimes, we learned, the student population today includes a Black student or two. But overwhelmingly, the faces are white, even in these Cotton Belt counties, where most people are Black.

Robert "Tut" Patterson was booster in chief of these schools. At age thirty-three, he founded the nation's first Citizens' Council in Indianola, Mississippi (in the county studied by Powdermaker and Dollard), just two months after what local whites called "Black Mon-day," the day the *Brown v. Board of Education* decision was handed down. That year, 1954, the organization established its national headquarters in neighboring Greenwood, with supporting chapters sprouting up across the South as whites rallied to fight the federal mandate to integrate public schools, which some white locals re-ferred to as the "second reconstruction." In its stronghold of Mis-sissippi, the Citizens' Council was initially highly successful in its fight to keep the public schools segregated in the wake of *Brown:* not a single school desegregated in the decade that followed. As late as 1961, three states—Mississippi, Alabama, and South Carolina—had not one integrated classroom.

But in 1963, with the Civil Rights and Voting Rights Acts in the offing, white segregationists, led by local Citizens' Councils, shifted their strategy away from resisting public school integration and set about creating an alternative: all-white private schools. In 1964, the Citizens' Council ran a story in its monthly magazine, *The Citizen*, offering step-by-step instructions on how to start a "private school." Tut Patterson then turned his attention to establishing a segregation school in Greenwood, founded in 1966 and named Pillow Academy, for the planting family that donated the land. Journalist Richard Rubin writes that "Patterson, and by extension Greenwood, came to symbolize the last best hope of segregation in Mississippi."

That same year, over in Phillips County, Arkansas, the newly founded Marvell Academy—the first of its kind in the state—would enroll its first seventy-three white students. Three years later, *Time* magazine reported that of the more than two hundred similar whites-only schools that had "blossomed" in the South "for the sole purpose of excluding Blacks," few were as "openly redneck," to use the author's language, as Marvell Academy. Its founders—members of the local Citizens' Council—proclaimed that "integration is the corruption of the true American heritage by concept and ideology." Harold Corkran, who led one of the county's public schools, Marvell High, told the *Chicago Tribune* that he had watched the number of white students in his school dwindle each year since desegregation, while enrollment at Marvell Academy, just across the cotton field, grew. Yet Corkran confidently told the *Tribune* that the academy would not survive, "because anything that's based on hate can't exist, alone—especially when it's preached day after day [in school]." Nonetheless, in 1970, the same year Corkran predicted their demise, the number of segregation schools throughout the South doubled. That year, Phillips County would add a second segregation academy, DeSoto School. All three segregation academies—Pillow, Marvell, and DeSoto—along with dozens of others across the Cotton Belt South have persevered to this day, each still enrolling hundreds of students.

Historian Michael Fuquay writes that in some instances, "entire student bodies moved from formerly all-white public schools to new private schools," built with public funds, legally and otherwise. "Private" was largely a "romantic subterfuge designed to evade the requirements of federal law without sacrificing the benefits of public support." Until it was deemed unconstitutional, the State of Mississippi provided tuition vouchers and other resources to help finance the schools.

Books and other school materials were transferred to the new schools, along with desks, blackboards, and even buses, secured via hastily organized "purchases" for pennies on the dollar. In 1970, the *New York Times* reported that eight hundred textbooks had been transferred from a public school in Jackson, Mississippi, to Woodland Hills Academy, a new segregation academy opening just outside town. Often, these unlawful seizures were aided and abetted by white school officials. When confronted by federal authorities, R. B. Layton, the assistant superintendent of the Jackson public schools, claimed, "These are surplus books we don't need because of our reduced enrollment. I don't see what the fanfare is about."

Yet the private schools seized more than just books and furniture. They also tried to steal the identity and legacy of the local public schools. "They took along the trappings of the old school, its colors, its teams, mascots, symbols, its student newspaper, leaving behind the shell of the building," write educational historians David Nevin and Robert Bills, who authored the authoritative text on the topic, *The Schools That Fear Built*. Some teachers followed their white students to the private schools as well. Debbie Hewitt Smith, who as a teen was part of the wave of whites fleeing the local public high school in Leland, Mississippi, for a segregation school, remembers these blatant attempts at appropriation: "Pep rallies were positively depressing compared to what they had been at Leland High. There was no pep band, no victory torch, no *tradition*. In fact, when it came to creating traditions at Leland Academy, we basically stole them from our old public school. For the new school mascot, the student body came up with the Bruins, only a baby step away from the public school's Cubs. Our fight song was the same one used at Leland High, just substituting the old school colors of maroon and white with [the] new colors red and blue."

Among the Cotton Belt counties, it was in the Delta, rich in income and property, where whites were best positioned to donate the land for, fund the construction of, and pay the tuition for the new schools. Mississippi whites in other areas of the state, however, soon followed suit as the United States Supreme Court's 1969 decision in *Alexander v. Holmes County Board of Education* led to immediate integration in thirty school districts in Mississippi and the eventual integration of every public school in the state. In less than a year, all but two of Mississippi's school districts had been forced to adopt desegregation plans. A mass exodus of whites from public schools followed. In Mississippi alone, enrollment in private academies— standing at about 20,000 at the end of the 1960s—more than doubled over the next five years. And in the Arkansas Delta, where Marvell was one of only a handful of segregation academies established in the 1960s, that number would more than triple in the next half decade. Nevin and Bills estimated that by 1975, approximately 750,000 white students were attending segregation academies in the South.

Delta whites weren't only the best resourced, they were also the most eager for the private schools. An obvious factor was the large Black majority in the region. Without segregation, not only would classrooms be predominantly Black, but properly educated Black people might regain the franchise by passing literacy tests. In 1971, Auburn University professors John Walder and Allen Cleveland reported that the "'white flight' [from public schools] continues to be especially strong in those areas where the school population is predominantly black. For example, in at least half a dozen [such] Alabama counties public school enrollment is now almost totally black. Only a comparative handful of white youngsters remain in the public schools. Resegregation is virtually complete in these districts."

Whites in Lowndes County, Alabama, where Blacks in the county seat of Hayneville outnumbered whites four to one, established Lowndes Academy, enrolling its first 265 students the same year Pillow and Marvell opened. While in many other Cotton Belt communities some level of integration was achieved, at least for a brief period, Hayneville School had not a single white student by 1970. Meanwhile, nearby Lowndes Academy enrolled 335 white students in twelve grades.

As Charles S. Johnson and the other researchers studying the Cotton Belt in the 1930s had shown, Black-majority counties were characterized by a distinctive set of social relations: namely, the obsessive monitoring of the color line. While inequities were rife across the South, in the majority-Black Cotton Belt counties there was a huge chasm between the facilities, per-pupil funding, length of term, and teacher preparation for white schools and those for Black schools. In these places, the prospect of integrating the schools was especially terrifying for whites because the education of Black children had been so degraded.

Segregation academies were also ideal vehicles to ensure that white supremacist beliefs were passed on to the next generation. Central to the mission of these academies was to inculcate the mythic history of the white, Protestant South, the myth of the "Lost Cause," and the supposed horrors of Reconstruction. This was especially necessary in the 1960s, as the civil rights movement succeeded in shifting the national political culture to one that "viewed white supremacy as evil and its defenders as un-American." In this context, according to historian Michael Fuquay, "segregationist parents hoped to recreate the social, cultural, and ideological environment of their own upbringing and thus nurture in their children a set of beliefs then being rejected by the outside world."

Segregation academies were supported (and sometimes financed), as we've seen, by the Citizens' Councils, once described as the "uptown Klan." White churches as well, from a variety of denominations but especially the Southern Baptists, rushed to lend support. With academies springing up almost overnight in little towns, the Sunday school classroom was very nearly the only spot academy classes could meet. As one expert put it, segregation academies found not just space but legal legitimation, too, "under the umbrella of the church school movement." The NAACP Legal Defense and Educational Fund reported that of the private schools and "education centers" that had been opened for white students fleeing the Memphis public schools, fully twenty-six of forty-three were sponsored by or housed in Southern Baptist churches. The same report noted that twenty Baptist churches operated segregation academies in South Carolina, that dozens of Louisiana's segregation academies were Southern Baptist enterprises, and that Catholic, Methodist, Lutheran, Episcopal, and Seventh-day Adventist churches also operated segregated schools.

While segregation academies may have been created in response to desegregation mandates, their defenders only rarely made this explicit. It is important to note the coded language used then, as it still is today. A 1969 feature in *Time* magazine profiled Sandy Run Academy, a segregation school in Swansea, South Carolina, just outside the state capital of Columbia. Headmaster William Jackson, a retired public school teacher, insisted that he and his staff were motivated purely by concerns about quality. "We're not concerned with integration, de-integration, or whatever," he stated. "We're concerned with quality education." Appealing to "quality" was indeed the most common justification voiced for these schools. Despite such denials, *Time* reported that several segregation academies in the state honored their graduates with diplomas and pins that featured a Confederate flag with the word "survivor" engraved across it.

Many Citizens' Council members were less subtle. In 1964, W. J. Simmons, a prominent Citizens' Council leader known as the brains behind the group, was featured in *Esquire*. Under the headline "The Segs," the blurb reads: "Perez, Harris, Shelton, Maddox, Simmons, the five most influential men in the southern resistance, tell you exactly what they think." In 1966, Simmons wrote in the Citizens' Council publication *The Citizen*, "[Parents] want their children to be raised and educated free from the tensions of racial conflict in the classroom, free from the frustrating drag of mass mediocrity, and free from the blight of self-styled progressive educators whose avowed aim is to turn young Americans from the established inheritance of their fathers to alien theories of collectivism and anti-white racism."

Not all segregation academies were created equal. In 1973, the *Yale Law Journal* identified three classes of segregation schools, roughly corresponding to the socioeconomic conditions of the white community: lower-class "rebel yell" academies; white community schools; and upper-class day schools. Rebel yell academies were organized by poorer white families and provided only a rudimentary education. Teachers did not have professional training. These schools were located in private homes, churches, or vacant commercial buildings. White community schools catered to middle-class families. Some may have eventually adopted an "open enrollment" policy, as required by the IRS to claim tax-exempt status, but their student population was almost entirely white. Tuition was occasionally waived for poor white families whose children would otherwise be forced to attend desegregated public schools. Finally, upper-class day schools offered complete academic programs. They creamed staff from public schools, sought accreditation by state and regional authorities, and built modern campuses with amenities such as athletic fields and science laboratories. These schools offered guidance counseling and foreign language instruction alongside other academic courses and the ubiquitous Bible classes.

Despite these distinctions, many of the schools failed to provide a basic education. In 1970, the *New York Times* reported that at southern segregation schools, "curriculums are generally not on a level with public schools in the same area. Their teachers as a rule earn less and are therefore not usually as qualified as their public-school counterparts. And their facilities and equipment are seldom comparable to those available in the public system." A 1976 study came to a similar conclusion. "Analysis conducted on the eleven schools indicates that the schools operate under severe handicaps," the study noted. "They frequently have an insufficient pool of children from which to draw to assure adequate financial support, inadequately prepared teachers, weak headmasters who lack training and experience in administrative roles, and a restricted curriculum." Yet the report also pointed out that parents had strong positive attitudes toward segregation schools. "The schools offer solutions to situations which the parents believe would be catastrophic for their children," it concluded.

As part of an oral history project, former pupils at segregation academies reflected on their schools' deficiencies. Renee McCraine Taylor, who attended a Citizens' Council–funded school in Jackson, Mississippi, said of her experience, "I started fourth grade at a just-organized private school operating at Hillcrest Baptist Church. Later on, I moved to Citizens [sic] Council School Number 2, later known as McCluer Academy. . . . The overnight all-white schools had bare-bones curriculum and resources. . . . There were no foreign language or art classes at McCluer. No tennis courts or volleyball teams either. There were very few advanced classes available to students." Others noted darker aspects of these schools. In a follow-up to an online essay that went viral in 2019 titled "Are You a Seg Academy Alum, Too? Let's Talk," Pillow Academy graduate Ellen Ann Fentress wrote, "In my school in the '70s, slurs and racist jokes were as common as acne and eight-track tapes. Yet running even deeper was a persistent unspoken pathology: a willed ignorance to the world beyond our chosen white one. I never knew any Black kids my age in my Mississippi hometown, which was split racially 50-50."

We could not ascertain the degree to which the Lost Cause and other elements of white supremacist ideology have been passed down to the current generation of segregation school students, whether explicitly or obliquely, although there is some evidence this is so. Fentress wrote of the Pillow Academy curriculum in the early 1970s: "What we learned in Pillow history class was distorted. . . . Enslaved people had enjoyed good treatment and Reconstruction—the brief years when black Mississippians held office and voted in substantial numbers—was an era of white suffering like the Civil War itself.

None of us heard a word about the lynching of Emmett Till in our hometown's backyard, although the visiting Chicago teen's death had drawn international coverage in 1955 and launched the civil-rights movement. When I finally heard about the Till case—I was 25, living 260 miles away. . . . I recognized the last names of classmates I'd known whose parents and grandparents had been in law enforcement or led the winning defense of Till's murderers. . . . Bryant's Store, the site where Till allegedly flirted with the owner, was nine miles from my former public school."

We could not learn much, either, about the current quality of the education in these private schools, which are not required to administer standardized tests. While the website of Pillow Academy boasts nearly 100 percent college attendance, the website Niche, which rates thousands of private schools through reports from students and parents, suggests that only about half of Pillow's graduates go on to a four-year school and few of those leave the state. Niche gives the academy a B grade. Indeed, the quality of the private academies has been questionable from the outset, according to Michael Fuquay. "Remarkably, although private school advocates emphasized that their primary interest was educational quality, no one expressed concerns about the quality of education that would be provided by an under-resourced, upstart school run by admitted novices. Segregation was the first and last word in educational 'quality.'" In fact, Fuquay found, the racism of white families meant that children ended up going to worse schools than they would have if their parents had supported integrated public schools.

No comprehensive list of the South's segregation academies exists, but researcher Christine Jang-Trettien's archival research conducted for this book shows that for the 140 most disadvantaged counties in the South as measured by the Index of Deep Disadvantage, nearly half (65) mounted a full-frontal attack against desegregation by forming at least one all-white private school. Jang-Trettien documented a total of 136 such schools in these counties. The reports of such low educational quality in the segregation academies themselves and the rapidly declining performance of the public schools they left behind suggest a question: Is one central mechanism linking places of deepest disadvantage to their pasts the degree to which school systems have remained segregated by ethnicity and race?

CHICANO RESISTANCE AND WHITE FLIGHT

In the Winter Garden region of South Texas, Rochelle Garza, now in her early fifties, told us that she and her nine siblings, like so many other South Texas children of migrant workers, missed weeks of school each fall, delayed from returning home by the northern harvest. Come spring, the kids missed more school, as soon as the field work began in the cotton-growing regions of Texas or even farther north. Of her five-year-old brother, Garza recalled, "They'd give him a little bucket and he knew what he had to do [to help with the harvest]."

In communities across South Texas, this pattern repeated itself. "Home" was a place where a family stayed for only a season. Agricultural work was available if the parents were willing to traverse the country with their family in tow—often in a rickety bus or even the back of a pickup truck. In the Winter Garden, the Anglo minority controlled everything in these migrants' hometowns. Elections were held in the summer, when the large Mexican American majority was away. Across South Texas, public office and key community leadership roles such as school board and city council membership were held exclusively by Anglos. Many in the Mexican American community felt they had no choice but to go along with the whites in power, because the Anglos were the source of all the jobs. Over time, more Mexican American citizens remained in Crystal City year-round, some working at the giant Del Monte canning plant or for other employers around town. Faced with *Brown v. Board of Education*, the Anglo minority had to figure out how to maintain power over the Mexican American majority in the key social institution of the schools.

They were good at it. In the wake of *Brown*, both the Carrizo Springs school district in Dimmit County and the Crystal City schools just down the road chose to desegregate, but both maintained de facto segregation in the elementary schools (the only somewhat integrated elementary school was the white "American" school). Several other South Texas school districts followed suit, including Brownsville and Laredo.

By the end of the 1960s, the vast majority of students at Crystal City High were of Mexican origin—roughly 85 percent. Yet a look at the yearbook from the time clearly indicates that most of the roles of distinction within the school—homecoming king and queen, for example—were reserved for Anglos. As the number of Mexican American students enrolled in high school rose, one Mexican American cheerleader was allowed on the squad, but the other three spots were reserved for Anglo girls. "It wasn't a written rule, but everybody knew," one student at the time, Diana Palacios, recalled when we spoke with her in 2021. Palacios had been a cheerleader in the segregated junior high school she attended. Once she enrolled in the "American" high school, though, she knew exactly what to expect: "The one Hispanic that got in would be [on the squad] until she graduated, and then someone else would come in."

At about the same time, a new generation of Hispanic leaders began to gain influence in Crystal City. Adopting the identity of "Chicanos," these activists were looking for ways to challenge the system. One, Jose Gutiérrez, had grown up in Crystal City before becoming the rare Mexican American kid from town to go to college and earn a graduate degree. Once back home, he started a newspaper for the Chicano community, which "became very, very successful because people could read about themselves for the first time ever. You could make the front page, [which they] never did in the other [papers], unless you killed somebody or you were charged with a murder," Gutiérrez told us in 2021. He and other young leaders wanted to fight what they saw as an unjust system: unfair voter registration laws, unfair labor practices, systemic racism in all its forms. But, as Gutiérrez explained, "people don't understand that bullshit." Instead, he said, "tell somebody, 'They don't want your daughter to be a cheerleader because she's got brown legs, those are ugly, only white legs are pretty,' [and they will understand that, because] no father has an ugly daughter."

In the spring of 1969, Diana Palacios wasn't going to try out for the cheerleading squad because the Mexican American slot was already filled by her friend Diana Teres. But, she told us, another friend "kept after me, 'You should try it out. You should try it out.' I didn't want to because I knew it was useless. Then she finally convinced me, [and] I thought . . . 'What do I have to lose?'" Palacios's father was a business owner, so his job wasn't at risk, but the family knew there could be other consequences. In the 1950s, when Palacios's father had run for Zavala County sheriff, "he got a beating from the Texas Rangers. They wanted him to take his name off the ballot," she told a newspaper reporter in 2001.

Even though she knew what she was up against, Palacios decided to try out. Once again, the teachers judging the girls filled three of the four slots with Anglos. "The students [were] upset, and they started talking about a walkout," Palacios told us. The powers that be offered the students both a stick and a carrot. The stick: walk out and you lose all course credits for the term. The carrot: a larger team with three Anglos and three Mexican American girls. While they opted for the latter, Palacios said, "we weren't satisfied because three and three is still not fair because we're eighty-five percent of the student body!"

Over the summer and into the fall of 1969, the students continued to meet. They decided not to back down. In fact, they upped the ante: not only should cheerleaders be selected on merit rather than the color of their skin, but the school also needed Hispanic teachers and counselors. "Most of the [Anglo] counselors, they would advise us to be a beautician . . . or be a maid in a hotel. Heaven forbid that you want to be a doctor, lawyer, or something!" Palacios recalled. "What happened with the cheerleaders opened our eyes to the actual discrimination, and how we were being shortchanged. . . . It got to the point that we're like, 'No, we're not accepting that.' And we're also not accepting that we can't speak Spanish in school. We [needed] books that gave us our history; any time [our textbooks] talked about a Mexican, he was having a siesta under a tree. It was always a lazy Mexican."

That fall, the students planned their offensive, partnering with Chicano movement leaders, including Gutiérrez. "We started going to school board meetings asking for things to change, but it all started escalating. When our parents went to a meeting and [the school board members] wouldn't listen to them either, we decided to walk out," Palacios recalled. Many of the student leaders' parents—mostly independent business owners—were already known for their civil rights activism, a story we tell later in the book. The tension built to a crescendo on December 8, 1969: "Everybody started chanting: 'Walkout! Walkout!'" After that day, Palacios said, "every school day started at the steps in front of the school. We said the Pledge of Allegiance and a prayer, and the rest of the day we walked around the school, [some of us holding posters reading], 'Brown legs are beautiful, too, we want Chicana cheerleaders.'"

Over time, more and more students and families joined their ranks. Gutiérrez recalled that "by the end of the seventeenth day of the walkout, we had like seventeen hundred kids out, almost eighty percent of the school." They carried signs that read, "We are not afraid to fight for our rights," "Chicanos want to be heard," and "Education and discrimination don't mix." As momentum built, those who had been hesitant to challenge the power structure lent their support. Parents "would bring us tacos and coffee and water. They'd be out there to watch [so] the police wouldn't beat us," Gutiérrez remembered.

Members of Congress brought the student protest leaders to Washington, DC, to discuss the matter. Diana Serna Aguilera, another cheerleader, told us she remembers asking for Senator Ted Kennedy's autograph: "It meant a lot to me because he was a Kennedy. . . . Mexicans just love the Kennedys." When the cheerleaders returned home, the local media were waiting. "We answered questions about what we did in Washington, what we accomplished. And that's when we informed the community that . . . the federal government was going to come down to mediate because the school board had refused to meet with us, even though we were legally on the agenda. And it was our right to be heard and to petition the government."

Finally, on January 9, 1970, in the face of federal scrutiny, the board caved in to the students' demands. The victory was far bigger than an extra spot on the high school cheerleading squad. This shift in the political winds was as strong as a twister. With one exception, before the 1971 elections only Anglos had served as city manager. But from then on, only Mexican Americans held that position. While the school superintendents had all been Anglo before 1971, they were all Mexican American thereafter. Yet Anglo backlash was as severe as it was sure. After the Anglos lost control of the schools, nearly all the Anglo students moved to nearby Carrizo Springs High School, which had a larger proportion of whites than Crystal City High, transferred to private schools, or left the area altogether. While the school had been roughly 85 percent Hispanic before these pivotal events occurred, the figure rose to 98 percent following the protests and white flight.

Nevertheless, what is now known locally as "the cheerleader revolt" or simply "the walkout" is still a point of pride in the town, and for good reason; it was a moment of great awakening for the girls and the Mexican American community at large. Soon after, Diana Serna Aguilera was part of the first all-Chicano cheerleading squad at Crystal City High. When that team went to the regional competition, she recalled, "we won superior ratings. . . . We brought home all these ribbons and all that [even though] we were competing with mostly Anglo girls. . . . It was so exciting and so affirming that 'Hey, there was really no reason to keep us out of cheerleading.' [We could] cheer as good or better than [the Anglo girls; the exclusion] was just because we were brown."

QUALITY EDUCATION

These days at Marvell Academy in Phillips County, Arkansas, the homecoming court is all white. So are the football and basketball teams. The cheerleading squad is all white. Yet the website reassures prospective students and parents that the academy was "founded on Christian principles" and that it strives to foster empathy, among a list of other virtues. At DeSoto School nearby, there are no students of color. Its website features an all-school photo with the youngest pupils in red, those a little older in blue, and the high schoolers in white, matching the flag in the foreground. The school's purpose? A familiar refrain: "simply and directly stated as quality education." The website tells us that DeSoto strives to give students "an understanding of our cultural heritage and respect for our country" along with "a strong moral character."

Like many segregation schools in Mississippi and elsewhere, Greenwood's Pillow Academy adopted a nondiscriminatory admissions policy in 1989 to gain tax-exempt status and to qualify for grants, but a decade later there had yet to be a single Black student, according to the *New York Times Magazine*. Today, the academy has more than seven hundred K–12 students, roughly 90 percent of whom are white and only 3 percent African American. Pillow's website features an all-white administrative and teaching staff. The school's diversity statement reads, in part, "Diversity is key to the mission of Pillow Academy. . . . Pillow Academy will continue its commitment to include diversity among the students and staff along with their perspectives into curriculum and activities." To live this out, however, the school will have to address its long and shameful legacy.

Meanwhile, there are ample data on how the public schools in Leflore County are faring. In 2018–19, less than a quarter of the students in the school district tested proficient in math and less than a fifth in reading, compared to 47 and 42 percent, respectively, statewide. Leflore's graduation rate lagged well behind the state's average, and the proportion of students deemed college or career ready was less than a third of the state average. ACT scores at Greenwood High averaged 15, considerably below the minimum (18) needed to attend one of the four leading state universities.

Mississippi schools in general perform below the national average, according to Quality Counts 2020, *Education Week*'s system for rating the nation's schools, although Mississippi has made positive strides in recent years. Indeed, education officials have lauded the state's improvement on the National Assessment of Educational Progress, which charts student achievement nationally in core instructional areas. In school districts across the Delta, however, low scores on state tests are still endemic. According to data from the Mississippi Department of Education, well over a dozen Delta school districts merited an F grade in the 2018–19 school year—the one just before the COVID-19 pandemic, after which education statistics became skewed or were not collected at all. Another dozen or so earned a D, and a few more rated a C. A smattering achieved higher grades, such as the Western Line School District in Washington County, which got a B. Schools in this district are far closer to evenly split between Black and white students. Outside the Delta, several Mississippi districts with a diverse student body earned an A grade, and there are numerous districts where Black students score at or above state averages in English and math.

The challenges faced by schools in Mississippi's Cotton Belt are shared by other Cotton Belt schools. Of the Alabama public schools labeled failing in the 2018–19 school year, 43 percent were in Cotton Belt counties, a disproportionately large share. Sharp educational deficits are seen in the Georgia Cotton Belt as well.

Surprisingly, none of our low-income interviewees in Leflore County complained about the schools. We can't say for sure, but perhaps this is because lower-income Black families have been exposed to segregated, low-performing schools for so long that they have become inured to the reality. However, Angela Curry, a Black community leader chairing the Greenwood-Leflore-Carroll Economic Development Foundation, sees a big problem: "Our public schools are probably ninety-eight percent African American. It's not diverse at all. I see that being a problem within itself, because that's just not the way the world is."

In the first decade of the 2000s, the city contemplated elements of the new Greenwood Comprehensive Plan and held a series of community forums. Attendees complained that the schools were "dated" or even "terrible." Nonetheless, they noted that voters would not support a bond issue to renovate them. A report concluded that "public meeting and stakeholder input indicates that outmigration is due primarily to the perceived lack of quality of the public education system in Greenwood." These stakeholders also noted that strong schools are key to recruiting new industry.

Teacher shortages, which are rampant in the Delta, are an important factor affecting the quality of education. One recent study found that the odds that a school district in the Mississippi Delta will have a teacher shortage is 115 times greater than in a non-Delta district in the state. Here again, in the challenge of teacher recruitment and retention, there is a direct link to the region's past. As Michael Fuquay notes, "In communities where the academy became the *de facto* white public school, white elites, who had always resented the expense of public education, suddenly found it possible to dramatically slash property tax assessments." The *Hechinger Report*, a publication that covers inequality in education, notes that, due to low stakes for whites, bond issues to build new high schools in Delta counties have failed to gain support. The publication points to Holmes County, adjacent to Leflore, where "educators and students . . . dream about what new school buildings, enough licensed teachers, new books, or even just a fresh coat of paint on peeling classroom walls would mean for them."

In the modern structure that replaced the historic 1930s-era Crystal City High School (now a middle school) where the cheerleader revolt occurred, only a handful of the school's students are white.

This situation is not unique to Crystal City: across Texas, more than a million Black and Hispanic children attend schools with few or no white peers. News stories regularly feature the ongoing struggle for integration in Texas schools.

Yet Crystal City High School, with its brand-new auditorium, is the "pride point of the town," helping "students have more pride in their school, not having to come into a run-down building," one school official told us. "Our town is known for its high school band. More so than the athletics, . . . [the] band has always been the gold star for our talent." Before, the band had to perform in an "old, run-down auditorium" that eventually became a storage area. Now, the auditorium is worthy of showcasing the young talent in town.

In 2019, that venue hosted a celebration of the fiftieth anniversary of the cheerleader revolt. Many of the original protesters and "dignitaries from all over the place" were on hand, Dr. Maricela Guzman, a guidance counselor at the high school, told us. "Then, of course, our [whole] town participates, so that's something really neat."

School pride is also the glue that holds the community together in Brooks County, in the Trans-Nueces region of South Texas, where Falfurrias is the county seat. A recent graduate of Falfurrias High told us that people in his community are always eager to "hype up [the school teams or the] academics. . . . If one of our teams makes it to [a] playoff, they'll decorate the town all in green, the school's color. It's like, 'Who would do that?' In this town, we do that. . . . We're just very supportive in this town." In dozens of conversations with Falfurrias residents, we heard stories of school spirit again and again.

We gleaned no such narrative from those interviewed in Greenwood, Mississippi. But as Dr. Tamala Boyd Shaw, founder and head of school at Leflore Legacy Academy, the city's new charter high school, explained, it is hard to build community pride when the schools are so divided by race. There are five high schools serving the small community: two public, which are nearly all Black; one private, which is almost all white; one for students with disabilities

(North New Summit School); and one for boys who have struggled in the public schools (the privately run Delta Streets Academy). Further, there is little collaboration across the schools. During the COVID-19 pandemic, Boyd Shaw suggested to her peers that "we should be talking about 'What is it that you're doing to prevent the spread of Covid in your schools?' 'How are your virtual classes going?' 'What are the subjects that you offer at your high school?' We should be asking Pillow, 'How is it that all of your seniors are getting these scholarships . . . ?' [But] there [is] no collaboration. Everybody's cordial, but . . ."

Boyd Shaw, a Greenwood native and graduate of the city's all-Black Amanda Elzy public high school, is an experienced administrator who returned to Greenwood in her early forties to "give back." In college, despite earning one of the top GPAs at her high school, she learned that "my peers were leaps and bounds beyond my knowledge." She said, "I had teachers who did the very best they could with what they could. But at Amanda Elzy High School . . . we had books that were . . . reject books, the old books that other kids had [had]. Like my name would be the last name [in a textbook with] ten spaces to put a name. The books were that old. . . . But over at Greenwood High School, air [conditioning], beautiful buildings, tissue in the restroom . . . and majority-white at that time."

Boyd Shaw aims to provide all students at Leflore Legacy Academy—including white kids whose parents can't afford Pillow's tuition—with the resources and enrichment she was denied. "What we want to do at Legacy is, we want our scholars to go play soccer . . . to go get on the softball team. We want them to go to [the] theater. Somebody can tell me, 'So Dr. [Boyd] Shaw, you just basically want to turn this into a Black Pillow Academy?' Call it what you may. We want to improve outcomes for children." If her school does manage to attract a more diverse student body than others have, and if Pillow Academy welcomes more Black learners, even these small gains in integration should be counted as progress against the seemingly immutable patterns of the past that have mired the community in educational mediocrity, not to mention robbed the town of a source of pride.

Meanwhile, in South Texas, the good news is that the public schools—still nearly all Hispanic—boast high graduation rates, a sharp departure from the past. The bad news is the poor student performance on standardized tests. As a result of the low test scores in both the Falfurrias and Crystal City districts, some of the elementary schools earned an F rating from the State of Texas in 2018–19, though both high schools in these districts merited a B. The school administrators we talked to were hard-pressed to explain the contradiction between high graduation rates and low test scores. But one read is that the paradox is simply another example of the present being linked to the past, when children spent precious little time in school but were sent on to the next grade nonetheless.

Dr. Guzman, one of the guidance counselors at Crystal City High, believes that tests themselves are the problem: "Those tests are not developmentally appropriate," she told us. "So at a very young age, our kids get discouraged, because teachers are under pressure, campuses are under pressure, principals are under pressure to just make the grade on accountability." Due to the pressure, she said, the kids "get their own stigma, 'Oh I'm always going to fail,' and you do have kids that have failed every single time. . . . Our kids in poverty tend to be the ones who score the lowest, and so they get discouraged." She complained that, due to government mandates, teachers must "teach for the test. We should be teaching more creatively, like we used to." Her school district is not alone in struggling to recruit and retain "our stronger teachers, because again, finances. [Because of the low pay] we lose good teachers sometimes. And we don't develop [our new teachers] as well as we should, . . . so [their students] don't do well on these standardized assessments."

But the quality problem may go deeper than the perceived troubles with the tests themselves. In interviews with nearly three dozen Zavala County residents, we heard one refrain repeatedly: Graduates from Crystal City High can't make it at a four-year college. To catch up, they have to start at a junior college. Those few who told us they had transferred out of the Crystal City schools to a district in another region were shocked at the differences in students' educational progress, as were those who had transferred in. Graduates who had gone to college often completed their degrees only in their thirties, or even into their forties, after multiple tries. The young women involved in the cheerleader revolt, each of whom received scholarships to a prestigious school, completed college only after stopping and starting multiple times, as they told us when we interviewed two of them.

But there is another potential explanation for the problem. Many of the grandparents and some of the parents of kids who are now in school completed so few grades that they may struggle to help their kids with homework. In South Texas, adult literacy rates are among the lowest in the nation, just as they were at the height of the internal colony that operated there. In Brooks County, fully 55 percent of adults are at or below level one literacy, roughly comparable to that of a first grader just learning to read, while the figure is 60 percent in Zavala County. Student test scores in reading are especially low, perhaps a reflection of this reality.

Undaunted, Dr. Maria Casas, superintendent of the Brooks County schools, has been busy putting together a college readiness curriculum. Early results, she told us, have been dramatic. "Last year, for the first time in the history [of the school district], we had ten students, which is ten percent of the [twelfth-grade] student population, graduating with an associate [of arts] degree. Ninety percent of our students graduated with college hours and/or certifications. . . . One hundred percent of the students graduated with a financial aid application and applied for college. . . . We did that with an investment of less than $10,000." Brownsville, Texas, has had a similar program in place for years. Despite poverty rates that nearly rival those in Brooks County, test scores regularly exceed the state average (though that average is admittedly low). What may seem impossible, Dr. Casas insists, can be done.

Andi Guerrero, principal of Dr. Tomas Rivera Elementary School in Crystal City, described her school as a "campus of joy." Even so, the school has faced severe challenges. "Texas will rate your campuses on an A to F scale, and my campus has been rated F . . . ever since I've been principal," she said. The extraordinarily high rate of child poverty across much of South Texas poses challenges that are hard to overcome. Over the five-year period between 2016 and 2020, roughly a third of the population in Zavala County lived in poverty. For children, the rate was more than twice the national average.

Prior to the COVID-19 pandemic, Guerrero was optimistic that the necessary partnerships were forming; momentum was building for major change. While her school has a long history of students failing to meet state standards, Guerrero told us that the elementary and high schools are working "hand in hand" and seeing positive effects. When the pandemic hit, "everything kind of came to a standstill," Guerrero said, but she hasn't given up hope: "I think [the momentum is] on pause. I don't think we've lost it."

One day, she hopes, there will be more to be proud of in Crystal City than the six-foot Popeye statue downtown. Meanwhile, the embedded history of separate and highly unequal education in South Texas is a key mechanism through which the deep disadvantages of the past are replicated in the present.

It's worth remembering that these stories from the Delta and in South Texas represent only a microcosm of the narrative of American education nearly seven decades after *Brown*. Today, America's schools remain sharply segregated by ethnicity and especially by race. As economist Rucker Johnson powerfully illustrates in his book *Children of the Dream*, American schools have been rapidly resegregating while academic performance has been falling, which suggests how profoundly the two may be linked. Johnson quotes a 1983 Reagan administration report, *Nation at Risk*, which concluded, "If an unfriendly foreign power had attempted to impose on America the mediocre educational performance that exists today, we might well have viewed it as an act of war." Johnson found that "the racial makeup and social conditions of our public school classrooms are nearly identical to those of the Jim Crow era."

What are the consequences of this lack of economically and racially integrated schools for Black, Hispanic, and white children? Johnson studied this question by following the story of the desegregation of schools after *Brown*. Bringing together data from surveys and from administrative records of each school district's level of integration in a given year, he captured what is known as each individual's "dose response"—in this case the number of years Black and white students were exposed to a school system under a desegregation order, ranging from zero for most people born before 1950 to up to twelve for those born later. He wiped out differences in family background or other variables by creating "virtual twins" who had experienced segregated and desegregated schools.

Johnson's work sheds crucial light on a critical question: What if the places we have written about in these pages had made different choices about desegregation? What differences might it have made in the outcomes of their children today? He documented that following a desegregation order, segregation levels fell markedly, per-pupil spending increased dramatically, and there was a sharp reduction in class size.

Johnson then contrasted the experiences of Black students who had no exposure to court-ordered desegregation with those of students who experienced the full twelve-year desegregation dose. His statistical models found that twelve years of desegregated schooling for Black children was enough to eliminate differences in Black-white educational attainment. Next he asked whether these benefits reverberated across a student's lifetime. By comparing the average effects of five years of exposure to a desegregation order among Black students to no years of exposure, he found an increase in annual work hours and wages that combined to produce a 30 percent bump in annual earnings in adulthood, a significant decrease in poverty, large improvements in marital stability, and a sharp increase in the likelihood of being in good or excellent health. Perhaps more profoundly, given the structural cycle of violence described later in this book, he documented that for Black children, being exposed to a desegregation order beginning in the elementary grades yielded a 22 percent reduction in the probability of being incarcerated as an adult. These gains were driven by the increases in resources available in desegregated schools, the goal that animates the work of Dr. Boyd Shaw. Meanwhile, white children who experienced desegregation did as well on all these metrics as those who had not been exposed to a desegregation order. The conclusion: no one lost. Although Johnson's analysis didn't include the gains to Hispanic children from desegregation, there is no a priori reason the story should differ, as the patterns of segregation within their schools were so similar in the years before *Brown*.

The failure of separate schools in America is that they have never been even close to equal. Ongoing segregation and resegregation—both the resegregation we have seen in the Cotton Belt South, aided and abetted by segregation academies, and the resegregation in South Texas that has occurred due to Anglo flight—are the results of colossal human and policy failures. Segregation is a key mechanism whites have used to undercut the chance that Black and Hispanic children can do better than their parents. The implications of Johnson's results are that those who don't have the benefit of attending equal schools will experience harms that extend beyond childhood into adulthood. School segregation casts a very long shadow—from before *Brown* to the present. Without decisive action, that shadow will persist.

3

Nothing to Do Here but Drugs

KEN BOLIN—A SOLIDLY BUILT sixty-something man with gray-blond hair and a scruffy beard, known locally as "Pastor Ken"—has led Manchester Baptist Church, in the county seat of Clay County, Kentucky, for many years. In 2019, he vividly recounted the events that finally spurred him to action in an interview with Bill Estep of the *Lexington Herald-Leader*. A twelve-year-old girl had started hanging around the church. It is hard to keep a secret in a small town, so Bolin knew her mom suffered from addiction and supported her habit through prostitution. He tried to find the woman help, but treatment beds were scarce. When he finally found a placement, she refused to go. Just days before Christmas 2002, she set out on foot to a drug dealer's house to score, then collapsed on her way home. She died in the cold. Bolin officiated at her funeral on Christmas Eve. "It was devastating to me," he told Estep. The death of that young mom instilled a deep conviction in Bolin that Clay County's churches must step up to fight the scourge that, even in those early days of the opioid epidemic, had already begun to consume this mountain community.

Meanwhile, Doug Abner, pastor of one of the local Pentecostal churches, was learning of youths who were getting addicted, overdosing, and even dying. These kids weren't only from tough backgrounds. Some were children of local business owners and other community leaders—even the daughter of the school superintendent had come close to death. For Abner and the whole community, what was happening to these young people was a real wake-up call: "When your kids start dying, you look at things different."

Thus began a regular Saturday prayer meeting where a small group of pastors gathered to pray for the community. More and more people—not just clergy but also parishioners, some with loved ones who had perished—joined the group. Quickly, they realized they had to take a public stand. They decided to organize a march to confront the dealers who had taken over the town and the corrupt public officials who were complicit, willfully turning a blind eye.

On May 2, 2003, the day of the march, the weather turned rainy and cold. Bolin, Abner, and the other organizers feared turnout would be low. That morning, Abner told the *Lexington Herald-Leader*, one local official—Abner wouldn't say who—had called warning him that children shouldn't attend. There was a rumor that a drug dealer planned to plow a truck through the crowd. "It was another one of those veiled threats," Abner recalled. He hung up on the caller.

That afternoon, congregants from roughly sixty churches arrived at the parking lot of Eastern Kentucky University's Manchester campus to walk to City Hall. As the *Manchester Enterprise* reported in a 2019 retrospective commemorating the event, "Nobody could have predicted what would happen that day. 3,500 people showed up for what many say was the largest single gathering in our county's history. Nothing before had brought that many people together for one purpose. . . . It was evident to all, this group meant business. They weren't intimidated by the political structure or power. This was an effort to save our county, our children and our families."

America's internal colonies are some of the sickest places in the nation, but the sickest region of all is central Appalachia. The most disproportionate cause of death here compared to the nation as a whole is the sharp rise in mortality due to drug overdose over the past thirty years. On November 17, 2021, local listeners tuned in to regional newscaster Carrie Hodousek's reporting that following the onset of the COVID-19 pandemic and the rise in substance use that accompanied it, "yearly overdose deaths have topped 100,000 for the first time . . . according to new federal data published Wednesday." While overdose deaths increased nearly 30 percent between April 2020 and April 2021 nationwide, "Kentucky ranked third with a 55 percent spike." Hodousek concluded, "Nationwide drug overdoses now surpass deaths from car crashes, guns, and even flu and pneumonia. The total is close to that for diabetes, the nation's No. 7 cause of death."

From the earliest days of the opioid epidemic, Clay and its neighboring counties have seen some of the highest opioid prescribing rates in the nation. When we began our fieldwork there in 2019, thirteen pharmacies were operating in the tiny hamlet of Manchester, a city of only eighteen hundred residents, all but two opening since Kentucky expanded Medicaid in 2014. Apparently, there has been plenty of business to go around. Even in 2019, when the dangers of opioids were well-known, 1.3 prescriptions for these powerful and addictive painkillers were filled annually for every person—man, woman, and child—in the county. Residents we spoke with reported high rates of concurrent substance use (e.g., methamphetamines and prescription opioids) and believed that methadone and buprenorphine (commonly known by the brand name Suboxone) were increasingly used recreationally. By the early 2020s, black tar heroin had arrived in town, a cheap but potentially lethal substitute for prescription opioids. Research has shown that most people who start using heroin were previously using prescription opioids.

The drug epidemic in central Appalachia is the fallout from a modern-day extractive industry—led by Big Pharma—that in many ways mimics industries like Big Coal and Big Timber that have come before. We tell the story of these other industries later in this chapter, but here we focus on the modern-day version of capitalist extraction, one in which capitalists depend on the local family practitioner—and the pharmacist willing to turn a blind eye—to do their bidding. Witting or not, the resource these accomplices extract is the health and well-being—really the bodies—of their own community's most vulnerable residents. The wreckage of the timber and coal industries pockmark the topography of the region, with its hillsides washed clean of topsoil, with its muddy streams, flat-topped mountains, piles of slag, rusted tipples, and ruins of former company stores. Everywhere, too, are the signs of the human wreckage of opioids—on the roadsides, in the emergency rooms, and at the morgues.

Why central Appalachia? It is tempting to look no further than the easy cultural stereotypes that flow from memoirs such as J. D. Vance's *Hillbilly Elegy*, which can be read as a reprise of the age-old notion of the backward mountaineer. Instead, Princeton economists Anne Case and Angus Deaton have attributed part of the rise in fatal overdoses and other "deaths of despair" (suicide and liver-related mortality) to a long-term decline in the life chances of the white working class, a trend as evident in this region as anywhere else. Surely the infiltration of drugs was driven by a surfeit of local demand caused by worsening economic conditions. But the bituminous coal region didn't become an epicenter of opioid addiction as a result of long-term economic decline alone. Other researchers point out that these same economic conditions characterized other regions as well, yet the epidemic didn't manifest in those places to nearly the same degree.

Patrick Keefe, author of *Empire of Pain: The Secret History of the Sackler Dynasty*, places the blame squarely on Big Pharma. Keefe found that Purdue Pharma intentionally chose the back roads of central Appalachia to market its new blockbuster long-acting opioid OxyContin. Why? Long before OxyContin was approved by the Food and Drug Administration in the mid-1990s, enduring problems in the region had laid the foundation for an unprecedented human catastrophe. These vulnerabilities put a target on central Appalachia's back.

Purdue "targeted certain regions in particular—places where there were a lot of family physicians," whom they assumed would be more naive and thus more susceptible to persuasion, notes Keefe. Central Appalachia fit the bill, as nearly all the doctors there were family physicians. A related factor weighed heavily as well: central

Appalachia topped the nation in disability claims. People on temporary (Workers' Compensation) or permanent (SSI or SSDI) disability automatically qualify for Medicaid—providing a means to pay for prescription painkillers even before the Medicaid expansion of 2014. Many had qualified for these programs due to chronic pain.

Keefe describes how Richard Sackler himself, the president of Purdue, led the marketing campaign for the new drug, and how he said the company "focused our salesmen's attention" on physicians "who write a lot of prescriptions for opioids." A doctor who did so was an invaluable asset to Purdue. "Like casino employees talking about an especially profligate gambler," Keefe writes, "the sales reps referred to these doctors as 'whales.'" Physicians in the region had been prescribing, and probably overprescribing, other, less potent forms of opioids such as morphine, combined with Valium, well before the epidemic. Indeed, the pattern may well have gone back generations. In his 1963 classic, *Night Comes to the Cumberlands: A Biography of a Depressed Area*, Kentucky lawyer Harry M. Caudill writes that "pain-masking sedatives became commonplace in the region's coalfields decades ago as doctors, stretched thin and pressed to help legions of injured miners and sick poor people, handed out 'bags and bottles of pills.'"

By most early measures, the May 2003 church-led march in Manchester was a remarkable success. It sparked a federal RICO (Racketeer Influenced and Corrupt Organizations Act) investigation into the corruption of public officials. Drug dealers went to jail, along with some complicit politicians who had provided protection for dealers—a theme we will explore in more detail later in the book. But in one vital respect, the march failed. Three years afterward, in 2006, when the rate of opioid prescriptions had begun to take off nationwide, there were 258 opioid prescriptions for every hundred people in Clay County, nearly three and a half times the national average. The impact of these prescribing practices across central Appalachia was seldom subtle. According to Patrick Keefe, some "communities began to resemble a zombie movie, as the phenomenon claimed one citizen after another, sending previously well-adjusted, functioning adults into a spiral of dependence and addiction." Research has found that state laws targeting "pill mills"—pharmacies that prescribe a disproportionate number of opioids—are linked to thousands of lives saved from prescription opioid overdose.

We saw a bit of the devastation of addiction firsthand when we stopped for gas while visiting Clay during a bitterly cold January day in 2019. A woman, pale and rail thin, with no winter coat, hat, gloves, or even shoes, approached our car asking if we could give her a ride home. She told us she had walked to town in search of cigarettes, yet we noticed that the package she was holding held none. When we delivered her down a narrow dirt road to her address, it became clear that she was living not in a house, but in a car parked on the side of the road. Repeatedly, Clay residents across the class divide had warned us about the danger posed by "walkers," people living in the hollows (small groupings of homes amid the hills) who, they alleged, appeared in town—zombie-like—to buy, beg, or steal for a fix.

Today, nearly thirty years after OxyContin was first marketed in central Appalachia, these high-potency opioids are still prescribed, albeit in a more tamperproof form. Across the nation, the prescription rate peaked in 2012 at 81 prescriptions per 100 persons and then declined. Yet as of this writing, there are still more opioid prescriptions than people in Clay County. Several of the many pharmacies there will still fill those prescriptions. And Big Pharma continues to rake in enormous profits from its sales in the region.

In the months our team spent in Clay County during the summer of 2019, we would learn that part of what made the human field so fertile for this modern-day form of extraction was that there was "nothing to do here but drugs." It was a singular refrain—voiced over and over by the dozens of residents we spoke to. In a word, the crumbling social infrastructure of the area was seen as a reason for the drugs. We asked dozens of residents across the class spectrum what would help the community the most. The top recommendation for change was jobs. After that, it was places providing things to do, like a community center, a movie theater, or an arcade—these topped the list.

Truth be told, the first few times we heard "nothing to do" as a cause of the epidemic, we dismissed it as unlikely, a cliché. Yet after hearing the same claim repeatedly, we began to take it seriously. Perhaps we needed to look beyond economic factors, government policies, and the behavior of Big Pharma to understand fully the sources of vulnerability to the epidemic. What if having "something to do"—something to knit the community together and give young people the sense of belonging that could fend off the anomic allure of drugs—was a vital, yet unrecognized, contributor?

One Manchester resident who goes by the nickname Sweet Pea* put it this way: "There's really nothing around here for kids. That's why they go to drugs." Her house sits at the end of a well-kept gravel road. Its two shades of vivid pink are the result of a well-meaning group of "missionaries" visiting the area who didn't realize they had bought two different hues. When we spoke, she wore two versions of her favorite color (a bright purple T-shirt and eggplant-colored sweatpants) while leaning back in her plastic chair and flashing an infectious smile. Nothing at all to do in Clay and not much across the county line either, she told us: "There's nothing [there] anymore, since their skating rink burned . . . they don't got anything except one movie theater."

Political scientist Robert Putnam, following the nineteenth-century French political writer Alexis de Tocqueville and others who have argued that voluntary associations are the key to building social bonds, made famous the decline of the bowling league. He warned it was a harbinger of the eventual degradation of democracy. But in the small rural hamlets in central Appalachia, it wasn't that bowling

---

* All community residents are referred to by pseudonyms to protect confidentiality. Throughout the text, to avoid revealing personal identifying information, minor details have sometimes been altered.

leagues had fallen out of fashion. Rather, there was no longer a bowling alley at all.

Dolly's small hands shook as she dipped her spoon in the bowl of soup on offer at God's Closet, a homeless shelter and multiservice center run by Pastor Ken's congregation. Her bright blue glasses were a little too large for her face. When we asked her what people should know about her community, she offered, "I just want things to change. I mean, better for the kids, better for the teenagers; stuff that the teenagers can do instead of getting on drugs. Parks for the little kids, something for the teenagers to do to get them out of trouble. Stuff that they can do." Crystal, whom we also met at God's Closet, offered a similar analysis: "There's nothing really here for kids, and then they wonder why they get on drugs. Because there's nothing for them to do. Like we had the movies a long time ago. And like I said, [the movie theater has] turned into a church. And there ain't nothing here really for young'uns to do."

Travis lives with his girlfriend, Helena, in a trailer lacking air-conditioning and running water. The structure sits on her family's land; the two live there free of charge in exchange for working to fix up the place. He offered us a Mountain Dew from a dorm-sized fridge perched precariously on a countertop while a pair of kittens frolicked amid a stack of DVDs borrowed from the library. A horror movie played silently on the TV. This slight man with short brown hair told us he wasn't fond of his hometown and didn't have happy memories of growing up here. "There ain't nothing around here to do," he said, slouched in a chair tucked in one corner of the stiflingly hot trailer. "One time when I was younger, we was [hanging out] in Walmart's parking lot, just listening to our stereos and stuff, [and] the cops come and run us off. . . . That's the big flaw around here. That's why I think everybody turns to drugs around here."

Marie moved to Clay County from Indiana while in her teens. She told us she is desperate to go back because "[they have] more stuff for the kids. . . . Down here, they just want to build roads and . . . drugstores, so it's not nothing that you can really do down here."

Middle-class and poor, resident after resident in Clay County linked the opioid crisis to the loss of the bowling alley, the roller-skating rink, the swimming pool, and the movie theaters. Several noted that even the one park with a playground for young children had recently been bulldozed for the construction of a new highway through town. In his 2018 book, *Palaces for the People*, sociologist Eric Klinenberg argues forcefully that "the future of democratic societies rests not simply on shared values but on shared spaces: The libraries, childcare centers, bookstores, churches, synagogues, and parks in which crucial, sometimes life-saving connections are formed." These spaces, including something as seemingly simple as a beauty salon in a neighborhood or town, play a vital role in forging the human connections that weave communities together. They can provide a tailwind that lifts people's chances in life and, like a net for a tight-rope walker, can catch them when they fall.

Klinenberg opens *Palaces for the People* with the story of the Chicago heat wave of 1995. As the temperature rose to 106 that July, the Centers for Disease Control and Prevention recorded almost 740 more deaths in Chicago than usual, "roughly seven times the toll from Superstorm Sandy and more than twice as many as in the Great Chicago Fire." The morgues overflowed. To understand who was most vulnerable and what could be done to prevent a similar tragedy in years to come, researchers descended on Chicago, visiting hundreds of homes, comparing "matched pairs" of victims and survivors. Not surprisingly, a working air conditioner cut the risk of death by 80 percent. But social isolation also proved deadly. In Klinenberg's own research, he used "matched pairs" as well—but of similar communities rather than of comparable people. Through the course of his work in the aftermath of the heat wave, he writes, "I'd discovered that the key differences between [like] neighborhoods . . . turned out to be what I call *social infrastructure:* the physical places and organizations that shape the way people interact." He concluded that in the heat wave, living in a neighborhood with robust social infrastructure was "the rough equivalent of having a working air conditioner in every home."

Klinenberg shows that some forms of social infrastructure—like public libraries and community centers that offer regular programming, plus churches and schools that provide space for recurring interaction—foster durable relationships. Others, such as playgrounds and parks, support looser ties, connections that may grow as people form deeper bonds. "Countless close friendships between mothers, and then entire families, begin because two toddlers visit the same swing set," he writes.

"But when the social infrastructure gets degraded, the consequences are unmistakable," Klinenberg warns. People hunker down and stop frequenting public spaces. Social ties atrophy. Disorder and crime rise. Old folks grow lonely, and the young get high. Mistrust increases. Civic participation, such as volunteering and voting, fades. This description fits closely with community residents' claims about what has happened in Clay County.

We don't mean to overdraw the portrait of Clay as a place utterly lacking in anything to do but drugs. In all of our interviews, we collected detailed information on what people do for entertainment and recreation. Cable television is key: almost all, whether middle-class or poor, have subscriptions to basic cable, as well as to streaming platforms like Netflix and Hulu. One could argue that it's far more isolating to stream personal content than to consume content the old ways, where families watched TV together or young people from across the community attended the Saturday matinee. But there's at least some social contact built into the fact that some residents cannot afford the cost of these subscriptions and so depend on someone else's Wi-Fi to download movies onto their phones. Helena, for example, lives with Travis in the trailer owned by her mother-in-law, Margie. She doesn't have a car, so her social calendar is limited. When asked what her daily routine is like, she replied, "[I'll] walk up to

Margie's [in the morning] and get on the internet, download a couple movies [that I'll watch later on]." The internet is also a huge pastime, though people also blame it for all manner of ills, including marital breakups.

Seventy-one-year-old Susie practices the time-honored Appalachian ritual of sitting on her porch "visiting" with her neighbors in the evenings. Her children visit on Sundays, she told us. "My kids, they come every Sunday and have dinner after church. And I get to see them and my grandbabies." Stephen and his wife also have a weekly visiting ritual: "We hang out and stuff on the weekends [at the home of a friend], and he's got a pool at his house and it's kind of what we do. . . . We made ribs last weekend . . . and cake."

While visiting the area, we were surprised at the number of aboveground pools we saw, often fronting 1970s-era trailers or tiny, century-old Jenny Lind coal camp homes, holdovers from the company towns that once dotted the area. Even more frequent were trampolines, a poor family's substitute for a visit to the pricey Air Raid trampoline park in London, a city with considerably more amenities about forty minutes away.

Middle-class families in Clay have access to a greater range of leisure activities than poor families. Biking, car racing, fishing, and ATVing are all popular, and there is an emerging music scene. But these activities require equipment, some of it costly. In 2020, the price of an ATV ranged from $5,000 to $11,000. Also, while some residents use fishing and ATVing as ways to get together with others, there are no official, maintained spots for these activities. Jake is among the 4 percent of county residents who are Black. He is an avid fisherman, but, as he explained to us, it doesn't earn him many social connections: "There's a lake at the end of Beech Creek. If you didn't know where you were going, you'd get lost. It's not in plain view. . . . There's no garbage cans out there. There's no Porta Potties or anything like that out there. It's just a lake."

Many in Clay County go to considerable lengths to seek out things to do. Jake regularly takes his three children to the movie theater in

London. Angel drives to David's Steak House and Buffet in Corbin, nearly an hour away, for special occasions. Scarlet's kids attend an arts program at Eastern Kentucky University's Manchester campus, though she told us that the enrichment activity is only open to a few: "You've got a lot of people here who don't participate because maybe they don't have the gas money to get there. [Manchester would be a much better place to live] if they had the programs and could do the funding and know how to write grants for music and for arts and things."

A few local traditions are still alive in the area, though. Angel lives with her daughter and her daughter's boyfriend, who spends some of his free time working at cockfights, preparing the animals and watching over them during events. Despite its illegality (not to mention cruelty), this is okay with Angel because "if that makes [the kids] happy and gives them something to do, and it ain't drug-related, go ahead, peck them chickens, baby." Aurora has a boyfriend who raises and fights chickens for extra income: "[He'll] chicken fight during the summer, and [the owners] give him money for taking care of them. . . . He'll help tag them, he trains them, and he'll fight them. . . . He don't have the money to get in there and [fight his own chickens]. But yeah, if they win, which they've won a couple times, [he gets some of the winnings]."

While gatherings with a few kin or friends on a porch or at a cook-out are not rare, what is notable about other forms of entertainment in Clay is that, with the exception of cockfighting, which can draw big crowds, they either involve solo pursuits—watching TV, streaming a movie—or are usually done with a close friend or relative, as with fishing or ATVing. For a while, one rural church congregation hosted a youth soccer league, but that fizzled.

Chad's Hope, a faith-based addiction recovery program established in the aftermath of the 2003 march, is perhaps one of the town's most important antidotes to the "nothing to do but drugs" scourge. The program's modest space was built on land donated by local businessman Charlie McWhorter, who joined Bolin and Abner's prayer group after he lost his son Chad to a drug overdose. When the *Manchester Enterprise* ran an ad seeking volunteers for Chad's Hope, ninety people showed up.

Among the lower-income residents we spoke with, the institution on most people's lips was Pastor Ken's church. Under his direction, it operated the nonprofit God's Closet, offering used clothes, hygiene products, and—on Mondays—a noon meal, until the COVID-19 pandemic closed it down. It is perhaps due to the charity work of this church that Pastor Ken is the most beloved figure in town, according to our interviewees.

Not only does Manchester Baptist Church provide sustenance to the needy, it also offers vital opportunities for community engagement. Volunteers include middle-class parishioners and welfare recipients alike. When the soup kitchen was open, moms on welfare could complete their community work hours ladling soup or folding and organizing the used clothing at God's Closet. For some, the opportunity to volunteer has been a literal lifesaver. James, who lives in the church's homeless shelter, told us that volunteering for Pastor Ken was his only opportunity to interact with others. Prior to the pandemic, he helped with the Monday meal, but he also worked with out-of-state mission teams who often travel to the area to do home repairs and install wheelchair ramps for those in need. James said the work was important to him "because I'm not sitting [around] all day. I could never do that. I would commit suicide if I had to do that. Yeah. I don't even have a wife, you know. Ain't nothing [else] to live for."

Could it be true that such a mundane establishment as a soup kitchen could count as the kind of social infrastructure that can turn the tide against the allure of opioids? Political scientist Michael Zoorob and epidemiologist Jason Salemi have found that the density of nonprofits and civic organizations, plus voting and other behaviors within a community are indeed strongly tied to overdose death rates. But they did not capture what are likely the key sites of social infrastructure in a community, such as its bowling alleys, movie theaters, beauty shops, and arcades.

For our own investigation, we partnered with sociologist Michael Evangelist to exploit a unique form of government data—a census of all US businesses. Using these data, we measured losses (or gains) of key sites of social infrastructure in every US county between 1996 and 2015. We then examined whether there was a relationship between changes in the presence of these forms of social infrastructure and changes in the overdose death rates (which are more reliably measured than addiction rates) during those same years, all else held equal. These data have big limitations, chief among them being that they include only institutions that have at least one paid employee other than the proprietor, leaving out many barbershops, churches, and other one-person operations. Parks and libraries are excluded, too. This isn't a statistical analysis that we are ready to bet our careers on. Yet even with these imperfect data, we have found evidence that places that maintain spaces that promote interactions at the community level have seen a lower rate of overdose deaths. This is true to an extent rivaling the effects of other, more well-accepted economic factors, such as wages and unemployment rates. While far from definitive, our research provides some support for the view of so many of the people we talked to in Clay County—that when these spaces are lost, the civic safety net a healthy community forms to catch people when they fall is torn apart.

As further evidence for this claim, Klinenberg points to what he characterizes as "a growing body of neurological research showing that opioids are, chemically speaking, a good analog for social connection." In a *New York Times* guest essay, "Opioids Feel Like Love: That's Why They're Deadly in Tough Times," science writer Maia Szalavitz offers a summary of this research: "Opioids mimic the neurotransmitters that are responsible for making social connection comforting—tying parent to child, lover to beloved. The brain also makes its own opioids. These endogenous ones include endorphins and enkephalins that are better recognized for their roles in pleasure and pain but are also critical to the formation and maintenance of social bonds."

While opioids may impersonate love, it is clear from our research that they increase the agony of social isolation. At the neighborhood level, responses to widespread addiction have made strangers out of neighbors and kin. Scores of marriages have broken down. Parents have been separated from their kids and desperately struggle for the sobriety that might help them regain custody. Anyone who drives the back roads of the region will note the plethora of placards affixed to telephone polls advertising for foster parents. With the breakdown in social ties at all levels in central Appalachia, it is hard to imagine a place in the nation where social isolation among the poor is more pronounced, where social cohesion is more fragile.

Demographer Emily Miller and sociologists Liv Mann and Lanora Johnson—all collaborators on this research—embedded in Clay County during the summer of 2019, combining forty-seven in-depth interviews (with twenty-two low-income families and twenty-five community leaders) with over fifty hours of participant observation in three months' time. Repeatedly, they were struck by the forcefulness with which many of the lower-income participants emphasized that they kept to themselves, as if it were a point of pride, or even a signal of morality. As they would learn, nearly all of these experiences and attitudes are colored by the scourge of drugs.

Aurora is afraid that her relatives, many of whom suffer from addiction, will be a drain on her limited resources: "I've had people that they'll come down, 'Well let me stay a night or two?' And then we end up with them for months. . . . You let them borrow a little bit of money and . . . they won't pay you back. And then there's just some that you can't be good to. No matter what you do, you can't be good to them, [or else] they'll steal from you. Let's see, I had one little girl that . . . was kin to [my husband], and she stayed a couple weeks with us, but she robbed us [to buy drugs]." Similarly, Miranda has a sister who is battling addiction and "takes advantage of me sometimes. . . . She'll come and steal something and sell it. . . . I have to watch her. She aggravates me when she comes over because she goes through my stuff. I tell her not to, but she won't listen to me. So I have to stand over her and watch her, every move she makes."

For some, the sheer prevalence of drug addiction has led to wholesale withdrawal from the community. "You can't hang out with people anymore because half of them is on drugs and stuff," Lulu said. "When they ain't on drugs, they're drinking. That's what they want to do. . . . I don't want to hang out with people with drama and crap like that." For similar reasons, Helena claimed she has no close relationships. She used to live in Ohio with her mother until she realized she had to get her daughters away from local kin, many of whom were addicted to heroin. Ironically, due to her husband's kinship ties, the family landed in opioid- and methamphetamine-rich Clay County. Another participant said she will no longer open the door to neighbors if they come calling for fear that they are using and might harm her.

Addiction also tears at the fabric of the nuclear family. After several years of dating, Crystal finally married the father of her youngest child. A year later, they divorced because "he got on drugs. . . . Drugs took over, and I'm not like that. I don't do that." Similarly, Lulu described what happened when her husband, whom she had been with since she was fourteen, became addicted: "Money started disappearing. He was staying out, staying out all night, getting high and stuff like that. His priorities just weren't with me and the girls. . . . One day . . . when he was gone . . . I left. Got [in] my car. I left everything there. Didn't [take anything with me]. Took off."

Especially poignant are the stories of mothers who became addicted and lost custody of their kids. Four in our small sample saw their children taken by the state. All claimed they were working hard to stay clean and regain custody. Loretta, a mother of two, told us, "I just knew that if I got out there on drugs [again] that I wouldn't get to keep my kids, or I wouldn't have a life for them. And it was either my kids or the drugs." Paige, a mother of three, said, "So I'm staying clean and trying to do the right thing for my kids."

This brings us to the role of churches, so numerous in Clay County that they are difficult to count. Despite their role in building social capital, we found that these key institutions—consciously or not—can also function in ways that inhibit social cohesion across the community. Klinenberg acknowledges that institutions can "set boundaries that define who is part of the community and who is excluded. They can integrate or segregate, create opportunities or keep people in their place."

To illustrate how this can occur, Klinenberg draws on the history of America's municipal swimming pools, chronicled in historian Jeff Wiltse's 2007 book, *Contested Waters.* "Swimming pools and other social infrastructures with potential to facilitate sustained, intimate interaction across group lines can easily be used to segregate instead," Klinenberg writes. According to Klinenberg, Wiltse shows how swimming pools have been places both of cohesion and conflict, precisely because they are spaces in which residents not only build a sense of community belonging but also define the boundaries of who is an insider and who is an outsider. When integration came, many southern towns chose to fill in the municipal pool with cement.

Our statistical analysis described earlier in this chapter revealed that on average, the continuing presence of churches is a net positive and associated with a lower level of opioid deaths. Some churchgoers—mainly those from the middle class—described to us the deep sense of belonging these institutions foster. Lindsay, for example, told us, "I've lived here my whole life, and I have been a member of the same church my whole life. It becomes a family. . . . My church family is as close to me as . . . what a lot of my biological family is."

Yet it's not clear whether a majority of people living in central

Appalachia feel as welcomed by the churches as Lindsay does. Despite the abundance of churches in the region, membership has always been notably low.

Few of our low-income interviewees said they are involved in local congregations. Marie told us that while God played a big role in her life, church did not. "I just don't go to church, because a lot of churches are hypocrites. . . . Most of the churches I've went to they've always talked about me, or my makeup, or pants. So I just don't go." Miranda said that God is the most important thing in her life, a virtue she hopes to instill in her children. But when it comes to church, she said, "Problem is with church, there are people that look down on people. If there weren't people like them, there'd be more people in the church. I'm not judging those people because that's their business. That's between them and God. But if it weren't for people like that, I think a lot of people would go to church. I know I would."

The Christian faith is an important source of identity in the community. Aurora, for example, told us, "I would say ninety percent of the people [in Manchester], they believe in God. They might not go to church, but they all believe in God." Dolly reminisced about her childhood in the hollow as one of thirteen children whose family practiced subsistence farming. To Dolly, faith is part of Manchester's DNA: "God is the most important thing in this little town we got." Yet as Klinenberg points out, "Social cohesion develops through repeated human interaction and joint participation in shared projects," not just from "principled commitment to abstract values and beliefs."

Manchester Baptist Church, with its many charitable endeavors, has clearly been a critical source of social cohesion. Other congregations seem effective at reaching across the class divide in meaningful ways as well. Sweet Pea has had three husbands. She attends a Holiness church every Sunday. "I was born Catholic," she explained. "Then I met my kids' dad. He's Baptist, or whatever you want to call it. . . . And then I met the guy I've got now, he's a holy roller. . . .

[When I first visited his church], you could feel love when you walked in the door. . . . And they help you out. Like, my husband had a stroke. After he came home, and within about a week, we went to church and everything. . . . They took an offering up and gave it to us and we wasn't even expecting it. Just to help us. They gave us close to $200 and we weren't expecting it."

There is clearly power for good in Clay County's places of worship. Indeed, the 2003 march against drugs would not have happened without them. Members of more than sixty area churches, presumably both the more established ones and the "holy roller" variety that Sweet Pea and her husband attend, participated in the march. Fully 3,500 people showed up—roughly one in seven county residents and nearly double the population of the town of Manchester. This suggests that it wasn't just well-to-do parishioners who came out. Indeed, when we mentioned the march, our low-income interviewees uniformly praised it.

THE COLLAPSE OF BIG COAL

This is not the first time central Appalachia's communities have experienced an implosion of social infrastructure. In a dramatic upheaval seven decades ago, much of the social infrastructure that existed in this region collapsed all at once, leaving only remnants found in county seats like Manchester and in the larger towns. The collapse came with the shuttering of the company towns.

Big Timber and Big Coal provided much of the early social infrastructure as the internal colony here began to develop and expand. For a time, the company-owned movie theaters, bowling alleys, and other institutions that brought people together and shaped interactions. Due to near-complete segregation by race, however, these institutions were never truly inclusive of all those living in the towns. Furthermore, the pluses of living in a company town came at a heavy price: sharp limits to autonomy placed on the residents of these places. Still, their benefits were felt.

Coal towns began to appear across the central Appalachian landscape as early as the 1880s. Construction peaked in the 1920s. Hundreds of company towns dotted the map of central Appalachia during that time. Towns were often named after the mine owners, their wives (or mistresses), or other officials. Commenting on this feature of the Appalachian landscape in a 1970s oral history, local activist and historian Warren Wright exclaimed, "We really honor our exploiters here, we mountain people do. Almost every town in the area is named for some bastard from outside the region who gutted it."

Life could be tough in the early days of the industry, especially in the smaller mining operations, like the string of fourteen independently owned coal camps that began just south of Manchester and moved west along Horse Creek, as well as the rough-hewn coal camp of Barwick, Kentucky, where Robert F. Kennedy visited that one-room school. But in places where the mines were owned by large corporations such as US Steel and International Harvester, the towns were often planned with worker satisfaction in mind. In southwestern Virginia, Stonega Coke and Coal was the force behind many of the company towns. SC&C was convinced that paternalism—what some corporations called "contentment sociology"—was the key to securing a stable labor force and keeping out the unions.

Knowledge is exceedingly scarce about what life was like in many of these SC&C and other coal towns, including in Clay County. Yet we know a great deal about Wheelwright, a model coal town in eastern Kentucky's Floyd County, built by the Elkhorn Coal Company in 1916 and later purchased by Inland Steel. Town manager E. R. "Jack" Price was a huge believer in contentment sociology. Under his direction, Inland modernized the town by building a water system, filtration plant, and sewage system and, in 1942, installing flush toilets in every home. That same year, a lot on which a boardinghouse had stood was transformed into a swimming pool, and a bowling alley was built. Inland loaned the county $15,000 for the construction of a high school. Under Jack Price's deft management, the town grew and prospered, boasting a fine library, an inn and restaurant, a hospital, a movie theater, and a department store. There was even an eighteen-hole golf course available for miners' use. Many came to call Wheelwright "the town that Jack built."

Life in these towns was often far superior to that of a subsistence or tenant farmer, especially once the "frontier stage" of the coal towns was superseded by the "paternalist phase," which came with greater mine consolidation and labor shortages during the First World War. White miner Melvin Proffit grew up in a farm family but went to work in the mines in 1921 when he was seventeen. When he married, Proffit returned home from the mines just once a month. "I had to do that in order to support the family," he said. In his home county, "there has been a number of people to starve and almost went naked. Where I worked on one of these farms for seventy-five cents a day to [buy my] bread and meat, well I was making seven to ten [dollars] in the mines."

In 1944, young Melba Kizzire, from a Black tenant farming family in Tennessee, moved with her parents to a mining town on the edge of central Appalachia. She said that it was the first time she had ever seen a telephone or a "flushing john" or had lived in a painted house. What really struck her, though, was the wallpaper. "The most beautiful wallpaper I had ever seen," she remembered. "I was stunned for about a week. It was like I had gone to heaven you know." As the paternalistic period advanced, medical care and education were also far superior to that received at the county facilities because salaries were paid by the company, and the clinics, hospitals, and schools were run by it as well.

Not all amenities were accessible to everyone. Like most coal towns, Wheelwright was thoroughly segregated by race. Hall Hollow was the name of its Black settlement. In *Coal Towns*, historian Crandall Shifflett tells the story of Hilton Garrett, a Black miner who came to Wheelwright from Alabama in 1923: "When asked why he could not go to the soda fountain and be served, Garrett explained it was due to Jim Crowism. The interviewer responded: 'I never heard of that. How'd that get started?' Garrett replied in a way that suggested he believed the interviewer had to be putting him on." Wheelwright's Black students had their own school on the periphery of town, well away from the white school in the town center. It had only three or four teachers. When the swimming pool was built in 1942, Black families were not allowed to use it, and there were separate facilities for churches and recreation, too.

No coal town was without a company store, the "social and economic nexus of the company town." Not only goods and clothing but furniture, appliances, buckets, nails, radios, garden tools, and household gadgets were some of the items available in a typical company store. You could get your hair cut and styled, have a shoeshine, and get your laundry done. A 1947 government report characterized the role of the company store as the "mecca for everyone in every coal camp. Even when the store is closed, the men gather there in their free time, frequently after working hours, and on Sundays and holidays. It is a common sight in summer to see miners, and often the women and children in the community, sitting or squatting on the porch or steps of the store, relaxing in idle talk." It was the only place of relaxation for the wives of the miners, where they would "learn and dispense the local news, read their mail, and meet their friends, as well as buy their groceries and supplies. . . . It is commissary, club room, and bulletin board rolled into one."

The company church was also part and parcel of contentment sociology, just like the schools and all the leisure and recreation amenities. In Wheelwright, there were Methodist, Baptist, Church of Christ, and Church of God churches, often two of each kind for both Black and white congregations.

As company towns across central Appalachia closed in the early 1950s, much of this company-owned social infrastructure came crashing down in just a few years. The churches, whose operating costs had been covered by the company, were left to fend for themselves, as were the schools and hospitals, whose relatively high-skilled staff had usually been paid a premium to work in the model towns. Those movie theaters, bowling alleys, and the like? All owned by the company. Few survived. Same with the inns and restaurants. All of it, within just a few years, gone.

Hilton Garrett, the Black miner hailing from Alabama, described the mammoth changes in Wheelwright in the span of just a few decades' time. According to him, Wheelwright in the 1930s was loaded with "a good bunch of people" and "a bunch of youngsters." But in the 1950s, few people remained except the elderly. "Gone too were the filling stations, shoe shops, a soda fountain, and the bathhouse. The trains no longer came through. Even the train station disappeared," Garrett said.

The story of the demise of social infrastructure is richly—and poignantly—illustrated by the case of baseball. Prior to the Second World War, the Sunday afternoon baseball game was the most revered social ritual in a company town. It was the miners' sport. Every little town had a team. Picnic baskets of corn bread and fried chicken were enjoyed by all. Children cavorted while their mothers gossiped and cheered for the home team. Mine operators engaged in stiff competition to lure the most talented players to their camps. Even today, as we noted on visits to the region, nearly every municipality has a baseball field in the center of town. Yet the same forces that beset the coal towns led to the decline of baseball. Shifflett explains: "When the UMWA [United Mine Workers of America] organized the miners, the coal operators ceased to sponsor the teams, buy uniforms, and organize leagues. Without company backing, the number of teams dwindled. . . . In the 1950s, the closing of the company towns virtually ended the sport." It is remarkable that so much social infrastructure was destroyed all at once, like during a war.

A question remains: How did the loss of these places, and the bonds they fostered, get etched into the bodies of the residents and the fabric of the community there? Across a broad array of diseases, central Appalachians die younger and more often than people in other parts of the country. The myriad health problems facing the region have been severe for many years. Even before the opioid epidemic, exposure to environmental toxins, limited access to health care, and risky health behaviors such as smoking were all challenges the region faced. We see evidence, though, that the loss of social infrastructure also played some role. Possibly because social infrastructure is difficult to measure, we know of no research linking its demise to a decline in health outcomes, other than the nascent work tentatively linking the loss of social infrastructure to drug overdose deaths reviewed here. Yet given what we've learned about the social determinants of health, we think the idea is worth exploring.

This chapter started with a march against drugs that took place on May 2, 2003, in Manchester, Kentucky. In another southern town, Selma, in the heart of the Alabama Cotton Belt, a march took place nearly forty years earlier, on March 7, 1965, for the cause of civil rights. Its participants also numbered in the thousands.

We visited Selma as part of our 2021 tour. The city was to be our headquarters for exploring the cluster of Cotton Belt counties there. Determined to avoid yet another meal at one of the ubiquitous chain restaurants one finds on the main drag of nearly every small southern town, we headed to what promised to be the fanciest place to dine in Selma—the Tally-Ho. Like scores of other eating establishments across the South, this hunting lodge turned supper club had resisted integration by becoming "members only." To eliminate the possibility that any Black Americans not in the know would dare try to dine there, the original owners installed a solid door with a peephole—or so the former owner (his son-in-law now owns the restaurant) told us when he stopped by our table to ask where we were from and what we were doing in town. Even in this town of 18,000, drivers with out-of-state license plates are clearly the object of curiosity.

Quickly, the Tally-Ho's former owner launched into what was obviously a favorite story. As a salesman from Columbus, Ohio, whose territory included parts of the Deep South, he had frequently traveled to Selma. On one trip, he learned that the infamous Tally-Ho, still members only in the mid-1980s, was for sale and jumped at the chance to buy it. The first thing he did was tear down that door and integrate the club, he told us. While we were dining, several other regulars stopped by to say hello, both Black and white, including the president of Selma's Rotary Club, a Black entrepreneur who has a business near the foot of the Edmund Pettus Bridge, site of the 1965 march. She was eager to describe what the club was doing for the city. For instance, they had recently installed an attractive bench near the bridge.

Then we got to chatting with our waiter, also Black, who was very interested in hearing about our research. He asked whether we were going to visit Selma again. We hoped to, we said. He replied, "Next time, you've got to bring something with you for our city." We asked what Selma needed most. He paused, considering, then declared, "A bowling alley! We're short of that sort of thing around here. There is nothing for young people to do in this town."

A Tradition of Violence

ON A HOT, SUNNY DAY in late June, we headed from Memphis down into Tunica County, Mississippi, and to the little town of Dundee. Here we crossed the Mississippi River on US 49 and drove into Helena, Arkansas, the Phillips County seat (home to Marvell Academy and DeSoto School, both mentioned in chapter 2). Our GPS pointed us to the courthouse, standing just shy of the levee. Steps from this edifice, on the courthouse square, we stumbled upon a memorial meant to reflect the features of a church, its centerpiece a 14,000-pound granite slab resembling an altar. The engraving read: "Dedicated to those known and unknown who lost their lives in the Elaine Massacre."

On this visit, part of our 2021 fourteen-state road trip, we had been in the Delta for about a week. From our Airbnb farm stay in Shaw, Mississippi, 122 miles south of Memphis, we headed out each day to explore the dozens of counties in the Delta regions of Mississippi, Louisiana, and Arkansas, which ranked among the most disadvantaged on our index. In place after place, we discovered astonishing stories about the industries that fueled the rise of our nation, the workers who sustained them, and the histories of human suffering they wrought. We then traveled to Memphis, from which we could investigate the Delta's northernmost counties. Here we learned that Phillips County, first on our itinerary on this day, was the site of one of the most violent acts of retribution by whites against Blacks in American history.

A quick Google search revealed that on the evening of September 30, 1919, roughly one hundred Black farmers gathered in the Hoop Spur church near the town of Elaine for a meeting of the Progressive Farmers and Household Union. Late in the evening, as they discussed how to negotiate with their white landlords for fair pay, a car with one Black and two white passengers pulled up outside. Shots were fired and returned, leaving one of the white men injured and the other dead.

As rumors spread of an impending race war, an armed white mob amassed and descended on the county. The mob was joined by more than five hundred soldiers from nearby Camp Pike, dispatched by Arkansas governor Charles Hillman Brough, who personally accompanied the troops and gave orders to "round up" the "heavily armed negroes" and "shoot to kill any negro who refused to surrender immediately." Accounts indicate that hundreds were slaughtered, not only men but any women and children unfortunate enough to be caught in the crossfire. One Black ex-soldier wrote that it was like the victims were "nothen But dogs."

Hundreds of Black Americans were hauled off to jail, where many were beaten and tortured. The first twelve tried, known thereafter as the "Elaine Twelve," faced charges ranging from murder to nightriding. After deliberating for a matter of minutes, all were sentenced to the electric chair by the all-white jury. Their appeal would eventually work its way up to the United States Supreme Court, which would vote six to two to overturn the convictions.

For years, the story whites spun about these events was patently false: that it was a planned insurrection. They claimed that Black folks were out to kill white people, hardly anyone ended up dead, and order was quickly restored. But Ida B. Wells secretly interviewed members of the Elaine Twelve while they were in jail. She offered a different account of what took place in Phillips County, labeling it an "orgy of bloodshed." The Equal Justice Initiative has documented 245 Black killings—considered lynchings due to the mob violence—in Phillips County, more than in any other county in the United States. The death toll from Elaine rivals estimates for the better-known 1921 Tulsa Race Massacre, which range from twenty-six to nearly three hundred killed.

Reading histories of the Cotton Belt, we came across other stories like that of the Elaine Massacre, some well-known, some not. What became clear was that these events should be understood as a fact of life in the region for decades, an ever-present reality, not an occasional tragedy. Lynchings were built into the very fabric of Cotton Belt society, serving an explicit goal of racial subjugation. Thumbing through historian John Willis's *Forgotten Time: The Yazoo-Mississippi Delta After the Civil War* while trapped at home during the early months of the COVID-19 pandemic, we came across a brief mention of an event described as the Leflore Massacre. We would soon learn that twenty-nine years and eleven months before the massacre in Elaine, a strikingly similar set of events took place in another Delta county on the other side of the Mississippi River. The backdrop was an economic crisis: cotton prices were falling, threatening the solvency of Black and white farmers alike. Meanwhile, the number of independent Black farmers—and Black farmers' unions—was on the rise. This led to a growing sense of unease among whites that would come to an explosive—and deadly—head on August 30, 1889.

As in Phillips County, the inciting spark was the meeting of a union, the Colored Farmers' Alliance, organized by a man named Oliver Cromwell. The goal of these farmers was to "improve themselves financially," which involved, among other things, encouraging other farmers to stop purchasing from local merchants and to give their trade instead to the Farmers' Alliance cooperative store. Local whites took notice of Cromwell's activities and began to spread rumors about him and to send him threatening letters. How many attended the meeting that August day is not known, but the number may have been as high as three hundred, many of them armed due to fears of white retaliation. A group of union members marched to show their support for Cromwell. Rumors about the events swirled in the white community, and an armed group of whites seeking retribution began to organize. Fearing a race war was imminent, the sheriff telegraphed Mississippi governor Robert Lowry. Three divisions of the National Guard arrived, accompanied by Lowry himself, ostensibly to persuade the white vigilante mob to disperse.

What happened next remains unclear. One white witness, a traveling salesman, claimed he had seen men, women, and children pulled from their homes and "shot down like dogs." Exact numbers were impossible to come by as Black witnesses were too terrified to speak. Meanwhile, members of the National Guard remained tight-lipped about what they had seen—and done. Four leaders of the Colored Farmers' Alliance were shot and then hanged, according to several news sources. Without irony, news outlets reported that their crime was "resisting arrest." These deaths, perhaps as many as one hundred, are not all included in the Equal Justice Initiative's count of lynchings due to the murkiness of the historical record. Nonetheless, Leflore County, where this event occurred, is tied for second in the nation in the number of documented lynchings between 1877 and 1950—forty-eight Blacks murdered in extrajudicial killings by white mobs.

Back in Phillips County, Arkansas, on September 29, 2019—exactly one hundred years after the first victim of the Elaine Massacre was slain—the historical narrative was finally set right when the memorial we came upon during our travels was erected in remembrance of the hundreds who were murdered. There is no memorial in Leflore County to commemorate the Leflore Massacre, and none in many locations where other horrific episodes of mob violence erupted in the Cotton Belt South with unnerving regularity for generations following the Civil War. These atrocities remain unacknowledged or, in the case of the Leflore Massacre, all but lost to memory outside of the Black community. Yet one lesson we have taken away from our study of these places is that the economic and social relations that marked these communities many decades or even a century or more ago still shape their fortunes today. In this chapter, we will show that violence is one key mechanism linking the events of the distant past to the present.

The well-known and horrific sin of human bondage in the United States was most concentrated in the Cotton Belt. Legions of enslaved Black people—outnumbering whites by large margins—were required to bring in the cotton crop, and the presence of large Black majorities in the region today reflects this past. Precious little changed for the Black majority once Reconstruction surrendered to Jim Crow and tenant farming. Lynching—the ultimate tool whites used to keep Blacks down in the Jim Crow era—was especially common and particularly brutal in Cotton Belt counties like Phillips and Leflore. Lynchings are often associated with the history of Black Americans, but they are equally fundamental to the history of white Americans. Nearly always, it was whites who made the accusations of Black transgressions. White people gathered the mobs and pursued the victims, while white law enforcement either turned a blind eye or was actively involved. White people committed these murders in brutal and heinous ways, and whites made up stories in the aftermath with the goal of absolving themselves of guilt. It was white perpetrators who almost always escaped blame.

Government bodies controlled by whites allowed lynchings to occur without any real fear of punishment. Northern white policy makers were all too willing to accept promises by southern states to crack down on lynchings despite not having any reason to think any such efforts would materialize. Over the course of more than a century, there were nearly two hundred failed attempts to enact an anti-lynching law before the federal government finally passed the Emmett Till Antilynching Act in 2022.

Part of reckoning with this history is acknowledging it publicly and grappling with its brutality. Another important step is to understand precisely how violence operated in the Cotton Belt, *then and now*. Across America's internal colonies, the historical record is sometimes thin, but a rare treasure trove of interview and ethnographic data collected during the late 1920s and 1930s by Black and white researchers who were embedded in communities across the Cotton Belt offers a rare window into the ongoing role violence played during that period. These narratives were written during the very years when this internal colony—like the others we write about in this book—reached its peak.

Charles S. Johnson was trained at the University of Chicago by the eminent urban sociologist Robert E. Park. His first work, commissioned by the Chicago Commission on Race Relations, was a close analysis of the Chicago race riot of 1919. His second, initiated once he joined the faculty at Fisk University in 1926, where he would go on to become the institution's first Black president, was the first comprehensive study of the Cotton Belt's tenant farmers. During the late 1920s and early 1930s, Johnson and his team interviewed roughly 600 tenant farmers cultivating cotton in the fields surrounding the county seat of Tuskegee, in Macon County, Alabama. His book *Shadow of the Plantation* (1934) offers a rich description of the family life of these farmers: their economic straits, schools, and health conditions, along with the role of the church. The sequel, *Growing Up in the Black Belt* (1941), draws on interviews with more than 2,000 Black youths across the Cotton Belt South, including those in Macon County, Alabama; Greene County, Georgia; and Bolivar and Coahoma Counties in the Mississippi Delta. In that book, Johnson's goal was to illuminate the devastating impact of Jim Crow on the well-being of Black youths.

At about the same time, two white scholars from Yale, anthropologist Hortense Powdermaker (whose work was facilitated by Johnson) and psychologist John Dollard, chose Sunflower County, next door to Leflore, to conduct their ethnographic studies. Powdermaker's *After Freedom* (1939) and Dollard's *Caste and Class in a Southern Town* (1937) focused on the family, economic, social, and religious lives of those living in the county's largest town, Indianola, and the rural areas surrounding it.

In 1933, two couples, one Black and one white, trained in anthropology by the community scholar W. Lloyd Warner, moved to Natchez, Mississippi. Allison Davis and his wife, Elizabeth, and Burleigh and Mary Gardner immersed themselves in the local cultures of their respective "caste groups" for nearly two years, meeting on deserted rural roads in the dark of night to compare notes. Their landmark work, *Deep South* (1941), documented the lived realities of American racism. Allison Davis would go on to become the first Black scholar with a full faculty appointment at an elite white university (the University of Chicago). The authors were aided by research assistant St. Clair Drake, who would later coauthor the classic work about Chicago's Black communities, *Black Metropolis* (1945).

The counties where these studies took place were between 60 and 80 percent Black. In each county, most Black men, plus their wives and children, toiled on tenant farms. The significantly outnumbered white elite maintained an aggressive stance toward their Black neighbors. Writing about this dynamic in *Deep South*, Davis and colleagues reported that the culture required that a white person "must always be ready to maintain his superordinate position, even by physical violence." Black people lived "under the shadow of an ever-present threat [that] whites can and will enforce their authority with punishment and death."

The severity of the violence whites unleashed on the Black majority was far beyond what was required to maintain the color caste line. Whites' "real and neurotic fear" compounded to "build up a permanent necessity for severe measures against Negroes on the part of the white caste," Dollard observes in *Caste and Class in a Southern Town*. Those in the white caste perpetrated violence in both legal and extralegal forms. Whites controlled all means of official law enforcement—the local sheriff, the police, the judges, and the all-white juries. Everyone knew that the so-called law was merely a tool of oppression of Black people. Perhaps more important, though, were the ways whites deployed extralegal force. "There are no socially effective patterns which confine violence to the rational and measured tread of the law," Dollard writes—though in the Cotton Belt, "rational and measured" certainly overstated the merits of the law.

Black community members had to be vigilant. Should they make even the smallest misstep, they could suffer severe consequences. Whites punished any sign of social equivalence to an extreme degree. A Black person could not shake hands with a white person, could not enter through a white person's front door (even to collect the rent from a white tenant). Black people of all ages were required to call a white man "sir" and a white woman "Mrs." or "Miss," but were almost never accorded the same respect, even if they were professionals holding college degrees. Instead, whites referred to their Black fellow citizens in terms that reduced them to childish figures—through the use of "boy" or "girl"—or used overly familiar terms such as "uncle" and "auntie."

The litany of rules and restrictions were all but limitless. Powdermaker labeled these "the little things that prick." Underlying these codes of conduct was the fundamental myth that physical contact with Black people was polluting. "The belief in organic inferiority of the Negro reaches its strongest expression in the common assertion that Negroes are 'unclean,'" Davis and colleagues observe. Dollard notes that most white households provided separate dishes for their servants' use. Any show of economic success among Blacks was greeted with alarm. They could expect to be "challenged if seen dressed up on the street during week days; again their place is in the fields." Any Black person "who has achieved advancement beyond lower-class status . . . has been made aware of this envy and resentment at his aggressive mobility," and any actual successes "are punished as aggressive acts."

Lynchings were the white minority's ultimate tool because they reverberated so powerfully throughout the Black community, particularly among the young. Here it is worth quoting Charles S. Johnson's *Growing Up in the Black Belt* at length: "In some communities, incidents have occurred which have left a vivid imprint on the minds of youth. . . . Although some . . . are relatively quiet affairs and are accepted with resignation as 'private' concerns or as justified punishments for the indiscretion of some irresponsible Negro, others are mob outbursts which leave deep scars of horror, fear, and dismay.

Lynchings usually followed a pattern. The mob, the man hunt, the brutality, the terrorization of the entire Negro community are standard features. The effect on children is profound and permanent." Dollard concurs, writing that the "threat of lynching is likely to be in the mind of the Negro child from earliest days."

Both emphasize that the point was not to punish the individual, but to keep the entire Black community down. According to Dollard, "The posse wants to get the *right* man, of course, but it is not too serious a matter if it does not, since the warning is even more clear when it lands the wrong one. . . . Every Negro in the South knows that he is under a kind of sentence of death; he does not know when his turn will come, it may never come, but it may also be at any time."

Johnson calculated that between 1900 and 1931, lynchings were most common in the Mississippi Delta, where "the plantation system still flourishes. . . . In these counties lynching or the possibility of lynching is part of a cultural pattern. A type of adjustment to it exists. During and shortly after a lynching the Negro community lives in terror. Negroes remain at home and out of sight. When the white community quiets down, the Negroes go back to their usual occupations. The incident is not forgotten, but the routine of the plantation goes on. The lynching, in fact, is part of the routine."

White perpetrators deployed a trope to justify their actions, claiming that most lynchings were in response to the rape of a white woman by a Black man and thus deserved. That a Black man would soil a white woman's virtue was such a deep-seated paranoia in the Cotton Belt that the conventional wisdom whites espoused was that it was "safer to lynch Negroes than to endure a spreading epidemic of attacks on white women." Of course, the real rape victims were almost always Black and the perpetrators almost always white. Indeed, among the most disturbing aspects of reading historical accounts about this era in the South is the frequency of the rape of Black women by white men, with no consequence for the perpetrator or recourse for the victim. While Black-on-white rape was often the pretext, Davis and coauthors captured what may have been a common sentiment among whites in the Cotton Belt for many decades after the Civil War: "A very influential government official . . . felt that, 'when a [n——] gets ideas, the best thing to do is to get him under the ground as quick as possible.'"

Any Black person seen to have "ideas" about his standing was in danger. In Lake City, South Carolina, Frazier Baker was a Black citizen appointed as postmaster by President William McKinley before his assassination in 1901. About six months into Baker's term, witnesses reported that a posse of white men circled his home one night, set it on fire, and fired up to one hundred bullets into the dwelling, with Baker and his wife and six children inside. Baker was shot to death while trying to escape. As his wife fled carrying their daughter Julia, the infant was shot dead in her mother's arms.

Ida B. Wells was spurred to become a fierce anti-lynching crusader after a white mob murdered three Black owners of People's Grocery in Memphis, which was proving successful in enticing customers away from a white-owned competitor. Wells meticulously documented the circumstances of lynchings and asserted that they were means to beat back economic progress made by Black Americans. In fact, a Wells editorial making this case led to a riot and threats against Wells herself, causing her to permanently flee her hometown of Memphis.

Dollard devoted an entire chapter of *Caste and Class in a Southern Town* to the phenomenon of the widespread violence in Sunflower County, Mississippi. He advanced what would come to be known as the frustration-aggression hypothesis: "Some of the hostility properly directed toward the white caste is deflected from it and focused within the Negro group as well. . . . Since the hostility of the Negroes against whites is violently and effectively suppressed, we have a boiling of aggressive affect within the Negro group." While "against the white rivals he is helpless, [yet among] his Negro rivals he can fight and shoot, and he does."

Writing in the early 1930s, Charles S. Johnson described "a tradition of violence which seems to mark personal relations to a high degree. . . . A woman who was asked about sleeping with her windows closed replied that 'people do's so much killing round here, I'se scared to leave 'em open.' Another explained why they stopped attending dances: 'Dere's so much cutting and killing going on.' One notes either casualness or fatalism in recounting deaths in the family by violence. . . . 'My other boy got kilt. He was just stabbed to death. Oh, they sent the boy what done it to the reformatory.'" Johnson documents that, among the myriad possible causes of death in Macon County, including the many serious health conditions that plagued the Black community referred to earlier, violence was the leading cause of death according to health department records.

Dollard also advanced the argument that whites used strategic under-policing of Black areas to bolster the idea that Black communities were inherently more violent: "It is clear that this differential application of the law amounts to a condoning of Negro violence and gives immunity to Negroes to commit small or large crimes so long as they are on Negroes." He concludes, "It seems quite possible that lack of adequate legal protection of the Negro's life and person is itself an incitement to violence." Whatever the cause, he adds, "one cannot help wondering if it does not serve the ends of the white caste to have a high level of violence in the Negro group, since disunity in the Negro caste tends to make it less resistant to the white domination." Echoes of this line of reasoning can be found in the work of later criminologists, and especially in sociologist Jock Young's assertion that violence may function as a response to the humiliation of poverty and structural exclusion.

Most Americans think about violence as mainly an urban problem, yet this is not so. For example, between 1999 and 2013, gun deaths were most likely to occur in counties that were poor and rural, after accounting for population size. Similarly, in twenty-one of thirty-three states studied by criminologists between 2008 and 2014, homicides involving guns were just as common in rural as in urban communities—and in some cases more common.

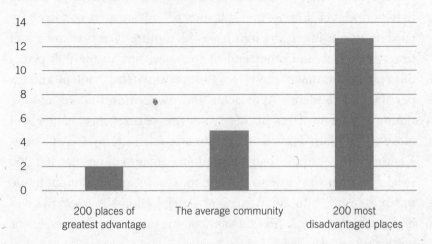

Deaths by Interpersonal Violence per 100,000
Residents in American Communities

Source: Authors' analysis of 2009–2014 data from the Institute for Health Metrics and Evaluation.

How violent are the most disadvantaged places in America? Comparing across communities is difficult. In some places, law enforcement does a poor job of reporting violent crimes. Legal entities sometimes misclassify or ignore crimes, and some violent acts do not come to the attention of authorities at all. Because we were concerned about these well-known problems in crime data, we turned instead to the Institute for Health Metrics and Evaluation (IHME). These data draw on official death certificates to provide counts of deaths by interpersonal violence, the violent killing of one person by another, along with other causes of death. Violent deaths are counted more reliably than other violent acts because a body must be reckoned with. With the IHME data as the basis for our analysis, we could bypass some of the issues of how effectively local law enforcement reports violence.

Using these data, we averaged the rate of deaths due to interpersonal violence for all counties in the United States between 2009 and 2014 (the most recent data available to us). By this measure, the prevalence of violence varied dramatically across the country. The average county saw 4.9 violent killings per 100,000 residents during that period, yet among the 200 most disadvantaged counties according to our index, the figure was 12.7, more than two and a half times higher. At the other end of the spectrum, in the 200 places of greatest advantage, the rate was approximately 2 violent killings per 100,000 residents. Appalachia and the Cotton Belt are among the most violent places in the nation (for reasons this chapter will make clear; South Texas is an exception to this pattern). Clay County, Kentucky, for example, had a rate of 9.2 violent killings per 100,000 residents. That was close to the rate for Cook County, Illinois, home to Chicago (10.5). In the Mississippi Delta, Leflore's rate was twice as high as Clay's at 19.2. Some Delta counties were even more violent by this measure.

In Clay County, some of the violence stems from the local corruption that we write about in chapter 5. Travis lounged on the couch in his Clay County trailer while his girlfriend, Helena, clad in rainbow leggings and a spaghetti-strap shirt, sat cross-legged on the floor. "A few years back, they had a couple of the high officials in the police department linked with drug dealing," he recalled. But as anyone who peruses the *Manchester Enterprise*, the newspaper serving the area, can attest, violent acts are routine among ordinary citizens as well. We met with Paige over coffee in a local diner, her blond hair pulled back into a ponytail. When we asked her to describe her relationship with the father of her youngest child, she told us he had been killed, "which I think made me go into my drug addiction even more."

Stevie shared an eerily similar story. She was in her mid-twenties when we met her, but she looked younger, with a heart-shaped face and fine, dark hair that she ran her fingers through as we talked. Speaking in a soft voice, she described how the father of her first child "had another child with someone else. . . . And [the other mother] was on drugs and he was taking her to court to get custody, and she paid two other men to [murder] him. . . . There's still not been a trial."

Pointing to a home near his own, Travis recounted how the "two people that lived there was actually shot and killed out in front of their house." Henrietta, whose thick black hair cascades over her shoulders, told us in a hushed, conspiratorial whisper about a neighbor accused of murdering his own parents: "They were shot and killed at the house that my daughter lives at [now]. . . . And [at the spot] where they had shot the guy outside, his cane was still there . . . and, you know, bloodstains [are] still there on the cement."

In a six-month period, from March through August 2021, we examined the weekly *Manchester Enterprise* for reported incidents of violence within Clay County. On March 10, a front-page story recounted how a group hunting for mushrooms in the tiny community of Red Bird, about twenty miles from Manchester, had found a skull. There was speculation that it might belong to any one of several people who had gone missing in the county over the past several years. Two weeks later, the newspaper reported that a second skull had been found in the same area by children playing in the woods.

"Indictments!" shouted a headline on April 28, referring to three persons charged with the murder of former Eastern Kentucky University football player Jeremy "Ta-Ta" Caldwell, gunned down in a parking lot in December 2020. The story noted that this was probably drug-related, as the victim had earlier been charged with possession of large quantities of methamphetamines and cash.

Almost a month later, the *Enterprise* reported both a murder and an attempted murder. In the small Clay County town of Oneida, two men got into an altercation. It ended with one reportedly shooting the other with a semiautomatic rifle. In the second story, a local man was charged with attempted murder for allegedly stabbing his own mother ten or eleven times and shooting her four times.

The following week's issue of the *Enterprise* recounted an act of unusual candor. A woman called 911 late on a Sunday evening to admit that she had just shot her boyfriend in the hip. She was charged with attempted murder and public intoxication. July brought news of a fatal shooting outside a Clay County residence, the result of a physical altercation between two middle-aged men.

Finally, August saw two more homicides resulting from altercations between male acquaintances. The first incident was the stabbing of a man in his thirties in his home; two men were charged with the crime. The second was a fatal shooting that occurred after one man threatened to enter the home of another and do him violence. When he entered the home, armed with a gun, both men exchanged fire and the intruder was fatally wounded. An unnamed woman also present was shot and taken to the hospital in critical condition.

Depending on where you go in town, you might never learn that Greenwood, Mississippi, is an extremely violent place. In the part of town that lies north of the Yalobusha River, the main thoroughfare is lined with more than a thousand oaks meticulously spaced to form a cathedral arch. The old homes along Grand Boulevard are surrounded by spacious lawns. On the sidewalks, pets are walked, babies are pushed in strollers, and an occasional jogger passes by. This is where most of the people who run things in town live. These people worry about how to stem population decline and lure newcomers, how to attract more industry, how to further beautify the downtown. Carolyn McAdams, just weeks into her fourth term as mayor, told us her top priorities were to finish a road-paving project and to put in a dock where the river passes through the downtown so fishermen can tie up to have lunch in one of Greenwood's upscale restaurants. When asked about the violence that was engulfing the city, she shrugged. There wasn't much she could do about that, she told us. Her diagnosis? It's the parenting.

McAdams's priorities were not on the radar for people living on the predominantly Black south side of town. There is a vacant feel to this part of the city, with empty lots far outnumbering occupied ones. The homes that still stand are aged one-story shotgun shacks—many strikingly similar, with clipped-gable roofs and cramped front porches—the houses packed in so tightly they almost pile up on one another, leaving little space for ventilation or light. Whereas North Greenwood's Grand Boulevard is so quiet you can hear the birds sing and the tree frogs emit their pulsing buzz of white noise, down in South Greenwood stereos blare from open car windows while old windowpanes shake with the vibration of the bass. Folks on this side of the river that divides the town told us that just days before our final trip to Greenwood in June 2021, a shooting by an unknown gunman had left a toddler dead and his mother and her three other children hospitalized. The family was simply driving along Champagne Street in the Rising Sun neighborhood on a Tuesday evening.

Indeed, while North Greenwood seems to slumber peacefully under those mighty oaks, South Greenwood is in the throes of a crisis that has caused many residents to withdraw into their homes, leaving the streets deserted even in the middle of the day. At regular intervals, the community finds itself mourning deeply for yet another victim of a violent crime. It is not unusual for kids to get caught in the crossfire. Because the south side is a place where everybody knows everybody, the mourning reverberates throughout the entire community. As one Black community leader we spoke with put it, "Everyone that's [involved in] gun violence down here, you either going to know them or know their parent."

That rings true for Ebony, whom we met at the motel where she lives on the edge of downtown Greenwood, next door to a deserted bowling alley. The place has seen better days, although Ebony's room is brightened by Mardi Gras decorations, which she found in a dumpster, arranged artfully on the wall, giving the place a celebratory air. When she opened the door, we crowded inside the room, two of us perched on the edge of the bed while the other took a seat in Ebony's wheelchair, parked near the entrance. Ebony presided over our conversation from the room's only armchair.

Ebony has lived here with her boyfriend, Lee, for several years. Nearly all the patrons of the motel are permanent residents. For most, it's here or the homeless shelter, she explained. The place has some advantages over other lodgings: no first and last required, no credit check, no lease. Utilities and phone are included in the $650 rent. Still, that puts quite a dent in her $771 disability check. Ebony needs a wheelchair to get around, and everything she needs is low to the ground, lined up in the narrow four-foot corridor between the wall and the bed: toaster oven, hot plate, deep fryer, Crock-Pot, and mini fridge. Dishes? "Oh, I wash them in the bathroom sink, there."

When we asked about her family, Ebony leaned over to rummage in a cabinet below the TV and extracted a clear plastic file folder with a purple flap. She pulled out a photo album with a blue-and-yellow-checked cover. Opening it, she pointed to a daughter, an aunt, a grandchild. She turned the folder upside down, and dozens of pictures spilled out onto the brocade bedspread: a kid's school photo, a daughter in cap and gown, a relative formally posed in front of the false backdrop of a library with leather-bound volumes, a father-daughter shot. This is when Ebony, in her late forties, told us that each of the three fathers of her four children was dead, all of them shot to death, one by his "daddy-in-law."

There were other documents reading "In loving memory" and "Order of Service." "So this looks like these are programs for funerals," one of us said. Ebony concurred and pointed to several yellowing news clippings. "Obituaries and stuff," she replied. She indicated one obituary: "This is my stepdad." She showed us another: "This is my cousin's wife." "That's my aunt Sara." "That's my uncle Ned." We pointed to another clipping, asking, "And how about this gentleman?" Ebony told us, "He had a shop. He used to be a drug dealer, like off the block. But he had a shop. And he died." We noted that he looked young in the photo. "Yeah. The street got him." Barely pausing, she moved on. "The [boyfriend] I got now, we been together about twenty-some years before his momma was murdered," she said, pointing to another clipping. "[Her husband] was a dealer. . . . I guess a friend told [him] she was ready to leave him alone, because she go to church and stuff. And I guess a friend told him about it, and he got in the car. . . . Killed her. Put her in a ditch out there. Shot [her] in the head. . . . He went to prison for all of it. . . . But he died over there."

Then Ebony related the story of a friend "who got killed just about a year ago. Last year, got shot over there at a little house, gambling. . . . Mr. Harold, we called him. He was like a son because he run with my children. He slept in the same bed, eat the same food, he come over when his mom gone or dad gone and come and be my kid. . . . But this child had growed up. He was a little dealer out there in the streets, they say. . . . Next thing you know, he was shot. . . . He drove himself to the hospital, and he died. It's like a little small Chicago now [in Greenwood]. Just that bad."

She shifted her focus. "I'm going to find my baby looking like a convict," she said.

Finally, after riffling through several newspaper clippings showing mug shots, she located one headlined "Man Charged in Fatal Killing." "Yeah, [he was only] twenty-seven. . . . Says [my son] has been charged with murder and the shooting death of a thirty-five-year-old auto mechanic. [That man] used to come stay here with us and eat and everything. I couldn't understand it, Lord! But he said he didn't do it. Whoever did, they shot the man's face off, Lord! It's so sad."

In 2019 and 2020, sociologist Ryan Parsons and other members of our team held extensive one-on-one conversations with Ebony and thirty-four other lower-income residents of Greenwood, nearly all living on the south side. Though we were prepared to engage in wide-ranging exchanges about their life experiences and views of the community, we hadn't planned to ask them directly about violence. Nonetheless, it kept coming up. When asked what they believed was Greenwood's biggest challenge, every one of the Black residents we interviewed put violence at the top of the list.

Sandy, fifty-eight, described how her son usually walked to and from work at a fast-food restaurant. He was getting a ride home from a coworker one night, she said, "and as he was getting out the guy's truck, somebody shot all in the truck." Her boy was hit three times. "I was at Jackson [hospital] with him for four weeks until they was able to get him back on crutches and stuff because he had to learn to walk all over again."

Jarvis, twenty-one years old, lives with his uncle and works odd jobs. He recalled two close calls in 2017; both times he was shot at in the middle of the day. "I'm coming across Zhen Market . . . and I got shot at. [Just two days later] I was going to visit my sister on Avenue I. Somebody parked across the street, and they was shooting at me. Luckily, they missed."

Rena, forty-nine, is no stranger to violence. She grew up in Compton, California, in the late 1970s, when her neighborhood was "gang central." She told us she witnessed five people die on the streets when she was young. Yet on a recent evening, she said, this was the scene at the motel where she lives: "Everybody was in here on the ground because somebody was out there talking about shooting each other, and they were pretty loud. . . . And I was like, 'This is crazy. Who would've thought I'd be in here on the bathroom floor like I'm in Los Angeles?'"

When Sandy first moved with her husband to Greenwood's Mc-Laurin neighborhood, she was thrilled by the proximity to a park, not realizing its notorious reputation for drugs and violence. "I was like, 'Oh my God, there's a park right here that my kids can go to. . . .' And then . . . I started hearing gunshots going across the park. You got to run [to] try to get your kid off the park. I can remember being in the middle of the park on my knees praying. [The neighbors are] like, 'Oh, she crazy, she stupid.' [No,] *you* need to be praying, too, because they [are] shooting past your house as well!"

These accounts were underlined by reports in the local daily, the *Greenwood Commonwealth*, which we tracked for two years. The first homicide of 2019, on January 15, was a fatal shooting of a man at the Curtis Moore Apartments, a low-income housing complex on the edge of town. A second man was shot in the same apartment complex that day in a separate incident, though he survived. Most shootings occurred on public streets or commercial areas with innocent bystanders present: at the Williams Landing Apartments, on George

White Circle; at the W. J. Bishop Apartments; at the Greenwood Gin; at the Wash Time Car Wash. Four people were shot at 5:30 P.M. on August 12, right behind a small grocery store in the south side's Baptist Town neighborhood.

Gun violence continued into 2020. Ten homicides were recorded in the first five months of the year in this city of 13,000 residents. Kenton Johnson was the first victim, killed on the corner of Broad Street and Avenue I in the middle of the afternoon, just as our researcher Ryan Parsons was conducting an interview a few hundred feet away. The second homicide occurred on Elzy Road at 3 P.M. on February 25. Three men were shot around 1:20 P.M. on March 1 in front of the Shell gas station on Highway 82. One of the year's only non-gun-related homicides took place on March 28 when Labrandon Baugh was beaten with a baseball bat on the corner of Main and McGhee. He was taken to Greenwood Leflore Hospital, pronounced brain-dead, and taken off life support. The suspected perpetrator in the killing had participated in local anti-violence rallies and had written letters to the editor of the *Greenwood Commonwealth*, urging fellow citizens to take a more active stance against violence.

June 2020 began with relative calm. Then, on the tenth, police were called to the intersection of Avenue H and McLaurin around 9 P.M., where they found two victims with multiple gunshot wounds. A half hour later, another call came in; shots had been fired at the Curtis Moore Apartments along Martin Luther King Drive. Two more gunshot victims were taken to the hospital. On June 16, a twenty-one-year-old male was shot outside the Curtis Moore Apartments around 9:30 P.M. He was pronounced dead at the hospital an hour later. A second victim was transported to a hospital in Jackson, about an hour and a half away. The following day, Valdemir Beverly, a twenty-two-year-old veteran who had served in Afghanistan and had only recently returned to town to take over a family business, was gunned down on Jackson Street. The shooting was a case of mistaken identity. Beverly died at the hospital around 12:40 P.M. On June 24, the *Commonwealth* reported that in the past two weeks, nine shooting incidents had occurred in Greenwood and the area just beyond the city limits. The following day, the newspaper announced another. The victim was a thirty-eight-year-old from a nearby county who had been visiting friends.

For those who live on Greenwood's predominantly Black south side, the fear of pervasive gun violence is palpable. Brent, age twenty-three, who works several part-time jobs, told us, "Greenwood's got too much violence. . . . Just like in Memphis!"

A week after Greenwood's first 2020 homicide, on January 23, the city finally took action, announcing it would install surveillance cameras around the south side. "This is the only way to get some [evidence] of the shootings and crimes in the city," explained an exasperated Mayor McAdams. In March, the Leflore County Board of Supervisors voted to allocate an extra $200,000 to the sheriff's office for additional staff and resources to aid in the investigation of gun crimes. At that meeting, board president Robert Collins exclaimed, "You can't even drive down the street without a bullet hole being put in your car. It's like World War II—shooting people, people laying out in the middle of the road."

In the wake of the many shootings, Lavoris Weathers, a six-foot-seven former all-state basketball player for Greenwood High, decided to take a stand. In June 2020, he organized Operation Peace Treaty, which sponsored a series of barbecues in several of the south side neighborhoods most affected by the shootings: at the Robert Moore recreation building down the road from the Boys & Girls Club; at the Greenwood Mentoring Group's building on Avenue G, near downtown; at the W. J. Bishop Apartments, a low-income housing complex whose light poles have no lights but plenty of surveillance cameras; at the M. A. Snowden Jones Apartments on the southern edge of town; at Broad Street Park ("Stokely Carmichael gave his Black Power speech in this park," Weathers pointed out); at a small park at the north end of Avenue A in the Baptist Town section; and at a car dealership near the intersection of Main and MLK. This last location was just steps from the site of a mass shooting that would occur a few months after the barbecue held there, at a family gathering in late October 2020 following a grandmother's funeral, leaving two visitors from Chicago dead and eight local residents wounded.

At each Operation Peace Treaty event, attendees were asked to fill out a short survey. The 527 surveys that were completed and tallied corroborated our own findings: nearly two-thirds of the respondents claimed gun violence was what they were most afraid of in their community, while only six respondents cited COVID-19. In open-ended answers, people noted that gun violence in Greenwood was arbitrary and that there was little one could do to avoid it. One five-year-old at the event complained that he was not allowed to come to the park to play because of all the shooting. Another community organizer active with Operation Peace Treaty, Shun Pearson, described how he spent summer evenings sitting in his yard listening for gunshots. Eugene, fifty-seven, had served for twenty years in the Air Force. He was retired and living on his military pension in the McLaurin section, one of the town's most beleaguered neighborhoods. He elaborated on this theme when we spoke with him: "You don't want to be in that part of town. You scared. You don't know what they've done to somebody else. And you don't know who's going to come through there shooting and you get hit."

Fredrick, thirty-four, was living in the same hotel as Ebony but was about to move to Texas with his girlfriend, in part because of the pervasive violence. As he deep-fried a pig's tail, he told our team, "That's why I don't really associate with nobody, because you don't know who to associate with. Everybody is beefing with everybody. So there's no need to put myself in that, in their way." As we talked in her motel room, Ebony declared, "I don't go to [church] picnics and stuff because, to me, these outings and stuff [are dangerous]. When you get around a lot of folks, it's going to be trouble." Evangeline, a fifty-one-year-old on disability because of lupus, told us much the same thing: "I don't participate in a lot of things in Greenwood. . . . I don't participate because I'm scared of the violence. A lot of things they have downtown, the Christmas parades and all that, I don't participate because I'm scared somebody might get to shooting or something might happen. When something is going on outside and the public is invited, I do not participate."

What were the reasons people gave for the prevalence of gun violence in Leflore County? Several pointed to interpersonal disputes. Brent declared, "People get angry over dumb stuff. People say something about your mama, and they get mad over it. I be seeing people talking about people, messing with people, every day. Ready to kill them when people get mad at them." Another resident put it this way: "It's just . . . we at the club, I might get into [it] with you. You from [the] Bishop [housing complex], I'm from [the McLaurin neighborhood]. Now here we go. And now we shooting at each other. Three, four times out of the week. . . . It's just about nothing. Because I don't like you and you don't like me."

But as he collected surveys one Saturday afternoon, Lavoris Weathers insisted it is not about the beefs or the drugs. There just isn't enough money in drugs to spark the level of violence seen in the community, he said, which he characterized as "worse than Chicago in the eighties." No, he explained, the cause of the violence is "mostly hunger"—hunger being a metaphor for lack of opportunity.

The violence felt in these communities today didn't appear out of thin air. It is baked into the histories of these places. A growing body of research has directly linked a history of violence to violence in the present day. Criminologist Steven Messner and colleagues have shown that in southern states, the frequency of lynchings is strongly associated with current rates of homicide, a finding that "underscore[s] the relevance of the historical context." Legal scholars Nick Peterson and Geoff Ward have found that violent opposition to the civil rights movement is related both to the lynchings that preceded it and to elevated homicide rates in subsequent years. Jhacova Williams and Carl Romer of the Economic Policy Institute also have found that counties where lynchings were more common (after accounting for population size) have higher rates of police officer–involved shootings today.

We have seen that sociologist Charles S. Johnson and anti-lynching crusader Ida B. Wells argued that lynchings were public spectacles used by whites—including prominent citizens and elected officials—to send a message to the Black community at large about the consequences of challenging the racial hierarchy. Both held that the primary objective was to keep the balance of economic power in whites' favor and, to use our terms, to shore up the internal colonies they had created. Their efforts were met with remarkable success: they managed to block the economic mobility of their Black neighbors for generations. Through the years, white elites used myriad other means to keep Black citizens down, as the other chapters in this book reveal.

Today, much as with lynchings, the fallout from police shootings is not limited to the people directly involved. These shootings send a message, intentional or not, to the entire community about how authorities view the value of Black Americans' lives. Using data from a survey of more than 100,000 Black respondents, public health researcher David Williams and colleagues demonstrated that Blacks who lived in a state with a recent police killing faced significantly more mental health challenges than those who did not. There are echoes of Charles S. Johnson and John Dollard in these results.

Research has shown that a child's exposure to community violence is linked to long-term trauma, delayed cognitive development, and problems at school. For example, sociologists Patrick Sharkey and Gerard Torrats-Espinosa have demonstrated that high rates of violence in a place limit the chances that poor youths growing up there can rise to the middle class. In essence, growing up with violence sharply constrains a child's life chances.

Thanks to Sharkey and Torrats-Espinosa's research, we can say with relative certainty that violence within a community hinders intergenerational social mobility—the chance that a child who grows up poor can rise to the middle class or beyond. But what if the opposite is also true? What if blocked mobility within a place incites violence? This is what John Dollard argued a century ago, and what Greenwood native Lavoris Weathers is asserting with his "hunger hypothesis"—that the high rate of violence in Leflore County is a response to blocked opportunity. The sense that it is nearly impossible to get ahead, plus the lack of ability to defend oneself against white reprisals, means that the anger boiling up in the Black community has no outlet except against those who are similarly oppressed. That the white authorities don't care only further stokes the anger.

Turning to big data, we decided to test Weathers's hunger hypothesis. Our team, led by researcher Liv Mann, examined whether simply growing up in a place where social mobility is hindered may itself spark higher rates of violence in that community. Consistent with Weathers's theory, nowhere in the nation is intergenerational mobility less common than in the Cotton Belt. Of the one hundred places with the lowest rates of mobility in the United States, more than half of them are in this region. Leflore County, Mississippi, has the ninth-lowest rate of social mobility of the 3,600 counties and large cities across the nation.

Drawing on mobility data gleaned from IRS records, plus the administrative data from a variety of sources, Mann examined the impact of rates of social mobility among kids born in the 1980s on the violent killing of one person by another when this cohort reached young adulthood. She compared the strength of this relationship to other, more common predictors of violence in a community. She found that a low probability that a poor child growing up in a given community could rise to the middle class was a powerful predictor of a high rate of violence in that community, a relationship that was more important than the number of police officers on the streets or the level of inequality in the community, and one that rivaled the community's poverty rate.

South Texas—which earned its place on our Index of Deep Disadvantage mostly due to the extraordinarily high rates of poverty there—has intergenerational mobility rates that actually exceed the national average. Even in Zavala and Brooks Counties, the rates are just below the national average. Perhaps due to the Anglo flight that occurred in the late 1960s and 1970s, these areas have been less successful in keeping the "have-nots" down. Nearly all the middle-class community leaders we spoke with there described childhoods as migrant laborers, yet many had earned advanced degrees. South Texas is the exception that proves the rule: its low rate of violence may well reflect the relatively high rates of mobility there.

Mann's results lend credence to Weathers's theory that a lack of opportunity for intergenerational mobility in a place will itself spark violence. But, as Sharkey and Torrats-Espinosa have shown, violence can then hinder mobility. Taken together, these dynamics can trap communities in a structural cycle of violence, with impacts that cascade through time.

Current estimates, compiled by the Equal Justice Initiative, of the number of lynchings in Leflore County, Mississippi, extend only to 1950. They thus fail to include what is most certainly Leflore County's most notorious lynching. In 1955, fourteen-year-old Chicago native Emmett Till was seized from a relative's home outside Greenwood, beaten with a tire iron, shot, tied to a cotton gin fan with barbed wire, and then drowned in the Tallahatchie River, all for the alleged crime of whistling at a white woman. Dr. Joyce Ladner, a Black sociologist who would eventually become a professor and interim president of Howard University, was a twelve-year-old girl living near Hattiesburg, Mississippi, at the time. In a 1987 magazine article, she explained that she was part of what she called the "Emmett Till Generation"—the group of young Black Americans growing up in the 1950s who bore indelible scars as a result of his murder. She recalled, "I had a scrapbook and I used to clip these articles from the local paper and from magazines. And I had a friend. . . . I used to go up to her house and we would talk about Emmett Till. We would lie on the floor and look at these pictures and cry. I would feel absolutely powerless."

A historical marker installed in 2008 memorializes the site where Till's body was recovered from the Tallahatchie River. The marker has been repeatedly vandalized—shot through with hundreds of bullets—replaced, and then vandalized again. In 2019, the marker was removed after an image surfaced of three white University of Mississippi fraternity brothers posing with guns next to the bullet-riddled sign. This time, it was replaced with a bulletproof marker and equipped with a webcam. The second of the four signs that preceded it is now on exhibit at the Smithsonian's National Museum of American History. It features 317 bullet holes.

For Ladner, agony over Till eventually turned from despair to activism. She became a volunteer for the Student Nonviolent Coordinating Committee. "I can name you ten SNCC workers who saw that picture [of Emmett Till's disfigured body] in *Jet* magazine, who remember it as the key thing about their youth, that was emblazoned in their mind," she recalled.

Another member of the Emmett Till generation, Ida Mae Holland, was growing up in poverty in the Gee Pee section of Greenwood when Till was murdered. In her memoir, *From the Mississippi Delta*, she writes, "After Emmett Till's death, I began to see, even if I did not understand it all, that we black folks had to be careful around whites, and mind never to get out of our 'place' around them." There were further scars. Holland recounts the story, passed down from generation to generation in the Black part of town, about the horror of an event that had occurred roughly ninety years before. "In my hometown . . . they celebrated as a holiday the Leflore County Massacre of 1889, in which . . . blacks seeking political rights had been slaughtered by white posses. Here, in this paradise lost, black people could take nothing for granted—not life, not liberty, not 'the pursuit of happiness.'"

Like Ladner, Holland, who was raped by her white employer at the age of eleven, would be transformed by her work with SNCC. There, she rubbed shoulders with Ladner, Bob Moses, Fannie Lou Hamer, Harry Belafonte, and Martin Luther King Jr. She helped

Even in the years of the Great Depression, Crystal City, Texas, prospered, with spinach production reaching roughly ten thousand cans a day. The city held its first annual spinach festival in 1936 and a year later proclaimed itself "Spinach Capital of the World," paying tribute to Popeye by erecting a full-color statue of him in the center of town.

Migrant workers, March 1939, in a spinach field in Zavala County, Texas. White school boards often would vote to end the school year early or begin it late for the children of migrant farm laborers in order to make them available for planting or harvesting.

This photograph taken in Zavala County in 1939 is titled *House of Mexican Family.*

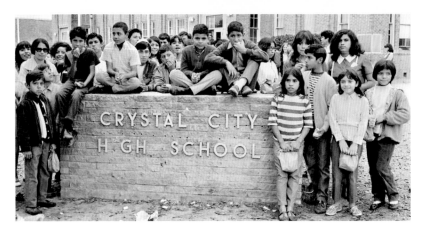

In 1969, Crystal City High School's Chicano students rebelled against unspoken ethnic quotas that allowed only one Mexican American on the cheerleading squad. A group that grew to include elementary and middle school students (*shown here*) walked out, demanding equal treatment in the schools.

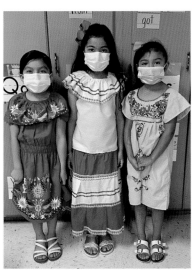

"We started going to school board meetings asking for things to change, but it all started escalating," said Diana Palacios, one of the student activists who spurred the historic walkout of seventeen hundred Crystal City students. A popular slogan of the boycott was "Brown legs are beautiful, too, we want Chicana cheerleaders." Palacios (*seen here dressed in white*) went on to become head cheerleader.

Students at Dr. Tomas Rivera Elementary School in Crystal City—principal Andi Guerrero calls her school a "campus of joy"—celebrate Cinco de Mayo while learning new vocabulary words. In Zavala County, nearly 60 percent of adults lack basic literacy skills.

Crystal City Spinach Festival royalty in 2018.

A wagon loaded with cotton in Greenwood, Mississippi, with the Leflore County Courthouse in the background, circa 1920, around the time US cotton production had reached an all-time high. It was in the Mississippi Delta, and in Greenwood in particular, that the antebellum cotton kingdom was most faithfully reproduced long after the Civil War.

Dr. Charles S. Johnson was one of the most prolific sociologists of his time, authoring nearly a dozen works on Black tenant farmers, Black youths growing up in the Cotton Belt, and other related topics. In 1947, Johnson became the first Black president of Fisk University.

Dr. William Boyd "Allison" Davis; his wife, Elizabeth; and a white couple—all anthropologists—moved to Natchez, Mississippi, in the mid-1930s to study the folkways and mores of the Deep South. In 1942, Davis became the first Black American appointed to a full-time teaching post at an elite and predominately white university (the University of Chicago), one year after the publication of his and his colleagues' landmark work, *Deep South: A Social Anthropological Study of Caste and Class.*

Pillow Academy football practice, August 2020. When the COVID-19 pandemic resulted in public schools suspending in-person learning—thus canceling the football season—some of the other private academies in the Delta capitalized on the situation, recruiting sidelined Black players to their nearly all-white rosters.

The September 1964 issue of the Citizens' Councils of America's magazine, *The Citizen,* offered step-by-step instructions for starting a segregation academy.

The late Democratic state representative Mack McInnis, who helped push through the mandate to make so-called ring-around uniforms Mississippi state law in 1994, told the Associated Press, "It was my intention to make those prisoners look like prisoners. And I know you psychologists and all . . . say, 'Well, that's humiliating.' Well, that's damn good. I want it to be."

Andrew Johnson, sixty-seven, spent two decades working for Pitt Farms, which stopped employing its Black labor force after the 2019 harvest, opting for white H2-A visa holders from South Africa instead.

Dr. Tamala Boyd Shaw (*center*), founder and head of school at Leflore Legacy Academy, told the *Greenwood Commonwealth*, "I am blessed beyond measure to have my dream of coming back and giving back to my hometown become a reality."

This ad from 1942 features the "naturally milder leaf" of the bright leaf strain of tobacco grown in Mullins, South Carolina.

Tenant farm women stringing tobacco in Florence County, in the Pee Dee region of South Carolina, 1938. Tobacco farming was even more dependent on tenant labor than cotton farming.

Mayor Barbara Hopkins of majority-Black Sellers, South Carolina, inspects the mold-infested home of one of her constituents. Three severe weather events, including hurricanes in 2016 and 2018, led to hundreds of millions of dollars in damage to thousands of homes.

An improved home sits next to an unimproved home in Sellers. An analysis by the State of South Carolina following Hurricane Matthew in 2016 identified Marion County, where Sellers is located, as the "most impacted and distressed area" in the state.

In Wheelwright, Kentucky, established by the Elkhorn Coal Company as a model coal town in 1916, town manager E. R. "Jack" Price practiced contentment sociology—the belief that productivity could be increased by investing in town infrastructure, civic life, and recreation, including an eighteen-hole golf course available for miners' use.

Black schoolchildren at recess in Wheelwright, September 26, 1948. The 1930 census enumerated 226 Black Americans living in the town, many of them hailing from spent tenant farms. Racial segregation in school, at church, and in all forms of social life outside of the mines was the norm.

A resident of Manchester, Kentucky, witness to a collapsing coal economy, was captured in this November 1, 1963, photograph. The following year, President Lyndon B. Johnson famously made the case for his War on Poverty from an eastern Kentucky porch.

Senator Robert F. Kennedy visiting the tiny school in Barwick, Kentucky, February 13, 1968. In smaller eastern Kentucky towns like Barwick, many of the schools were one-room affairs like this one, serving students from kindergarten to third grade. More than twenty years later, on June 9, 1989, the Supreme Court of Kentucky declared the state's public school system unconstitutional due to funding disparities between eastern Kentucky's schools and those in other parts of the state.

Pastor Ken Bolin, head of Manchester Baptist Church. In May 2004, he and other clergy in this city of only eighteen hundred residents organized a march to confront the drug dealers who had taken over the community, as well as the many corrupt public officials they felt were complicit by turning a blind eye.

organize Freedom Summer, then traveled to Atlantic City as a representative of the Mississippi Freedom Democratic Party at the Democratic National Convention in 1964. The MFDP demanded that they, instead of the official Mississippi delegation, be seated, due to the lack of voting rights for the state's Black citizens. Holland, who later added "Endesha" to her name, toured the country advocating for civil rights and went on to become a prizewinning playwright and professor of African American studies at the University of Southern California.

Resistance in the face of repression is not the exception. It is emblematic of each of the regions where the deepest disadvantage in our nation is felt. But resistance has been costly, as we will show in the coming chapters.

Little Kingdoms

"MISSISSIPPI IS REJECTING Nearly All of the Poor People Who Apply for Welfare and the State Won't Explain Why," read the headline of an April 2017 article on the website of the progressive Washington, DC, think tank ThinkProgress. The 2016 analysis found that roughly 11,000 families had applied for the state's Temporary Assistance for Needy Families (TANF) program—known colloquially as "welfare"—which offered a maximum of $170 per month to a family of three, by far the lowest benefit of any state. Of that number, only 167 applications were approved—a rejection rate of over 98 percent.

This anomaly caught the eye of veteran reporter Jimmie E. Gates, who was covering the government beat for the *Clarion-Ledger*, a statewide daily published in Jackson. He sought verification from the Mississippi Department of Human Services. Paul Nelson, the MDHS spokesperson who confirmed the numbers, told Gates, "There are many reasons . . . an application should be denied." But state representative Jarvis Dortch wasn't buying it: "The question is we have a lot of poor people in Mississippi so why are there just under two percent being approved for TANF?"

Gates's story piqued the curiosity of a newbie on the *Clarion-Ledger*'s staff, investigative journalist Anna Wolfe. She embarked on a quest that would take her far beyond where she might have imagined at the start. "Over the next two or three years, I filed dozens of public requests . . . fought the agency while they put up big walls . . . lots of secrecy. . . . They would send me these very meager, vague reports . . . about how they were spending the money. And it didn't show which entities were receiving funds or what they were doing with the money. And so, it was just a constant fight for years."

Ironically, Wolfe never unearthed the drivers of Mississippi's 98 percent welfare rejection rate; that remains a mystery. But she did find out where many of the state's welfare dollars were going. Her queries revealed a sprawling public embezzlement scheme, the largest known in state history, one that ensnared a family of all-star wrestlers, several retired professional football players, and a state university's athletic foundation, among others.

It all started when Greenwood native Nancy New, founder of the nonprofit Mississippi Community Education Center and a darling of Mississippi's then governor Phil Bryant and first lady Deborah Bryant, conspired with the director of MDHS, John Davis, to embezzle or redirect millions of dollars from the TANF program. They allegedly misspent tens of millions more of funds meant to aid the poorest Mississippians—$77 million according to state auditor Shad White and independent forensic auditors.

Some of the money went into the bank accounts of celebrity athletes who hailed from the state, such as former Los Angeles Rams running back Marcus Dupree, who ran a nonprofit with the mission of providing "equestrian activities for underprivileged children." Nancy New's nonprofit signed a six-year lease agreement for Dupree's newly purchased fifteen-acre ranch, which included the five-bedroom home where Dupree resided. We can find no evidence that any robust programming actually took place, although Dupree continues to deny any wrongdoing.

Meanwhile, retired World Wrestling Entertainment star Brett DiBiase, son of the all-star wrestler Ted DiBiase, "the Million Dollar Man"—whose memoir is ironically titled *Every Man Has His Price*—contracted with the state to provide drug addiction classes for an upfront fee of $48,000. Instead, he ended up in rehab himself, clocking four months in a luxury facility in Malibu, California. According to a forensic audit, this treatment was paid for with TANF funds—at a cost of $160,000. TANF dollars were also flowing into the coffers of Ted DiBiase, who ran a Christian organization called Heart of David Ministry with his other son, Ted Jr. (also a retired celebrity wrestler). State auditor Shad White ordered the ministry to repay $722,299 to the State of Mississippi, while Ted Jr. must reimburse the state $3.9 million.

But what really grabbed the headlines was a scathing 2020 state audit alleging that NFL Hall of Famer Brett Favre, the quarterback who led the Green Bay Packers to a Super Bowl victory in 1997, was paid $1.1 million by New's nonprofit for speaking events. According to the state auditor, no record of such events exists. Favre vehemently denies the state's claim.

Subsequently, some of Favre's text messages were released to the public, including one where he asked Nancy New, whose nonprofit was the conduit for the money, whether there was any way the media could become aware of the payment to him. She was quick to offer assurances that they could not. Favre later informed New—in a message punctuated by emojis—of his excitement concerning the money's arrival. Favre has since paid back the money he received—but not the interest that the state says he owes.

Welfare money was also funneled—again via New's nonprofit—into a new volleyball stadium at Favre's alma mater, the University of Southern Mississippi, where his daughter was on the volleyball team at the time. New's nonprofit sent $5 million in TANF dollars to the project with the thin justification that the facility would host "activities that benefit the area's underserved population." The single such event we are aware of is a Healthy Teens rally held at the Coliseum in October 2018. Money was also invested in a pharmaceutical start-up Favre was involved in called Prevacus.

How was all of this possible? Since a significant reform to the nation's welfare program in 1996, funding for states' welfare programs come largely from a federal block grant. This means the federal government sends a set amount to the states based on how many families got cash aid in the early 1990s, no matter how many families they serve now. To spend the funds to help needy families, the states must navigate myriad rules and reporting requirements. But to use the money for other purposes, they need only justify that the expense is relevant to one of the core purposes of the program: to increase self-sufficiency, curb nonmarital births, or promote marriage. These criteria leave a lot of wiggle room, to say the least. Mississippi, a state that ranks among the most corrupt by any measure, took that wiggle room to the extreme.

Not surprisingly, the state's welfare rolls have fallen dramatically in the years since 1996. While nearly 34,000 parents and children received benefits in 2000, that number plummeted to 11,387 in 2016, then dropped again to 6,125 by 2019, covering only a tiny fraction of the nearly 200,000 children living in poverty that year. Mississippi had the highest official child poverty rate in the nation in 2019, at 28 percent. That year, only 5 percent of the state's welfare dollars were being spent on cash assistance for those needy children and their caregivers. Meanwhile, MDHS director John Davis and Nancy New were traveling the country garnering attention for how, under their leadership, the state had embarked on a "multi-generational, collaborative approach which addresses barriers associated with poverty."

In fact, Davis essentially privatized the state welfare program in 2017 when he funneled tens of millions of TANF dollars into two nonprofits, including the one run by Nancy New. In the words of *Greenwood Commonwealth* editor Tim Kalich, "One person at the Department of Human Services, John Davis, was given nearly limitless authority to decide how tens of millions of dollars in [TANF] grant money was awarded. If that one person was either incompetent or corrupt, not only would massive amounts of taxpayer money be squandered, but the poor would be worse off. Welfare . . . executed this way, would increase poverty, not relieve it."

In 2020, Nancy New and her son Zach New, welfare commissioner Davis, and three other codefendants were charged with multiple crimes, including conspiracy to embezzle, embezzlement, making fraudulent statements, and conspiracy to commit mail fraud. Then in 2021, new charges were brought against both News at the federal level, this time for defrauding the Mississippi Department of Education out of $4 million in public education dollars for students not actually enrolled in New's New Summit schools—which received state dollars for serving children with disabilities—and for teachers not employed at these schools (including New herself). Mother and son were charged with conspiracy to commit wire fraud, money laundering, and conspiracy, among other charges. They faced sentences of up to 218 years in prison and $5 million in fines each. It was not until the spring of 2022 that Nancy and Zach New pleaded guilty in both state and federal court, and agreed to testify against Davis and the other codefendants, potentially including others who have not yet been charged. Their guilty pleas saved them from the prospect of spending any time in the notorious Parchman Farm or another of the state's barbaric penal institutions.

The celebrity "welfare recipients" involved have been ordered to pay restitution despite claims they have done nothing wrong and didn't know where the money originated. Nonetheless, Brett Favre insisted he "would never do anything to take away from the children I have fought to help!" Anna Wolfe questioned that claim in a conversation with former US congressman Ronnie Shows on his radio program: "So where did they think the money was coming from . . . ? [It was from] a nonprofit, so how do you get a million dollars from a nonprofit? I mean, nonprofits are charities." When asked by Shows to reflect on all that her reporting had revealed, she said, "It's kind of mind boggling to me . . . that the folks who rail against these social safety net programs . . . are often the same people who are making their careers at the government trough, privatizing these programs and getting cushy jobs for their [friends]."

Corruption is a common theme across America's internal colonies and is a key mechanism through which the sins of the past continue to wreak havoc on these places today.

In the Brooks County seat of Falfurrias, in South Texas, Mayor Pro Tem Letty Garza became embroiled in an illegal gambling scheme in the 2010s, landing her and her coconspirators in federal prison. Illegal casinos like the ones she abetted are all too common in the communities we visited in the region. Over in Zavala County in 2016, the mayor, the city manager, and three current or former members of Crystal City's city council were charged as part of a conspiracy and bribery scheme. Another council member had previously been indicted on human trafficking charges. That left only one councilor to run the town of 7,300. News coverage implicated not only the city but also the region: "Why is Public Corruption So Common in South Texas?" A *Washington Post* headline proclaimed, hyperbolically, "This Might Be the Most Corrupt Little Town in America."

Meanwhile, in September 2009, over in the Pee Dee region of South Carolina, a story in Charleston's *Post and Courier* heralded the good news: "A county with one of the highest unemployment rates in South Carolina is getting a jobs boost." According to a news release from the South Carolina Department of Commerce, Georgia-based Softee Supreme Diaper Corporation was investing $6 million in Marion County and bringing in 262 jobs. Several years later, another headline revealed the bad news: "Foul Smell for Taxpayers in S.C. Diaper Plant Project." In 2015, plant owner Jonathan Pinson, a former South Carolina State University board chair, was sentenced to five years in prison on multiple counts of embezzlement, bribery, kickbacks, and filing false papers. Later on, some of these convictions would be vacated while others would stand, and his sentence was reduced to four years. According to the indictment, Pinson and others "devised a plan to submit falsified invoices to Marion County for engineering services supposedly provided to the diaper plant, illegally billing Marion County at grossly inflated rates for work which was not always completed."

In the interim, there had been more bad news. On October 18, 2011, the Florence, South Carolina–based news source SCNow ("The

Voice of the Pee Dee") reported that "Former Marion School District 2 Superintendent Dr. Nathaniel Miller will spend six years in prison for theft of more than $500,000 in public funds."

But of all of the regions examined in this book, it is in eastern Kentucky where the corrosive effects of corruption are most keenly felt. As we will show, for generations the region's penchant for rampant political corruption has been a millstone around its neck, stunting economic growth and thus miring the region in disadvantage so deep that it has persisted even in the face of substantial federal aid meted out during the War on Poverty and beyond.

Nowhere is this tale of Appalachian corruption more lurid than in Clay County, which, along with Kentucky's other counties, functioned as a "semi-autonomous state" from its inception—a "little kingdom," to use historian Robert Ireland's colorful description, plagued by a "tradition of parochialism, corruption, and inefficiency" and a "prevailing lawlessness." When we first spoke with Carmen Lewis, former one-term mayor of the Clay County seat, Manchester, in the summer of 2019, she pointed to the area's poor showing five years earlier in a *New York Times* analysis, which had named Clay the "hardest place in America to live." The *Times* averaged every US county's rank on a grab bag of indicators: education, income, unemployment, disability, life expectancy, and obesity. Clay County topped the list. In this community, it all boiled down to a single dynamic that had been centuries in the making. Since as far back as the early 1800s, Clay's citizens had been held captive by a corrupt political elite they kept voting into office.

TWO CENTURIES OF CORRUPTION IN CLAY COUNTY

It began with a vital commodity, salt, leading to the first capitalist enterprise in central Appalachia. Recall that salt, mined from the brine along the banks of the county's Goose Creek starting around the turn of the nineteenth century, was the commodity first linking Clay County to regional markets. For a half century, its role in this community (and several others across central Appalachia) was akin to that of cotton in the Deep South. The salt industry, as with cotton in the Delta, laid the foundation for the political and social order still at play in Clay.

From the colonial era, salt was in constant demand, tying early settlers to the coast and limiting westward expansion and development. One cannot overstate the significance of salt, which played a key role in the development of roads, the improvement of river transport, the commercialization of the livestock industry, and urbanization. Furthermore, "salt was the one commodity readily converted into cash and the one commodity readily accepted in barter. Participation in the salt trade, therefore, proved requisite [for trade in that era]," writes historian John Jakle.

In Kentucky's salt industry, Clay County quickly took center stage. As early as 1810, four salt capitalists there were generating 7,000 bushels of salt each year, a fourth of the state's entire output. That figure would skyrocket to nearly a quarter of a million bushels at the industry's peak in the 1840s. Not only did salt link antebellum Clay County to markets beyond its borders, it led to the importation of hundreds of enslaved Americans and enabled the rise of a local elite that would come to exercise control of the region from its founding, in 1807, to the present day.

Abner Baker was one such member of the local elite. The younger son of a Virginia slaveholder with a large estate, he left Virginia for Kentucky to seek his fortune in 1793. After a decade and a half in the Bluegrass region, Baker found a foothold in the newly formed county of Clay when he was appointed clerk of the county and circuit courts. A cousin would soon begin to mine salt along Goose Creek, and Baker would eventually join him. He was perhaps the first to discover the key to control of the region: the twin pursuit of both political and economic power. In this way, the Baker family soon rose to the top of Clay's highly stratified social order.

The Road to Poverty, sociologists Dwight Billings and Kathleen Blee's lucid analysis of the roots of long-standing poverty in the central Appalachian region, takes Clay County as its case study, and the story as relayed here is deeply indebted to their work. They note that during even the very earliest days of its development, Clay was vastly unequal, due to the great inequality not only between enslaved people and their owners but also between capitalists and subsistence farmers. As John Campbell, one of the earliest chroniclers of the history of the region, observes, the success of the early saltworks contributed to the "picture of wealthy landlords . . . living on baronial mountain estates in almost feudal fashion, surrounded by slaves and retainers."

The most important of these backcountry elites other than the Bakers were the Whites and the Garrards. James White, a wealthy Virginian, first learned about the opportunities for salt mining in Clay while serving in the Revolutionary War. Just after the turn of the century, he and his brother Hugh, along with the scions of other rich slave owners, acquired land and built up the salt industry on the county's riverbeds. Hugh made the county his home and would become one of its most powerful men.

Like Abner Baker, Hugh White built power not only in the economic but also in the political sphere through a series of public offices he and other members of his family held. White's descendants would serve in pretty much every local political post over the next two centuries, as well as in the state legislature and the halls of Congress. Hugh White's son John was speaker of the US House during the Twenty-Seventh Congress. Meanwhile, the Whites would mine salt using the labor of enslaved people and amass vast tracts of land—roughly 20,000 acres by 1860.

For James Garrard, who became Kentucky's second governor, the story was much the same. Hailing from the Bluegrass region of the state, Garrard sent his son Daniel to Clay County in 1806 to establish a salt mine. The Garrards also secured more than 45,000 acres of land for farming. For Daniel, involvement in local politics quickly followed. He and his sons James and "T.T." would also rise to the highest level of the power structure in Clay. Together, the "Whites and the Garrards, along with a few other families, thus established economic and political dynasties in Clay County based on enslaved labor, salt manufacturing, commerce, and large-scale farming that persisted throughout the antebellum and early postbellum periods and, in some cases, even into the modern era."

Before the Civil War, these salt capitalists had enormous power. As highway commissioners, they could direct the building of roads in ways that linked their mines to regional transportation. They could compel locals to undertake road maintenance and improvements. Records show they reimbursed themselves for making the river improvements needed to transport salt—at local taxpayers' expense. They had the authority to appoint patrols to monitor the activities of the people they enslaved. As justices, they were charged with administering relief and widows' pensions, but they also had the standing to remove children from the homes of poor families, binding them as apprentices to the wealthy, not an uncommon practice at the time. Across central Appalachia, as scholar Mary Beth Pudup documents, "the intersection of professional occupation, political office, county-seat residence, and property ownership—all within the compass of a certain few families—was the rule, not the exception."

Ostensibly, it was the murder of salt miner Daniel Bates in 1844 by Abner Baker's son Dr. Abner Baker Jr. that precipitated one of the more infamous Kentucky mountain feuds: the war between the Garrards, who believed Baker Jr. was insane and thus could not be executed by law, and the Whites, who wanted to see him hanged. Baker Jr. had accused his wife—James White's daughter Susan—of adulterous affairs with several men, including Bates. But as many Appalachian scholars have argued, this feud, like so many others in the eastern Kentucky mountains, stemmed less from the revenge motive of a husband who believed himself a cuckold than from competition between economic elites. Ultimately, the Whites won, and Baker was hanged. According to historian Altina Waller, who has written the definitive text on the topic, "Conflicts identified as feuds or vendettas were conflicts between gentlemen of property and standing." The consequences of the White-Garrard feud for Clay County were both formative and tragic, for the conflict deformed the local government and public spheres, and Clay's society was altered to reflect the rivalries among these warring factions.

During the mid-1800s, the salt industry began to collapse in the face of competition from other regions where the commodity was easier to extract and bring to market. During the Civil War, Goose Creek's saltworks were destroyed by the Union army for fear they would be seized by the Confederates. This dealt the industry a death blow. After the war, "the county slipped into an era of deepening economic and geographical isolation that lasted more than a generation." At the same time, subsistence farming was becoming an unviable way of life. Between 1875 and 1900, the population grew because of the extraordinarily high fertility rates among farm families, which required subdividing the land. Thus, food production per capita fell sharply. Harry M. Caudill quipped, "The stork outran the grubbing hoe and plow." This not only reduced living standards but, in the words of historian Paul Salstrom, softened residents up "for later industrial exploitation."

Meanwhile, little changed in the trench warfare between the Whites and the Garrards. Billings and Blee recount the story of a traveling preacher who arrived in Clay County in 1897 hoping to win souls. While his message of salvation fell on deaf ears, he was able to record an outbreak of violence that coincided with his arrival: two killings along the banks of a local creek, an ambush-murder-arson, a gun battle, an assault, a murder by a mob of "Ku Klux," plus "quarrels, brawls and pistol drawings . . . too tedious to mention. . . . As I sat in my room in the second floor of the Lucas Hotel, I could hear the bullets whiz through the air." He would soon learn that the violence was far from random. It was driven in large part by the stiff competition for political power between the two rival clans. Billings and Blee observe that "for the first decades after the Abner Baker conflict, these wars of position took place through local elections and the offices of congressman, clerk, treasurer, and state representative oscillated between the Garrards and Whites."

Between the late 1880s and 1920, a massive, systematic drive to clear-cut the central Appalachian Mountains by the American timber industry revived a regional economy that had floundered after the twin collapse of the salt industry and subsistence farming. In fact, by the turn of the century, the region was producing 30 percent of the hardwood in the United States. Logging had long been a side occupation for local farmers who culled a limited number of hardwood trees each year. Now it became a full-time job as companies assembled large crews and housed them in logging camps and towns. By 1920, the "virgin forest was gone, except for the pathetic remnants of a few hundred acres." Meanwhile, many loggers had completely abandoned their farms.

While the leading families pursued timbering and mining to a limited extent, they had neither the capital nor the credit to do so on a large scale. It was absentee capitalists rather than the local elites who would go on to become the principal industrial ownership class. Due to their hegemony over the political and social order, however, mountain elites like the Whites and Garrards were ideally positioned to benefit from connections to the corporations that invaded central Appalachia in successive waves during those years. Because these elites owned much of the land, they profited handsomely from real estate speculation and the leap in land values as corporate interest in the region's potential mineral wealth grew. It was Clay's elites—with their preexisting advantages in the old economy—who profited most from the arrival of the railroad in 1917. Both a Garrard and a White reaped huge profits by selling rights-of-way for the new lines. Summing up the period, Mary Beth Pudup chronicles how, among the mountain elite, some "maintained their holdings to become coal owners and operators on their own account, others sold out and made a fortune, while others traded their land for equity positions in new coal and land firms."

Taken together, neither the timber boom nor the arrival of Big Coal did much to bridge the chasm between the tiny cadre of elites and the much larger numbers of struggling subsistence farmers and wage laborers employed in resource extraction. Rather, these industries fostered what has been called "the development of under-development" in central Appalachia. Historian Ronald Eller, author of *Miners, Millhands, and Mountaineers: Industrialization of the Appalachian South, 1880–1930*, writes, "By the turn of the century, the Appalachian South had become the economic colony of the urban northeast."

The patterns of political corruption and elite capture of resources from the early 1800s onward were richly on display a century and a half later, when Clay's Republican leadership controlled the patronage in the county—especially jobs in the schools, the largest employer—while its Democratic leadership controlled state programs, such as the maintenance of local highways, another prominent source of employment. Political patronage served both to reward and threaten—with promises of jobs and threats of dismissal used as tools to maintain political power. In the early 1960s, business leaders formed the Clay County Development Association to attract new industry to Manchester. Douglas Arnett, a historian who studied the program, reported that "the local elite was willing to tolerate the work of the development association as long as the innovations . . . [wouldn't] threaten the social structure."

Later that decade, the War on Poverty would infuse more than $1.5 million in federal funds into the community but also would require that the county ensure what the War on Poverty architects referred to as "maximum feasible participation" among all groups, including the poor. This requirement was a "direct challenge to the local political machine and its control over patronage," according to Billings and Blee. To meet the perceived threat, the school superintendent attempted to co-opt the efforts of the US Office of Economic Opportunity (OEO) by incorporating an entity that would be the conduit of federal funds. Arnett described how, when this failed, local officials mounted an intimidation campaign to ensure that the populace voted for the political machine's representatives to serve on the board of the OEO's Community Action Program (CAP). Due to persistent corruption, Clay's CAP was the first in the nation to be defunded for self-dealing, as well as an utter failure to achieve "maximum feasible participation" of the poor to any meaningful degree. It later merged with a multicounty CAP the OEO hoped would be less vulnerable to elite exploitation. As we will show, that would not be the case.

Throughout this period, just as in other internal colonies, local officeholders relied on the denial of suffrage—in the form of vote buying and voter intimidation—to retain power. Historian Thomas Kiffmeyer described the experiences of an anti-poverty group that began its work in the region just before the launch of the War on Poverty. These volunteers witnessed myriad instances where contentious elections resulted in both discriminatory hiring and firing, with the end goal of controlling local voters. When local elected officials felt threatened, they resorted to the use of bribes of food, moonshine, and cash to bring voters around.

In 1997, graft in the now regional Community Action Program was alleged. *Lexington Herald-Leader* reporter Karen Samples wrote, "Strange things were going on at the Daniel Boone Development Council [the regional CAP] when state officials arrived in September, 1996, for an annual review." Some of the poverty relief agency's money was ending up in secret bank accounts controlled by a private company, records show. "A truckload of donated floor tile had gone to Clay County residents who weren't poor . . . middle-class folks had been renting the council's vans for vacation trips—even though the agency's mission is to help the disadvantaged."

In the following decade, public corruption continued. Daugh White, Manchester's long-serving mayor and direct descendant of the early nineteenth-century Clay County settler Hugh White, pleaded guilty to racketeering conspiracy in 2007 for demanding kickbacks from companies bidding on city contracts. The companies had been coerced into making the payments to the city manager, a position created by Daugh and filled by his son Kennon. While serving time, Daugh was also implicated in a scheme in which a drug dealer burned down a vacant home in Manchester, which allowed the city to then purchase the property to build a new police station.

As was true in antebellum Clay County, the power of local officials in eastern Kentucky is nearly absolute these days, too. They still control most of the well-paying jobs. Clint Harris, a circuit court judge, told us he was offered his job as an assistant county attorney because he was "Jack Harris's kid." Harris explained, "I was getting ready to . . . go take the bar exam, and [the county attorney] called me and he said, 'I talked to my daddy, and Daddy said, Call Jack Harris's boy. He's in law school, so I believe he'd be a good one." Favoritism in hiring is most noticeable in the schools. One high school employee told us that cronyism in hiring is ubiquitous: "In this town, it's more likely that someone will get hired because of who they are more than they can do their job well. It will always be like that because that's your friend's dad or son." This is not new, as the historical record attests: "Over the course of the nineteenth century local political office-holding in the mountains gained a high premium. . . . The distribution of teaching positions in each county became one of the most closely guarded patronage preserves."

Many among our low-income interviewees know full well that a person needs to have connections—preferably family ties—to get one of the good jobs in town. Paige put it this way: "It's all about who you know." Jake described Manchester as a "family-owned town [where] they only care about [themselves] and their money. . . . They don't care about everybody else. . . . The rich gets richer, the poor gets poorer. . . . Really, there's probably four or five big names, and they run the town as far as jobs and businesses . . . they allow to come in and don't allow to come in. . . . It's always been like that, honestly, it really has."

But Clay's experiences in recent years vividly illustrate how control of local offices enables public servants to facilitate any number of illicit moneymaking schemes—some of which may risk their constituents' lives. Most shocking has been the willingness of Clay elites to make common cause with criminals, bringing drugs and illegal painkillers into the county.

Despite years of allegations of corruption, it wasn't until Daugh White was under federal investigation that he was finally unseated after seven terms as mayor. Daugh's family patriarch Jennings White, who served as county clerk, pleaded guilty to laundering money for one of the largest known cocaine and marijuana drug rings in eastern Kentucky, headed by kingpin Kenneth Day, a Manchester pawnshop owner. Day also served on the county board of elections in the 1990s and held the post of Republican election commissioner, a position that allowed him to select precinct officers. These positions were instrumental in the Whites' ability to buy their way into public office year after year. Denver Sizemore, a convicted drug dealer, testified that Jennings White gave him $25,000 to kill one of White's political opponents—a charge White still denies. Vernon Hacker, a city councilman and director of 911 operations, who was also aligned with White, used his position to tip off dealers and facilitate the illicit sale of OxyContin and cocaine. A number of our interviewees relayed stories about police arriving to raid a drug house and finding that the last call received there was from their own police department, presumably warning about the impending raid.

By 2002, circuit judge Cletus Maricle and school superintendent Doug Adams, both of whom had daughters who had fallen prey to illicit pain pills, had had enough. They decided to wage war against the Whites. The 2002 election was a particularly violent one, as the *New York Times* reported: "In one of the bloodiest election seasons in more than 50 years in these fabled Kentucky hills, Sheriff Edd Jordan of Clay County is watching his back."

Violence included the "riddling of County Clerk Jennings White's van with bullets," although later court testimony revealed that White shot up his van himself in an attempt to gain the sympathy of voters. That election cycle also included the attempted murder of the man Denver Sizemore testified he was paid to kill but didn't. The target was a private investigator who—whether by Sizemore or someone else—was shot six times in the back (and yet somehow survived) on his way home from Indiana where he was said to have gotten some dirt on White. Violence wasn't limited to Clay County in that election cycle; in another nearby county, the *Times* reported that "two candidates in sheriff's races have been killed," and yet other races in the region were "punctuated with gunfire and fistfights, and there [were] widespread accusations of swapping votes for liquor, cash and even the addictive prescription pain-killer OxyContin."

After the 2002 election, the opioid crisis in the county—as well as the collusion by officeholders—only intensified. A coalition to defeat the Whites and their allies continued into the elections of 2004 and 2006. Problem was, in their quest to unseat the corrupt White clan, crusaders Cletus Maricle, Doug Adams, and their allies relied on an age-old eastern Kentucky tactic—vote buying—perhaps believing that the ends justified the means. In 2006, newly minted Manchester mayor Carmen Lewis (who had refused the coalition's backing and would later accuse it of extortion) and her chief of police, Jeff Culver, chose to cooperate with a federal investigation of the vote-buying scheme of Maricle, Adams, and their allies. In the end, the prosecution relied on testimony from none other than members of the White slate, who agreed to testify in exchange for lesser sentences on their own convictions.

The story of public corruption in Clay County is a cautionary tale bringing into sharp relief how, even in one of the most deeply disadvantaged places in our nation, there are still plenty of spoils ripe for elite capture. If a place has even the basic elements of local government—schools, city and county government, and local law enforcement—blood can be squeezed from a stone. In Clay, the graft has been obvious—even flamboyant. Yet for nearly two centuries, Clay's citizens have mostly stayed silent. As one of Mayor Carmen Lewis's chief supporters, a former high school principal, told us, "You speak up, you lose your job. . . . Your family doesn't eat."

Mayor Lewis and Chief of Police Culver probably risked their lives to help end the corruption so pervasive that it had stifled any prospect of economic progress. Both received death threats and lost their posts in the next election (a new chief of police was appointed by the incoming mayor). They became, in Lewis's words, "two of the most hated people in Clay County." Meanwhile, corruption of this kind was occurring across central Appalachia. In 2010, when Maricle, Adams, and their codefendants were all convicted, Clay was just one of eleven eastern Kentucky counties in which officials were charged with corruption. Lewis referred to it cynically as "mountain politics."

During the sensational trials of those on the Maricle-Adams side, Lewis told us, locals minimized the crimes as "only vote buying," which they claimed was "not that bad"—or at least not as bad as committing arson for profit, accepting kickbacks, tipping off drug dealers, and laundering money for a drug cartel while in public office, crimes for which some of the White clan and their allies had been convicted. She said ruefully, "It is as if the whole traumatized populace is still in the grip of Stockholm syndrome," referring to the rare psychological condition where traumatized victims bond with their abusers. In line with these observations, on a trip to Greenwood, Mississippi, in June 2021, we spoke with several local leaders who mentioned Nancy New. They played down her alleged crimes and praised her schools, especially the New Summit Academy in Greenwood, which does "so much good."

FROM TURNING A BLIND EYE TO ABSOLUTION

Much as many of Greenwood's community leaders tend to downplay the violence on the south side while also blaming it on those who live there, a number of Clay County's leaders seem willing to turn a blind eye to rampant public corruption while blaming the poor, or the government programs that serve them, for the community's problems.

In his 2018 book, *The Left Behind: Decline and Rage in Small-Town America*, sociologist Robert Wuthnow describes the dozens of rural communities he studied as places that, while rich in favorable attributes, tend to exclude those who don't belong, often "the poor who townspeople figure are on welfare and probably up to no good." These include "newcomers of different ancestry who don't quite fit in." Paul Bowling is a fifty-four-year-old principal officer of the Clay County Cancer Coalition, a nonprofit that relies on government grants to help with the gas bills of cancer patients who must travel significant distances for treatment. Clearly an insider, he explained to us that as "friendly as people are, when you're an outsider, you're an outsider. . . . Our people are our people."

Another prominent scholar of rural poverty, Cynthia Duncan, refers to this state of mind in rural America as one of "good rich people" and "bad poor people." But in America's internal colonies, where inequality is among the highest in the nation and has been for generations, how does the moral community operate? Here, our evidence suggests, divisions between the haves and the have-nots may be reinforced to an extreme degree. This in itself may be a mechanism by which the life choices of people today are hindered—through racial, ethnic, and class cleavages that have persisted for hundreds of years. For the poor of eastern Kentucky, there is an extreme level of social exclusion that has a lot in common with that seen today in the Cotton Belt and in South Texas. For elites, the dividing line between the classes is defined as a moral—rather than a racial, ethnic, economic, or political—divide. This construct offers an absolution of sorts, for the moral narrative shields the elite from having to grapple with the grinding poverty in this poorest white-majority place in the nation, with the history of extraction and exploitation that has marked the lives of the have-nots for generations, and with the very real corruption that is crippling the community and perpetuating the class divides.

For the community leaders we spoke to in Clay County, the divide comes down to one central distinction: Do you work or collect a government check? Government checks, said Pastor Ken Bolin of Manchester Baptist Church, make people feel entitled. They no longer know what it feels like to work for a living, he told us. Nearly every other community leader agreed. Almost all extended their critique to child disability. Government benefits are choking the educational aspirations of poor children, they claimed, because poor kids' parents coach them to do poorly in school so they can qualify as disabled and collect "stupid checks."

Stories about "stupid checks" were on nearly every community leader's lips when we were conducting fieldwork in Clay. The term is perhaps an echo of a centuries-old program authorized by the Kentucky legislature in 1793 that provided those deemed "pauper idiots"—many of them children—with modest financial support.

Nicholas Kristof, reporting from neighboring Breathitt County for the *New York Times* in 2012, quoted a local school district official, Melanie Stevens, who said, "The greatest challenge we face as educators is how to break that dependency on government. In second grade, they have a dream. In seventh grade, they have a plan": to draw government assistance for life. Christy Rice, a Clay County High School guidance counselor, shares the belief that what she sees as government dependence is due to "culture." While acknowledging the high rate of poverty in the county, the many health challenges, and the lack of well-paying jobs, she told us she doesn't approve of those who claim government checks, which she believes have "alienated" generations from the "culture of work."

It is worthwhile to consider whether the numbers lend credence to these assertions. Among our participants, some had certainly applied for SSI (Supplemental Security Income) on behalf of their kids. Yet of the roughly 4,200 children in Clay County in 2020, only 213 were getting a check from the SSI program, a rate of about

5 percent. Only 185 kids in Breathitt County received SSI in 2019, a rate of about 6 percent. Meanwhile, local nonprofit leader Jason Bailey writing for The Daily Yonder, a rural Appalachian news outlet, wondered in 2013 whether the school district's woes might have a different cause: "Breathitt County's school system was recently taken over by the state due to corruption and mismanagement at the top. The superintendent was indicted for vote-buying; he is the eleventh county leader (including the sheriff) to have been recently convicted or pled guilty to illegal activity associated with political battles among county elites." What is really holding back children from success in school in Breathitt County? A relatively small fraction of children receiving a modest monthly check, or persistent and rampant corruption in the institutions charged with serving them?

Joe Farmer, the forty-six-year-old founder of the Axis Coffee Shop & Gathering Place in Manchester, battled both poverty and addiction in his younger years. Now a business owner, he, too, blames government assistance for Clay County's woes, telling us that it has "killed our communities. It really has. The War on Poverty began in the Appalachians . . . and people are worse off because [they] have forfeited their rugged individualism that made this country great."

Fifty-two-year-old Jeff Culver, Carmen Lewis's former chief of police, is now head of security at the Manchester hospital. He also is eager to condemn government checks, as he explained to us: "Help us, but don't give it to us. . . . We're a very proud country. When you take someone's pride from them, you've stripped them of their dignity. Feed us but feed us with jobs. Feed us with hope. Feed us with a life to look forward to, to get up and go to work. To make something. To be productive in your community."

One cannot dismiss these narratives out of hand. Clay County ranks third in the nation in adult disability claims, when adjusted for population size. As of 2019, the county's official labor force participation rate was only 37 percent, on a par with most of its eastern Kentucky neighbors but far below the national average of 63 percent. Among the working-age population, we estimate more than 20 percent receive some form of disability. Furthermore, Culver's comments are not completely at odds with our low-income interviewees' accounts. Seven of twenty-two were receiving SSI, while another was benefiting from her husband's SSDI (Social Security Disability Insurance). Many of them described their boredom and isolation.

None were making as much money from the program as some of the local elites who have taken advantage of the program have, such as Eric Conn, a lawyer specializing in disability claims in eastern Kentucky who was convicted of defrauding federal disability programs. Conn was indicted for conspiring with doctors who falsified medical records and with a Social Security Administration appeals judge who pleaded guilty to taking more than $600,000 in kickbacks in exchange for approving Conn's cases. Conn—who cut off his ankle bracelet, fled to Honduras, was captured, and pleaded guilty to conspiracy to defraud the government and to retaliation against a witness—is now serving a twenty-seven-year prison sentence. His clients continue to face the fallout of his crimes. One of them, Bryan McCown, told a local reporter that he had "fractured his neck and back in a fall from a truck at a Pike County coal mine." He claimed he was wholly unaware that Conn was bribing a judge on his behalf, but that didn't keep the Social Security Administration from cutting off his disability payment after the fraud was uncovered.

While there may be some whose desire to work is sapped by the lure of a government check, it is also true that blaming government benefits for breaking the spirit of the poor is just the latest guise in a long history of elites blaming Appalachian highlanders for the region's problems. In fact, most of the low-income people we spoke with told us they were desperate to do more than rely on a disability check. Even those with severe disabilities hoped to have a job one day so they could contribute to society.

Paige believes that the lack of jobs is the real problem: "If they had more jobs besides just restaurant work, or something like that, it would help a lot of households." Jake concurs: "It all comes down to more jobs, more jobs for people to survive and live, because if not, man, everybody's going to be on welfare. . . . That's what most people turn to." One Clay County resident admitted he had given up: "I tried working and they don't really pay enough to actually survive down here. So I do a lot of little side hustles, I guess," including selling his prescription Suboxone on the black market to pay his rent. Yet others, like Stevie, said that she was so determined to work that she would "walk to work in the rain, in the snow. The police picked me up a couple of times and asked me what I was doing out because it was storming." Similarly, Helena described her determination to keep her job, which meant walking to work, even while eight months pregnant.

To claim that government assistance has led to a decline in people working also poses a "chicken and egg" problem. Which came first? A report examining the decline in workforce participation prepared by the Kentucky Chamber Foundation concludes that the causes "are many, including demographic change, poor health outcomes, substance abuse, incarceration, among many others." "Demographic change" refers to the aging of the population: the share of adults in or approaching retirement in the region has grown relative to younger individuals in their prime working years. The report does mention government benefits, though this is not high on the list. Even then, the problem is cast as one of bad economic trade-offs faced by beneficiaries rather than moral failings. That is, even given their meager benefits, disability programs may offer a more stable and livable income than most available jobs, at least for those without connections or a college degree. Given that, is the right solution to cut off the one income source providing some stability? Or is it to increase opportunities for living-wage jobs for those able to work?

Isolated rural locations such as Clay County have low living costs, which is a plus when a disabled individual's income ranges from $840 to $1,200 per month, depending on which disability program they qualify for. For those with limited incomes, places like Clay are "sticky"—meaning that people can seldom afford to move away. Real differences in morbidity are also at play. Economists Anne Case and

Angus Deaton, among others, have found that reports of pain are sky-high in Appalachia and several other rural regions possibly as a result of the history of physically demanding work in these locales. Among the twenty-two low-income Clay residents we interviewed, fully three-quarters reported a disabling condition, about three times the number claiming disability benefits. In fact, their disorders were often serious and overlapping. Three had been diagnosed with cancer, three with hepatitis C (possibly related to past drug use), and two with arthritis. Three were on medication for high blood pressure. Other conditions included seizures, epilepsy, diabetes, high cholesterol, migraines, degenerative disc disease, lupus, Raynaud's disease, Graves' disease, bulging discs, and fluid on the hips. Eight were being treated for one or more mental health disorders, including bipolar disorder (two), anxiety (four), depression (three), and schizophrenia (three). These underlying vulnerabilities are precisely why places like Clay County were targeted by pharmaceutical companies like Purdue for the rollout of OxyContin and other painkillers.

Each of the communities we examined for this book suffer not only from a legacy of grossly underfunded and often racially segregated schools, violence, and a collapse of the local social infrastructure but also from weak and often corrupt local government. In this way, America's internal colonies are similar to former colonies established by foreign nations around the world, where government corruption "has deep historical roots that go all the way back to their colonial experience." In Clay County, public corruption has emerged in an especially virulent form, arguably due to unique historical processes, including the formation of a political and economic elite that coalesced well before the Civil War.

Corruption is a seldom recognized form of exploitation in which an elite few are allowed to live off the spoils of public office and to preserve the status quo. Under these conditions, it is nearly impossible for a community to improve. In 2011, the *Lexington Herald-Leader* editorialized, "How does a business know it can count on roads being maintained, public utilities providing the best service at the lowest cost, the police and courts treating all fairly, schools hiring the best educators they can find?" An editorial in the same newspaper opined, "Economic development will be hard, if not impossible, in places governed by small-time political machines that maintain power in ways that can't bear scrutiny." It noted that the "State Department recently devoted an issue of 'The Foreign Service Journal' to the topic of corruption. . . . Former secretary of state John Kerry was quoted as saying, 'Corruption is an opportunity destroyer because it discourages honest and accountable investment; it makes businesses more expensive to operate; it drives up the cost of public services for local taxpayers.'" What is true around the world is most certainly true in Clay County, Kentucky, and America's other internal colonies.

The Invisible Hand

MONTHS AFTER THE 2016 FLOODWATERS of Hurricane Matthew had receded, seventy-eight-year-old Billy Jones of Nichols, South Carolina, was still reeling. "Everything is gone," he told a local reporter. "The duct work, the heat pump, they disconnected the water and the sewer. They tore out the flooring, the kitchen cabinets, piled them in the street." Many months after this retiree had been forced to flee his home, he was still unable to return. Photos of his house from that time show an inviting brick fireplace seemingly undisturbed by the destruction, and a large living room window with light streaming in. These features might have made the room appear almost pleasant, except for the missing flooring planks and the fact that the bottom half of the drywall had been ripped off the wall due to mold, revealing the wood framing and another damaged room beyond. Jones's upright piano, too heavy to move, is his sole possession in view. (He said the piano, while a bit worse for wear, was still mostly in tune.) Jones's income is limited to Social Security, so he didn't have the money to rebuild. Meanwhile, he claimed, the government agency charged with aiding victims of disasters had deemed him ineligible for help because the home is located in a floodplain and was uninsured. "It's overwhelming," his daughter said, "just to try to figure out what to do."

Billy Jones's hometown of just under three hundred people, in the heart of the Pee Dee region, had already been rocked by another major flood the year before Matthew, and the area was about to be battered again in 2018 by Hurricane Florence. Other homeowners told the local news how they invested everything they had to rebuild after Matthew, only to be flooded out again. It wasn't the high winds from the hurricanes that caused the damage. It was the flooding. Nichols sits near the meeting point of the Lumber and Little Pee Dee Rivers. Each time these rivers breach their banks, water comes pouring into town.

Slammed by floods from three extreme weather events over the course of just a few years, dozens of residents of Nichols and other parts of South Carolina's Marion County could recall the flood-waters reaching halfway up the first-floor windows of many homes, and the tops of many traffic signs that were barely visible. We talked to locals who had seen cars completely submerged. Some surveyed the damage in boats they typically used to tool up and down the Lumber River. Helicopters scanned the devastation from above, looking for stranded residents. Many people were rescued by boat or by National Guardsmen who drove through town in high-water rescue vehicles—tan military-grade monster trucks sitting atop massive wheels.

The mayor of Nichols, Lawson Battle, recalled the story of one young man trapped on the roof of his SUV and shouting for help. A resident who worked for the regional agricultural retailer Carolina Eastern, the largest employer in town, described water forty inches deep inside the business's warehouse. "It was pitch-black dark in the warehouse since there are no skylights back there. . . . I saw dead fish on the floor in here when we first got back in. They had fifty-gallon barrels of mold cleaner at Town Hall, and we would go up there and fill up five-gallon buckets of it to wash down the walls," he told a local reporter. Pace's Pharmacy, an anchor in Nichols's downtown for generations, closed permanently after Matthew.

Well into 2019, many Marion County families still weren't back in their homes. Meanwhile, many wondered what had happened to the $95 million that had been designated to help the region. "We don't know where to turn to get help," one victim said. While some had managed to get aid from the Federal Emergency Management

Agency (FEMA) or other government entities whose job is to help in the aftermath of a disaster, many more had been told that the agency could do nothing for them. Some claimed they had been told by FEMA that to get any aid, they would have to raise their flood-zone homes six feet or more above sea level, at a cost of at least $40,000 for even a modest home. One landlord in this predicament was contemplating walking away from his two rental homes: "The houses are worth but about $50,000 to start so, if I have to do that, I'll just take a bulldozer and run through them." A homeowner with a more substantial property explained, "We can't use our existing foundation. We have to put in a new one. . . . And it's going to cost us anywhere from $130,000 to raise our house." These disaster victims were caught between multiple government agencies, each with its own byzantine bureaucracy, trying to navigate the process of re-claiming their homes. By the time we got to know some of them in 2019, many felt that their prospects did not look bright.

Deep structural inequalities are so baked into the legacies and cul-ture of our nation's most disadvantaged regions that they can be taken for granted. Only in a crisis are they fully revealed, a lesson brought home in our study of the Pee Dee region. Marion County has much in common with our other regions of deepest disadvantage. It is mostly rural and agricultural, dominated at first by cotton, then by tobacco, and now by a mix of crops and, on vast swaths of some of the former plantation land, solar farms. Disadvantage in the Pee Dee has deep historical roots, just as it does elsewhere across Amer-ica's internal colonies. The Pee Dee is in mourning over the loss of social infrastructure, from the emptying out of its Main Streets to the shuttering of a much-loved community school. During our time in the Pee Dee, though, the residents and community leaders we got to know were dealing with the fallout from a very different kind of challenge than we had encountered elsewhere, one that brought the dynamics of systemic inequality—what can only be called structural racism—into full view.

Marion, South Carolina, is a rural community of about 31,000 just inland from Myrtle Beach and the Atlantic coastline. The majority of the county's residents are Black. At number 138 on our Index of Deep Disadvantage, it is a bit further down in our ranking than either Mississippi's Leflore County or eastern Kentucky's Clay County. You can feel that little bit of difference when you arrive. Driving into the city of Marion—the county seat and home to about a fifth of the population—we found ourselves wondering if there had been a mistake in our numbers. The poverty that comes more quickly into view in other places we've gotten to know is not quite so evident in this hub. Sure, there are a few vacant buildings on Main Street, but the avenue boasts a series of striking, well-maintained edifices, too, including an elegant, pillared city hall.

Sometimes people assume that the class structures of poor rural towns are flat—that is, that the only people who live in poor rural places are poor themselves. Thus, they believe that these communities are fundamentally different from big cities like Los Angeles, where the poor and the rich coexist. Measures of inequality such as the Gini Index can quantify the divide between the haves and the have-nots. The Gini Index is a metric used by the federal government to assess inequality in the United States and by the World Bank and United Nations to measure inequality worldwide. When we began this research, we, too, were guilty of the assumption that inequality would be worse in places like LA and New York than in the rural South and the other regions identified by our index.

In fact, while central Appalachia, the Pee Dee, and the Delta might lack a Jeff Bezos or Bill Gates, we found that, by the most commonly used measure of income inequality, the Gini Index, the divide between the haves and the have-nots in America's internal colonies is just as wide, sometimes even wider, as it is in highly unequal cities. According to this measure, Marion County is about as unequal as Los Angeles and is more unequal than tech-rich Seattle. Similarly, Leflore County, Mississippi, is more unequal than New York City by quite a bit. At the other end of the spectrum, as we will show in chapter 9, the places of greatest *advantage* according to our index are also typically the least unequal.

Outside the county seat of Marion, the inequality and entrenched poverty in the county come into full view. For researchers Jasmine Simington, Meg Duffy, and Lanora Johnson, who conducted field-work in Marion County for several months in the summer of 2019, it would become abundantly clear that our index's rankings highlighted monumental challenges there—difficulties that well might be missed by a cursory drive down Marion's Main Street. Marion County has less poverty than Leflore County, but its poverty rate is still far above the national average. In recent years, average life expectancy was just over seventy-two years, nearly six years below the national mean.

After tobacco production in the Pee Dee waned, the region saw an influx of several small manufacturing plants in the late twenti-eth century. A Russell Stover factory known locally as "the candy plant" provided stable, middle-class jobs for three decades. When it closed in 2000, it rocked the local economy to its core. SOPAKCO, a company that makes rations for the US armed forces, and a couple of auto parts factories are among the few manufacturers that have survived. Solar farms have brought some jobs to the region, although they do not pay the rank and file as well as other employers in the energy sector, so they may not prove to be a viable path to building a middle class.

We began to understand better why Marion County lands where it does on our index as we got to know the smaller municipalities of Nichols and Sellers. Though extraordinarily hard hit by the three severe weather events that battered the region one after another, Sellers went unmentioned by the county leaders we met and ap-peared only sporadically in news coverage of the storms. According to Mayor Barbara Hopkins, "Sellers has been forgotten." A Black woman who exudes charisma and infectious energy, she had been serving as mayor of Sellers for nearly a decade when Jasmine and

Lanora talked to her. When they offered her a handshake at their first meeting, she protested, saying, "Let me get a hug, baby!" and proceeded to envelop them in a warm and enthusiastic embrace.

Hopkins acknowledges that the community has innumerable challenges. For many years, she has been trying to secure funding to get indoor plumbing for all the residents, including some families with children who live in homes that have only outhouses. The challenges of the community's two hundred or so residents, virtually all of them Black, have only intensified since the fall of 2015, when the region was hit with what many residents call the "thousand-year flood." Those floodwaters killed nineteen South Carolinians and caused $1.5 billion in damages all told. Hopkins herself lost her home when an electrical pole fell on it, setting it on fire. One year later, almost to the day, Hurricane Matthew arrived, skipping along the South Carolina coast. Matthew was followed, as we've seen, by Hurricane Florence in 2018. As the Lumber River, a tributary of the Great Pee Dee River, rose again, it caused severe flooding in Sellers and elsewhere across the county. These two hurricanes led to hundreds of millions of dollars more in damages to thousands of homes. An analysis by the State of South Carolina following Hurricane Matthew named Marion County the "most impacted and distressed area" in South Carolina.

No resident we spoke with explicitly made the connection between this onslaught of severe weather events and global climate change, but many described how they feel constantly pummeled by severe weather. As the planet continues to warm, the southeast coast of the United States is expected to face some of the most severe and increasingly violent weather events. While the western portions of the United States will likely face increasing periods of drought coupled with extreme heat, with the attendant risk of forest fires, the Southeast can expect both periods of drought and extreme rainfall. Marion County, and Sellers in particular, fit the profile of the type of places that will be hit the hardest, according to the EPA: rural, low-income communities of color.

Mayor Hopkins told us stories of the flooding in Sellers that echo those from Nichols. "It was back-to-back [disasters]," she explained. "Sellers has a total of forty homes right now that people have not moved back into. Some people are still staying in [their flooded-out homes], but they are dying because of that mold and stuff still in their homes."

The roads leading into Sellers are lined with open drainage ditches that were supposed to provide an outlet for floodwaters like those the community had experienced. But as Hopkins noted, "I'm sixty-seven years old; they only cleaned the ditches out once since I was a little girl." Over time, they have become a dumping ground for everything from cast-off furniture to broken-down appliances. When the floodwaters rose, much of the junk floated out of the ditches and onto the roads. Highways became blocked, and traffic backed up, horns blaring. Hopkins's own muscle, plus that of a couple of public-spirited senior citizens from town, was required "to clean that highway off," the mayor recalled.

At the height of the flood, Hopkins gathered the community in a church on high ground to wait things out. As the water ebbed, volunteers made repeated trips to "bring food and stuff, which we needed because [we] didn't have no food, no lights for about three weeks in this town." Authorities came to assess the damage. In Hopkins's words, "They had someone come by to put the signs on the homes. [They] said if they're a red sign, you are not supposed to be in them. If it's a yellow sign, you can clean it up. [If] it was a green sign, it was okay. But most of the . . . community as a whole had red signs." Just as in Nichols, standing water rose in those homes, seeping into the walls, spoiling the carpets and floorboards. People should have evacuated, Hopkins said, but they had nowhere to go. While government officials were eager to tell people to do so, there was no one in those early days offering much in the way of resources to help residents comply with the orders. As a result, many simply remained in their homes.

In the summer of 2019, Mayor Hopkins took us to visit Jerry

Testle in his home of nearly seventy years. He was watching television when we arrived. Like many of his neighbors' homes, Testle's house had flooded not just once, but multiple times. We saw black mold crawling up the bottom half of the walls. Crossing the front threshold, some on our team had immediate symptoms of respiratory distress. For the last few years, Testle had lived mostly in his living room, because even though it was pretty bad, the rest of the house was worse. He slept lying down on the couch by night and sat propped up against the armrest by day. When we visited, he had just gotten a pacemaker to deal with heart problems that had developed since his house flooded. As Hopkins explained, "He can't breathe because he's still living in the mold!" Medicare had covered the cost of the pacemaker, but Testle hadn't gotten any help to address what was almost certainly one source of the problem that had led him to need one.

In the wake of the three flooding disasters, FEMA allocated millions of dollars for disaster relief in Marion County to repair and replace homes through programs such as the Individuals and Households Program (IHP). The IHP fact sheet explains that the agency "provides financial and direct services to eligible individuals and households affected by a disaster" who do not have adequate insurance but do have "serious needs." Yet only a small portion of residents in Marion County had received much aid by the summer of 2019. Testle had gotten no help at all. His primary obstacle was that he could not prove that he owned his home. Testle has paid property taxes for decades and had records showing he pays the light bill and other utilities. But the property came into his possession through what is referred to as "heir's property," meaning that he assumed ownership when his father died. He didn't go through the formal process of inheriting the property. There wasn't a will, and there were no lawyers involved. No government entity recognized the transfer of title. Volunteers counseled those seeking help to repair damage from the floods to secure a quitclaim deed (referred to in the community as a "quick claims deed"), but this process is arduous and just a single step in a much longer process of applying for aid.

At that time, FEMA had a color-blind policy concerning who needed a title or who needed to raise the foundation of a house, but the adverse effects of these policies fell disproportionately on Black people. In this case, treating people equally led to a sharply inequitable outcome. After first learning about heir's property through this project, sociologist Jasmine Simington became an expert on the topic. She learned that in some cases when a property owner dies, the extended family effectively splits up the plot of inherited land, putting smaller houses on the property surrounding the original home. In other cases, the family is happy to treat the land as communal property. Sometimes one family member takes over responsibility for the property, as Testle did. No one was looking to contest Testle's claim, and the county had been perfectly happy to accept his property tax payments. Yet because the home was still in the name of relatives from an earlier generation, he could not prove to FEMA that he owned it. Technically, this meant that another immediate family member might be able to claim partial ownership. This possibility might extend to the descendants of those who owned the home many generations back if the property had been passed down informally over many years. After the property was improved with government dollars, these other potential claimants might then decide to stake their claim. In sum, FEMA rules were such that Testle was ineligible for the aid he so desperately needed.

FEMA's regulations were no doubt based on a certain logic, but they also seemed completely disconnected from Testle's situation, not to mention that of many of his Black neighbors. To have any hope of crossing this eligibility hurdle, Testle was told he must obtain a copy of his father's death certificate, document his own payment of property taxes since his father's death, and file other necessary paperwork. Those were steps that appeared to be too much for him, at least without a lot of help. Testle's father had been dead for decades.

Mayor Hopkins described how she and Testle "went to Florence to try to find a death certificate. They didn't have one. They told me I had to go to Columbia [the state capital]. And I had to take [Jerry Testle] with me when I go, to verify who he was." All to no avail.

There are no solid estimates of how common heir's property is in the Pee Dee or elsewhere. Different studies have estimated that anywhere between 30 and 60 percent of all land owned by Black Americans in the South might be held as heir's property. This tallies up to millions and millions of acres of land valued well into the billions of dollars. Heir's property is also prevalent in Appalachia. One 2005 survey of Letcher County, in eastern Kentucky, about an hour from Clay County by car, found that as many as one in four respondents held claim to land that could be construed as heir's property. Beyond creating a barrier to getting help after a natural disaster, not having clear title also makes it extremely difficult to secure many of the benefits of ownership, such as a bank loan. Thus, it really limits the value of the asset that is most people's chief form of wealth.

Deep structural reasons may be behind the fact that heir's property is so common among southern Blacks and white Appalachians. Some might reasonably point to low literacy as a cause, and that may well be a piece of the puzzle. In Marion County, more than a third of adults older than twenty-five have literacy rates equivalent to that of a beginning reader. Working through complicated paperwork, as well as processes that require significant written comprehension, would be challenging for a considerable fraction of Marion County residents who might find themselves in need. Describing the pickle Jerry Testle was in, Mayor Hopkins told us, "He cannot read, cannot hardly hear, and he can't hardly see. He has no family here. Mother dead, daddy dead. He's the only sibling." She was the only one with any power who was looking out for him.

In addition to the challenges of completing paperwork, establishing title can be costly. Paying for a lawyer who could oversee the process of securing legal title to Testle's home would be prohibitively expensive for him. If it weren't for Hopkins, even the $12 required to obtain a copy of his father's death certificate would have presented a significant challenge—even if Testle could have gotten to a bank to get the required money order or cashier's check to send to the proper government office. There are no banks in Sellers, so Testle would have needed to get a ride of some distance just to do that.

To go deeper in our understanding of why one form of land title—heir's property—strips so many Black Americans (and some white Americans as well) of their rights to federal aid, it is necessary to understand a place's past. The clouded title of small plots of family land in rural South Carolina could be viewed as the fault of the individual. But this doesn't take into account nearly a century and a half of context. Some scholars have argued that the informal transfer of property across generations among Black Americans in the South has been shaped by cultural traditions, perhaps from West Africa, where land has been passed down within families without government involvement for centuries. Among the families we got to know, however, no one described long-standing cultural traditions as a reason for avoiding formal means of inheritance. No one said, "This is how our ancestors did things," nor did we hear such accounts from community leaders, white or Black. In contrast, we heard a lot about distrust of government, especially in Sellers, where many Black residents were having such a hard time getting any help after the floods. There is ample reason to think that this distrust—more than cultural mores—is driving the continuing tradition of the informal transfer of land.

Before the Civil War, when whites considered enslaved Black Americans property, the vast majority of Black people could not themselves own any property, especially land. In the immediate aftermath of the Civil War, it looked as though the United States might embark on a very different path forward, through the federal government's only large-scale effort at reparations for slavery in our nation's history. During the war, General William Tecumseh Sherman's Special Field Order No. 15 provided for the provision of forty-acre plots of land to freed Blacks and designated an inspector of settlements to "ensure legal title of the property for the Black settlers."

The genesis of this order, which is the source of the famous adage "forty acres and a mule," was a meeting attended by Sherman, Secretary of War Edwin Stanton, and a group of prominent Black ministers held in Savannah in the early days of 1865. Sherman and Stanton convened the group to discuss how millions of newly free Blacks with no assets to speak of might be supported. Historian Henry Louis Gates Jr. recounts that the spokesman for this group, Baptist minister Garrison Frazier, told Sherman and Stanton that the best path forward was for them "to have land, and turn it and till it by our own labor. . . . We want to be placed on land until we are able to buy it and make it our own." Gates writes that when asked if the Black community preferred to live separate from or among whites, Frazier responded, "I would prefer to live by ourselves, for there is a prejudice against us in the South that will take years to get over." President Lincoln approved the plan. At that moment, it appeared as though a transformational shift was in the making.

In March 1865, the newly established Freedmen's Bureau was charged with carrying out this vision. In addition, the bureau helped Black southerners negotiate wages for their labor and legalize marriages, along with providing a host of other services. All of these efforts met with considerable resistance from southern whites. Even so, the bureau accomplished a lot in a short amount of time. On April 15, however, President Lincoln was assassinated. President Andrew Johnson's sympathies lay with southern whites, and in a matter of months, he had rescinded Sherman's order and directed any land set aside to be returned to its former owners.

In this monumental reversal, the federal government abandoned its plan to provide land to formerly enslaved Americans. Although the government did pass the Southern Homestead Act of 1866 to help newly freed Blacks acquire property, almost all land made available to them was unsuited for agriculture, and the program was inadequately staffed. All told, only 4,000 Black families acquired homesteads in the three years of its operation. After Reconstruction, subsequent policies and programs actively worked against the goal of increasing landownership among Blacks. Despite all this, many among the newly freed Black men followed Frazier's call to secure land and did so to an impressive degree. Black landholdings stood at an estimated 16 million acres by 1920. In that year, fully 14 percent of all farm owner-operators were Black Americans, up from virtually none just a few decades before. W. E. B. Du Bois quoted one observer from the time writing about those who eventually became owners: "The first year, they worked for bare subsistence [as tenant farmers]; the second year, they bought stock—mules, implements, [and so on]; third year many rented land; and now the fourth year, large numbers are prepared to buy."

Most scholars place the peak of Black farm ownership somewhere between 1910 and 1920, nearly all of it in the Cotton Belt, where so many had toiled as enslaved people. Over the course of the twentieth century, these trends reversed sharply, as the vast majority of this farmland was lost. Writing in *The Atlantic*, journalist Vann Newkirk reported that while most of that loss of title was achieved through ostensibly legal means, it was precipitated by pressures that were discriminatory and, in many cases, illegal. These pressures included New Deal administrators who denied aid to Black farmers during the Great Depression, banks that refused to lend at reasonable rates, unwarranted tax assessments, and an inability to retain legal counsel when issues arose. The Great Migration to the North in the face of violent suppression by southern whites also played a large role. Newkirk concluded that "mass dispossession did not require a central organizing force or a grand conspiracy. Thousands of individual decisions by white people, enabled or motivated by greed, racism, existing laws, and market forces, all pushed in a single direction."

Back in Marion County in 2019, as residents were struggling to rebuild after a massive flood and two hurricanes, this centuries-old history provides context for why some Black Americans might be cautious about bringing questions of property ownership to the attention of predominantly white authorities. What's more, with property values low, Black families could go for decades before experiencing any sort of penalty for not holding clear title on a small parcel of land or a house in this poor, rural, southern community. In all that time, they might never have known that there was any question as to who owned the home. Yet in a moment of crisis, who holds legal title can matter a great deal.

Many of the residents we spoke with were downright angry about how they were treated by the government entities that claimed they had come to help. Others were caught in the catch-22 of being approved for aid but, due to red tape, unable to claim it. Eliza Harrison, a ninety-year-old lifelong Marion County resident, had been displaced since Hurricane Florence hit in 2018. She heard that FEMA representatives would be coming to a local event to talk with residents about the process of getting help. It was their presence that made her decide not to attend. "I got mad, and I ain't talk to them no more. Then they had another meeting in [town]. I said, 'Who is this here?' They said, 'FEMA.' I said, 'I don't want to talk to them because they ain't going to do nothing.'" Sitting across from Jasmine and Meg at her daughter's kitchen table, she said, "They promised me they'd give me a house, but they have never given me one."

Most of the families we got to know in Marion labeled the totality of the federal government's response to the flood and hurricanes as "FEMA." In truth, the systems meant to help people after a natural disaster span more than a dozen different federal agencies, all with their own paperwork and rules. Two of the important players are the US Department of Housing and Urban Development (HUD) and the US Department of Agriculture (USDA).

Even so, it was commonly believed that FEMA was responsible for all the shortcomings of all these agencies—for providing help that was slow in coming or, according to one community leader we spoke to, for outright denying assistance to "almost every other person" who applied for help. In fact, records our team uncovered suggest that just about 50 percent of those who completed an application in Marion County got help. One resident told us there were still "a lot of people now not even got help yet." Speaking of a neighbor, a Sellers resident noted that the government "didn't help her. They help other people like [white people in] Nichols, they helped them." Unlike Sellers, Nichols is more than half white. A community leader close to the process discussed how these denials of aid deepened distrust among folks like Eliza Harrison, explaining that "people were traumatized from these storms. Traumatized. And FEMA came in riding on these white horses like they're going to save the world and almost every other person that went to them were denied. And [in] a small place like this, news travels like wildfire. And so, from the denials, people [were] talking, 'They don't care about us.'" Sometimes people got help, but it seemed paltry and was at times even perceived as a slap in the face. One interviewee said, "I already had been applied for it after Matthew came through. White man came to my house, came here looked at my house and told me, 'You don't qualify, but I can give you four boards on your porch. . . .' He told me, 'That's all you qualify for,' and walked off."

In recent years, scholars, community advocates, and affected families alike have raised the issue of eligibility for disaster relief for those living on heir's property. As a result of their work, starting in fall of 2021 FEMA now allows families to self-attest to their ownership of property. This change should be celebrated. It does not remedy the situation, though, for residents of Sellers and Nichols who were subject to the previous rule. In addition, as researcher Meg Duffy found, while it is true that proving ownership was a major barrier to getting help in those towns, FEMA might give literally dozens of other reasons for rejecting an application. In a pattern that was common in Sellers and Nichols, help might be denied if government representatives determine that a home in question was worthless by market standards before the disaster. Indeed, the amount of aid FEMA will provide is directly pegged to the market value of a home, part of why higher-income families claim the bulk of the resources as a general rule. FEMA may also deny aid if an applicant misses an inspection appointment. The process and language used to communicate these procedures and rules is itself a barrier to success. As one local leader described it to us, "It was like the government agencies was talking Chinese, and the people in the community was talking Spanish. And we just kind of became their interpreters."

One report on the experiences of low-income residents in Texas following Hurricane Harvey in 2017 showed how myriad technicalities disproportionately excluded low-income applicants. This study found that FEMA deemed 46 percent of applicants with incomes below $15,000 ineligible for help, compared to 10 percent of those making more than $70,000. This dynamic seemed to play out in Marion County, too, where white, generally more affluent homeowners were much more likely to receive aid. New, neat brick homes with sturdy brick foundations rose in the white parts of the county, while most homes in the Black sections of Nichols and pretty much all of Sellers were left to cave in, often consumed by mold. Sharing her perception of how each town fared after the disasters struck, Mayor Hopkins concluded, "We was worse than Nichols, [but they] got all that money. They didn't give Sellers nothing."

Bishop Michael Blue, the Black pastor of the Door of Hope Christian Church in Marion, got involved early in the recovery and went on to become chairman of the Marion County Long Term Recovery Group. Even under the best of circumstances, Blue described to us, the federal government's response as of 2019 was slow: "The relief that comes from the federal government is slow. We've not received a [Hurricane] Florence dollar yet. We just learned that Florence money had been allocated, but . . . I'm not aware of a dollar from Florence having made it here yet. . . . I'm not indicting anybody, I'm just saying, that's what makes it problematic. It takes so long for it to happen." Mayor Hopkins told the story of one woman who "stayed in a molded home and she went to FEMA and they finally passed it for her that she was going to get a [new] home, but [she] never received the home. She died in her [old place]."

Hopkins described how Sellers residents are sometimes caught between the competing demands of different public officials, different federal agencies, and the competing demands of the county, state, and federal governments. For example, much of the land in Sellers and Nichols has been officially designated as a floodplain. Because of this, as we've seen, many residents who want to undertake renovations on their homes are required by county ordinance to elevate them well above sea level. This rule has logic to it; homes that are raised are much less likely to flood. It is a commonsense preventative measure, but one that comes at considerable cost. FEMA does offer a program to help defray the cost, but it doesn't go to residents directly. Instead, the aid takes the form of grants made to local governments, which then create their own programs with their own rules, eligibility criteria, forms, and application processes—and the attendant headaches.

Families in Sellers who were aware of this locally administered option and explored the possibility of getting help from Marion County's version of the program learned it would cover only 75 percent of the cost to elevate their homes. The other 25 percent had to be financed by the homeowners or come from some other source. Our reading of the fine print revealed that there might be circumstances in which this match wouldn't be required, but none of the residents or community leaders we talked to seemed to be aware of any such loophole. Simple math suggests that this matching requirement means that residents would still be on the hook for at least $10,000, a no-go for pretty much everyone. As Mayor Hopkins explained, "Most everybody in the community now been trying to do a mitigation grant that will elevate these homes with a twenty-five percent matching fee, and these people ain't got that. Because they [elderly or] ain't got no job. And then, too . . . if you elevate it, they're going to fall apart anyway because they're so old."

As our researchers on the ground during the summer of 2019 spoke with more and more community members, they found that the news of frequent rejections and the slow pace of aid disbursement spread fast. The resulting rumor mill created a policy feedback loop, whereby experiences with a program by some residents led other residents to avoid it. Frequent and confusing rejections meant that people assumed they wouldn't get help even if they asked for it. Thus, many didn't even bother to apply. Some had heard that applying for help might raise questions about the ownership of their homes. By asking for help, they might lose their residences entirely, they feared. True or not, what counted in the end was what people believed to be true. According to Bishop Blue, "There was such a distrust among our people of the people who were doing the intake, people who got to write down your information and see your proof that you occupied a place. Rural people maybe in general . . . tend to be suspicious of governmental officials and all that kind of thing." One grant writer from the county administration office told us that even when they were conducting a community needs assessment some years back, "you didn't [even] have to sign your name, address, telephone number, Social Security number, just tell us what you think is needed in the area. They wouldn't even do [that]. And it's sad." Misinformation proved to be such a barrier to successful disaster recovery in Marion County that following Hurricane Florence, FEMA dedicated a page on its website to dispelling rumors.

Even when government representatives came to present residents with information, people still did not believe that they would actually get help. To lift depressed application rates, FEMA reached out to local leaders for assistance. A volunteer for Bishop Blue's group explained to us how "FEMA came to us and asked, 'How can we reach the people? Can you all help us?'" The group set up a community meeting at Marion High School. "And at that meeting, there were quite a few people in there that was already denied and some that had not even signed up yet. So what the man from FEMA was saying— 'We can build you a brand-new home, we can get you a brand-new trail[er]. We can do this. We could do that'—well, they were sitting there like, 'Oh, that ain't going to happen. That'll never happen.'"

Data bear out the perceptions of Marion County residents. A *New York Times* investigation by Christopher Flavelle concluded that "a growing body of research shows that FEMA . . . often helps white disaster victims more than people of color, even when the amount of damage is the same." In one study, white families in places where FEMA aid was distributed saw their wealth *increase* relative to similar white families in unaffected communities. In contrast, Black families in places that received FEMA aid saw their wealth *decrease* compared to similar Black families in other places. Put simply, in the long run a natural disaster was a financial boon for white families, on average. For Black families, it was more often a financial catastrophe. The very government agencies responsible for helping Americans recover from disasters are exacerbating preexisting inequalities, not reducing them.

Take the experiences of Nichols and Sellers. As we've noted, most residents in Nichols are white, although there is a sizable Black population as well. We've also seen that virtually all of the residents of Sellers are Black. Although Nichols is bigger than Sellers, both are small towns. Both were hit hard by Hurricanes Matthew and Florence. Yet official records indicate that after each extreme weather event, FEMA inspected only a small fraction of homes in both communities. In Nichols, however, FEMA approved a much higher percentage of inspected homes for help. Among those who qualified, the value of the aid they received was three to seven times higher in Nichols than in Sellers. By 2021, an analysis conducted for us by the research organization Texas Appleseed found that homeowners in Nichols collectively had received $4.7 million in aid from FEMA's IHP program, while those in Sellers had gotten only $429,000. That equates to 2.7 times more aid per inspected home in Nichols compared to Sellers. We don't want to minimize the fact that Nichols suffered serious damage from these natural disasters. These weather events were traumatic for residents of the town, and many white residents like Billy Jones, mentioned earlier in this chapter, also experienced serious challenges in getting aid. But in the end, there is strong evidence that long-standing inequalities in Marion County were magnified when floods, then FEMA and other government agencies, came to town. Racism has been baked into the very policies of these agencies that were supposed to help.

Natural disasters represent only one source of environmental challenge facing America's most disadvantaged places. It is an understatement to claim that the industries most tied to these places are themselves sources of environmental degradation. Not too far away from Marion County, hog farms in southeastern North Carolina are disproportionately clustered in Black and low-income communities. A study conducted by researchers at the Duke University School of Medicine found that communities located near these farms had higher rates of mortality from any cause, higher infant mortality rates, and elevated levels of kidney disease, tuberculosis, and septicemia, even after controlling for other factors. When hurricanes hit the region, the winds and floodwaters spread the waste from these hog farms to even more communities, further polluting the air and water.

More broadly, industrial agriculture as practiced in South Texas, across the historic Cotton Belt, and into the Pee Dee region consumes fossil fuels and water at unsustainable rates. It pollutes the air and water, depletes the topsoil, leads to reduced biodiversity, and creates unlivable conditions for aquatic creatures swimming downstream of agricultural runoff. Pesticides used to boost crop yield are especially harmful to all living things, including people. Exposure to these pesticides can come through residues in food, drinking water, and the air. Glyphosate, the most widely used herbicide in the world, has been linked to cancer, hormonal disruption, and damage to microbes that are beneficial to digestion. Not surprisingly, health impacts from pesticides are particularly acute for children in rural settings. The effect may be profound. Research has found that there are linkages "between early life exposure to pesticides and pediatric cancers, decreased cognitive function, and behavioral problems."

The routine practice of spraying pesticides from airplanes onto fields below, a shockingly imprecise practice, leads to serious drift of these pesticides through the air. Studies show that 95 percent of applied pesticides miss their targets, reaching unintended ones including waterways and nearby soil.

Mining has gained notoriety for the severe environmental impacts it has wrought. Today, mining corporations routinely blast the tops off central Appalachia's mountains to expose coal seams below. First the forests are clear-cut. Then explosives are used to reach the coal. Forest, rock, and soil debris are simply dumped into the valleys and mountain streams. Clearing the land of vegetation eliminates natural habitats for wildlife and reduces biodiversity. Deforestation has long-term impacts even after the scars of these blasts are filled in and the forests replanted, as the soil holds concentrations of metals that many plants simply can't tolerate.

Michael Hendryx, a health scientist, has been working for more than a decade to assess the deleterious health impacts of mountaintop removal on the surrounding population. He has found that compared to areas of Appalachia where mountaintop removal hasn't been practiced, those areas where it has been used have seen an additional twelve hundred more deaths than would be expected per year since the 1990s, adjusting for demographic factors such as age and behaviors such as smoking. Practices that degrade and poison the environment are literally killing people. In these areas, self-reported rates of cancer and mortality from diseases of the heart, lungs, and kidneys are also significantly elevated. Rates of birth defects are much higher than on average. Given the very high rates of poverty in central Appalachia, it is hard to avoid the conclusion that the poorest Americans in the country are the ones paying the highest price for the environmental effects of resource extraction and degradation.

Meanwhile, in job-starved areas like those we focus on in this book, community leaders—who are often, but not always, white—usually push for more jobs at any cost, regardless of the environmental impact. Then, when a natural disaster strikes, government policies, rather than helping to ameliorate the racial and socioeconomic inequalities endemic to the region, deepen them in the aftermath of the disaster. The structural racism that permeates the regulations of federal agencies such as FEMA is built on decades or even centuries of discriminatory practices. Importantly, as Vann Newkirk concluded in his *Atlantic* article mentioned earlier in this chapter, this need not be the result of a grand conspiracy. It is instead a toxic alchemy of government policy, market forces, good and not-so-good intentions, and preexisting differences in wealth and other resources. When combined, these pressures—what might be called the invisible hand of structural racism—all push in one direction: toward the deepening of inequalities.

Federal relief in the face of disaster is but one of the myriad ways that the persistence of disadvantage is achieved, and one of the many mechanisms whereby the assets of the less advantaged—especially poor Black Americans like Jerry Testle—are rendered useless. Nowhere is this more true than in the places we write about here.

Revolt and Retribution

AMERICA'S INTERNAL COLONIES are marked by unequal schools, violence, a dearth of social infrastructure, public corruption, and the invisible hand of structural racism. In the face of these challenges, and in places where those who are subjugated vastly outnumber those in control, you may ask: Why don't they—the majority—revolt? Truth be told, periodic revolt is in the very DNA of these places. So, as we will see, is violent retribution by those desperate to retain power.

Because history is written by those who win, such revolts—much like the Leflore Massacre—are often all but lost to collective memory, even if they make national and international news at the time. In this chapter, we tell the stories of several revolts that have taken place in our regions of deepest disadvantage, the first two during the early years of the Great Depression and two more during the civil rights era. These revolts have undoubtedly paved the way for increased unionization and southern Black and Hispanic citizens' ability to secure the right to vote, among other historic gains.

In central Appalachia on the eve of the Depression, demand for coal plummeted. While much of the economy was riding high until Black Tuesday, in October 1929, when the stock market famously crashed, bituminous coal had been in decline since 1923 because of overproduction, competition from Europe, new sources of energy, and other factors. Yet things got even worse as the nation entered the Depression. Unemployment in the mines reached a twenty-five-year peak;

average per capita earnings among coal miners plunged from $851 in 1923 to just $235 a decade later. Harlan County miner Tillman Cadle recounted what life was like for miners in 1930: "Some companies worked a few days each week, some resorted to dumping coal on the ground to allow [enough for] a few miners to live on. . . . Some people just 'starved by,' as we called it. I don't think they themselves knew how they managed."

While coal crumbled, cotton also staggered under the one-two punch of a sharp fall in cotton prices in the 1920s and Wall Street's 1929 collapse. These woes coincided with a terrible drought across the South: in Mississippi, Louisiana, and Arkansas, summer rainfall in 1930 was the lowest then ever recorded. The Red Cross distributed food, but its efforts were overwhelmed by the depth of the disaster. Meanwhile, Republican president Herbert Hoover—for whom the "Hooverville" shantytowns that sprang up during his tenure were named—continued a long tradition of the federal government by refusing calls for assistance. In January 1931, hardest-hit Arkansas was the scene of a "food riot" in Lonoke County, just west of the Delta region of the state, with three hundred hungry families marching to the town of England to demand that local merchants supply them with groceries.

In this dry tinder of depression and drought set against the inhumane cruelty of the elites—coal operators and cotton planters alike—the spark of revolt was lit.

The first blaze erupted in 1931, in eastern Kentucky. In February of that year, mining companies in Harlan County, just southeast of Clay, announced a 10 percent wage reduction to the already suffering mine families. Local representatives of the near-moribund United Mine Workers of America (UMWA) seized on the moment to reestablish the union there, circulating handbills urging miners to resist the pay cuts.

On Sunday, March 1, more than 2,000 Harlan and Bell County miners rallied in Pineville, the county seat, on the southern border of Clay County. District 19 president William Turnblazer promised the miners that if 10,000 dues-paying members joined, the UMWA would support a strike. Miner and later union balladeer Jim Garland recalled attending the Pineville meeting with an uncle: "As we were walking in, we spotted the foreman from [the mine company we worked for], who was obviously stationed at the door to check if any of his men were there. . . . Sure enough, when my uncle and I reported for work the next Monday, we weren't allowed to enter the mine." These miners were not alone, as coal operators across the county fired and evicted hundreds of attendees of the Pineville meeting in the following weeks.

Most of the displaced families found refuge in towns like Evarts, one of the three municipalities in Harlan County that was not a company town, swelling the population from 1,500 to more than 5,000. Turnblazer sent a telegram to President Hoover imploring him to sanction the coal operators' behavior. Hoover declined. The Red Cross refused to distribute food to the starving population, citing its policy not to intervene in labor disputes.

In desperation, 2,800 men, women, and children marched into the city of Harlan. Likely inspired by the farmers of England, Arkansas, they demanded that merchants supply them with food. Tensions mounted as coal operators brought in strikebreakers and posted armed guards at the mines. By April, the increasingly anguished miners began to rob and loot local grocery stores. On May 5, tensions culminated in what is known as the "Battle of Evarts," where roughly 100 armed miners fought dozens of sheriff's deputies, leaving one miner and three lawmen dead. To restore order, the governor sent in 370 National Guardsmen.

Sociologist Shaunna Scott, who conducted an oral history in Harlan County in the late 1970s, describes the tactics coal operators employed against the miners in those early months of 1931: "The testimonies, oral histories, and memoirs of Harlan union activists abound with tales of pistol whippings, midnight abductions, dynamitings, drive-by shootings, torture, murder, and false arrest, all suffered at the hands of local law enforcement agents and company-hired guards." Those paying close attention to the events that unfolded in Harlan County during this time may have felt a keen sense of déjà vu. The "mine wars" of West Virginia in 1897, 1912, and 1920 had featured the same plot and the same characters: militantly anti-union coal operators firing and evicting miners and their families, miners battling armed guards, county sheriffs and their deputies beating and intimidating union organizers, the governor sending in the National Guard.

In the aftermath of the Battle of Evarts, forty-three unionists were charged with murder. But the confrontation only emboldened the miners. Twelve days later, 5,800 miners from Harlan and Bell Counties walked off the job. Only 913 remained to work in the mines. Despite the successful mobilization, UMWA president John L. Lewis reversed course and declared that the union did not have enough money to support the strike. He urged striking miners to go back to work, and by late July all but 800 of the striking miners had returned to the mines.

New unions, such as the communist-affiliated National Miners Union (NMU), rushed in to fill the void, establishing soup kitchens for impoverished miners and their families, including one in Evarts. The usual campaigns of harassment ensued, including arrests on fabricated charges and shootings. The Evarts soup kitchen was destroyed by dynamite in late summer. According to one visiting investigator, "The effort to break the strike through starvation did not stop there. In the Black Mountain Coal camp near Evarts, pigs were shot by deputies to prevent hungry strikers from using them for food." Florence Reece, whose husband had joined the NMU, grabbed a wall calendar (she had no paper in the house) after she and her children had been terrorized in their home by union busters and penned the enduring militant ballad "Which Side Are You On?"

In early November, a group of celebrated writers arrived to report on conditions in Harlan and Bell Counties. Headed by well-known novelist Theodore Dreiser and including John Dos Passos and Sherwood Anderson among others, the group garnered much attention from the national press. The writers interviewed "Aunt Molly" Jackson, who had married at fourteen and practiced nursing in Clay County before moving to nearby Harlan and becoming a midwife, reportedly delivering 884 babies over the years. Mining accidents had killed her first husband and several others in her immediate family. At a meeting of the NMU local at a Baptist church on Straight Creek, Aunt Molly testified to the committee that during the summer months, miners' children were dying at the rate of four to seven per week from "cholera, famine, flux, stomach trouble brought on by undernourishment." She also performed her composition "Kentucky Miners' Wives' Ragged Hungry Blues" for Dreiser and the others. The lyrics would be featured in their report, *Harlan Miners Speak*, published in 1932. A week after the visiting group left, a Bell County grand jury indicted each member of the delegation for "criminal syndicalism"—working for radical social and economic change. It was a felony and an extraditable charge that carried a maximum penalty of a $10,000 fine and twenty-one years in prison—though the writers were never tried.

After turning a deaf ear to the suffering of tenant farmers, miners, and others among the growing ranks of the poor, Hoover lost to Franklin D. Roosevelt in a landslide in the 1932 presidential election. During the early months of his administration, Roosevelt backed two key pieces of legislation that promised relief for the nation's farmers and industrial workers. One of these, the National Industrial Recovery Act (NRA), signed by Roosevelt on June 16, 1933, guaranteed the right of employees to join a union of their choice and to bargain collectively. The NRA did not extend this right to agricultural and domestic workers, however. Sociologist Arthur Raper has estimated that at the time, three-fourths of the Cotton Belt's Black workers toiled in those sectors. Although the act benefited few Blacks, the effect of the NRA on the mostly white coal miners of central Appalachia was immediate and phenomenal. The UMWA's organizers blazed through the company towns like wildfire. One historian describes how in "only seventeen days, one organizer created forty-two new locals. At one meeting at Williamson, West Virginia, forty-two hundred miners from 'Bloody' Mingo County, a notorious antiunion stronghold, joined the UMW. Within weeks after NRA's enactment, the UMW had boosted its membership from fewer than one hundred thousand to five hundred thousand and had organized 92 percent of the country's coal miners."

Roosevelt's other major initiative, the Agricultural Adjustment Act (AAA), which was also passed in 1933, sought to raise cotton and other farm commodity prices by paying farmers to reduce the acreage they planted. The act proved to be a boon to white planters but not their tenants, a group that Charles S. Johnson and colleagues estimated included 5.5 million white and more than 3 million Black farmers. In a nation of 123 million, this amounted to roughly 7 percent of the population. According to AAA rules, the government would compensate landowners for held-back acreage, with the expectation that they would pass on half of the money to their tenants. This system was ripe for abuse, as landlords were used to cheating their tenants at settlement. It should have been a surprise to no one that many planters did not play by the rules, refusing to pass on the farmers' fair share. Instead, they pocketed the money to cover supposed "past debt," downgrading tenants' status to that of wage hands (making them categorically ineligible for payments), or simply evicting them from their land (with the same result). No doubt, the scales were tipped in favor of the landlord in part because the financial manager of the AAA was none other than Delta planter Oscar Johnston of the massive Delta & Pine Land Company—the largest cotton plantation in the nation, with 9,000 acres under cultivation in Bolivar County, Mississippi, two counties west of Leflore.

In their 1935 assessment of these and other New Deal recovery programs, Charles S. Johnson and coauthors conclude that "for the landowners there is no doubt that the program was a success." Cotton prices rose and owners' income more than doubled. Noting that the white landlords had seen their debts relieved by the federal government yet still demanded debt repayment (which may or may not actually have been owed) from their tenants, Johnson and collaborators dryly observe, "There is a New Testament parable on this subject, but the quoting of Scripture in economic treatises has never gained much vogue."

The founding of the Southern Tenant Farmers Union (STFU) was sparked by the actions of one such landlord, Hiram Norcross of Fairview Plantation, a property of 4,500 acres near the small town of Tyronza in the Arkansas Delta, roughly one hundred miles north of Elaine. In 1932, Norcross evicted forty sharecropper families from his land. In early 1934, the tenants who remained were informed that they would receive only a third of the AAA "plough-up" money rather than the half they were owed.

The aggrieved tenants knew whom they could turn to for help. Clay East and Harry Leland Mitchell, both white, were small businessmen in Tyronza who had campaigned for the Socialist Party's presidential candidate, Norman Thomas, in 1932. It was Thomas, an outspoken critic of the AAA, who had suggested the idea of a sharecroppers' union when he visited Tyronza in mid-February 1934. Historian Jerold Auerbach describes the STFU's beginnings as follows: "On a sultry July evening a small group of white and Negro croppers, encouraged by Mitchell and East, gathered in a rickety schoolhouse on the Norcross plantation to organize the first local." Several, in fact, "had been members of a Negro union wiped out in the Elaine massacre fifteen years earlier; some of the whites were former Ku Klux Klan members." Hiram Norcross's evictions and greed may have given rise to a class solidarity among his tenants that prevailed over racial divisions.

The preamble to the new organization's Declaration of Principles presented its view of the situation: "On the one hand we have a small owning class who depends upon exploiting the working class by rents, interest and profits. On the other hand, we have the actual tillers of the soil who have been ground down to dire poverty and robbed of all their rights and privileges." Within a few months of its first meeting, the union could boast 1,400 members in five Arkansas counties, an achievement that did not go unnoticed by the planters. The very fact that a union had been established posed a potent threat to the status quo in Arkansas. Howard Kester, a white minister and board member of the national YMCA, joined in the efforts of the STFU in its early days. His book, *Revolt Among the Sharecroppers*, with a foreword by the famous theologian Reinhold Niebuhr, describes some of the violence directed at members of the union. Shots were fired into the home of union attorney C. T. Carpenter. A mob of forty fired a machine gun into the home of a union chaplain. Kester reports several lynchings and attempted lynchings. In addition to the violence, union speakers were frequently arrested and charged with "anarchy," "blasphemy," and even "barratry"—"the persistent incitement of litigation." Local officials throughout northeastern Arkansas passed ordinances prohibiting all public gatherings.

In early 1935, Harry Mitchell and four union members—two white and two Black—traveled to Washington, DC, to make their case before Secretary of Agriculture Henry Wallace that the AAA was leading to mass evictions of tenant farmers. In Mitchell's autobiography, he recounts that because of the interracial nature of the group, the five decided to make the nearly thousand-mile trip through the South without stopping. Even though they had no appointment, Secretary Wallace listened to their concerns. Mitchell writes, "I told Wallace that every time the sharecroppers complained, their complaints were turned over to the plantation owners, the very men whom they wanted investigated."

Wallace promptly ordered a thorough inquiry. Attorney Mary Connor Myers, who had participated in the Treasury Department's investigation of Chicago gang boss Al Capone, delivered a report substantiating these charges to Wallace. Despite these findings, the report was kept secret; no copies appear in the National Archives even today.

In September, the STFU declared a strike for higher wages. Planters agreed to raise tenants' profits from 40 cents per one hundred pounds of picked cotton to 75 cents. When its second convention rolled around, the union could count 25,000 members in 200 locals across 6 states. Another strike for higher wages in 1936 was not successful. Planters were tightening the screws by continuing to evict masses of tenants who joined the union. Other tenants were threatened with the loss of credit needed to secure seeds, fertilizer, and equipment. Local lawmen arrested strikers for vagrancy. One Arkansas Delta planter not only had thirteen tenants arrested but held them in a stockade on his property, forcing them to work off their "sentences" on his land. The US Department of Justice indicted him for peonage. He was eventually convicted and fined $4,000, which his fellow planters paid on his behalf.

Perhaps the high-water mark for publicity for the union and its tenant constituents was the action of January 10, 1939. To dramatize the plight of evicted tenant families in the bootheel of southeastern Missouri, the Black preacher and activist Owen Whitfield set up a tent colony along Missouri Highways 60 and 61, midway between Memphis and St. Louis. Two hundred fifty families—1,160 people— were in place on that cold winter day, their destitution on display for all the travelers passing through. "Embarrassed public officials at the state and federal levels searched for ways to disperse the sharecroppers and remove forlorn faces from the pages of newspapers from New York to Los Angeles," historian Van Hawkins writes. The squatters were evicted from their tents on January 14 by Missouri State Police for violating public health codes.

Assessing the accomplishments of the STFU is a difficult task. In his foreword to Harry Mitchell's 1979 autobiography, author and social critic Michael Harrington observes, "In one sense the Southern Tenant Farmers Union . . . was defeated, and there is no use trying to walk around the fact. But in that defeat, pressure was generated which left its mark on American history." A more thorough assessment of the union's legacy comes from historian Jason Manthorne: "At its peak in 1936 [the STFU] claimed upward of thirty thousand members across the South concentrated in Arkansas and Missouri, but as far afield as Oklahoma and Texas. It would roil the east Arkansas countryside with a series of strikes in 1935 and 1936. It dramatized the 'plight of the sharecropper' for the entire nation and influenced the creation of the Farm Security Administration (FSA) in 1937. . . . Its members courageously withstood the brutal 'reign of terror' that landlords and law enforcement visited upon the union. Perhaps most notably, the STFU practiced interracial solidarity when to do so was largely unthinkable and quite possibly deadly."

FROM "BLACK MONDAY" TO BLACK POWER

The best-known story of revolt and retribution in America's internal colonies began to unfold two decades after the miners' union rebellion. It took place in the Cotton Belt, following the 1954 Supreme Court ruling in *Brown v. Board of Education*. The ruling opened a new chapter in the Delta town of Greenwood's history. Greenwood played a crucial role on three fronts during the civil rights activism that persisted throughout the 1960s: school desegregation, voting rights, and the integration of workplaces and public accommodations.

While the battle over school desegregation was initiated by a decision made in distant Washington, DC, the voting rights struggles in Greenwood had a much closer origin: the small Leflore County town of Money, Mississippi, near where Emmett Till was murdered in 1955. Sam Block was a young Black man from Cleveland, Mississippi, who had wanted to get involved in the civil rights movement since hearing about the Freedom Rides in 1961. In the spring of 1962, Block was approached by the Reverend James Bevel of the Southern Christian Leadership Conference (SCLC) and Bob Moses of the Student Nonviolent Coordinating Committee (SNCC) to set up what the organizers called "citizenship schools." Moses had been organizing in McComb, in the southwestern part of the state, and wanted to spread the movement to the Delta. He recruited Block to lead the charge and asked where he wanted to go. Block replied, without hesitation, "'Greenwood, Mississippi.' I wanted to do something in Leflore County where Emmett Till was killed."

After a two-week training at the Highlander Folk School in Tennessee—a program readying Black and white southerners for action for social change—Moses dropped Block off in Greenwood in June 1962. His first task was to build trust and connections among the fearful Black community. For months, his efforts seemed to bear little fruit, but "when Sam Block began walking the streets of Greenwood," historian John Dittmer writes, "he set in motion a movement that would involve thousands of Delta blacks in a militant campaign to overthrow a system that had oppressed them since the days of slavery." In 1960, Leflore County had just over 47,000 residents, nearly two-thirds of whom were Black. Whites owned 90 percent of the land in the county. Only 250 Black residents were registered to vote.

Since 1957, the county had participated in a federal surplus food program that provided basic foodstuffs to poor residents throughout the year, adding more recipients to the rolls during the lean lay-by period of January through March. In 1961 and 1962, more than 5,000 residents received the surplus commodities all year, while more than 22,000 were helped in the winter months. But in retribution for the inroads Sam Block was making in bringing small groups of Black residents in to register to vote, the Leflore County Board of Supervisors voted in July 1962 to discontinue the surplus food program, citing the costs of administration as the reason. The commodities were warehoused. The fallout the following winter was as predictable as it was severe: many residents were starving. SNCC, feeling responsible, put out a nationwide call for help. Singer Harry Belafonte held a fundraiser at Carnegie Hall, and comedian Dick Gregory began making trips to Greenwood with a chartered plane loaded with food.

White resistance intensified. On February 20, 1963, four buildings in the Black business district next to the SNCC office were set on fire. This only increased the determination of the civil rights workers and the Black community. After a mass meeting, more than 150 Black people went to the courthouse to register to vote, "the largest single registration effort in Mississippi since Reconstruction." After white gunmen shot into a car full of volunteers on February 28, seriously wounding one of them, the Greenwood movement was further galvanized. According to Bob Moses, "It seemed to be the only way to answer this kind of violence: instead of letting up, to pour it on; instead of backing out, to move more people in." Reacting to the shooting, Black civil rights activist Wiley Branton, who headed the Voter Education Project, wired Attorney General Robert Kennedy demanding immediate action by the federal government. Branton asserted, "Leflore County has elected itself the testing ground for democracy."

March saw an escalation in violence. Greenwood police chief Curtis Lary formed an auxiliary force with the power to make arrests, boasting that the auxiliary "doubled the size of the police department." On March 24, SNCC's headquarters were almost destroyed by fire. Two nights later, buckshot was fired into the home of the Greene family, the most prominent Black supporters of the right-to-vote campaign. On March 27, a crowd of 150 marched on City Hall, where the police let a German shepherd loose on protesters and jailed ten leaders of the Greenwood movement. The following day, 100 people went to the courthouse to register to vote. The police turned their dogs on the civil rights protesters once again, this time as they made their way back to the gathering point at Wesley Chapel. National media attention was now riveted on Greenwood, forcing the Kennedy administration's hand. On March 30, the Justice Department filed suit against the city—the first time the department had interceded to protect the rights of civil rights demonstrators.

White Mississippians responded in force. On April 2, Mississippi's US senators John Stennis and Jim Eastland made impassioned speeches on the Senate floor denouncing the lawsuit and demanding that it be dropped. On April 4, the day scheduled for the federal court hearing in Greenville, Branton got a call from Justice Department attorney John Doar telling him that the government had settled the case. The only thing the Justice Department demanded was the release of eight of the jailed SNCC workers until their hearing in October. As Dittmer notes, "The Justice Department retreat shocked and saddened black Greenwood." White citizens were jubilant over the turn of events.

Some observers have claimed that the movement collapsed in the face of this setback, as celebrities left town and SNCC workers dispersed. In his history of the Greenwood campaign, though, sociologist Charles Payne counters this narrative. He documents that "more people were arrested for activism in early June than in March, and they were local people" who "went right back to the slow process of building a solid movement, with more confidence than ever." The county quietly resumed distributing surplus food to needy residents, but only after the USDA agreed to pay the administrative costs. Despite the easing of tensions, Greenwood had emerged into the national consciousness as a crucible for civil rights. In July 1963, members of one of the most prominent Black families in the movement hosted a folk festival on their farm featuring Pete Seeger, Theodore Bikel, and Bob Dylan, who sang "Only a Pawn in Their Game," about the murder of Medgar Evers.

The following year brought renewed attention and tension to Mississippi and Greenwood, as the Council of Federated Organizations (COFO) and SNCC rolled out the Mississippi Summer Project, more often known as Freedom Summer. The Summer Project brought mostly white and northern college students to Mississippi to work in voter registration and teach in what they called Freedom Schools. Organizers divided the state into regions, setting up offices in each one. Greenwood was chosen as headquarters for the Delta region. SNCC also made Greenwood its national headquarters for the duration of the project. While the influx of summer volunteers helped voting rights advocates reach farther into places like the Delta's Issaquena County, where no Black residents had been able to register to vote, the project met with deep resistance from whites.

One of the Summer Project's main objectives was to challenge the legitimacy of the Mississippi Democratic Party and to create a parallel institution, the Mississippi Freedom Democratic Party (MFDP), which would put up an alternate slate of delegates at the National Democratic Convention in Atlantic City. Although the MFDP slate ultimately failed to be officially recognized at the convention, losing out to the all-white official Mississippi delegation, the organization survived and continued its work through the decade.

As for voter registration, of the 17,000 Black Mississippians who tried to register, only about 1,600 were successful. But in the long term, the denial of suffrage came to an end, with the project no doubt playing a role. The impact of the Freedom Schools is harder to assess. Perhaps the effort to enfranchise Black people through educating them led at least indirectly to the passage of the Civil Rights Act of 1964 and the Voting Rights Act of 1965.

Stokely Carmichael (later Kwame Ture), twenty-two at the time, was a recent graduate of Howard University based in Greenwood for the duration of the project. Carmichael, in a move that signaled the growing militancy of SNCC, was elected in May 1966 to replace John Lewis as the head of the organization. In early June, James Meredith, the first Black student to enroll at the University of Mississippi, announced his March Against Fear, intending to walk from Memphis to Jackson to show it was possible for a Black man to do so. He was shot and wounded on the second day of the march. Civil rights groups vowed to press on. Meanwhile, Carmichael was back in Greenwood, which lay along Meredith's route, trying to arrange permission for marchers to pitch tents on the city's school grounds. He was arrested but bailed out of jail by Father Nathaniel Machesky, the white priest at St. Francis of Assisi, a local Catholic church. That evening, Carmichael showed up at a rally in Greenwood. He was fired up, telling the crowd it was time to stop chanting "Freedom Now" and to start demanding "Black Power." As the Mississippi Freedom Trail marker now on the site of the rally in South Greenwood notes, he repeated this phrase five times during the speech. Many people mark it as a turning point in the larger fight for civil rights. The ranks of marchers swelled to fifteen thousand upon the group's arrival in Jackson, making it one of the largest protest gatherings ever held in the region.

Greenwood's Black residents during this time knew that the new civil rights legislation, just as with the *Brown v. Board of Education* decision a decade earlier, would be meaningless unless they challenged the inevitable resistance to it with action. At the end of the summer of 1965, the Greenwood NAACP formed a "testing committee." They "would go up one side of Howard Street, the main business corridor, and down the other, testing each business in turn. In the beginning, they were consistently refused service, they were ignored, had hot coffee thrown on them, and were attacked by mobs," writes Charles Payne. But by the end of the year, most businesses were at least trying to look like they were complying with the Civil Rights Act, although one restaurant, the Crystal Grille in downtown Greenwood, was converted into a private club. Another, Lusco's, charged its Black customers $5 for a cup of coffee (roughly comparable to $45 in 2022).

The MFDP took up the work of boycotts, which became the focal point of civil rights activity in Greenwood in the mid- to late 1960s. After several earlier boycott attempts, in 1967 the movement recruited an important ally, St. Francis's Father Machesky, the priest who had earlier bailed Stokely Carmichael out of jail. In Greenwood, the Freedom Democratic Party changed its name to the Greenwood Movement and recruited clergymen from several Black denominations, as well as Mary Boothe, a St. Francis parishioner. The movement was run from the Saint Francis Center, an outreach effort of Machesky's parish. Nuns from the church were active on the picket lines. For the next two years, boycotters kept up the pressure on store owners, despite the Saint Francis Center being shot up repeatedly and firebombed once. Payne notes the hard-won accomplishments of the Greenwood Movement by mid-1969: "The city, pressured by the boycott as well as lawsuits filed by the various civil rights groups, began hiring Blacks, paving streets in Black neighborhoods, putting up streetlights, and so forth. It was hardly the millennium; whites continued to employ a variety of strategies to hold on to power, but by the end of the decade raw white supremacy was going out of style."

WAR FOR CONTROL IN THE WINTER GARDEN

"There is one Texas that is . . . rich," a *Look* magazine article titled "The Other Texans" claimed in 1963. Yet the vast majority of the population, the article continued, was "at the bottom of the scale on virtually every criterion measuring health, wealth, education and welfare." Nowhere was this more true than in Crystal City, Texas, where by the early 1960s, Mexican Americans outnumbered Anglos by a margin of four to one. Yet the "rich" Texans in Crystal City—the tiny Anglo minority—controlled nearly every aspect of life for the "other" Texans living there.

In his account of this era in Crystal City, political scientist Armando Navarro details the many reasons why Mexican American laborers came to recognize that far from having their best interests at heart, the city's Anglo leaders were corrupt. In one scheme known as the "Veteran's Land Board Scandal," speculators took advantage of a program providing low-cost land loans to veterans by purchasing land at rock-bottom prices and reselling it to program participants at egregiously inflated prices, with some government officials allegedly taking a cut. The scandal, which was brought to light in 1955, involved Zavala County officials and other county bureaucrats all the way up to high-ranking state officials. Another point of contention dating to the late 1950s involved federal urban renewal dollars, which, at the direction of Anglo leaders, were spent to improve the Anglo-dominated business district, while roads remained unpaved in Mexican American neighborhoods and half the town lacked a sewage system. Then, during the harsh winter of 1962, a freeze wreaked havoc on crops, leading to widespread unemployment among farm laborers. More than a hundred Mexican Americans marched to demand that the county offer a surplus food program. The authorities approved the program but refused to extend it after the first thirty days, fearing that if the program continued, the laborers might be less willing to remain in the fields.

Inspired by news of civil rights activism in the Cotton Belt, a group of Mexican Americans in Crystal City decided they wanted more say in the community. In their minds, that started at the ballot box. The first step was to get more people registered to vote, a goal hindered by the $1.75 poll tax. In early 1963, a poll-tax drive—an effort to raise money to cover the poll tax for Mexican American voters—was organized by the Teamsters Union in partnership with a group called the Political Association of Spanish-Speaking Organizations (PASSO). One historical account describes how mothers made tamales from ingredients donated by Mexican-owned stores, with young people selling them door-to-door for $1.75—the amount required to pay the poll tax for one person. Women organized boycotts against stores that refused to donate ingredients. The local Catholic church's parish hall was pressed into service as a venue for dances and cakewalks. The price of admission? $1.75. PASSO trained young leaders like Jose Gutiérrez (who would go on to play a role in the 1969–70 cheerleader revolt) in the art of electioneering. PASSO also insisted that the city appoint Mexican American registrars, with young activists doing much of the work of registering people to vote by knocking on their front doors.

The efforts proved to be a spectacular success. For the first time in history, Mexican Americans became the majority of registered voters in Crystal City—1,139 of 1,681. One local man, Juan Cornejo, who had left a job at the unionized Del Monte canning factory to work full-time for the Teamsters, emerged as a leader. The voter drive fundamentally changed the face of the electorate, but finding candidates who would step forward on behalf of the Mexican American community was another matter.

Many middle-class Mexican Americans in town did not support

the campaign, aligning themselves instead with the existing Anglo power structure. The town's Mexican American Chamber of Commerce went so far as to join with the Anglo chamber in running an advertisement in the *Zavala County Sentinel* condemning these efforts, explaining that they were "against tactics designed to create racial issues." Juan Cornejo recalled that the "educated Latins did not want to join with us" and so "we poor Latin-Americans with fifth-grade educations had to run [for office]."

One member of PASSO, Juan Martin Garcia, said that he was disappointed by how few people showed up at the early meetings the group hosted, but that "there were others watching through the windows of the meeting hall and listening outside the door, all afraid to participate." Several people were asked to run but declined; they were afraid of losing their jobs and worried about their families' safety. Finally, five candidates who came to be known as "Los Cinco" stepped up. Juan Cornejo led the slate. Joining him on the ballot were Antonio Cardenas, Manuel Maldonado, Mario Hernandez, and Reynaldo Mendoza. When they arrived at City Hall to file their candidacy papers, a white clerk claimed there were no more forms left. A Mexican American who worked at the courthouse slipped the men the needed paperwork.

Anglo resistance was stiff. The Del Monte canning factory—by this time the largest employer in town—dismissed Mexican American employees for wearing campaign buttons, but union lawyers were successful in getting them reinstated. Anglos branded the activists' efforts the work of "outside agitators or communists" and sought to weaken Mexican American support for the slate by appointing a few Hispanics to government jobs. The Texas Rangers harassed the newly registered voters on their way to coalition meetings. Then, in the days leading up to the election, the Anglo government announced it would spend half a million dollars to pave the streets in the Mexican American part of town, a last-minute move to sway the Hispanic vote. On Election Day, April 2, 1963, farm owners—in an effort to keep Mexican American voters from the polls—offered field hands double wages for a full day of work in the fields.

Despite all these tactics, "hundreds of Crystal City Mexicans gathered round the statue of Popeye," and "one by one, Mexicans crossed the square and lined up at city hall to vote, many for the first time in their lives." They continued to gather in the town square to await the results, despite the fact that the Texas Rangers ordered them to disperse. To the surprise of everyone—including the Mexican American candidates themselves—every one of them won. When the results were announced, within seconds "there was pandemonium; the winners hoisted upon shoulders . . . handshaking, horns blowing, but then suddenly [everyone] dispersed under the gaze of the Rangers." Later that night, the Rangers crashed an informal victory party at a local bar and ordered everyone to vacate the premises.

Retribution was swift. Upon winning the election, Manuel Maldonado was summarily fired from his job at a local store. His employer claimed he had campaigned on Election Day instead of reporting to work. Antonio Cardenas, a truck driver, was told by his employer that his wages would be cut in half. Mario Hernandez, who also lost his job, was allegedly found to have bounced checks. Maldonado, who received the most votes, should have assumed the post of mayor, but he couldn't due to financial difficulties stemming from the loss of his job (the position of mayor paid nothing), so Juan Cornejo, secure in his employment with the Teamsters, took the top post instead. Captain Alfred Young Allee of the Texas Rangers reportedly had the only key to the council chambers. When Cornejo, as duly elected mayor, requested it, Allee refused to comply. Cornejo told the *San Antonio Express* that Allee slapped him and pushed him up against the wall. "He told me that was only a sample. If I didn't keep my mouth shut to the [news]papers, it would get a lot worse."

To say that the new administration had trouble governing would be an understatement. Many Anglo municipal workers resigned in protest. This was a particularly devastating blow because the new council had no idea how to run a city government, a challenging task even in the best of circumstances and many times harder with Anglos (and many middle-class Mexican Americans) working against it at every turn. Historian John Shockley argues that "the inexperience of the candidates, the dependence upon [PASSO and the Teamsters], and the vulnerability of the Mexicano community in a town which had always been dominated by Anglos came back to haunt all those who had worked for the electoral success." Though the unions had shown local Mexican Americans how to get elected, they hadn't equipped them with the tools they needed to govern.

In the next election, a new group made up of both Anglos and middle-class Mexican Americans defeated the incumbents. For a moment, some version of the old order was restored, but it wouldn't last long.

THE RISE OF RAZA UNIDA

We have already told the story of the Crystal City cheerleader revolt and its legacy for educational equity in South Texas (see chapter 2). When we spoke with Jose Gutiérrez in 2021 about the walkout, he related that even back then, he was focused on issues much bigger than who made up the high school cheerleading squad. What's more, he was skeptical that any real change was in the offing, even after the school board finally bowed to many of the students' demands. Gutiérrez recalled that the board's concessions were all provisional: "'We will institute the bilingual education if funds are available.' 'We will begin serving Mexican food if we can find suppliers. . . .'" That was "all bullshit," he told us. "We knew from past experience that if we went back to the classroom, it was going to be the same superintendent, same school board, same principal, same racist teachers, same everything." So he and other young activists decided to form a political party to "boot them out."

Gutiérrez and his allies started registering more people to vote—"100 per day" was their slogan. This action marked the birth of La Raza Unida Party. (The literal translation of "La Raza Unida" is "the united race.") In short order, La Raza Unida took control of the Crystal City school board and municipal government. The party quickly gained a presence statewide and even made headway in advancing the status of Mexican Americans in other states, like Colorado and California.

The new Mexican American leadership in Crystal City tried to enforce the federal minimum wage and demanded that contractors working for the city hire locally. They sought to employ Hispanic teachers to ensure that those at the front of the classroom reflected the student population and that schools offered bilingual and bicultural instruction. In the early years, more federal funds began to flow into the town, allowing party leaders to establish a health clinic and construct public housing.

La Raza's leaders weren't looking for the approval of the Anglo community. Gutiérrez, who was elected head of the school board, told us how board meetings "got to be more popular than the Friday night football games; . . . they were packed. They would see me rule the white board members out of order or scold them or jump on the superintendent, who was white at the beginning. They just thought it was a fun show."

According to newspaper accounts from that time, Anglos weren't conciliatory either. Some charged that La Raza was a communist party and that the new teachers were teaching "racial hatred." The Chicano takeover "brought bitterness to many white people," who, in response, opened their own private school; others moved elsewhere. Many Anglo parents, according to one source, were unwilling "to subject their children to Chicano dominance and bilingual education." One local critic was quoted as saying that unless residents "wake up, we'll be worse than in a state of Communism."

The Texas Classroom Teachers Association sanctioned the school district in 1971 for moving toward bilingual and bicultural instruction, as well as for the district's efforts to diversify the teaching staff. The association urged teachers statewide to boycott the school system. When a local Catholic priest joined in several protests organized by La Raza, nuns at his church gathered five hundred signatures for a petition demanding that he be replaced by "a spiritual leader rather than political priest." The priest stayed, while the nuns left in protest.

One front in the contest to control Crystal City involved a building that had once been part of an internment camp that held Japanese, Italian, and German American families during World War II. When the city acquired ownership of the building after the war, Anglo leaders rented it to a whites-only private country club at below-market rates. When La Raza gained control of the city government, the new leadership refused to recognize the lease and demanded $14,400 in back rent. The city then closed the facility, citing racial discrimination. Rival lawsuits ensued, and though the country club prevailed in court, Chicano leaders eventually used eminent domain to raze the structure.

Many business owners claimed the unrest made it impossible to run their businesses and moved out of town. Some claimed La Raza was blacklisting merchants who didn't abide by its demands. One, quoted in the *Zavala County Sentinel*, claimed that industry "had shunned Crystal since La Raza took over." The white Chamber of Commerce declared that there "wasn't any use" in meeting until "some of this stuff blew over." The same was true for the Rotary Club. In June 1971, some of the major white landowners went on a tax strike, further crippling the town's finances.

Dolph Briscoe, who became governor of Texas in 1973, famously referred to Crystal City as "Little Cuba," promising that he would block federal grants to the Crystal City Development Corporation. His tactics further isolated the city's business community from the flow of state and federal dollars and were a factor in forcing the local hospital to close. Chicano leaders focused on providing small-business loans to Hispanic entrepreneurs, but it was an uphill battle to create enough jobs.

Conditions in the town had become increasingly bleak. The mayor knew he couldn't expect any help from the State of Texas, so he called on Mexico instead. In response, Mexican president Luis Echeverría dispatched his director of the Office of Rural Industry to San Antonio to meet with delegates from the city to brainstorm new ways to establish industry there and to bring technical assistance to teach "new skills to the poor."

In 1975, the party suffered another blow when the *Wall Street Journal* ran an exposé of La Raza Unida, alleging that Jose Gutiérrez and others were paying themselves and their relatives exorbitant sums. Gutiérrez did not deny the charge; he pointed to the fact that he was only doing what Anglo leaders before him had done.

Tensions came to a head in 1977, when city officials refused to assent to an increase in the rates charged for natural gas by the city's supplier, the Lo-Vaca Gathering Company. The Texas Regulatory Commission had given Lo-Vaca permission to raise rates significantly, but Crystal City officials claimed they had previously signed a long-term contract at a much lower rate. Furthermore, they argued, Crystal City residents were too poor to afford the increase. They sued the company but lost their case. The city council voted unanimously to defy the company's ultimatum to pay up or have service cut off.

On September 23, 1977, when Lo-Vaca terminated service to the entire town from its Corpus Christi control room, the action marked the first time in American history that an entire community was disconnected from an energy source en masse. Those who were able purchased electric heaters. Some thought Lo-Vaca was trying to make an example of Crystal City because of its leaders' radicalism. Others laid the blame for the disruption on the city government. As the shutoff dragged into January 1978, the mayor traveled to Washington to seek help. Senator Edward Kennedy had read about the situation and remembered the school walkout a decade earlier, when he had met the cheerleaders on their trip to the capital. Kennedy was instrumental in bringing in the Community Services Administration. Although federal officials helped secure propane tanks to provide heat, public gas service has never been restored in Crystal

City. Many residents we spoke to still remember the small, wood-burning stoves that were distributed to residents during those early months; some still have them.

In 1976, the Texas Rangers and a task force from the Texas attorney general's office launched a special investigation into alleged misappropriation of funds by city leaders. They indicted eleven city officials, including former school superintendent Angel González, who had already left town for a post at the US Department of Education. González was acquitted of these charges by a jury—a fact that went virtually uncovered by the press. Some argued forcefully that these and other indictments were politically motivated. Yet stories emerged in other communities that cast doubt on the party: two La Raza candidates arrested in Starr County for possession of narcotics; twenty officials in Nueces County indicted for encouraging members to vote twice, once in the Raza Unida primary and again in the Democratic one; a county commissioner in Cotulla replaced after being accused of misappropriating funds. Then the party's popular nominee for governor, Ramsey Muñiz, was convicted of conspiracy to smuggle roughly 6,000 pounds of marijuana into the country. He fled across the border to Mexico but was apprehended and would eventually serve a five-year prison term. A former supporter told the press that Muñiz's conviction "just about put the cap on our disillusionment with continuing efforts on behalf of the party." La Raza Unida effectively died in 1978 when its poor showing at the polls led to a loss of state funding.

Today, Crystal City residents hold a range of perspectives on the history of the town. A close relative of the city's first Mexican American mayor, Juan Cornejo, told us, "A lot of the white people ended up upset, maybe, that the Hispanics had taken over. And they probably felt like, 'Okay, if they think they can run it, we'll let them all run it and see how they do.'" In this woman's mind, that didn't go very well. "To me, . . . after La Raza Unida took over, it just was a total mess. It still is."

Not everyone sees it that way, however. One of the cheerleaders who led the school walkout told us, "There was a lot of organizing [among the Anglos] from not just Crystal City, but a lot of Anglos [in the] surrounding [area], and the governor, Dolph Briscoe . . . got involved. And it was shocking to Mexican Americans how deliberate and forceful they responded when they feared the minorities were going to elect their own representatives." Luis, an older Mexican American man we talked with as he was tending a small garden of fruit trees in his yard, also doesn't believe that La Raza's actions were the cause of the community's problems. He lays the blame on the Anglo "teachers in the schools. They were real bad with Hispanic people. They would whip them and all that stuff." Luis emphasized that La Raza Unida was only created because Anglos "were treating the Hispanic people like dirt." Elena, whose family has called Crystal City home for generations, remembers being told by her elders as a kid about the 1950s and '60s, when Mexican Americans were not allowed on Lake Street, one of the main commercial thoroughfares. "If they had to go down this road because they had a friend that lived [across town], they had to run through there, or they would get attacked by the whites," she said she recalled hearing. Plus, "they had a separate theater for the Mexicans. And the theater that used to be downtown was only for whites. And then of course the Mexicans weren't allowed to be in the band. They were not allowed to be cheerleaders. . . . So it was bad back in the day."

Gabriel, a middle school social studies teacher, summarized the white backlash against the cheerleader revolt and the rise of La Raza Unida Party this way: "There was a lot of discrimination and prejudice," but then when the walkout made national news, the story the local elites told was that the activists "drove the Anglo people out, and they drove the businesses out. Supposedly back then, Crystal City had a Sears, they had a hospital, they had car dealerships, they were a city that was growing." When white business left, they "took the connections that make any city, any community, thrive and progress." Today, Gabriel said, you can feel the difference between

Crystal City and other nearby communities without a reputation for activism, like nearby Carrizo Springs. "You can feel the progress. You drive . . . in and you see Holiday Inn, Ramada Inn. . . . You see construction. You see revitalization. You see all these things there, but [not in] Crystal City. It's night and day." He puts this down to ongoing discrimination against the town for its history of activism.

Dr. Maricela Guzman is a 1989 graduate of Crystal City High who, after completing a bachelor's degree, went back for a master's degree and then a doctorate in educational leadership. Now a guidance counselor at the high school, she speaks eloquently about how, despite the struggle, the events of the 1960s transformed the lives of the city's Mexican Americans. She, too, lays the blame for the city's current woes squarely on the Anglo community.

"Back then, the people who had money were the white people, because they were landowners. . . . They had all the high positions in town. [The Mexican Americans] were [patronizing] their stores even though they had to wait [until] after hours or they were followed around [because the Anglos] thought they were going to steal. [The Anglos] were making money. . . . They were not going to stop making money because now somebody else was on the school board or because now somebody else was city manager. . . . If they wanted to keep their businesses, they could have. They would not have lost money, because our people were still going to rely on those products. . . . [Their actions were] racist, because [it was] 'Unless I have you under my thumb, you can't buy from me.'"

Yet despite the scars remaining from Anglo retribution, Dr. Guzman is grateful for how much was gained. "Yes, there was political strife. [But] I wouldn't trade that [walkout] for the world. What changed for the school was that now we got to learn about our culture and be proud of it. We got to speak our language without being paddled. We got to . . . learn both English and Spanish. Oh my gosh, so many good things came from that movement. . . . I'm a product of [those gains]. And you're going to tell me that it wasn't good? I mean, you're really going to tell me that, [when] I went to university and got my degree? I went even further and so did my siblings, and we were migrants [as kids]! I mean, we have suffered consequences, [but that's] because we won."

Revolt and retribution can be seen as a stage in the life cycle of every internal colony we discuss in this book. Those who lead revolutions are as human and imperfect as the rest of us, as the historical record of any revolt shows. As was the case with Juan Cornejo and the 1963 Los Cinco coalition, new leaders may not have the resources or institutional support to govern, even though their intentions are good. There will be those who succumb to corruption, as perhaps some among La Raza Unida did. Yet the authorities charged with investigating the Chicano leaders were the same authorities that had overtly attempted to prevent Mexican Americans from seizing political power in the first place, the Texas Rangers. So who can be certain?

Even today, the prevailing story of Crystal City is one of brown radicalism run amok—the view the fleeing Anglos and some of the more-educated Mexican Americans who opposed the actions of La Raza Unida long espoused. What if we assume that La Raza was, in fact, driven by patronage, just like their Anglo predecessors who had controlled Crystal City for generations? The Anglo leaders who came before were known for doling out resources based on racial allegiance. This was visible to every Mexican American who saw those urban renewal dollars being used to beautify the downtown while they still had to use their privies out back, lacked streetlights, and had to make do with dirt roads. For all its alleged faults, La Raza Unida didn't expend government funds to subsidize a private country club, where four out of five residents were barred from entry because of the color of their skin. Instead, the party tried to enforce the federal minimum wage, create jobs, lend support to Chicano entrepreneurs, diversify teaching staffs, bring in bilingual and bicultural instruction, secure resources to build affordable housing, improve health care, and gain equitable pricing for public utilities. Whatever La Raza's faults, it is hard to argue that its members weren't working for their constituents.

Perhaps those new leaders should have been guided by higher principles. That is what society expects of those who newly claim the mantle of leadership, even if the leaders have grievances by the score. Yet state leaders, from the governor to the Texas Classroom Teachers Association to the middle-class Mexican American establishment, were actively working against the new leaders, hoping to bring them down. The white business leaders who pulled out, the state government that blocked resources from the town, the federal government that swooped in during moments of crisis only to retreat when things calmed down—none of them have been called to account.

In the Cotton Belt during the era of Reconstruction, Black Americans held office at higher rates than would be seen for decades to follow. Those leaders fought for progressive taxation, investments in public schools and other public goods, and redistributive policies. Yet in some southern communities, Black Americans assumed office at much higher rates than in others.

What can explain these differences? Political scientists Megan Stewart and Karin Kitchens point to the Black Americans who escaped slavery during the Civil War and sought the protection of the Union army as it moved through the South. Without the authority to offer those Americans their freedom—but not wanting to return them to their slaveholders—the Union army established "contraband camps," deeming the people to be confiscated property. The camps were largely self-governing. While they were far from ideal in many respects, Stewart and Kitchens argue that they offered Blacks new opportunities for leadership that included "organizing the labor of Black persons, serving as justices of the peace, acting as sheriffs, or holding town hall–style meetings to debate political events." Camp leaders also connected to northern political networks "and cultivated local political coalitions."

Stewart and Kitchens found that the communities where these camps were located and the "social infrastructure of political participation" they allowed went on to have almost twice the number of Black officeholders as compared to similar communities in the same state without a camp. While these gains were lost during Jim Crow, they are nonetheless instructive. Shielded from interference by those who want them to fail, leaders who rise up from a subjugated group can thrive. With technical support and opportunities to hone the craft of leadership, new leaders across the country might succeed in doing right by their communities. All too often they get none of these benefits. Then, when they fall short, society uses it as evidence that they shouldn't have been allowed to try in the first place.

8

The Sins of Our Fathers

IN THE MISSISSIPPI DELTA, much has changed since the reign of King Cotton came to an end. Thanks to the efforts of Black Delta activists in the 1960s, as well as others, Black residents now vote in large numbers. Their vote is influential enough that although Donald Trump easily won statewide in Mississippi in the 2020 presidential election, virtually every Delta county went for Joe Biden. Black Americans sit on school boards, serve as local leaders, and represent their districts in the state legislature. In 1986, Mike Espy was elected to the US House of Representatives, the first Black Mississippian to hold elected federal office since Reconstruction. He served three terms before becoming secretary of agriculture in the Clinton administration. Espy lost his bid for the US Senate in 2018 to Cindy Hyde-Smith. Congressman Bennie Thompson earned recognition as chair of the House Select Committee to Investigate the January 6th Attack on the United States Capitol, although he is only the second Black Mississippian elected to the US House of Representatives since Reconstruction.

Yet much has also remained the same in the Delta. By the mid-1960s, the region's cotton economy was in total free fall. From that period to the present, Leflore County has survived by replicating the model of the industrial company town, with only one or two large employers dominating the labor market at any given time. This has left the community ever vulnerable to the ups and downs, the booms and busts, of global markets, as was also true when it was in the thrall of King Cotton. Likewise, in many ways these industries have pursued labor relations that are not unlike those of the plantation system: a large, relatively unskilled Black labor force, a very few white-owned firms dominating the labor market, and a high degree of inequality between the white owner-manager class and Black labor. While the community had some success in its transition to manufacturing—at least initially—and in diversifying the local economy, that trend was brought to a screeching halt by a dramatic shift in the Democratic Party's approach to trade policy during the 1990s.

In 1962, the creator of "America's Favorite Piano"—the Baldwin—set up shop in Greenwood, manufacturing spinets and uprights. It was the first significant manufacturing concern to come to town since the city's founding in the mid-1800s. Three decades later, the plant was turning out 31 finished pianos, 137 cabinets, and 20 Baldwin clocks per day, with 450 people on its annual payroll. To boost sales, the company ran numerous newspaper ads, including one captioned "Your Child Deserves the Best . . . A Baldwin Piano" and another "This Christmas Make It a Musical One with a Baldwin Piano and Organ."

In the mid-1990s, the demand for pianos began to drop. To grow local interest, Baldwin, at the direction of company president Harold Smith, partnered with Greenwood's Davis Elementary School to create a pilot program to introduce the piano keyboard as a teaching tool for students in the second grade. Far beyond teaching the piano, he told the *Union Appeal*, a local newspaper, the program would teach children what he called the "three C's—concentration, coordination, and confidence"—three qualities, he insisted, that were essential for success in school. Despite these efforts, the demand for pianos and organs continued to dwindle. The Greenwood facility closed in 2001, ending a run of forty years. Soon after, the company opened two factories in China.

It was at about the same time Baldwin came to Greenwood that a Mississippi native built the state's first catfish pond, the beginning of what would become a multibillion-dollar industry over the next twenty years—a high-risk, high-profit venture much like planting cotton. The farm-raised fish that is now ubiquitous on restaurant menus across the South is a different animal than it was prior to the 1960s. That is when farmers, fish processors, and researchers at land grant universities teamed up to improve the catfish's image by changing its taste, through modifying the pond environment. According to one study, "This process moved the catfish from the ranks of a muddy-tasting wild fish mainly associated with the poor, to a tasteless, cheap food consumed by all classes and ethnicities." By the late 1970s, when the first Leflore County catfish pond was built, the industry had already "invade[d] the land of cotton" in neighboring Sunflower and Humphreys Counties. Leflore County's first processing plant, in Itta Bena, led the county to experience rapid growth in catfish production, soon making it among the top producers in the state. A second Itta Bena plant opened in 1996.

Soon the president of the Catfish Farmers of America would tell Greenwood's Rotary Club, "The goal of catfish farmers is to put their product on the table of every U.S. household at least once a month." Enthusiasm for the new "crop" was extreme: in a 1986 op-ed, the catfish was described, only a bit tongue in cheek, as "the greatest of all domestic piscine delicacies." Cooking magazines such as *Southern Living* and southern cuisine cookbooks featured recipes that celebrated the fish for its versatility, suggesting creative ways to spice it up. A *New York Times Magazine* writer claimed in 1988 that "catfish has made the leap from poor folks' food to haute cuisine."

By that time, neighboring Sunflower County's processing concern, Delta Catfish, had claimed the title "world's largest catfish processor," while in nearby Humphreys County, the town of Belzoni had proclaimed itself the "Catfish Capital of the World." Both were cheered on during National Catfish Month by catfish-loving celebrities Maureen McCormick (who played Marcia on the television series *The Brady Bunch*) and novelist John Grisham.

Mississippi was producing about 70 percent of the US total by the mid-1990s. During this heady time, catfish farming was a $4 billion enterprise and "one of the fastest growing agricultural enterprises in Mississippi," according to the *Greenwood Commonwealth*. In the early 2000s, the industry continued to grow, but in just a few years, catfish farmers' profits were increasingly being undercut by foreign competition, motivating producers to lobby Congress to restrict use of the label "catfish" to fish raised and caught in the United States. Despite its efforts to shut out competition, the industry continued to shrink. By 2014, production had fallen to about half its 2003 peak. In 2015, to preserve Mississippi's market share, Senator Thad Cochran succeeded in persuading Congress to require on-site inspections for foreign catfish producers exporting to the United States (as was already required for domestic producers).

Legislative maneuvers are perhaps the only reason why the catfish industry survives in the Delta today, albeit in diminished form. A few aquaculture farms remain scattered across Leflore County, along with the processing plants in Itta Bena. One Leflore County farm and plant founded in 1983 by a Black catfish farmer named Ed Scott, who fought discrimination in the industry by creating one of the first vertically integrated operations, did not survive, in part due to alleged racism in the industry.

The remaining farms and fish processing plants continue to provide about four hundred jobs in Leflore County, though conditions at the processing plants are harsh for the line workers, who are predominantly Black. Routine tasks include stunning, decapitating, gutting, skinning, filleting, breading, freezing, and packaging the fish.

One of our lower-income interviewees told us her daughter had been working at one of the plants for thirteen years but was currently making only $8 per hour, and only after a recent raise. Despite the low pay, several others we spoke with described friends and relatives who were faithful to these jobs. One elderly interviewee told us, "They talk about how cold it is. . . . They would have to wear a lot of clothes and rubber boots because it's wet and cold. . . . But they must love it, because my friend . . . she gets up faithfully [every day] and goes to work." Another, younger person we spoke with, who had experienced setbacks but was determined to "move forward" with her life, said, "Even if it take me going to the fish house and work . . . you just got to buckle down and do what you got to do. Because all money is green."

The late 1990s and early 2000s were nearly as disastrous for the Delta economy as the collapse of cotton thirty years earlier. This was due not to choices by community leaders, but to decisions made by the nation as a whole, ostensibly in the name of the greater good. Just as Baldwin shuttered its factory and the catfish industry began to decline, five other manufacturing concerns in Greenwood also shut their doors. The Sunbelt felt the heat after the North American Free Trade Agreement (NAFTA) took effect in 1994, opening up a free trade zone consisting of Canada, the United States, and Mexico. This was followed by a boom in manufacturing in China, which accelerated in the early 2000s. Both these events made US products less competitive on the global market.

As white Greenwood city councilman Johnny Jennings told us, "At one time, [Greenwood] had Baldwin Piano and Organ Company. We had Medart Lockers, and we had a bunch of other industry. . . . There was something for everybody at any level they wanted to get into. [Now] you can go through every little Delta town and see a little factory that's an empty building. . . . They used to make garments. Made fabrics. There used to be a blue jean factory. . . . I would say probably the biggest [factor was] foreign countries, competition."

The local economy would be rescued this time by an innovative Greenwood native named Fred Carl Jr. Years before Baldwin and the other companies closed, he had begun tinkering with old ranges in his basement after his wife expressed a desire for a commercial range for use at home. In 1989, Viking Range moved its nascent manufacturing operations to Greenwood, and three years later, in 1992, opened a small state-of-the-art plant there. Even in those early years, it could already boast that meals cooked in the private White House kitchen were prepared on a Viking range and that the kitchens of

Oprah Winfrey, Ted Turner, and Willie Nelson were graced by the brand.

By 2001, Viking had grown to become the city's largest employer. The company spurred additional economic growth when it annexed thirteen buildings on historic Cotton Row in downtown Greenwood and began opening ancillary businesses there: a design center, a training facility for appliance dealers, an award-winning luxury hotel and spa, a cooking school, and a retail kitchen store. These amenities in turn attracted new shops and restaurants, reinvigorating the struggling downtown and upping Greenwood's appeal as a tourist destination.

Yet when demand for high-end ranges was pinched by the Great Recession of 2008, Viking laid off almost 20 percent of its workforce. By 2010, Leflore County unemployment surpassed 15 percent. Again, the local economy needed help. Badly. That help came in an unusual form when the city was chosen as the site for the movie *The Help*, filmed in Greenwood in 2010. The business it brought was a short-term boon to the revenue-strapped town. In the aftermath of the popular movie, *Help* tourism boomed, too. Experience Greenwood Mississippi, a tourism booster group, created the self-led "Help Tour" in which the opulent homes on the white side of town, as well as the modest dwellings of the historically Black Baptist Town neighborhood in South Greenwood, are featured.

After Viking downsized, Milwaukee Tool became the town's industrial savior. The company had first earned acclaim a century before, in the early years of the auto industry, by designing a lightweight drill for use on the assembly line. Founded in the Milwaukee, Wisconsin, area, as its name suggests, the company moved some operations to Jackson, Mississippi, in 1974. In 2002, chasing cheaper labor, it expanded its Mississippi footprint to Greenwood. Representatives from Milwaukee Tool and the Greenwood-Leflore-Carroll Economic Development Foundation, the entity that lured the firm to Greenwood, were unapologetic about the role labor costs played in the company's decision to eliminate relatively well-paying jobs in the Milwaukee area while adding the same number of jobs in Greenwood at roughly half the pay. In 2001, the *Mississippi Business Journal* reported that in the part of Wisconsin where the company was located, the average manufacturing wage was almost $20 per hour, and the local unemployment rate was below 5 percent. By contrast, the average manufacturing wage in Mississippi was half that, and Greenwood had double the unemployment rate. "They'll be saving nearly $10 an hour here. . . . That's a tremendous savings for the company. And there are a lot of people looking for $10 an hour jobs," Donnie Brock Sr., then chairman of the economic development foundation, told the *Journal*. The wage scale and benefits, he said, were patterned after those of Viking Range—one indication of that firm's limited compensation.

As Viking bled jobs due to the slump in sales during the Great Recession, Milwaukee Tool's Greenwood operation would eventually stanch the town's wound with a significant expansion in 2013, followed by yearly growth between 2014 and 2017. That brought the job count to nearly 1,000—a huge operation for a town of less than 15,000 residents. "Thank God for Milwaukee Tool," Anjuan Brown, Leflore County supervisor for District 3, told the *Greenwood Commonwealth* in 2019. As of this writing, Milwaukee Tool has moved 1,200 jobs to Mississippi as it has continued to reduce its workforce in Wisconsin, where earnings had once lifted employees to the bottom rung of the middle class. Meanwhile, the wages offered to Mississippi workers are so low that they can't lift a family of four out of poverty. Yet most of the low-income people we spoke with agreed that for non-college-educated workers, "Milwaukee Tool. . . . That's the only [decent job]."

Angela Curry, the current director of the economic development foundation, told us that she is deeply concerned about the lack of middle-class jobs here: "What we're missing are the white-collar jobs. A college graduate is not going to come back here to work at . . .

Milwaukee Tool on the assembly line. . . . It's . . . chicken and egg, though. Can you recruit the jobs first without having the people, or how do you get the people here [when you] don't have the jobs?" In the low-wage sector, she claimed, the local economy had reached job market "saturation" by 2019 and would have difficulty expanding.

Meanwhile, the State of Mississippi has assured employers that they will have a ready supply of cheap labor in another way—through its imprisoned population, as it has done for more than a century, now through so-called restitution centers. These community-based residential centers house nonviolent offenders who agree to pay restitution for their crimes. Debts tend to be relatively low, yet even modest amounts can take years to pay off. This is because about three-quarters of the wages workers earn are subtracted for room and board (around $300 per month) and other obligations, such as child support. If an offender is unable to work due to sickness, their debts continue to accrue for room and board. Inmates work in fast-food restaurants, meat processing plants, and taxidermy shops, or as handymen or landscapers for private citizens.

Inmates at the Greenwood County Jail can be granted work release as well when there is adequate demand for their labor. These prisoners are highly visible in town, given their green-and-white-striped "ring-around" uniforms, which are nearly identical to those worn by forced laborers on chain gangs during Reconstruction and a century ago in the fields of nearby Parchman Farm. Parchman, a notorious penal farm still in operation, once provided a significant amount of revenue to the state through forced labor. Mississippi Department of Corrections buses deliver these prisoners to their worksites. They get a lunch break at Community Kitchen, the local soup kitchen, where they line up with the city's needy for the free noon meal, even though the program charges them for room and board. As Community Kitchen is not reimbursed for these meals, this practice is little more than bald-faced graft by the system at the prisoners' expense.

When speaking with community leaders, we repeatedly heard the claim that Milwaukee Tool—far and away Greenwood's largest employer by 2019—and other low-wage employers in the area were struggling to find employees. Yet the assertion seems at odds with official statistics. At the end of 2019, the strongest year for the US and Mississippi economies in recent memory, Leflore County's unemployment rate was still 7.1 percent, nearly twice the national average. More telling, though, are unemployment figures that include people not actively seeking work by the government's definition. In the boom year of 2019, nearly 54 percent of working-age adults were not in the labor market—they were neither working nor looking for work—compared to 43 percent statewide and an average of 37 percent nationwide.

There are several possible explanations for why the labor force participation rate is so low here. First, the schools may be failing to produce graduates who have the skills needed for some of the jobs available. During the summer of 2020, when we observed the activities of Greenwood's Operation Peace Treaty, the anti-violence group that sponsored barbecues for residents who were asked to respond to a short survey, we noted that a number of people were unable to complete the survey without assistance. Some of the older residents could do little more than write their names. One low-income resident we interviewed told us that people she knew couldn't get jobs at Milwaukee Tool because of "the tests that people are failing," a reference to a certification system administered by the local technical college that rated potential employees' skill levels.

There is a second possible explanation for the county's low labor force participation. Given the high prevalence of violence in Greenwood and elsewhere across the Cotton Belt, potential workers may be hampered by their criminal records. Several of the low-income residents we spoke with said that they had been refused employment because of past criminal convictions. Yet some community leaders contested this narrative. One skeptic told us a story about several men who claimed they had been denied jobs due to their criminal records but were told by an employer in town, "Well, I've got a company, and all they do is hire. . . . They'll put you through truck driving school. . . . That's all they take is felons. You'll start out [at] $62,000 a year!" According to the storyteller, all of the men, race not indicated but clearly implied, just shrugged and said, "Well, let me think about it." While this story is hardly credible—median family income in the county is just $27,000, well under half the salary quoted by the skeptic—apocryphal tales such as this echo white planters' accounts of allegedly "lazy" Black people refusing to work in the days of Reconstruction and Jim Crow.

This story is reminiscent of something we heard in Clay County, Kentucky, where one pastor cited welfare as the cause of low labor force participation rates: "[People on welfare are] enabled to stay poor and they're enabled to stay where they are by our government system." An employer we interviewed there also cited government benefits as the cause of low labor force participation, lamenting that "we don't have a viable workforce. People just don't want to work." Later in our conversation, she claimed that she had personally witnessed welfare recipients driving "really nice cars," a reprise of the myth of the "welfare queen" that helped Ronald Reagan attain the nation's highest office in 1980.

Welfare is not likely to be keeping workers away from jobs at Milwaukee Tool or any other employer in Mississippi. The state has the lowest benefit levels in the nation, a record it has maintained since the 1930s, when the program began. Due to a recent increase in benefit levels, it offers a maximum of $260 a month for a family of three with no other source of income—if, that is, the family can actually get approved for the benefit, a rare feat, as we showed in chapter 5. That family could expect to claim $586 per month in SNAP (Supplemental Nutrition Assistance Program) benefits, but they can't pay their landlord with their SNAP EBT (Electronic Benefits Transfer) card, or buy clothing, school supplies, toiletries, over-the-counter or prescription drugs, or any other nonfood item at the local Walmart. Mississippi offers no cash aid to able-bodied adults without dependents (including noncustodial parents), called ABAWDs for short, nor can they get SNAP for more than three months every three years unless they meet the program's work requirements. Nationwide rates of Americans accessing disability benefits have grown and are especially elevated in much of the Delta, though less so in Leflore County. However, the rates are nowhere near high enough to be the key driver of the very low rates of labor force participation here.

Another possible explanation for low participation in the labor force lies in the nature of the work available—the assembly line, the processing plant, the isolated catfish farm—which "young people aren't into," according to one business leader we interviewed. The mind-numbing nature of these jobs was recognized by Delta Catfish, the giant catfish farm in neighboring Sunflower County. In the early 2000s, management there began offering CD players and audiobooks to workers to help them pass the time. While some workers were pleased with the program, such strategies might not be enough to compensate for the many downsides of these jobs.

There is yet another, more obvious explanation. What if employers are overstating their inability to find workers as a way to divert attention away from the low wages they provide, or to undermine social welfare programs that might be seen as discouraging employment? If worker supply were truly a barrier to production, wouldn't the employers just leave?

Whatever the cause, we invite you to join us in the following thought experiment: What if Milwaukee Tool's Greenwood employees were paid what their counterparts in Wisconsin had earned in the years leading up to the initial relocation to Mississippi—which would amount to roughly $40,000 per year for a full-time employee? It is hard to imagine that any position would remain unfilled. Furthermore, if this were true, one can imagine a virtuous circle where hundreds would be lifted out of poverty, where families could purchase or upgrade homes, contribute to the local tax base, and boost the economy. In this virtuous circle, families would be stabilized, health improved, and school revenue expanded. The intergenerational mobility that might result could be just the right remedy for the violence on the streets of South Greenwood.

You may be wondering what place agriculture currently plays in the region's jobs picture. Massive fields still blanket the landscape in the Delta regions of Mississippi, Louisiana, and Arkansas, with the crops varying according to market conditions. In the rest of the Cotton Belt region, including swaths of Alabama, Georgia, and South Carolina, millions of acres of land are no longer cultivated; the land there has been stripped of the rich topsoil accumulated over millennia by the rapacious planting of tobacco and cotton. This is not a new phenomenon. When Frederick Law Olmsted traveled through these states in the 1850s reporting for the *New York Times,* he wrote about passing many farms where the soil had been used up. Some abandoned plantations bore signs with the letters "GTT"—Gone to Texas. Only over in the Delta, an ecosystem endowed annually with the rich nutrients delivered by the Mississippi River and its tributaries during annual floods, do the fields remain fertile and vast. Yet in a striking departure from the past, the land today sustains few people economically except for the planters who own it and the banks that lend to them.

Given the high degree of mechanization in agriculture these days, one might expect that the extraction of labor from a subjugated people is a thing of the past. Not so, though the story has a twist. Depending on whom you believe, either labor shortages or the desire to rid themselves of the trouble of dealing with local Black labor has led many of the remaining Delta planters to seek out field hands from South Africa—where the unemployment rate has approached 30 percent in recent years. For about a decade, these white South Africans have been turning up at the Greenwood Walmart in the evenings and on the weekends, identifiable, several locals told us, by their habit of wearing very short shorts. Delta planters use middlemen to recruit these workers by the hundreds each year through the

US government's agricultural guest worker program, known colloquially as H2-A. Meanwhile, scores of Black adults in the surrounding area remain jobless.

In 2021, the *New York Times* reported that several longtime Delta field laborers had filed a lawsuit against Pitt Farms, located just west of Leflore County, in Sunflower County. The plaintiffs alleged that they were asked to train guest workers and then were subsequently themselves let go. The lawsuit is ongoing at the time of this writing, and Pitt Farms denies all the allegations. Richard Strong, one of the claimants, told the *Times* he had worked for the Pitt family for a quarter of a century, like his father, his grandfather, his grandmother, and an uncle before him. All told, the Strongs had labored for the Pitts for roughly sixty years. In 2021, Pitt Farms paid its Black workers the legal minimum wage—$7.25 an hour ($8.25 on the weekend)—plus an occasional bonus. But they paid their South African workers $11.83 an hour, a discrepancy that violated the terms of the H2-A program (both groups must be paid the wage set forth by the government for guest workers). Employers are also required to pay travel costs and lodging for their South African "guests," which involves thousands of dollars in additional outlays.

"I never did imagine that it would come to the point where they would be hiring foreigners, instead of people like me," Strong told the *Times*, which reported that H2-A visas, though initially unpopular among planters due to the hassle and cost, had grown from only about 56,000 in 2011 to more than 213,000 in 2020. "It's like being robbed of your heritage," Strong said. According to program guidelines, farmers who participate in the H2-A program must prove they have tried and failed to recruit domestic workers to fill the jobs, which the lawsuit alleges Pitt Farms failed to do. "I gave them half my life and ended up with nothing," Strong concluded.

Ty Pinkins, a fellow at the Sunflower County branch of the Mississippi Center for Justice, concurs: "Unfortunately, this case is emblematic of a disastrous pattern in the South. Our research indicates that farm owners are increasingly abusing the H2-A program and denying opportunities to U.S. workers. . . . The case also reflects our nation's deep, ugly history of exploiting Black labor."

Given the additional costs of securing South African workers, what is their appeal? Industry experts put it down to their work ethic and high literacy rates, but there are probably unsaid motivations on the part of employers as well. Two South African migrants sued Kyle Mills and his company, Kyle Mills Trucking & Custom Harvesting, LLC in Winona, Mississippi, located about thirty miles east of Greenwood, for luring them to the United States for agricultural jobs but instead making them drive trucks across the Southeast to deliver fertilizer and grain. The suit alleges that they worked ninety-five hours on average each week and that the owner failed to reimburse them for their travel costs to the United States. While the South Africans were paid $11.33 an hour—the approved rate for agricultural work under the H2-A program—local drivers were charging $18.25, according to Mississippi Today. Mills agreed to pay $34,000 to resolve the claim, including $13,000 in back wages, but at the time of this writing had only paid $15,000, promising to come up with the rest by January 2023 or face contempt hearings. Could it be that one additional motivation for employers is that these workers, far from home, are simply more exploitable than Mississippi's Black Americans, who have finally achieved a minimal set of protections since the end of Jim Crow?

Meanwhile, in the face of brutal global competition, the Delta's catfish industry has also turned to migrants from South Africa. Echoing the suit against Pitt Farms, five Black catfish farm workers filed a lawsuit in 2022 against a local catfish farmer, Harris Russell Farms, after losing their jobs to migrant workers on H2-A visas. This case was settled out of court in December 2022.

While the region is locked in a desperate struggle to attract and maintain employment, its calling card of low wages, low taxes, and lack of state regulation virtually ensures that poverty wages will continue. One mainline Protestant clergyman told us that Greenwood has "created a situation where even having a full-time job is not enough. . . . What I would hope for Greenwood is to have an economy strong enough that folks who are willing and able to work [can] make a living for their family and have work with dignity." In the meantime, however, a Black community leader put it plainly: "Basically . . . it's a low-income area, here. . . . Let's not try to put a wedding dress on a skunk."

Some white community leaders are more sanguine about the city's economic future. One told us, "I think [Greenwood] is a very iconic symbol of the culinary arts. . . . The cooking school, the Alluvian [luxury hotel] and Giardina's [its upscale restaurant], Lusco's [restaurant], the Crystal [Grille]. . . . You don't find that in a lot of southern communities." Another community leader, the director of the Main Street Greenwood initiative, placed her bet on tourism, pointing to the many civic events that bring revenue into the city on the weekends, noting that "the economic impact is huge." She referred to the importance of providing "that authentic experience" and those "Instagrammable moments."

As we have seen in Greenwood, segregation, including school segregation, is nearly total. According to the white clergyman who also mentioned the problem of poverty wages, it is "the most intractable problem." On the broader issue of segregation, he told us, "We're divided racially in Greenwood [and can't] constructively solve problems together in any way, shape, or form. The inability to . . . trust fellow citizens . . . that's the kind of stuff that just leads me to despair. . . . We're enriched by diversity. That is a resource to be tapped, and if we can harness it, there is a greater opportunity [for the community to thrive]."

Several community leaders complained to us that racial divisions dominated local politics, making it hard to get things done. Some white leaders were vocal critics of some of the more outspoken Black politicians. One said, "I'm going to say this as PC as possible: Have there been horrible stories of racial inequalities in the Mississippi Delta in the past? Yes. Do some people hold on to those wrongdoings too tightly? Yes . . . because a lot of times, it serves as a tripping block to progress in the Delta. It's still trying to make up for wrongdoings."

A white evangelical pastor defended the separation of the races on "cultural" grounds, claiming, "I think the greatest challenge in this community is not color but culture. . . . The Black culture historically from the Old South is a very frustrating thing for the established white culture to try to identify with. I mean, we see it in the community, even how a house is taken care of, a yard is taken care of. There's just a complete different way in which people accept or practice what they believe to be okay."

Other leaders denied that race and segregation are problems at all in Greenwood. One employer told us, "I don't consider it that we have huge . . . racial issues. I think there's a lot of segregation, but I think that it's on both [sides]. I don't think it bothers either. I think it's just accepted, and I don't . . . think anybody around here feels like it's a horrible place. . . . I just feel like everybody's kind of used to how it is, and they don't do anything. There's not a lot done to change it." In keeping with this view, decades after *Brown v. Board of Education* and the civil rights movement, which flourished in Greenwood, the city is characterized by "a strange calm," as one *New York Times Magazine* reporter wrote twenty-five years ago: "Former members of the Citizens' Council and civil rights groups cross paths every day at gas stations, supermarkets, Wal-Mart. They do not hide from one another. A cold war has given way to a cold peace."

What is most striking about our interviews with Greenwood residents is the extreme disconnect between the views of the mostly white leaders and those of many of their Black constituents, who struggle, as we have seen, with schools in free fall, dire health issues, and pervasive violence. Equally striking is the lack of vision for the city itself, the resignation that Greenwood is a dying town, and the view that there is little that can change that trajectory. Then there is the failure to grapple with the lack of avenues for upward mobility in the labor market. As one Black community leader put it, "See, this place is all about just having some sex, having a car, doing—you know—menial shit [jobs]." Finally, as is true in many other parts of the country, there is the high tolerance for the racial separation—in schools, neighborhoods, churches, and nearly every other community institution—that many people believe is at the root of the region's woes. No one we spoke with seemed hopeful about tackling that problem.

Growing reflective, Councilman Johnny Jennings, who represents North Greenwood, told us, "We are paying for the sins of our fathers right now about public schools and private schools. That was the mind-set then [in the 1960s]: 'The government is not going to tell us what to do and how we're going to do our schools.' But today, we pay for those sins. . . . If we would have gone to school [together], learned how to play football with each other, learned how to go get a milkshake and a cheeseburger [together], and go to somebody's wedding or be in their wedding. We turned our back on that deal. [Instead of integrating the schools, people said,] 'I'm fixing to build me a [segregation academy] out here.' Bad mistake. Nobody knows how that chemistry would have worked, but as an end result, I think we probably would have been . . . better off."

One clergyman summed up how he sees the region's dilemma as follows: "I think white Mississippians are often stuck in the cycle of defeat, and shame, and defiance. So we . . . defy the rest of the world in terms of the direction . . . we should be going, though we perhaps at some level know that it's the right way to go. We have to be forced to do what's right [by the] federal government [which makes us feel defeated]. And then that leads to this place of shame—that just makes us more defiant. We're defensive and defending ourselves. . . . We would rather lose than admit when we've ever been wrong."

Down in South Texas, the fields are vast, but farmers are becoming hard-pressed to stay in business. The newest industry to appear on the scene is fracking, a boom that has marred the landscape throughout the Winter Garden and the Trans-Nueces region with thousands of oil wells. One farmer we spoke to in Crystal City has been holding out on giving his land over to fracking because he knows the hundred or so people he employs would immediately be out of work. But it sure is difficult to say no to all that money. The water-intensive process of fracking plus an extended drought has led to a catastrophic drop in the water levels in the huge aquifers that once ensured the prosperity of the region. Even so, the industry is booming. The flood of temporary workers for fracking jobs has been so great that the hospitality industry in the region can't keep up. Hotel room prices are soaring, and new eateries, like the 5D Steakhouse just west of Crystal City in Carrizo Springs, have sprung up in temporary structures to meet the demand.

Across both the Trans-Nueces region, where Brooks County lies, and the Winter Garden, some of the remaining Anglo farmers and ranchers—who often live in a world apart from their Hispanic neighbors—are taking an entrepreneurial turn. They are converting some of their fields—land that is still mostly white owned—into a new brand of economic venture: hunting grounds for the rich, some of whom arrive on private jets at private airstrips. Throughout South Texas today, hunting resorts are a niche industry on its way to becoming a regional economic development strategy. At Four Seasons Ranch just outside Pearsall, in the Winter Garden county of Frio, visitors are promised "A Touch of Texas Paradise." Four Seasons' massive yet simply constructed thirteen-bedroom lodge boasts a lounge with a soaring stone fireplace, leather chairs, and a full bar, plus a wraparound porch where clients can relax. Chef Andrew, who will see to your every culinary need, claims to provide meals so rich that "most people leave here gaining ten pounds." Happily, those wishing to avoid the weight gain can hit the facility's gym. But the hunting is the draw. "In addition to world-class whitetail deer and dove hunting, Four Seasons Ranch offers exotic hunting for those wishing to experience a 'Texas Safari,'" the website entices visitors. You can kill "addax, aoudad sheep, axis deer, blackbuck antelope, fallow deer, gemsbok, scimitars, horned oryx, and zebra."

Just a few miles north of Zavala County, Ox Ranch offers "18,000 acres of the best Texas Hill Country Hunting. . . . A few of the species you will encounter on your visit include giraffes, zebras, kangaroos, axis, bongo, kudu blackbucks, elk, hogs, red stags, and of course record-breaking whitetail deer." If shooting rifles at exotic animals is not sufficient entertainment, you can also drive and fire the resort's World War II tank. Website photos of Ox Ranch show an impressive stone lodge, soaring stone fireplaces, an antique bar, and vaulted timbered ceilings. The lodge overlooks a lake stocked with fish. Cordon Bleu–trained Chef Eric specializes in French food and exotic game. Guests stay in quaint log cabins with Jacuzzi tubs; one has a private hot tub and pool. The website claims that accommodations "rival many of the world's finest resorts." To say the experience is pricey is an understatement. However, as of 2022, hunting zebras ($7,500) is cheaper than hunting native whitetail deer ($10,000).

Finally, it is impossible to spend any time at all in either Brooks or Zavala County without noting the overwhelming presence of the US Border Patrol. While the constant surveillance casts a pall, local eateries are boosted as clusters of uniformed agents crowd around tables. Suspicious vehicles (including ours) are pulled over at regular intervals, often for technicalities such as failing to signal, failing to maintain a single lane, or making an unsafe lane change. But in reality, locals say, agents are looking for subtle signals, such as signs that a vehicle is carrying an unusually heavy load. Several times a week, any number of what law enforcement officials call "undocumented aliens," or "UDAs," can be found huddling in the back of a vehicle or stacked atop each other there. Such vehicles are impounded (a boon to a local towing company that seems to get most of this business), according to police reports in the *Zavala County Sentinel*. The drivers are jailed and the occupants—sometimes from as far away as Africa and Cuba—are turned over to Border Patrol. In Falfurrias, the Brooks County town that lies just up the road from a border checkpoint, the county morgue is so burdened by bodies of migrants who have died trying to make it around the checkpoint by traveling through parched ranchland that it has bankrupted the county. The State of Texas has had to provide a mobile morgue. Some have referred to the area as "Migrant Death Valley," as more migrant deaths are recorded here than in any other place in the country.

Over in eastern Kentucky, Clay County leaders and Manchester boosters alike have settled on a different flavor of tourism than that of the Texas luxury ranches. When we last spoke with Michael White—the former high school principal who now heads the Clay County Historical Society, not to mention brother-in-law of former mayor Carmen Lewis—in March 2022, he had good news to share: US representative Harold "Hal" Rogers had successfully secured a $2.2 million federal earmark for the Downtown Manchester Market Place. The new facility will provide citizens and visitors with activity space centered around the music and culture of the region. Rogers said, "I am proud of the ongoing work to revitalize the City of Manchester, nearly twenty years after holding the region's first drug-free rally on Main Street. Great things are happening in Clay County as a result of proactive citizens who continue to actively work to drive out a deeply rooted drug culture and turn their community around for a brighter future."

The Downtown Manchester Market Place complements another new venture, Impact Outdoor Adventures, a campground offering RV sites with electric, water, and sewer hookups. It is situated on abandoned mine land and supported by a $700,000 pilot grant from the state's Abandoned Mine Land Fund. Campers can enjoy archery, mountain biking, kayaking, and hiking. Roy Rice, board president of Impact Outdoor Adventures, explained, "[We] started as an outreach for our young people in Clay County, to provide fun activities for them to do right here in our backyard. Thanks to this . . . grant, people are now coming to Clay County to stay in our new RV park, camp under the stars, eat in our restaurants, and experience these hills like never before. We are excited about our future in the City of Hope."

Several volunteer groups have been diligently working to clean up the downtown, renovating run-down buildings and spiffing up store-fronts. One such group, Stay in Clay, has rebranded the county as the "Land of Swinging Bridges" in homage to the eighteen picturesque bridges that span some of its many creeks. The city has hired a director of tourism, and in May 2022 he publicly unveiled a new master plan for downtown Manchester—garnering more than $4 million in additional state funds—to a crowd that included state senator Robert Stivers, Congressman Hal Rogers, and Governor Andy Beshear. The Clay County Historical Society operates an impressive museum with the name "The Clay We Were," along with a series of historic murals under the same name. Recently, the historical society purchased a bus to offer daylong history tours of the county for $45. Sales exceeded expectations. "The question of whether or not we can do something never enters our mind," said Michael White, in his role as head of the historical society. "We just think about how we're going to do it." All over central Appalachia, local governments and other groups in community after community are similarly looking for ways to bring tourists into their communities by developing hiking and ATV trails.

As of this writing, Manchester has a new shine—fresh coats of paint, new welcome signs, and several new murals—although the progress has not been without pain. An aged apartment building and several other rental spaces that were within walking distance of the hospital and grocery store and were once home to around thirty residents, many of whom were disabled or fostering children, have been razed to make room for the revitalized downtown. While plans are still uncertain, proposals for the redeveloped space include retail shops, a couple of units for transitional housing, and several Airbnbs. A nonprofit group, Volunteers of America, has assigned a case manager to relocate the evicted families, but given the area's housing shortage, the displaced residents will not likely be able to secure new housing in Manchester. Some options include housing in neighboring counties fifty-plus miles away and far removed from the residents' social support systems.

Meanwhile, this small municipality still supports thirteen pharmacies plus numerous walk-in and urgent care clinics, where people go to get prescriptions for painkillers like OxyContin, as well as several addiction recovery centers. Many of those making up the medical elite live on the hill overlooking town, as did the coal camp executives of old. Given the dominance of medical and addiction-related ventures in the local economy, efforts to spur tourism will require a success of massive proportions to overcome the local economy's dependence on pain and drugs.

Across America's internal colonies, it does not seem likely that these newer endeavors revolving around tourism will bring into the middle class those who have, for decades if not centuries, been relegated to the ranks of cheap labor.

Appalachia, the Delta, the Tobacco Belt, South Texas—despite considerable change in the years since the 1960s, when the reign of King Coal, King Cotton, King Tobacco, and Popeye all came crashing down—still retain, to a greater or lesser degree, features of the internal colonies they once were. The company town of Greenwood, Mississippi, exporting Milwaukee Tool's Sawzall reciprocating saws and Viking's luxury ranges all over the world, is one or two trade wars away from the next economic crisis, while the failing schools threaten the town's ability to retain—much less attract—a middle class. The fracking industry in South Texas has brought boom times to the region in some years but busts in others, with the locals we interviewed reporting huge income swings from year to year. Meanwhile, votes are still bought and sold or rendered meaningless on the state and national level due to gerrymandering, though some local activists have been successful in fighting back. While the violent suppression of the have-nots by the haves has changed form, violence continues to pervade these places where people have been kept down for so long. In sum, the exploitation of whatever resources remain in these internal colonies continues, and poor people's labor also continues to be extracted or, more commonly, is simply discarded.

To end our story of America's places of deepest disadvantage on such a pessimistic note, however, would not paint a true picture of America's internal colonies today. For all the injustices, for all the hardships, these places all have powerful, passionate leaders who are fighting against the current, standing up for the most vulnerable in their communities, and trying to turn the tide toward a brighter future. Take the Tobacco Belt county of Marion, South Carolina, where we met strong community leaders like Mayor Barbara Hopkins of Sellers, who serves as a powerful advocate for the Black citizens of her community in the face of climate disasters. Over in the Mississippi Delta, Dr. Tamala Boyd Shaw, after earning several advanced degrees and gaining expertise as a school principal and with the charter school movement, chose to leave a comfortable life in Memphis to come home to Greenwood, founding Leflore Legacy Academy in 2019. Ernest Adams, a Black Greenwood native who graduated from Greenwood High, and his wife, Debra, have recently given up successful careers in Atlanta to revive the historic Saint Francis Center of civil rights–era fame in Greenwood. Now called the Greenwood Community Center, it is teeming with activity every afternoon and on weekends in the heart of the south side.

Recently, Dr. Boyd Shaw and Debra Adams decided to attend the Junior Auxiliary of Greenwood's Cotton Ball, an event Boyd Shaw had never heard of before returning to her hometown. They were the only two Black people in attendance. "When I tell you the Greenwood Leflore Civic Center looked amazing, [I mean] it was amazing!" Boyd Shaw told us. "I don't mind breaking ceilings and breaking barriers." The next time the ball was held, Boyd Shaw bought a whole table. "I took ten people from my staff. . . . Some [people at the ball were] warm, welcoming, and . . . like, 'Hi, let's go get a drink.'"

Ten miles away, Cedric and Mary Williams, a middle-class Black couple who, through Mary's work as a chaplain for the Federal Bureau of Prisons (Cedric is an elementary school counselor), traveled the country, have also returned home to Leflore County, to the tiny town of Itta Bena. They are determined to bring proven anti-violence programs to the town.

In addition to this formidable group of Black leaders who have returned to the Cotton Belt, determined to claim it as their home, others have risen through the ranks locally, such as Angela Curry, who directs the Greenwood-Leflore-Carroll Economic Development Foundation. Today any number of Black elected officials sit on school boards or represent the region in the Mississippi legislature. The Cotton Belt belongs to them at least as much as it does to anyone in the white elite power structure. Indeed, its future rests with them. But they desperately need resources to have a fighting chance to succeed.

In a move meant to grapple with the injustices of the past, in June 2020 the Leflore County Board of Supervisors voted to remove the Confederate monument that stood alongside the Leflore County Courthouse and relocate it to a Civil War battle site. In addition, a sculpture of Emmett Till was installed downtown on October 21, 2022, and the site was renamed Emmett Till Square. State senator David Jordan, who secured $150,000 in state money to help fund the statue, said, "It is a sign of Greenwood and Leflore County acknowledging the past."

In the "City of Hope," as Manchester, Kentucky, is known today, many locals have shown that they simply won't put up with public corruption anymore. Indeed, the 2003 march in that city was as much a stand against corrupt public officials like the Whites and their cronies as it was against the drug dealers. Slowly, the centuries-old power structure is losing its stranglehold. As noted earlier, there is a palpable sense of boosterism in the town, perhaps due to the large infusion of state dollars—$4.5 million at last count—recently awarded to the city. While trying to lure tourists, local leaders are also trying to address the "nothing to do here but drugs" problem by building social infrastructure to give young people something to do in their own backyard. Whatever is done needs to extend beyond the calcified class lines that have bifurcated central Appalachian towns for generations, and must resist corruption.

What is most striking about Crystal City, Texas, is the solidarity one feels there, at least among the city's Hispanic residents. Nearly every community leader we interviewed was homegrown, and nearly always the son or daughter of a migrant worker. These leaders have fought for their credentials—many of them earning master's degrees and PhDs over many years, after many tries. They could no doubt succeed elsewhere (indeed, several have), but they have decided to devote their expertise to their hometown. One upside of the outmigration of Anglos is that the entrenched social divisions one sees elsewhere in America's forgotten internal colonies aren't as evident here.

Perhaps because of this, the local schools can truly be the "pride point" of these towns, to quote principal Andi Guerrero. In contrast, in Greenwood, five high schools compete with one another for enrollment. Schools that serve the whole community can be key sites of social infrastructure, bringing people from all walks of life together. In South Texas, at no time is this more evident than in June, as every high school graduate's home and the light posts lining the main thoroughfare are all festooned with large banners, each emblazoned with a student's name and picture, one for each graduate. In contrast, in many eastern Kentucky towns, it is the war dead who are featured on banners in the downtowns. Perhaps it is this solidarity that is partly responsible for the favorable health and mobility outcomes seen here (at least relative to our other deeply disadvantaged places) despite the very high poverty rates of many communities in the region.

All of these assets provide a foundation to build upon in each of our nation's regions of deepest disadvantage.

Healing America's Internal Colonies

BEFORE WE CONCLUDED OUR RESEARCH for this book, we felt it was important to spend some time exploring the other end of our Index of Deep Disadvantage—the places identified as those of *greatest* advantage. Once again, we were surprised by where the index took us. It was not Manhattan, center of world finance, or tech-rich Seattle. Neither is among the 200 most advantaged places in our nation by our measure. Instead, the list pointed us to the upper Midwest. At first, we had a hard time believing that this region was truly home to the places of greatest advantage. Shouldn't cities with the most colleges and universities—like Boston—top the list? But, in fact, it was numerous counties in Minnesota, the Dakotas, Nebraska, Iowa, and Wisconsin—roughly a dozen per state—that came out on top. We found that poverty rates in these places are usually very low, babies are usually born healthy, most people live to a ripe old age, and a low-income child usually has the same chance to make it into the middle class as any other kid. Eventually, we stopped being so surprised.

Furthermore, we would learn, many of these states have made significant investments in schools, contributing to long histories of high graduation rates and college attendance. Using the best data available, we found that they have enjoyed the lowest rates of violent crime. According to a measure that includes the vital social infrastructure we've described, these counties are unusually rich in social capital: residents are connected to one another through volunteerism, membership in civic organizations, and participation in other community activities. The level of income inequality in these places is unusually low when compared to the rest of the country. And they experience some of the lowest rates of public corruption in the nation.

In the summer of 2022, we embarked on a second road trip, this time to visit some of these places of greatest advantage. Throughout much of the journey, the sky was a vivid blue, the deep browns of the soil—some of the richest on earth—barely visible beneath the burgeoning sugar beets and the dark green leaves of the soybeans. Then it hit us: in most places, we could see a dozen or more farmsteads. This was in clear contrast to the vast uninterrupted fields of the Cotton Belt or the Winter Garden. Farming in these communities is not without its challenges, but unlike the many untilled acres of the Cotton Belt regions of the Carolinas, Georgia, and Alabama, their nutrients exhausted, few fields here are devoid of crops, except those allowed to lie fallow to replenish the soil. The houses, usually modest, are sturdy and well-kept. Often, ranch-style dwellings have replaced older farmhouses. Alongside the common two- or three-bay garage, one family stores a boat, another several ATVs, and yet another a giant RV. One farm we passed had three of these parked next to the house. On these farmsteads, the house, often enfolded by a copse of trees, is usually the smallest structure. It's typically dwarfed by substantial outbuildings and huge aluminum silos—frequently half a dozen or more lined up beside the barn. In the towns, which are few and far between, huge grain elevators and sugar beet processing plants, along with other small manufacturing concerns, line the train tracks. These towns have few, if any, imposing homes.

What is striking about these landscapes is, well, nothing. Nothing strikes one at all except for the unrelenting sameness of the unending fields, occasionally interrupted by a few dozen acres of bright sunflowers. While the farmsteads are farther apart in the Dakotas than elsewhere, and the homes are more substantial in the rolling hills of Iowa and Nebraska than in southern Minnesota, these places of greatest advantage are mostly marked by a sheer lack of variety, perhaps reflecting the lack of inequality among them. To riff on

Tolstoy's remark about families, what we learned on this second tour was that while each disadvantaged region suffers in its own way, the most advantaged places are more or less alike.

The eateries here, such as the Sioux County Livestock Company in Sioux County, Iowa (ranked the fourth most advantaged place on our index), serve local fare—cheese balls, fried pickle chips, and a half dozen cuts of red meat. We came across a number of enterprises that would qualify as social infrastructure as well, such as the Hole in One Bar & Grill at the Forman Golf Course in Forman, North Dakota (population 509), where we found a good 5 percent of the local population on an August morning, drinking coffee out of Styrofoam cups while finishing off tasty-looking breakfast sandwiches.

In 2015, Christopher Ingraham, then a data reporter for the *Washington Post*, wrote about an obscure data source from the USDA called the Natural Amenities Scale, which rates every US county on indicators such as the weather, the topography, and the presence of lakes. Overall, Minnesota didn't fare well by this measure of desirability as a place to live. Ingraham pointed to Red Lake County, in the northwestern quadrant of the state, which ranked dead last in the nation. Like the rest of Minnesota, the winter temperatures there are frigid (one of the items on the Natural Amenities Scale), and the county, despite the name of the county seat, Red Lake Falls, has neither lakes nor waterfalls.

The citizens of Minnesota, especially those from Red Lake Falls, rebelled against Ingraham's story. They flooded his email with both vitriol and pictures of bucolic Minnesota scenes. One enterprising citizen invited him to visit, and Ingraham's editors agreed. He was so taken by the place that he moved there from the Baltimore suburbs with his wife and young twins. Though his bestselling book on his experiences, *If You Lived Here You'd Be Home by Now*, makes no mention of any of the indicators in our index as a justification for his decision, perhaps his instincts were right. Despite the fact that the place is several hours from the nearest international airport, Starbucks, or Whole Foods grocery store, the quality of life in Red Lake County,

Minnesota, is virtually unbeatable according to our index, where it is ranked among the 20 most advantaged places in the nation.

Across these counties of the upper Midwest, the land has provided sustenance to people for generations. Here farm families weathered the Great Depression, the ups and downs of the 1940s and '50s, the farm crisis of the 1980s, and more. Places like Red Lake Falls have had to adapt to the times, but according to rural sociologist Robert Wuthnow, who has conducted the most comprehensive history of the region, they remain economically vibrant.

The upper Midwest was originally home to Native tribes such as the Blackfoot, Sioux, and Chippewa. Throughout the eighteenth and nineteenth centuries, the US government seized their land through conquest and coerced treaties, many of which were later broken. The region was resettled in the mid- to late nineteenth century by German and Scandinavian immigrants, along with a smattering of southern European groups. Many among these white settlers secured their land at no cost from the government through the 1862 Homestead Act, probably the first major piece of federal social policy. Southern planter-politicians fiercely opposed the law, and it was only after the South seceded from the Union that the act was passed. It is ironic, though not surprising, that this act benefiting white settlers was passed just three years before General Sherman's Special Field Order No. 15—with its forty acres and a mule promise—was overturned by President Andrew Johnson, devastating the prospects of most southern Blacks, who were desperate to establish homesteads of their own. They have never been compensated for that loss.

A deep dive into these places of greatest advantage reveals few "firsts" or "mosts." They largely lack the symbols of a sole-commodity economy—like the Popeye statue in Crystal City—that dot the South Texas, Cotton and Tobacco Belt, and Appalachian landscapes. Instead, many of the symbols are whimsical. Paul Bunyan and his blue ox, Babe, are well represented in Minnesota (Babe's footprints are the source of the state's 10,000 lakes, so the story goes), and the state boasts not only the Willie Walleye statue in the border city of Baudette but the world's largest ball of twine in the town of Darwin (weighing in at 17,400 pounds and measuring 13 feet in diameter). Le Mars, Iowa, has dubbed itself the "Ice Cream Capital of the World," and there are fifty ice cream cone sculptures around town to drive home the distinction. Le Mars, a largely agricultural place, happens also to be home to a Blue Bunny ice cream plant—and indeed, more ice cream is made in that plant than in any other single location in the world, proof that if your definition is sufficiently narrow, "world capital" is not that hard to claim. Many towns in this region host festivals in the summer, a time for family reunions and get-togethers with old friends. There is the annual county fair, which is a chance for the farm families to show off their wares and for kids to ride the Tilt-A-Whirl. Mostly, these places have never been the true "capital" of anything. Perhaps as a result, great divides so evident in America's internal colonies never took hold here.

Counties that rank among those of greatest advantage on our index began as agricultural communities with modest-sized farms, many family owned. Nowadays, small-business owners, managers, administrators, doctors, nurses, and teachers make up the middle class, along with electricians, plumbers, and the more prosperous farmers. Mostly, there is no intergenerational elite. We don't want to aggrandize or romanticize these places; while some have gained modestly in population in recent years, others have suffered population loss. Many have experienced a "hollowing out [of] the middle"— sociologists Patrick Carr and Maria Kefalas's phrase for the brain drain when the local "high-fliers" go off to college and don't return. Local job opportunities for young college graduates are sometimes limited. Yet these communities have been more successful than most in preventing poverty, promoting health, and ensuring a level playing field for their children.

These places lack the racial and ethnic heterogeneity that adds such richness to the American experience. Clearly, the fact that the residents are almost all white means they have enjoyed access to more advantages—going back generations—than the many majority-minority communities we have written about in this book. In line with that reality, when we examined the relationship between whiteness and rank on the index, we found that a higher percentage of white residents is a significant predictor of a place's rank, not at all surprising when one considers that the good schools and the good jobs have long been bestowed liberally on whites while being denied to Hispanic and Black Americans. But it is not as predictive as the level of inequality, the unemployment rate, or the degree of educational attainment in a place. Furthermore, many places that are disproportionately white (given whites' representation in the population), in states like Ohio, Maine, Illinois, Indiana, Kentucky, Montana, Michigan, West Virginia, and Idaho, do not rank even among the top half of advantaged places in America.

One cannot fully understand the advantages enjoyed in America's most advantaged places, however, without considering the historic (and ongoing) exploitation of migrant labor that has gone on in them, mostly drawn from the US border regions (especially South Texas) and Mexico. As late as the early 2000s, an estimated 20,000 to 30,000 migrant workers traveled to Minnesota each year to work in the sugar beat fields, poultry processing plants, and dairy farms. Neither the suffering of souls whose permanent residence is elsewhere nor the forced transfer of Native lands to white settlers is captured in the official statistics of these places.

Some of these most advantaged places lie cheek by jowl with Native Nations, places that, as we have seen earlier in this book, often rank among the least advantaged. As part of our six-state upper Midwest tour, we visited the Crow Creek reservation in Buffalo County, South Dakota, which ranks as the fourth most disadvantaged place on our index. In 1863, its population was exiled from the rich land of southwestern Minnesota when Governor Alexander Ramsey expelled the state's Sioux after the bloody US-Dakota War, in which hundreds of settlers were slain. Native Americans also lost their lives by the hundreds, some in the war but most to starvation after they were forcibly relocated onto land mostly inhospitable to human habitation.

On Buffalo County's northeastern boundary sits Hand County, ranking 31st most advantaged on our index. Hand County has ample acreage suitable for farming, which was also true of some areas of Buffalo County until the US Army Corps of Engineers dammed the Missouri River at Fort Thompson in 1964, creating an eighty-mile-long reservoir that drowned the fertile bottomland. Stories like this on native lands abound and must be reckoned with, though they are not the ones featured in this book.

With important caveats about the most advantaged places in mind, the key lesson we have taken from our exploration of those places is that people seem to thrive—maybe not in wealth but in health and life chances—when inequality is low; when landownership is widespread; when social connection is high; when corruption of the kind seen in central Appalachia is virtually unknown; and when violence is rare. The social leveling that is characteristic of communities in the upper Midwest (a place where "every child is above average," as radio personality Garrison Keillor famously put it) is more than just a quaint cultural feature. It is the engine that drives the social and economic processes from which its citizens derive benefits.

How do we ensure that all American communities can confer upon their citizens the chance to thrive? How do we build not injustice, but *justice* into place? As professors who have spent much of our careers studying poverty and anti-poverty policy, it is almost instinctual for us to list a string of specific, evidence-based strategies that hold the promise of turning the tide for the nation's most disadvantaged places. Any such list juxtaposed against the centuries of extraction and subjugation perpetrated in America's internal colonies would pale in comparison. Yet we also believe that a data-driven understanding of the mechanisms linking the past to the present can lead us to promising new avenues for policy change. Indeed, discovering that the most advantaged places on our index are also the least likely to feature these very mechanisms has underlined our confidence in the findings in our book.

For America's former internal colonies to move forward, these legacies must be addressed. From our analysis, we have derived six principles for action.

END SEPARATE AND UNEQUAL SCHOOLING

Desegregating schools is a tall order. Yet economist Rucker Johnson's research demonstrates that the benefits of doing so are huge. We must remain vigilant in aspiring to this goal. What was possible once is possible again if we have the political will.

Short of this, there are other obvious strategies that can improve the public schools. Johnson's and others' research has revealed that some of the benefits to Black students from desegregation orders flows through increased teacher pay. There is strong evidence that increasing the pay of new teachers improves learning in schools. Today's teachers are forced to do odd jobs like drive for Uber or Instacart to get by. Wouldn't we rather they were able to own homes in the communities in which they teach, serve as leaders there, and enrich the tax base? At this writing, a movement for increasing teacher pay is sweeping across the South, but these efforts haven't gone nearly far enough yet.

Patronage in teacher hiring has plagued the Clay County, Kentucky, school district for generations, just as it has America's other internal colonies. The power of superintendents or school boards should not be absolute, nor should jobs in the educational sector be traded for votes at election time. School systems should be scrutinized for their hiring practices to ensure that the best talent gets the jobs and that nonlocal candidates—or those who grew up on the wrong side of the tracks—have an equal chance of being hired if qualified. Anti-nepotism laws in states without them (like Kentucky) could help, as could more stringent enforcement of existing laws.

In the end, however, it should be obvious that no measure that fails to recognize that separate cannot be equal will truly heal the ills of America's schools. Today, there is what might be called another secessionist frenzy mirroring the one that led to the establishment of thousands of segregation academies across the South. In 2022, Mississippi lawmakers once again tried to funnel federal money to segregation academies and other private schools—$10 million from the pandemic relief money the state received—but as was true decades ago, a state judge deemed the plan unconstitutional. At the time of this writing, the governor of Arkansas is trying to do the same. Further, some parents decry any public school curriculum that seeks to tell the story of racism in America, with the rallying cry of banning "critical race theory." Books that have been treasured, even revered, by children and teens have been banned. There are instances where the parallels with history run even deeper, as in the wealthy, mostly white Atlanta neighborhood of Buckhead, which is threatening to secede from the city and its schools. Vigilance is required in naming the wrong when new forms of segregation in schools emerge.

TO END VIOLENCE, SPARK MOBILITY

We have argued in this book that the extraordinarily high level of violence in many of our places of deepest disadvantage—especially in the Cotton Belt of the South, the Tobacco Belt of the Pee Dee, and the Coal Belt of central Appalachia—is rooted in a history of profound economic and social subjugation of the many by the few, relying on violence as the ultimate tool. Drawing on big data, our research has found that the rate of violent crime in a community is directly tied to the rate of intergenerational mobility in that place—a key indicator of how successful a community is, and has been, in keeping the oppressed group down.

Thus, the ultimate cure for violence can come only when the social and economic barriers between the haves and the have-nots, which have been maintained by, and for the benefit of, the haves, are breached. While the American Dream has been more myth than reality for many people throughout our nation's history, it must nonetheless be our goal, particularly in places where a history of internal colonialism has left such profound human scars. Neglecting this first principle in any anti-poverty strategy will only continue to mire a community like Greenwood, Mississippi, in a structural cycle of violence, where violence perpetuated across the generations has ensured low mobility, which in turn incites violence, which in turn ensures low mobility.

Indeed, the federal government has invested significantly in the economic development of some of these regions, especially in Appalachia through the Appalachian Regional Commission (ARC) and in the Delta through the Delta Regional Authority (DRA). The ARC provides grants for communities to pursue economic development strategies, publishes research on this work, and sponsors conferences. Its resources have been used to build highways and institutions such as hospitals and to invest in industry. The DRA makes similar investments in the Mississippi Delta. There is some evidence that these programs have benefited the regions, yet both have come under criticism for investing mostly in physical infrastructure and industry, with less attention paid to the human capital and employment outcomes of lower-income residents. An evaluation of the DRA in 2011, for example, found that while it had been modestly successful in increasing economic growth, it had had no discernible impact on rates of employment in the communities it serves. It could well be that the ARC and DRA may do more to help the haves than the have-nots in these vulnerable regions.

Communities need tools to cope with the high levels of violence that plague them today. Peacekeeping efforts of local activists like Shun Pearson and Lavoris Weathers, who started Operation Peace Treaty to respond to the high rate of gun violence in Greenwood, are a start. Recent research has shown that programs such as READI Chicago that address violence through both "interrupters" who can mediate conflicts and interventions that include cognitive behavioral therapy can have a dramatic impact on violent crime and recidivism. When used with high-risk high school students, similar programs—Becoming a Man and Choose to Change, to name just two—can significantly reduce violence and boost high school graduation rates. But most of these efforts have been deployed in cities like Chicago; they are needed in rural locales as well. This is especially true in the South, as Mary and Cedric Williams in Itta Bena, Mississippi, who are working to bring these proven anti-violence interventions to their town, know. There is some evidence that other youth-focused activities that build prosocial identities can be powerful tools in helping youths stay on track and avoid getting caught up in violence and crime. Such approaches have been criticized for "blaming the victim," but we see them as vital resources that should not be denied to those who are living in areas plagued by violence and who desperately need them.

Yet another strategy is to build collective efficacy—neighbors who are willing to intervene in their communities and on their streets for the public good. Today, people in both Manchester, Kentucky, and Greenwood, Mississippi, are hunkered down inside their homes. Most are afraid to get involved. While understandable, this response weakens a community's informal social control, rendering it more reliant upon formal social control—the intervention of police, the courts, and prison systems—to solve problems. Through key neighborhood institutions such as churches, community centers, after-school programs, and Boys & Girls Clubs, adults in the community can be encouraged to get involved—the way Pastor Ken has with God's Closet and the soup kitchen, or how Baptist Town native Ernest Adams and his wife, Debra, have by opening a community center on Greenwood's south side, or the way former Greenwood school board member Bill Clay has with the Greenwood Mentoring Group. All of these efforts have sparked participation by others in the community.

Bill Clay's after-school program, operating on a shoestring budget and funded mainly by his wife, serves dozens of South Greenwood children each day, marshaling the talents of retired teachers and other professionals to assist with homework and offer structure at the end of the school day. Clay told us, "Challenges? Sure. Challenges are everywhere you go. But I want [the program] to be a place where I feel like I made a difference. . . . Some of these people work jobs, two and three jobs. . . . It would shock a lot of people that a lot of these parents want the best education for their [kids]. [In a few weeks we're taking the kids on a] trip to New Orleans. You know what [one mother] told me? 'Mr. Clay, we done already started packing.' They want their children to have the very best. And they understand, 'A lot of the things I want for them, I can't provide for them,' and that's where we come in. . . . We're going to bridge that gap. We're going to level the playing field."

INVEST IN SOCIAL INFRASTRUCTURE

How does a community build back lost social infrastructure, and in a way that is inclusive, not divisive? Clay County's economic development plan is only one illustration of how tempting it can be to invest in a downtown as a tourist destination, rather than as a place that fundamentally alters the way community residents interact. In places divided by race or ethnicity, building equitable social infrastructure is a special challenge, as invisible lines have separated the spaces of Black and Hispanic residents from those of white residents for generations.

What would a truly inclusive Main Street look like? Nearly every place in America has a public library, often in or near the downtown. Following sociologist Eric Klinenberg, whose book title recalls Andrew Carnegie's vision that public libraries be "palaces for the people," we visited the public library in every place we could during our various trips to the most disadvantaged places on our index. At this writing, Greenwood's downtown public library offers one activity each week—a book club, bingo, a movie night, or crafts. The Marion County library system offers a weekly story time in its

Mullins and Marion locations, and its bookmobile brings reading materials to outlying areas like Nichols. The nicely appointed public library in Clay County has a bookmobile but no programming other than providing access to online learning resources. The public libraries in Brooks and Zavala Counties appear to have no programming and no web presence.

Contrast this with Klinenberg's account of an early morning visit to the New Lots Library in East New York, one of the poorest neighborhoods in Brooklyn. In this small library, flyers advertise events for everyone, including toddlers, English-language learners, and retired folks. There is a designated spot for the kids, there are tables pushed together for the English-language instruction on offer, and there is a classroom where any adult reading below GED level can get individual or group tutoring. A basement community room is a showcase for the creativity of the library staff: sometimes it's a library, at other times it's an art studio or community meeting space. On the morning Klinenberg visited, it was a virtual bowling alley, part of the Library Lanes bowling league, an initiative where older patrons of New Lots play against other libraries' teams. The example of New Lots suggests that with a little imagination, rural libraries could also become vital community hubs.

Other potential low-hanging fruit are Head Start and other local childcare centers. These facilities are key sites where parents gain social capital—a term used to describe how people benefit from their social networks. Head Start, which was piloted in the Mississippi Delta roughly seven decades ago, has the benefit of being a trusted institution in most poor communities. According to the research of sociologist Mario Small, Head Start centers already function as convening places for parents to gather information, express concerns, and solve problems; provide some of the key social glue that keeps a community together; and serve as social safety nets to catch people when they fall. With a modest expansion of their mandates, these centers could serve as vital social infrastructure.

Bookstores that hold readings and host community discussions, such as the beloved Turnrow Book Co. in Greenwood, can be key convening sites, as can restaurants and civic organizations that maintain community rooms for public use, like the Tally-Ho in Selma, Alabama. Governments and foundations could fund not only Main Street initiatives, like the Downtown Manchester Market Place in Clay County, but also the revival of a local movie theater or a new arcade.

Schools are obvious sites for creating social infrastructure. We were struck by the level of social infrastructure the schools provide in our two South Texas communities, where the high school is a "pride point" of the towns. Similarly, during the period when Greenwood High was briefly somewhat integrated in the late 1970s and '80s, a large contingent from town would follow the sports teams as they played rivals across the state, according to a memoir by Richard Rubin, who served as a sportswriter for the *Greenwood Commonwealth* for a year during that time. Great potential for social infrastructure was lost when white students left the Greenwood public schools. Finally, as we learned from the 2003 march in Clay County led by Pastors Bolin and Abner, there is tremendous, often latent, power for creating social infrastructure that is inclusive, not divisive, in places of worship.

ROOT OUT CORRUPTION

Carmen Lewis, the former mayor of Manchester, Kentucky, though born in Clay County, was viewed by the political establishment as an outsider with new, unwelcome ideas. She planted flowers and trees to beautify the bleak downtown, and she helped bring down eight corrupt community leaders. Though defeated in 2010 after only one term, Lewis left her mark on the city.

Across the country, organizations and programs such as IGNITE, New American Leaders, Ready to Run, and Run for Something help aspiring new leaders like Lewis to run for local office. Providing ways for new leaders—people not entrenched in corrupt practices such as using public office for private gain and vote buying—to emerge is one way to begin to loosen the grip of corruption that is present in America's internal colonies. But it is not enough to help new leaders get elected, as the Teamsters did for Juan Cornejo, the first Mexican American mayor of Crystal City. New leaders also need help to govern well.

Most often, emerging leaders trying to set a new course have the odds stacked against them—as was the case with Cornejo's coalition and later with the slate of La Raza candidates who came into office in South Texas in the early 1970s. People at every level are hoping for their failure: when they stumble, it is all the easier to blame the community for its own problems. Universities could certainly play a role in helping to equip local leaders with the tools needed to succeed, perhaps through a model like the USDA's community- and university-based Cooperative Extension System. Recently, one community leader told us that while his state's flagship university is not beloved in most rural towns, the extension service is immensely popular because it provides knowledge and resources the community values. Using university extension programs as a conduit for equipping local leaders might help higher ed prove its worth in many far-flung communities.

Better systems of funneling much-needed government resources to poor communities are a critical piece. Since at least the New Deal, according to historian Douglas Arnett, there has been an expectation in central Appalachia that resources from the government will not flow directly to the needy. Aid goes instead to local government, which then dispenses the goods: a recipe for corruption. This is why, Arnett argues, the War on Poverty, with its independent Community Action Program, was such a threat to local elites in the 1960s. A federally administered, expanded Child Tax Credit would be one way to get resources to parents today without having them flow into the open pockets of local elites. More-targeted investments in people must be implemented in this way as well, with full recognition that the risk of elite capture is real.

For decades, though, the US government has recognized that it must invest in places as well as people. This has usually been done through policies that force communities to compete for funds. This puts rural communities on unequal footing with urban areas, since in these places municipal and nonprofit staff are stretched thin and there is little access to professional grant writers. Christie Green, public health director of the Cumberland Valley District Health Department, serving Clay County, told us she was too busy replacing light bulbs and trying to repair faulty wiring in the building to write grant applications—while, ironically, her budget didn't even have enough wiggle room to hire an electrician to make those repairs.

Sociologist Laura Tach has added up all the place-based funding that each US county received from 1990 to 2015. What predicted which counties got more? Poverty was a strong correlate, as should be the case, since only places exhibiting a certain level of need are eligible for many of the grants. Percentage of minority residents was another—not surprising again, since Black and Hispanic people are so much more likely to be poor in the United States. But beyond these obvious factors, Tach found that the strongest predictor of funding was the number of nonprofits in a county—a rough proxy of how many skilled grant writers there are. Due to this fact, Boston—a rich city by any measure—received a disproportionate share of funding, while many of the places that rank high on our index got little to none.

Another problem with the process for dispensing government funds for place-based initiatives is that the proposals are bottom-up. Rarely is the process driven by experts in regional development. Instead, local elites—with their own self-interest—often control the process. This leads to wasteful boondoggles. One example is the county that received more place-based dollars per person in Tach's analysis than any other in the nation—Tunica County, Mississippi—at $16,000 for every man, woman, and child in the county. What was the money used for? To help attract a stainless-steel-pipe factory, which in the end provided only a few hundred low-wage jobs.

Meanwhile, the area hemorrhaged roughly 13,000 jobs when a casino closed, leaving it with some of the highest unemployment and poverty rates in the United States. Data, not cronyism, should determine the areas of greatest need, as well as the strategies that are most likely to lead to meaningful gains.

One way to give poorly resourced places a step up even in the current system was modeled by the Obama administration, which created federal task forces for local areas identified as being in acute need, including the city of Baltimore, which was reeling after the unrest caused by the death of Freddie Gray while in police custody in 2015. Partnering with local leaders, the Baltimore task force, consisting of senior officials from sixteen federal agencies, worked to find solutions for the city's pressing problems and prepare local leaders to better compete for available federal funding.

MAKE STRUCTURAL RACISM VISIBLE AND CONFRONT IT

When people think about how to combat poverty, a specific focus often emerges, such as job training or affordable childcare. Yet sometimes what impacts struggling families the most is a host of other issues. When we first arrived in Marion County, South Carolina, we didn't imagine that we would spend the next few years learning about how structural racism was so deeply embedded in the nation's natural disaster policy. We didn't know that in the wake of multiple natural disasters, we would meet Americans living in homes with mold crawling up the walls or still using outhouses. And we weren't aware that after many climate-driven events, predominantly white communities end up better off in the long run, while the outcome for predominantly Black communities is the opposite. In the case of disaster relief, the policies that lead to these disparate outcomes are not overtly racist, but they have an undeniably racist impact. Part of that can be attributed to the fact that these policies take no account of history—a centuries-old history of structural racism that means, for instance, that Black homeowners are more likely to have a legally tenuous claim to homeownership and are therefore at heightened risk of being denied help by the federal government.

Disaster recovery is the tip of the iceberg when it comes to structural racism, however. Recall how planters and catfish farmers across the Delta are allegedly abusing the H2-A visa program to replace their Black laborers with white South Africans, who in turn have accused their employers of exploitation. In an example closer to home, researchers have found that Black and Hispanic Americans are charged more for opening and maintaining a checking account. Black people are more likely to be denied approval for a home mortgage, all other things being equal. If they are approved, recent studies by scholars at MIT and the Urban Institute found that Black homeowners pay higher interest rates on their mortgages, even after accounting for other factors like credit score and income. They pay more for mortgage insurance premiums. They even pay more in property taxes, after accounting for all other factors. A recent study found that Black Americans with severe depression were more likely to be misdiagnosed with schizophrenia. Doctors on average don't take their reports of pain as seriously as the reports of white patients. This is just a small sample of the ways in which racism persists and is prevalent in too many dimensions of life to count.

When one of us (Luke) began to work with the city government of Detroit (one of the few cities among the 100 most disadvantaged places on our index) to reduce poverty and enhance intergenerational mobility, he and his team began by building a list of the policies that might impact low-income Detroiters most. Nowhere on the list was the cost of auto insurance. Yet it came up repeatedly in conversations with residents, city officials, and Detroit mayor Mike Duggan. Luke's team found that the same policy that cost $1,400 per year on average nationally was pricing out at $5,400 in Detroit. Low-income Michiganders across the state were paying rates that were unaffordable, but the problem was many times worse in Detroit. The single best predictor of how expensive auto insurance was in a Michigan community was the percentage of Black people who lived there. Such inequities should be routinely scrutinized. Responses such as "Because that's just the way it is" and "That's just how the numbers work out" should be challenged.

Confronting structural racism means rooting it out anywhere and everywhere. A necessary part of anti-racist reforms must be an audit of policies, programs, and regulations in federal, state, and local government to identify disparate racial outcomes; to delve deep into history to understand what factors have led to these outcomes; and to devise concrete solutions to address disparities. In all cases, such a structural racism audit would probably find that the devil is in the details. Indeed, it is impossible to ferret out structural racism without being deeply ensconced in those details.

BRING THE SUPPLY CHAINS HOME

We agree with Greenwood native Lavoris Weathers of Operation Peace Treaty, who advanced the "hunger hypothesis" to explain the violence in his city. The story of how to end violence begins and ends with real prospects for intergenerational mobility. That quest, of course, is vitally linked to a diverse economy that offers authentic opportunities for advancement. The nation must confront the fact that policy makers on both sides of the aisle have endorsed trade policies that have crushed the South's nascent efforts to industrialize and diversify its economies after the vast internal colonies that dominated these places began to break down. These policies include the North American Free Trade Agreement (NAFTA) and others that have driven the boom in manufacturing in China. During the COVID-19 pandemic, Americans became aware of just how risky exporting our supply chains could be.

NAFTA is easily one of the most contested policies in American history. Passed by a Democratic Congress and implemented by a Democratic president, Bill Clinton, in 1994, NAFTA represented a fundamental shift in the policy platform of the Democratic Party.

Prior to NAFTA's passage, Democrats were seen as protecting American manufacturing jobs from competition abroad. Many southerners weren't aligned with Democrats on social issues, but they voted with them on jobs. Three decades later, both researchers and policy makers continue to debate whether NAFTA was good policy. Most think it was neither as good as its proponents advertise nor as bad as its detractors claim. Recently, however, economists have come to the consensus that the agreement cost jobs in some parts of the nation. Huge numbers of jobs, in fact, according to a recent study. These job losses were concentrated in places like Texas's Winter Garden and especially in the Cotton Belt, along with a few other regions, including portions of central Appalachia. Communities such as Greenwood were devastated, and they have fought an uphill battle ever since. Many economists argue that while these places may have been hurt by NAFTA, the nation as a whole benefits from free trade. If true, this marks another in a long line of instances where the more prosperous among us have benefited from the pain of the less well-off. The exploiter in this case is the nation.

But the story doesn't end there. The ushering in of free trade by Democrats didn't cause only an economic realignment; it spurred a major political shift as well, according to recent research. In 1995, when Republicans took control of the House of Representatives just months after NAFTA went into effect, no Republican then in office had ever served under a Republican Speaker of the House. Democrats had controlled the chamber for decades, and the party's grip hadn't loosened much even in the run-up to the 1994 election. Going into the election, Democrats had 258 seats to Republicans' 176, a similar margin to what they had enjoyed going back all the way to the late 1950s. Since 1994, Democrats have been in the minority more years than not.

Before the trade deal, voters in counties that were the most at risk of losing jobs because of NAFTA were more likely than voters in other counties to choose Democrats in House elections. By 2000, these counties had flipped strongly to Republicans. Other recent studies suggest that the shifting of manufacturing to China in the 2000s has had a similar effect. Some twenty-two years after NAFTA took effect, opposition to the agreement would become a major plank in the platform of a Republican presidential candidate whom few people in Washington gave much of a chance. These voters were essential to his unexpected victory in 2016.

FOR THE SAKE OF THE CHILDREN

Despite the recurring themes we have uncovered across the communities featured in this book, each of them has its own unique story to tell.

While the repugnant history of the World War II internment camps in the United States is well-known, few have heard the story of the only camp built expressly for the purpose of interning Japanese, German, and Italian American families with children. This occurred in Crystal City, Texas, on the grounds of a former government-owned migrant labor camp, where the town's high school sits today.

Some of the kids who grew up in the Crystal City Internment Camp have penned accounts noting that conditions there were better than most might expect—two-bedroom dwellings, running water, electricity, iceboxes and stoves, adequate food, decent schools—amenities due to the dictates of the 1929 Geneva Convention plus strict oversight by the International Red Cross. Yet others are still traumatized to this day by memories of that time. "Fence sickness" was a term used to describe the despondency and depression that affected many of those living under armed guard.

Only traces of that world inside the barbed wire linger. But in recent years, a series of historic markers have been placed on the site commemorating the suffering of those unjustly denied their freedom due to their national origin—"a reminder that the injustices and humiliations suffered here as a result of hysteria, racism, and discrimination will never happen again."

Calls for reparations for these and other internees went unheeded for decades. Finally, in 1988, former Japanese American prisoners, but not Germans or Italian Americans, received an official apology and modest reparations. The nation has, at least to some degree, taken pains to acknowledge this wrong. John Tateishi, who led the movement for redress, told NPR's Bilal Qureshi, "There is a saying in Japanese culture, 'kodomo no tame ni,' which means, 'for the sake of the children.' And for us running this campaign, that had much to do with it. . . . It's the legacy we're handing down to them and to the nation to say that 'You can make this mistake, but you also have to correct it—and by correcting it, hopefully not repeat it again.'"

The acknowledgment of the wrongs committed and the reparations for these interned families and their descendants were long in coming. But the deep wounds of exploitation and subjugation suffered by those on the other side of the wire on the unpaved streets of Crystal City—and in all of America's former internal colonies—have not been addressed. It is beyond time to come to terms with these injustices. It is time to repair the wrongs that go back many generations. This work will not be easy or straightforward. But by applying a deep understanding of our nation's most disadvantaged places, with the knowledge gained from amassing an arsenal of big data, engaging in deep listening, learning from history, and publicly acknowledging the impact of generations of exploitation, we might finally follow a path to a renewed America that can make us all proud.

Acknowledgments

We are indebted to so many who contributed to this work. We thank Andrea Ducas and, later, Katrina Badger, our program officers at the Robert Wood Johnson Foundation, for sparking the idea of studying America's most disadvantaged places with an eye toward health and RWJF for generous funding of the project. Luke also thanks the Carnegie Foundation for generous support of his work on the project. At the University of Michigan, Kate Naranjo was exceptionally adept at project management, only to be equaled by Karen Otzen, who succeeded her. Kate also aided us in the end by formatting and providing key phrases for nearly seven hundred notes. At Princeton, Kris McDonald and Kristen Catena aided in a multitude of ways.

We thank Silvia Robles, Jasmine Simington, and Samiul Jubaed for major contributions in building the Index of Deep Disadvantage, and acknowledge the feedback of the entire research team. Liv Mann, then a first-year graduate student, was persuaded during a chance meeting at the communal coffeepot to spend the summer of 2019 in Clay County, Kentucky. She in turn convinced Emily Miller, also in her first year of graduate school, to join her. Liv's blog based on their interviews and observations was the first to point to the "nothing to do but drugs" theme in the data and to make the link to Eric Klinenberg's ideas about the importance of social infrastructure. Emily wrote a journal article (with Kathy) about the special challenges poor youth in eastern Kentucky face in making the transition to adulthood. We drew on both of these early analyses in this book. On the Michigan end, Luke learned that grad student Lanora

Johnson was from eastern Kentucky and intended to conduct her dissertation research there. She was also persuaded to join the team. Princeton postdoctoral researcher Christine Jang-Trettien conducted follow-up visits to Clay County in 2021 and 2022 to help us better understand the fallout from the ongoing drug epidemic there and how it shaped the local economy. Emily and Lanora returned in the summer of 2022 as well, conducting interviews on the role of disability programs in community life. They were on the ground to observe the many community development initiatives being rolled out in Manchester that we describe in the final chapters of this book, as well as the eviction crisis these efforts spawned.

Meg Duffy, a master's degree student at the University of Michigan's Ford School, and Jasmine Simington, a PhD student in sociology and public policy at the university, spent the summer of 2019 embedded in Marion County, South Carolina, sometimes joined by Lanora Johnson, who split her time between there and Kentucky. Based on an early analysis of the data gathered in Marion, Meg wrote a paper (with Luke) on the policy feedback loop that, she argued, partly explained why Black victims of the back-to-back flooding there were less likely to access relief than whites in the aftermath of Hurricanes Matthew and Florence. Jasmine identified a second key reason for racial differences in who received relief—the fact that so many Black homeowners' property had been passed down informally over the generations. She quickly became an expert on heir's property, wrote a blog on the topic, and is writing her dissertation on this theme.

Princeton graduate student Ryan Parsons, who was living in Greenwood, Mississippi, in 2019 while conducting his dissertation research in nearby Sunflower County, also joined our team. Sometimes accompanied by Kathy and Tim, he conducted interviews and observations there until early 2020, when the COVID-19 pandemic broke out. He resumed the research from May 2021 through the spring of 2022.

In December 2019, Meg Duffy and Emily Miller flew to McAllen,

Texas, then embarked on a nine-hundred-mile road trip across South Texas, including both Brooks and Zavala Counties, to identify research sites there. Kathy and Tim followed up, holding focus groups with community leaders in Brooks County in January 2020. During the pandemic, when it was not possible to do in-person research, Karen Otzen and Maricruz Moya, a graduate student in public policy at the University of Michigan, conducted several dozen interviews with people in Brooks and Zavala Counties over Zoom or by phone. When finally allowed by our universities to resume in-person research in May 2021, Maricruz, Karen, Christine, Luke, Tim, and Kathy all spent part of that summer in Zavala County conducting face-to-face interviews with dozens of residents.

Many of the hypotheses our ethnographic research generated led us back to big data, where they could be tested. For these analyses, we partnered with Columbia University postdoctoral researcher Michael Evangelist, Liv Mann, and Ryan Parsons. Some of this analysis has led to publications, additional grants, and even, in Liv's case, the seeds of her dissertation. In other cases, due to limitations of the data, the only credit these researchers will get for their efforts is this acknowledgment.

Christine Jang-Trettien took on the task of attempting to identify every segregation academy still operating in the fourteen southern states and was aided in this task by Ryan Parsons. Christine also helped trace the complex story of corruption in Clay County through myriad news accounts and court records. In addition, she analyzed transcripts of our interviews, coding what leisure pursuits people in Clay County engage in.

Karen Otzen's research into the origins of the American catfish industry shed light on this major economic driver in the Mississippi Delta. She also analyzed the interview transcripts from Zavala County that allowed us to tell the story of the cheerleader revolt and the rise of La Raza Unida in our interviewees' own words. Her final contribution was meticulously checking the accuracy of many notes.

We thank Elina Morrison and Hannah Pollack for research assistance. Elina read the whole manuscript a number of times, and she and Hannah gave incredibly helpful comments on many chapters.

Longtime colleague Stefanie DeLuca commented on every chapter of this book, sometimes multiple times, as did Philip Garboden, Sarah Gold, Meredith Greif, David Grusky, Michelle Jackson, Christine Jang-Trettien, Marybeth Mattingly, Reuben Miller, Karen Otzen, and Eva Rosen. We thank David Grusky in particular for his suggestions for appendix A. Each of the primary student researchers engaged in this project (Liv, Emily, Lanora, Meg, Jasmine, and Ryan) read the chapters relevant to their sites and offered ideas and corrections. Other incredibly helpful readers of chapters included Dan Bolger, Chad Brummett, Kristina Bryant, Lynette Clemetson, Hope Harvey, Eric Klinenberg, Vann Newkirk, Mara Ostfeld, Nicole Sherard-Freeman, Angela Simms, as well as Bill Estep and Anna Wolfe, who commented on passages related to their reporting. Dr. Shaunna Scott of the University of Kentucky offered helpful feedback on our work in eastern Kentucky. Blake Trettien amassed a two-thousand-page compendium of legal cases as part of our legal review.

In 2020, 2021, and 2022, students in Kathy's Poverty and Social Policy course helped us explore other deeply disadvantaged places where we hadn't conducted fieldwork, including the Pine Ridge Indian Reservation, the Central Valley of California, southern Louisiana, and rural Maine. One student's work convinced us we had to adjust our poverty measures to account for college towns where a significant portion of the students lived off campus (and thus counted in the census and other surveys as residents, unlike students living in dorms). While we did not draw explicitly from these students' original research, we benefited greatly from their efforts and the many conversations about these places in class.

Most important, this work was carefully shepherded by our wonderful and incredible agent, Lisa Adams, and our exceptionally gifted editor, Deanne Urmy, who never failed to grasp what we were trying to communicate and helped us do it better, without doing violence to the complexity of the narrative. Barbara Jatkola, our copyeditor, is in our view the very best in the business and we are deeply grateful for her careful work. After failing for more than a year to find a title for the book, our agent Lisa Adams came through with "The Injustice of Place." It was just right. We also offer our deep gratitude to Susie Shaefer, who, though not a coauthor of this book, probably felt like one from time to time. Her deep imprint is on this work.

Appendix A

The History and Theory
of Internal Colonies

INTERNAL COLONIES:
A TWO-HUNDRED-YEAR HISTORY OF A CONCEPT

Activists, intellectuals, and academics have promoted the idea of "internal colonies" and related concepts for at least two centuries. Sociologist Charles Pinderhughes locates it as early as 1830 at the first meeting of the Black Convention Movement in Philadelphia, with the promotion of the idea that Black Americans comprised a "nation within a nation." This wording was later picked up by thinkers such as Frederick Douglass and then W. E. B. Du Bois. Vladimir Lenin produced an early version of the internal colony theory in his 1899 work, *The Development of Capitalism in Russia*, and Antonio Gramsci and the Italian communists used the term in the 1920s to describe the subjugation of southern Italy and the nearby islands at the hands of the bourgeois of northern Italy. According to leading Cotton Belt Communist Party organizer Harry Haywood, the party built its appeal to Black Americans during the 1930s on the idea that they were a "subjugated nation."

The popularity of the colonial perspective grew dramatically throughout the 1960s, motivated primarily by four developments: (1) independence movements in former European colonies in Asia and Africa; (2) the publication of two influential books by intellectuals from former French colonies; (3) the escalation of US involvement in Vietnam; and (4) the shifting emphasis from integration to building a separatist power base among racial and ethnic minority groups within the United States.

In the global realignment after World War II, many former European colonies in Africa and Asia fought for and gained their independence, often under the leadership of charismatic figures such as Jomo Kenyatta of Kenya and Kwame Nkrumah of Gold Coast (now Ghana). These leaders and movements inspired people in the United States and elsewhere to think in terms of decolonization. Albert Memmi and Frantz Fanon were French colonial subjects born in the 1920s. Both were writers and intellectuals who drew on existentialism, psychoanalysis, and other perspectives current in the Parisian circles they frequented in the early 1950s. Fanon's analysis of anti-Black racism, *Black Skin, White Masks*, was published to much acclaim in 1952. Memmi's novel *The Pillar of Salt*, based on his experiences as a Parisian Jew raised in Tunisia, followed in 1955. It was each author's second book, however, both with an introduction by Jean-Paul Sartre, that had the biggest and most lasting impact on anti-colonial thinking and activism. Memmi's *The Colonizer and the Colonized* came first, in 1957. This book analyzes the two parties identified in the title as a "linked duo whose fates are intertwined, [and] both of whom are disfigured by an inherently poisoned relationship built on myths and lies, but also on the force of law and economic exploitation." Fanon's book, *The Wretched of the Earth*, appeared in 1961 with an almost literal call to arms, arguing for the necessity of violence to overthrow colonial systems. The book had far-ranging influence on revolutionary movements as diverse as the Black Panthers, the Irish Republican Army, anti-apartheid activists in South Africa, and even the 1979 Iranian Revolution. The deepening American involvement in Vietnam from 1966 onward led anti-war activists increasingly to characterize the United States as an imperialist power. It was a short step from there to viewing the history of the country's treatment of its own minority groups in a similar manner. Some Black activists on the far left identified with the Vietnamese insurgents, with some leaders even traveling to North Vietnam in a show of solidarity.

Stokely Carmichael personified each of these four developments. Elected president of the Student Nonviolent Coordinating Committee (SNCC) in 1966; disillusioned by his experiences attempting to register voters in Greenwood, Mississippi, and elsewhere; and inspired by African liberation movements as well as by Fanon's book, he became increasingly outspoken against the Vietnam war. Carmichael changed his name to Kwame Ture in honor of two early proponents of Pan-Africanism, Ghanaian Kwame Nkrumah and Guinean Sékou Touré. He also contributed to the analytic reach and popularity of the internal colony perspective with the publication of his 1967 book, *Black Power: The Politics of Liberation*, coauthored with Columbia political scientist Charles V. Hamilton.

As political agitators embraced the internal colonies framework, the approach began to influence activist sociologists in the mid- to late 1960s. In 1965, Pablo Gonzalez Casanova published the first sustained academic treatment of the concept in "Internal Colonialism and National Development," in which he analyzes the situation of Mexican Indigenous peoples, first under Spanish and then under Mexican rule. Robert L. Allen's *Black Awakening in Capitalist America* (1969) views the Black radicalism of the late 1960s through the lens of internal colonialism. Allen pairs the perceived threat of Black Power and its calls for uprising with the violence of urban communities, from Watts in 1964 through the uprisings following Martin Luther King Jr.'s assassination in 1968. He argues that the white establishment—consisting of government, foundations, and corporations—was trying to co-opt the Black Power movement by offering middle-class status and control to its leaders.

Yet it was Robert Blauner's influential 1969 *Social Problems* article that was the first to develop the concept of internal colonies systematically and apply it to the experience of Black people in the United States (and later of Hispanic people, in his 1972 book, *Racial Oppression in America*). Blauner distinguishes between the histories of "immigrant" and "colonized" minorities in the United States, arguing that the colonized groups of enslaved Africans and of Mexicans in the Southwest could not be expected to follow the same trajectory as that of the voluntary immigrants from Europe. Blauner's primary purpose was to explain the uprisings in the Black ghettos of the 1960s, but his articulation allowed for broader application—a capacity that was seized upon by scholars working on the Southwest, Appalachia, and beyond.

In 1970, Joan Willard Moore, a prominent Black sociologist of Mexican American life, critically applied Blauner's version of the concept in a comparative look at that population's history across three states: New Mexico, Texas, and California. That same year, Helen Matthews Lewis and Edward E. Knipe presented a paper arguing for the concept's use in understanding the underdevelopment of Appalachia. This served as the basis for the later collected work *Colonialism in Modern America: The Appalachian Case*. Several years later, Mario Barrera and coauthors wrote "The Barrio as an Internal Colony," and applied Blauner's approach to urban Mexican American neighborhoods. His follow-up book, *Race and Class in the Southwest*, is an ambitious attempt to use internal colonialism as a key to understanding racial subjugation in the United States. Influenced by both Blauner's and Casanova's earlier formulations, Michael Hechter used the framework to explain the persistence and resurgence of ethnic identity in advanced industrial societies, an argument he applied to the European Celts in his 1975 book, *Internal Colonialism*.

The late 1960s and early 1970s saw the internal colony idea proliferate across social science disciplines and applied to a multitude of ethnic groups and countries. The South African apartheid system and Native peoples in Ecuador, Bolivia, and Colombia were some of the first to be examined, but the use of the framework rapidly expanded to research of places across the globe, culminating in 1979. In that year alone, individual studies applied the perspective to Alaska, the Austro-Hungarian Empire, the Cherokee Nation, Finland, France, Palestinians in Israel, Quebec, Sudan, and Thailand.

While the phrase "internal colonialism" appears across all these studies, the concept to which the studies refer is less than unified or cohesive. Each author developed their own analysis usually based on a single case, and each addressed a range of empirical issues from a particular disciplinary perspective. As early as 1971, one of the most influential proponents of the internal colony concept, Michael Hechter, asserted, "There does not seem to be a general consensus on a small number of essential defining features of internal colonialism." By the mid-1980s, a comprehensive review of the literature on internal colonies concluded, "What the concept gains in flexibility and adaptability, its theoretical application loses in rigor. Many intractable problems confront the formulators of internal colonial theories, and these difficulties are recognized by scholars . . . whose theses are particularly influential."

Perhaps because of this incoherence, the concept had virtually disappeared from the literature by the 1990s, and several original proponents of the model, including Robert Blauner, later renounced their support for it. A few researchers have continued to argue for "the continuing relevance of internal colonialism theory" (the subtitle of Charles Pinderhughes's 2009 dissertation), and a more recent article on the history of South Texas points to its ongoing use across several historical cases.

Nevertheless, the rapid eclipse of the internal colony model meant that none of this history was known to us when we began this project. By the time we entered graduate school, the literature on internal colonies was not part of the curriculum, even for students of poverty and race. As we explored common features of the regions identified by our Index of Deep Disadvantage, we inductively hit upon the idea of internal colonies because of the features these places had in common, which we identify in the first chapter of this book: reliance on a sole commodity for export that is tied to global/national markets; outside financing with profits flowing outside of the region; and a continuous supply of cheap, pliable laborers, resulting in social, political, and cultural subjugation. In an ironic parallel to the European colonial powers, we had "discovered" new territory only to find that many people had walked this path before we arrived.

Some prior applications of the internal colony framework are anchored in place, while in others, place plays no role. Our approach is firmly grounded in the specific places featured in this book. In another departure from much of the earlier literature, our historical analysis inductively identifies the essential elements that all these places have in common rather than focusing on the features of a single region. Our ethnographic analysis pinpoints mechanisms that have reproduced disadvantage across generations in these regions, even as the original conditions have changed.

The heart of our approach to internal colonies lies in the regional dependence on an ample supply of exploited labor to produce a single export commodity tied to global markets. For that reason (along with the practical considerations outlined in the introduction), we have not included Native Nations in our analysis, even though many counties containing Native lands are high on our index. According to sociologist and Native American expert C. Matthew Snipp, "Unlike their South American counterparts . . . there is little to suggest that the labor of North American Indians, either as farmers or factory workers, made an important contribution to the development of American capitalism." Instead, Snipp, writing in 1986, suggested that the term "captive nation" was more appropriate until such time as individual tribal lands saw their natural resources such as coal, oil, gas, and timber developed for exploitation by outside corporations—a process that accelerated in the 1980s. This is not to say that Native Americans were never exploited for their labor. Historian Andrés Reséndez has documented the horrifying regularity with which Native people were captured in wars or raids and sold to Anglos and others, including US officials, in the western territories of New Mexico and California. Reséndez estimates that between 147,000 and 340,000 Native Americans were ensnared in what he calls "the other slavery" in North America (including Mexico) between 1492 and 1900. The majority of them were women and children, valued as domestic servants and sometimes even forcibly "adopted" into Mormon families in the new Utah Territory.

HOW IS THE INTERNAL COLONIALISM PERSPECTIVE DISTINCTIVE?

At first glance, internal colonialism theory may seem like a repackaging of other, earlier theories, such as resource curse, community-level trauma, what we'll call "toxic South" perspectives, continuing legacies of place, and the macro-level costs of inequality. In this section, we aim to show where our approach is complementary yet distinctive.

Resource Curse: Also known as the paradox of plenty, resource curse theory was originally advanced to explain the paradox of how nations with especially abundant natural resources tend to suffer more adverse outcomes both economically (in terms of GDP) and socially (in terms of degraded democracy and human rights) than those with fewer natural resources. This perspective has engendered lively debate, with contemporary experts acknowledging that a resource curse is not inevitable, but is rather contingent on certain conditions, such as the price of the commodity, the volatility of its market, and the quality of governance.

We argue that the conditions of extreme exploitation that we document in this book did not inevitably flow from the rich soil, mineral endowments, or natural aquifers of these regions. Nor were they merely contingent on market factors. Instead, in each region they also flowed from government policy (e.g., the misappropriation of Indigenous lands) and from the attitudes and behaviors of an elite class. Indeed, historian Sven Beckert has shown that cotton was cultivated in Egypt and India for centuries without the exploitative conditions practiced in the United States. Furthermore, according to economist Gavin Wright, crops such as cotton and tobacco could have been just as profitably grown on family farms as on large plantations.

Community-Level Trauma: Trauma theory posits that the trauma of the original sin (in the case of the United States, slavery and other less extreme forms of human exploitation) can be passed down through the generations via epigenetics—changes in gene expression due to exposure to extreme stress and material deprivation. While this may well be true, our analysis focuses on how the highly exploitative economic practices of America's internal colonies became inscribed in social relations and community institutions, persisting even today and reproducing conditions that perpetuate exposure to hardship. Could our approach be viewed instead as an institutionalist version of trauma theory in which the original sin of slavery and other, less extreme forms of human exploitation are passed on via institutions rather than epigenetics? This rendition comes closer to our argument, but we part ways with the implication that this original sin would *inevitably* engender a full-on embracing of exploitative practices. We can at least imagine a world in which the reaction to this original sin would be to repudiate exploitative practices rather than embrace them and inscribe them (and indeed, as noted in the next section, some subregions of the South were somewhat less exploitative than others).

Toxic South Perspectives: A number of influential scholars from the mid-1800s onward, such as journalist and, later, urban planner Frederick Law Olmsted (who conducted several tours of the South between 1852 and 1857 as a correspondent for the *New York Times*) and 1930s-era southern studies scholars Howard W. Odum and Rupert B. Vance, argued that, due to its unique history and its distinctive economic and social arrangements, the South is more prone to myriad forms of disadvantage than other regions of the United States. In 1938, these distinctions were cataloged in the US National Emergency Council's "Report on Economic Conditions of the South." This report led President Franklin D. Roosevelt to proclaim the South "America's No. 1 economic problem." We have found, however, that only some subregions of the South rank as "most disadvantaged" on our index, and we argue that particular subregions within the South have had especially exploitative histories that must be reckoned with.

Continuing Legacies of Place: Sociologist Robert Sampson has shown that within cities, neighborhoods have enduring legacies. Despite population turnover, advantaged neighborhoods tend to retain their benefits, while less well-off neighborhoods tend to continue to face challenges. This book provides an example of that phenomenon playing out in much larger units of geography—not just in neighborhoods within a given city, but in counties and cities nationwide. Our focus is on a particular type of place, namely high-exploitation regions within the United States. We suspect, though we cannot say for sure, that the legacies of high exploitation-based regions may be more likely to persist over time in these areas than in other types of places.

What can explain this continuity? Sampson and colleagues focus on the role of social psychological factors such as perceptions of disorder, neighborhood stereotypes, shared expectations, and legal cynicism. He argues persuasively that these, along with larger social forces, "may be underappreciated causes of community wellbeing."

Our analysis highlights several mechanisms that have operated in high-exploitation places, many of which have become inscribed on social relations and community institutions. Social psychological mechanisms are undoubtedly at work in these places as well, though they are unlikely to be the prime factors in the histories of social and economic subjugation we document here. We cannot test this hunch, however, as data on these mechanisms are not available for counties and cities across the United States.

Macro-Level Costs of Inequality: There's a growing scholarly consensus that, while some inequality may increase total productivity (because inequality is incentivizing), inequality becomes counterproductive when it gets too high. It is particularly problematic, some argue, when societies have high levels of "bad inequality" arising "from market failure in the form of corruption and sweetheart deals that benefit those at the top, and various labor market bottlenecks at

the bottom that prevent poor children from fairly pursuing opportunities."

In America's internal colonies, massive inequality between the
haves and the have-nots was (and continues to be) a key feature
by definition; their very existence economically was predicated
upon the availability of cheap, exploitable people to work the land
(whether above or under the ground). This book is further evidence
that "bad inequality" has long been pervasive in these regions. While
our findings complement research in this vein, we move beyond
this approach to document the deep historic roots of present-day
inequalities, as well as the complex array of mechanisms tying the
present to the past.

Appendix B

The Index of Deep Disadvantage

with Silvia Robles, Jasmine Simington, and Samiul Jubaed

We call the approach we used in this study "iterative mixed methods research." It builds on methods developed in Edin and Shaefer's 2015 book, *$2.00 a Day: Living on Almost Nothing in America*, where big data was combined with systematic, in-depth qualitative interviews and ethnographic observation, putting these research methods into conversation with one another. In *The Injustice of Place*, we added deep historical analysis to better understand the rich array of social forces that drive present-day realities in each of the regions identified by our index as deeply disadvantaged. In sites that were representative of these regions, we interviewed and observed low-income families in an effort to paint a vivid portrait of the lived experiences of the least advantaged residents in each community, as well as key stakeholders, including elected officials, civil servants, faith leaders, those in the nonprofit sector, and representatives of the business community. From these qualitative data, we sought to uncover the specific processes and mechanisms that serve to link present-day realities with the sharply exploitative systems that dominated these places in the past.

In the first stage of this project, we built a multidimensional index of disadvantage that we used to rank the level of disadvantage in all US counties and the 500 largest cities across the nation. Guided by the conceptual framework detailed in this appendix, our Index of Deep Disadvantage includes select data from surveys and administrative sources on metrics that are well measured across jurisdictions and averaged across multiple years. Our collaborator Silvia Robles suggested that we use a statistical technique called principal component analysis (PCA) to weight these variables (standardized for comparison). This method was ideal for our purposes, as there was no a priori way to weight the factors that make up the index. Instead, PCA uses machine learning to see how all these factors best fit together.

Based on the output, we ranked counties and cities on a continuum of disadvantage. To our knowledge, no other researchers have attempted an apples-to-apples comparison of US communities encompassing counties and cities, and few other studies have attempted to combine multiple indicators reflecting multiple dimensions of disadvantage across counties and cities. Readers might want to know why we did not include certain metrics in our index that might be particularly salient to them. After we reached consensus on the basic set of indicators to use, we tried to be as parsimonious as possible. These indicators reflect three dimensions of disadvantage of high salience in American society: *cyclical measures*, which vary with the economy (poverty, deep poverty); *cumulative measures*, which reflect how the long-term exposure to disadvantage shapes outcomes over the longer term, such as people's health (low birth weight, shorter than average life expectancy); and *structural measures*, which reflect the degree to which the labor market offers opportunities, among other things (the rate of intergenerational mobility). We did try including other obvious candidates, such as the Gini Index (a measure of inequality in a place), but doing so didn't alter our results in any significant way. To allow other researchers an opportunity to vet—and possibly improve—our approach, we've made the data publicly available on the Poverty Solutions website at the University of Michigan.

In constructing the index, and following the work of sociologist

James Coleman, we sought to identify the key macro-level dependent variables that would capture these three critical dimensions of disadvantage. We then relied on ethnography and historical analysis to tease out the key macro-level independent variable: whether a place was part of a region that had been an internal colony. We also used ethnography and history to identify the micro-level variables—the mechanisms—that linked these macro-level independent (was the place an internal colony?) and dependent (the index combining indicators of poverty, health, and mobility) variables. It is these micro-level dynamics, we argue, that can help to explain the continuity between the economic and social systems of the distant past with present-day outcomes.

CYCLICAL MEASURES OF DISADVANTAGE

To capture cyclical disadvantage, we included two measures of income poverty: the percentage of the population living below the poverty line and the percentage living under half of the poverty line. Importantly, poverty rates rise and fall within a place over time along with the strength of the local labor market and economic conditions. We chose the official poverty measure because a myriad of evidence, including our own past work, has demonstrated that income poverty is deleterious to well-being. We also noted how, over time, the official poverty measure tracks closely with measures of material hardship, such as food insecurity and difficulty paying for basic expenses. The official poverty measure, in fact, does a bit better on this count than alternative measures such as the supplemental poverty measure, and better than some prominent expenditure and consumption poverty measures. Finally, it has the benefit of being consistently available for all counties and cities using the American Community Survey (ACS). Deep poverty acts as a marker of the depth of poverty in a community. Research has found that deep poverty presents challenges above and beyond poverty.

CUMULATIVE MEASURES OF DISADVANTAGE

To capture cumulative disadvantage, we included two health measures, the percentage of infants with low birth weight and average life expectancy, thus capturing health at the beginning and the end of life. Low birth weight is known to reflect the cumulative disadvantages of children's parents, thus capturing some of the intergenerational disadvantage passed down from parents to children. In addition, children with low birth weight are more vulnerable to early mortality and a whole host of other deleterious outcomes in childhood and throughout life, so it is a predictor of future disadvantage. Shorter than average life expectancy reflects cumulative disadvantages experienced over a lifetime.

STRUCTURAL MEASURES OF DISADVANTAGE

Finally, to capture the structural dimension of disadvantage, we used the rate of social mobility—more specifically, the likelihood that a low-income child in a community will enter the middle class in adulthood. This indicator reflects the structure of a place. Does that community allow poor children the same chance to advance as other children who grow up with more resources?

WHAT IS NEW WITH THE INDEX OF DEEP DISADVANTAGE?

Many researchers have compared a single outcome or a set of outcomes in one domain across counties or neighborhoods in the United States. For instance, researchers at the US Department of Agriculture have documented that those counties with the most persistently high poverty rates are mostly rural, which is consonant with our findings. However, that research focused on only income-based poverty and did not account for the cumulative or structural dimensions of disadvantage. Nor did it rank cities in conjunction with counties. This is important because the affluence of a surrounding county can shroud a city's disadvantage, as is the case with Detroit and Wayne County. Conversely, others have argued that poverty is worse in cities than in rural areas because of the higher cost of living in urban versus rural places (though these critics often fail to account for the greater transportation costs and lower availability of health and social services for those living in rural areas). By including both counties and cities, and by using multidimensional indicators rather than a single metric, we sought to address both concerns.

Our multidimensional approach follows that of Nobel Prize–winning economist Amartya Sen, who called for a multidimensional method of poverty measurement. His call has yielded new tools, such as the US Census Bureau's multidimensional deprivation index. Yet that index still measures disadvantage at the *person* and not the *community* level. Thus, though a vital complement to our work, it fails to identify America's most deeply disadvantaged places, which the Index of Deep Disadvantage has sought to do. Public health researchers sometimes employ a tool called the social vulnerability index (SVI), which they use to gauge risk in a given neighborhood. Yet the SVI does not include cumulative measures such as health or structural measures such as social mobility, relying instead on the socioeconomic characteristics of a neighborhood. Additionally, neighborhood-based measures (usually based on census tracts) are not as useful as county-based measures in rural places.

Table A1 compares a series of outcomes for the 200 places of most disadvantage, the national average, and the 200 places of greatest advantage, all according to our index. All averages are population weighted. We estimate that 3.6 million Americans live in the nation's 100 most disadvantaged places. Roughly 11.3 million live in the nation's 200 most disadvantaged places. More people live in these 200 places than in any one of forty-two states in the Union.

The places of deepest disadvantage have roughly twice the rates of poverty and deep poverty as the national average, and rates of poverty that are many times higher than the 200 places of greatest advantage.

TABLE A1: SELECTED OUTCOMES FOR
COMMUNITIES BY INDEX RANK

OUTCOME	200 PLACES OF MOST DISADVANTAGE	NATIONAL AVERAGE	200 PLACES OF GREATEST ADVANTAGE
Poverty (%)	26.8	13.7	5.6
Deep Poverty (%)	13.2	6.2	2.6
Life Expectancy (Years)	74.2	79.1	83.1
Low Infant Birth Weight (%)	12.2	8.2	6.6
Social Mobility (Chetty-Hendren)	36.5	43.1	49.8
Non-Hispanic White (%)	37.9	56.6	70.0
Non-Hispanic Black (%)	48.4	13.3	3.7
Hispanic (%)	7.3	20.5	11.1
Less Than High School (%)	16.7	12.7	6.4
College Graduate (%)	22.8	32.7	48.6
Unemployment Rate (%)	9.5	5.5	3.2
Labor Force Participation Rate (%)	57.0	63.6	69.6
Gini Index (Inequality)	50.7	46.5	42.8
Severe Housing Burden (%)	17.8	15.0	10.9
Own Home (%)	51.9	60.7	72.0

Life expectancy is nearly five years shorter than the national average
and nine years shorter than in the places of greatest advantage. The
200 places of deepest disadvantage also have highly elevated rates
of low infant birth weight, life expectancy, and markedly low rates
of social mobility. Only 38 percent of residents in these places are
non-Hispanic white, while nearly one-half are non-Hispanic Black.
Interestingly, Hispanic Americans are underrepresented among the
nation's 200 most disadvantaged places. Rates of educational attainment are much lower and unemployment rates much higher in the
200 places of deepest disadvantage.

After we learned that the places of deepest disadvantage were
dominated by rural communities, we presumed that they would not
also exhibit high levels of inequality. This presumption is wrong; in
fact, they have rates of inequality that are somewhat higher than the
national average and markedly higher than the 200 places of greatest advantage. Another presumption was that poor residents of very
poor places would not have the housing affordability challenges of
those living in larger cities. Yet we found that the percentage of residents in these places who experience severe housing cost burden is
higher than the national average. It is equal to the average rate of
severe housing burden experienced in the 500 largest cities. Rates
of homeownership are also well below the national average and dramatically lower than in the 200 places of greatest advantage. Across
all the outcomes we examined, we see improvement as we move up
the index: outcomes look better for places ranked 201 to 400 most
disadvantaged according to our index compared to those ranked 1 to
200, and better still for places ranked 401 to 600.

Our Index of Deep Disadvantage reveals patterns that are broadly
similar to those based on any one of the index components, but together the factors tell us more than any one of them does by itself.
For example, Zavala County, Texas, would rank 50th if measured by
the poverty rate, but according to our index it ranks 140th because
it does better in terms of intergenerational mobility and health than
other counties with similar poverty rates. We believe this information

deepens our understanding of the circumstances of this community. An even more extreme example is Dimmit County, Texas, which would rank 45th by the poverty rate but is 534th on our index because of strong mobility and health outcomes. In contrast, Marion County, South Carolina, would rank 414th by the poverty rate alone, but it is 138th on our index because of its very low rate of social mobility and especially poor health outcomes. We believe that our index offers a richer way to assess disadvantage across cities and counties than other available methods.

MORE DETAILS ON SOURCES OF DATA FOR THE COMPONENTS OF THE INDEX

Income

We drew on traditional measures of income-based poverty recognized by the US Census Bureau, including (1) the percentage of the population reporting cash income that falls below the official poverty measure, which has been updated annually by the Census Bureau according to measures of inflation based on the consumer price index since the late 1960s; and (2) the percentage reporting cash incomes falling below 50 percent of the official poverty level, often referred to as "deep poverty." The estimates for counties and cities come from the 2019 ACS, five-year estimates. For these measures, the poverty threshold varies by household size, but not by geographic area.

To calculate poverty rates adjusted for the presence of postsecondary educational institutions, whose students may be only temporarily poor, we followed the approach used by Feeding America, using 2019 ACS five-year estimates of poverty disaggregated by postsecondary enrollment at the city and county levels. These estimates are based on the population that is at least three years old as their universe. Consequently, we used the same population in defining the population in our adjusted poverty and deep poverty rates. Thus, we computed the adjusted poverty rate by dividing the population (of at least three years old) living below the poverty line who were not enrolled in college by the total population (of at least three years old) who were not enrolled in college.

In applying PCA, we retained the unadjusted poverty and deep poverty rates in cases where there were not meaningful differences between those rates and the adjusted rates. To identify those places for which adjustment was needed, we calculated the percent difference between original and college-adjusted poverty rates and converted those to z-scores disaggregated by type of jurisdiction (i.e., county versus city). "Outliers" were marked as such if the z-score was greater than 3, in which case we substituted the college-adjusted poverty rate for the original.

Adjusting the deep poverty rate required more finesse. Since the income ratio disaggregated by school enrollment was not available through the ACS, we used a combination of estimates of the income ratio disaggregated by age and by school enrollment as proxy measures. We first computed the population enrolled in higher education (college/graduate school) by age bracket (18–24, 25–34, and 35+ years old), and the corresponding age bracket percentages for the population with a postsecondary degree. Then we imputed the population living in deep poverty for the same age brackets, which we multiplied by the percentage of enrolled students in each age bracket and summed to estimate the population of college students living in deep poverty. Finally, to calculate the adjusted deep poverty rate, we divided the total population living in deep poverty, minus the college deep poverty population, by the total population not enrolled in college. As we did for the poverty rate, we only replaced the deep poverty rate to adjust for students enrolled at colleges and universities in the same instances in which we replaced the poverty rate as described in the previous paragraph.

We note here that there are alternate poverty rates available from the Census Bureau, such as the ones available from its QuickFacts, which are derived from the Small Area Income and Poverty Estimates (SAIPE) program. The SAIPE methodology uses regression models to predict county-level poverty estimates by combining ACS single-year estimates with administrative records and census data. For city-level predictions, SAIPE aggregates estimates from the school district level. This produces poverty rates that sometimes differ significantly from the ACS five-year estimates. We opted to use the ACS five-year estimates in order to access finer disaggregate poverty rates such as education and age brackets, which are not available via SAIPE, and because ACS poverty rates are derived from reports from a representative sample rather than being model based.

Health

We utilized two measures of health, one that captures health at the beginning of life and another that captures health at the end of life. The county/city life expectancy level at birth was drawn from publicly available data from the 2019 University of Wisconsin County Health Rankings & Roadmaps and the City Health Dashboard. Life expectancy was estimated using de-identified, official death records from the National Center for Health Statistics (NCHS) and population counts from the Census Bureau, the NCHS, and the Human Mortality Database. Due to data availability, for counties life expectancy was estimated based on a three-year average from 2015 to 2017, while for cities life expectancy was estimated based on a six-year average from 2010 to 2015.

The low birth weight rate represents a county or city's share of live births weighing less than 2,500 grams. Once again, we drew these data from the 2019 County Health Rankings and the City Health Dashboard, which build on data from the NCHS natality files. The County Health Rankings documentation notes that "these data are submitted by the vital registration systems operated in the jurisdictions legally responsible for registering vital events (i.e. births, deaths, marriages, divorces, and fetal deaths). Missing values are reported for all counties where fewer than 20 births were considered low birth weight." For cities, low birth weight is calculated based on a three-year average for the time period 2015–2017. For counties (and due to data suppression concerns), the measure captures the time period 2011–2017.

Social Mobility

The measure of social mobility we used captures the likelihood that a child who grows up low-income in a community can rise to the middle class (or beyond) in adulthood. We used novel data drawn from federal income tax returns from a cohort of Americans born from 1980 to 1986. Raj Chetty and Nathaniel Hendren have made these data publicly available by a variety of jurisdictions, including counties and cities. These estimates capture the mean household income rank for children at age twenty-six whose parents were in the twenty-fifth percentile of the national income distribution. Adult income is defined as the sum of one's own and one's spouse's income. By focusing on people whose parents were in the twenty-fifth percentile of the national income rankings, we could capture the rate of intergenerational mobility specifically for lower-income populations who may be more vulnerable to variation in local conditions relative to high-income populations who can use their individual resources to insulate themselves from deficits in community resources. To estimate mobility for the top 500 cities, we used the same mean household income rank variable from the Chetty and Hendren team in our index, but starting at the tract level, our index aggregates up to the city level. We verified the legitimacy of the tract-to-city aggregation by also aggregating from census tract to county, then comparing the aggregated tract-to-county estimates with the publicly available county estimates. Less than 1 percent of counties had an aggregate tract-to-county measure that was one standard deviation away from the county estimate, giving us confidence that the tract-to-city aggregation is sound.

GEOGRAPHIC UNIT OF ANALYSIS

Defining "communities" is always challenging. In our case, the primary objective was to compare communities across a set of reasonably well-measured metrics—and so counties and cities became our primary units of analysis. To our knowledge, this is the first such index to compare both counties and cities on the same outcomes, thus our claim to a novel "apples-to-apples" comparison.

One might argue that some cities with extremely high rates of inequality, such as New York City or Los Angeles, will not appear on our index because the disadvantage in these places is hidden by their proximity to areas of affluence. Yet the same argument could be made for some counties. As we found, many of the counties that are high on our index also have very high levels of inequality.

In the event that the city and county were spatially equivalent units, we included only the county observation, while flagging in our data that it is also a city. Note that in these cases, we found that the city and county estimates are virtually identical, as should be the case.

We classified counties as urban or rural using definitions from the National Center for Health Statistics, which offer more nuance than census definitions. Furthermore, counties that include any form of federally recognized tribal land are flagged as such, using standard census and Office of Management and Budget definitions.

Dealing with Missing Data

The data set contained some missing values for the mobility, life expectancy, and low birth weight variables (but not poverty and deep poverty). In lieu of dropping these observations, we opted for imputation using a geostatistical technique known as "areal interpolation" in ArcGIS, which takes available data from a (source) set of polygons and predicts corresponding values at a (target) set of polygons. This technique is often used to interpolate variables that are available at a certain geographic level to another geographic level (e.g., estimating student obesity rates at the census tract level using rates at the school district level). In our case, our source and target polygons were the same: US counties to counties, and cities to cities.

We used ArcGIS's Geostatistical Wizard to apply areal interpolation layers using data from each of the three variables. For each variable, we adjusted the procedure's parameters of lag size and number of lags: for mobility, we chose a lag size of 7 and number of lags 8; for life expectancy, a lag size of 6 and number of lags 6; and for low birth weight, a lag size of 9 and number of lags 9. These parameters provided acceptable errors during cross-validation. We substituted the missing data with the predicted values for each region, after which we applied PCA to the newly complete data set.

For the cities of Covington, Radford, Petersburg, Martinsville, Galax, Danville, and Hopewell, all in Virginia, our visual audit did not square with their ranking on the index. We determined that given other demographic characteristics of the population, available values of life expectancy and low birth weight were almost certainly incorrect and should be dropped from the analysis. These values were then imputed using areal interpolation in ArcGIS as described in the previous paragraph. The parameters for running areal interpolation to impute life expectancy and low birth weight were a lag size of 5 and number of lags 6, and a lag size of 10 and number of lags 10, respectively.

Methodology

The Index of Deep Disadvantage is the first principal component from a PCA of the five factors in our index. PCA is a technique often chosen to reduce the dimensions being considered in prediction-style analysis. This made it a natural choice to summarize the information carried across the five factors we chose. The five factors, while highly correlated, also highlight different dimensions of disadvantage, as explained earlier in this appendix. PCA yielded a weighted average of the five features where the weightings were chosen to capture as much of the variation in the observed data as possible.

The first step was to gather the variables. PCA is sensitive to the magnitude of each feature included. Therefore, after merging all five factors into one data set, each feature was normalized by subtracting its mean and dividing by its standard deviation. The first principal component represents nearly 65 percent of the variation (or information) in the data. Interestingly, the weights on each variable were fairly even, with a slightly higher loading on the share of community residents in poverty.

Notes

Introduction

2 *less than $2 per person per day:* Kathryn Edin and H. Luke Shaefer, *$2.00 a Day: Living on Almost Nothing in America* (New York: Houghton Mifflin Harcourt, 2015).

2 *place is key:* William Julius Wilson, *The Truly Disadvantaged: The Inner City, the Underclass, and Public Policy* (Chicago: University of Chicago Press, 1987).

2 *made the case:* Matthew Desmond, *Evicted: Poverty and Profit in the American City* (New York: Crown, 2016); Matthew Desmond and Bruce Western, "Poverty in America: New Directions and Debates," *Annual Review of Sociology* 44, no. 1 (2018): 305–18.

3 *food on the table:* Gordon M. Fisher, "The Development and History of the Poverty Thresholds," *Social Security Bulletin* 55, no. 4 (1992), www.ssa.gov /history/fisheronpoverty.html.

3 *life expectancy:* H. Luke Shaefer, Pinghui Wu, and Kathryn Edin, "Can Poverty in America Be Compared to Conditions in the World's Poorest Countries?," *American Journal of Medical Research* 4, no. 1 (2017): 84–92. For life expectancy rates, see S. Jay Olshansky et al., "Differences in Life Expectancy Due to Race and Educational Differences Are Widening, and Many May Not Catch Up," *Health Affairs* 31, no. 8 (2012): 1803–13, doi:10.1377/hlthaff.2011.0746. Amartya Sen makes similar comparisons in his book *Development as Freedom* (New York: Oxford University Press, 1999).

3 *non-Hispanic whites:* Shaefer, Wu, and Edin, "Can Poverty in America Be Compared?"

3 *shaped more by their context:* Paula Braveman and Laura Gottlieb, "The Social Determinants of Health: It's Time to Consider the Causes of the Causes," *Public Health Reports* 129, suppl. 2 (2014): 19–31; Carlyn M. Hood, Keith P. Gennuso, Geoffrey R. Swain, and Bridget B. Catlin, "County Health Rankings: Relationships Between Determinant Factors and Health Outcomes," *American Journal of Preventive Medicine* 50, no. 2 (2016): 129–35.

4   *a particular community:* See appendix B for more details.

4   *do better than their parents:* Raj Chetty, David Grusky, Maximilian Hell, Nathaniel Hendren, Robert Manduca, and Jimmy Narang, "The Fading American Dream: Trends in Absolute Income Mobility Since 1940," *Science* 356, no. 6336 (2017): 398–406.

4   *used tax records:* Raj Chetty and Nathaniel Hendren, "The Impacts of Neighborhoods on Intergenerational Mobility II: County-Level Estimates," *Quarterly Journal of Economics* 133, no. 3 (2018): 1163–228.

4   *much better chance:* Chetty and Hendren, "Impacts of Neighborhoods."

4   *being held back:* Desmond and Western, "Poverty in America."

5   *a long way:* See appendix B for more details.

5   *"most disadvantaged":* Similarly, researchers at the US Department of Agriculture have documented that among counties, those with persistently high poverty rates are predominantly rural. "Rural Poverty & Well-Being," USDA Economic Research Service, last updated March 7, 2022, www.ers.usda.gov/topics/rural-economy-population/rural-poverty-well-being/. These findings, however, do not attempt to compare counties to the 500 largest cities. This is important because a surrounding county can shroud a city's poverty, as is the case with Wayne County, Michigan, and Detroit. Others also argue that poverty is worse in big cities because of the higher cost of living there. Our method is the first to seek to address both these concerns by comparing counties and cities directly and by using multiple factors in an index, rather than just one metric, to take a more holistic approach that mitigates arguments about differences in cost of living. Nobel Prize–winning economist Amartya Sen spurred efforts for a multidimensional method of poverty measurement, outlined in his book *Development as Freedom.* Yet such approaches typically still measure poverty at the individual level rather than for communities, as we do. Public health has a measure called the social vulnerability index used to gauge the risk of neighborhoods. Yet interestingly the SVI does not include measures of community-level health or social mobility.

6   *not one community:* To view an interactive map of our index, see "Understanding Communities of Deep Disadvantage," Poverty Solutions, University of Michigan, https://poverty.umich.edu/projects/understanding-communities-of-deep-disadvantage/.

6   *paying for housing:* According to our data, America's 500 largest cities report a rate of severe housing burden (meaning families are spending more than half their incomes on housing) of 17.7 percent. The rate of severe housing burden among the nation's 200 most disadvantaged places according to our index was 17.8 percent.

8   *county seat's name:* "A Brief History of Our City," Falfurrias, Texas, website, https://falfurrias.us/history/.

9   *"nation within a nation":* For a more thorough discussion of the concept of internal colonies, see appendix A. For a full history of Black scholars'

use of the framework, see Charles Pinderhughes, "Toward a New Theory of Internal Colonialism," *Socialism and Democracy* 25, no. 1 (March 2011): 235–56, https://doi.org/10.1080/08854300.2011.559702.

9   *build on this work:* See appendix B for a more detailed discussion.

9   *adult illiteracy rates:* See "U.S. Skills Map: State and County Indicators of Adult Literacy and Numeracy," Program for the International Assessment of Adult Competencies (PIAAC), National Center for Education Statistics, https://nces.ed.gov/surveys/piaac/skillsmap/. As we will describe in chapter 2, in Brooks and Zavala Counties, the percentage of adults who are at or below "level 1 literacy"—comparable to a first grader learning to read—is well above the national average.

11   *a century and a half ago:* See, for example, Rodney Andrews, Marcus Casey, Bradley L. Hardy, and Trevon D. Logan, "Location Matters: Historical Racial Segregation and Intergenerational Mobility," *Economic Letters* 158 (2017): 67–72; Avidit Acharya, Matthew Blackwell, and Maya Sen, "The Political Legacy of American Slavery," *Journal of Politics* 78, no. 3 (July 2016): 621–41; T. M. Tonmoy Islam, Jenny Minier, and James P. Ziliak, "On Persistent Poverty in a Rich Country," *Southern Economic Journal* 81, no. 3 (2015): 653–78; Thor Berger, "Places of Persistence: Slavery and the Geography of Intergenerational Mobility in the United States," *Demography* 55 (2018): 1547–65.

11   *reached its apex:* These authors' works are discussed in depth throughout this book.

11   *valuable insights:* James C. Cobb, *The Most Southern Place on Earth: The Mississippi Delta and the Roots of Regional Identity* (Oxford: Oxford University Press, 1992).

11   *Ned Cobb:* Theodore Rosengarten, *All God's Dangers: The Life of Nate Shaw* (New York: Knopf, 1974).

13   *After enslavement and disease:* Andrés Reséndez, *The Other Slavery: The Uncovered Story of Indian Enslavement in America* (New York: Mariner Books, 2016).

13   *disproportionate share of Native lives:* Rhitu Chatterjee, "Hit Hard by COVID, Native Americans Come Together to Protect Their Families and Elders," Shots, NPR, November 24, 2021, www.npr.org/sections/health-shots/2021/11/24/1058675230/hit-hard-by-covid-native-americans-come-together-to-protect-families-and-elders.

13   *declared the checkpoints illegal:* Lee Strubinger, "Native American Tribes Defy South Dakota Orders to Remove Checkpoints," *Morning Edition*, NPR, May 12, 2020, www.npr.org/2020/05/12/854363912/native-american-tribes-defy-south-dakota-orders-to-remove-checkpoints.

15   *Theodore Roosevelt praised:* Melissa Block, "Here's What's Become of a Historic All-Black Town in the Mississippi Delta," Our Land, NPR, March 8, 2017, www.npr.org/2017/03/08/515814287/heres-whats-become-of-a-historic-all-black-town-in-the-mississippi-delta.

15   *vast majority of Black farm owners:* Vann R. Newkirk III, "The Great Land Robbery: The Shameful Story of How 1 Million Black Families Have Been Ripped from Their Farms," *The Atlantic*, September 2019, www .theatlantic.com/magazine/archive/2019/09/this-land-was-our-land /594742/.; Joel Nathan Rosen, "Mound Bayou," Mississippi Encyclopedia, https://mississippiencyclopedia.org/entries/mound-bayou/.

15   *"Lynch Colored School":* "African American Schools in Harlan County, KY," Notable Kentucky African Americans Database, https://nkaa.uky.edu /nkaa/items/show/2797.

16   *decline in the demand for labor:* Harry M. Caudill, *Night Comes to the Cumberlands: A Biography of a Depressed Area* (Boston: Little, Brown, 1963).

17   *"The Great Society rests":* https://www.americanrhetoric.com/speeches /lbjthegreatsociety.htm.

Chapter 1: America's Internal Colonies

19   *honored the cartoon character:* The town fathers placed the Popeye statue on this spot in 1937 as a tribute to cartoonist E. C. Segar, whose 1929 creation Popeye the Sailor Man increased spinach consumption in the United States by fully a third between 1931 and 1936, according to industry experts—a boon to the town that was, by then, producing more spinach than any other place in the world.

20   *Cotton Ball:* Andy Lo, "King and Queen," *Greenwood (MS) Commonwealth*, March 1, 2022, 1.

21   *"the Coal Company House":* https://beckley.org/coal-mine/.

21   *markers of local pride:* Robert Wuthnow, *Small-Town America: Building Community, Shaping the Future* (Princeton, NJ: Princeton University Press, 2013), 352–55.

23   *separating the cotton fibers:* Long-staple cotton had seeds that were easier to separate, but most southern soil was not ideal for its cultivation.

23   *including Catherine Greene herself:* "Eli Whitney's Patent for the Cotton Gin," Educator Resources, National Archives, www.archives.gov/education /lessons/cotton-gin-patent#:~:text=Whitney%20Patents%20a%20 Cotton%20Gin&text=Whitney%20received%20a%20patent%20for, inventors%20of%20the%20cotton%20gin. See also "Catherine Littlefield Greene," Your Dictionary, https://biography.yourdictionary.com /catherine-littlefield-greene.

23   *great cotton rush:* The story of Whitney and the cotton gin can be found in Daniel A. Wren and Ronald G. Greenwood, "Business Leaders: A Historical Sketch of Eli Whitney," *Journal of Leadership Studies* 6, nos. 1–2 (July 1, 1999): 128–32, https://doi.org/10.1177/107179199900600110; David L. Cohn, *The Life and Times of King Cotton* (New York: Oxford University Press, 1956).

23   *moved westward:* Sven Beckert, *Empire of Cotton: A Global History* (New York: Vintage Books, 2014), 104.

24   *"twin hubs"*: Beckert, *Empire of Cotton*, 103.

24   *palatial mansion:* Jim Fraiser, "Greenwood Leflore's Malmaison: Prosperity and Power," *Greenwood (MS) Commonwealth*, November 7, 2001, www.gwcommonwealth.com/archives/greenwood-leflores-malmaison -prosperity-and-power#sthash.ilICjl9D.dpbs.

24   *"the Wilderness"*: Frank E. Smith, *The Yazoo River* (Jackson: University Press of Mississippi, 1954), 41.

24   *"exceptional fertility"*: Cobb, *Most Southern Place on Earth*, 8.

24   *human destiny unfolded:* The area is more accurately known as the Yazoo-Mississippi floodplain to distinguish it from where the Mississippi River empties into the Gulf of Mexico south of New Orleans.

24   *"King Cotton that is"*: John Willis, *Forgotten Time: The Yazoo-Mississippi Delta After the Civil War* (Charlottesville: University of Virginia Press, 2000), 1.

25   *"66 million pounds of cotton"*: Beckert, *Empire of Cotton*, 113.

25   *dependence on outside capital:* During this time, southern cities became the "regional branches of Northern and European sources of credit." Jack Temple Kirby, *Rural Worlds Lost: The American South, 1920–1960* (Baton Rouge: Louisiana State University Press, 1987), 26.

25   *5.6 million manufacturing jobs:* Jay R. Mandle, *The Roots of Black Poverty: The Southern Plantation Economy After the Civil War* (Durham, NC: Duke University Press, 1978), 21.

25   *"commercial dependence"*: Ulrich B. Phillips, "The Decadence of the Plantation System," *Annals of the American Academy of Political and Social Science* 35, no. 1 (1910): 39.

25   *"form of mysticism"*: David L. Cohn, *God Shakes Creation* (London: Harper & Brothers, 1935), 41.

26   *Queen Anne and Classical Revival mansions:* Donny Whitehead and Mary Carol Miller, *Greenwood*, Postcard History Series (Charleston, SC: Arcadia Publishing, 2009).

26   Travel Guide to the Magnolia State: Federal Writers' Project of the Works Progress Administration, *Mississippi: The WPA Guide to the Magnolia State*, American Guide Series (New York: Viking Press, 1938).

26   *half of these landowners' debts:* Thomas J. Woofter, *Landlord and Tenant on the Cotton Plantation*, Research Monograph No. 5 (Washington, DC: Works Progress Administration, 1936), xxv.

26   *offered this diagnosis:* Woofter, *Landlord and Tenant*, xx.

26   *"flat cotton fields"*: John Dollard, *Caste and Class in a Southern Town* (New York: Doubleday Anchor Books, 1937), 6.

27   *"decaying plantations"*: Charles S. Johnson, *Shadow of the Plantation* (Chicago: University of Chicago Press, 1934), 12–13. While the same patterns could be observed across much of the South, scholars argued that the economic caste system described in this book found its fullest form in the Cotton Belt. Three anthropologists of the day, Allison Davis, Burleigh

Gardner, and Mary Gardner, wrote that the "cotton kingdom represents virtually a culture of its own," one "built around the single commercial crop of cotton [and] its vast Negro population inherited from the plantation economy of slavery." This system produced a "rigid cycle of life" that yielded a "low level of living for . . . producers of the crop." Allison Davis, Burleigh B. Gardner, and Mary R. Gardner, *Deep South: A Social Anthropological Study of Caste and Class* (Chicago: University of Chicago Press, 1941), 40.

27   *tenancy after freedom:* Woofter, *Landlord and Tenant.*

27   *"settling up" time:* Dollard, *Caste and Class,* 123.

27   *discourage these laborers:* Hortense Powdermaker, *After Freedom: A Cultural Study in the Deep South* (New York: Viking Press, 1939), 81.

27   *laborers included women:* Cotton Belt landlords tended to avoid, if not outright exclude, white tenants not only because they "contrasted . . . unfavorably with the Negroes who 'know their place'" (Dollard, *Caste and Class,* 94) but also because "of the ability of white tenants to resort to legal defense against dishonest settlement, terrorization, illegal eviction, or illegal seizure of livestock and personal property" (Davis, Gardner, and Gardner, *Deep South,* 266–67).

27   *material deprivation:* Bruce H. Rankin and William W. Falk, "Race, Region, and Earnings: Blacks and Whites in the South," *Rural Sociology* 56, no. 2 (1991): 224–37; Gloria Ladson-Billings, "Landing on the Wrong Note: The Price We Paid for *Brown,*" *Educational Researcher* 33, no. 7 (2004): 3–13. Rankin and Falk failed to recognize, however, that differences in human capital may be the direct result of structural factors, such as Black-white differences in school funding prior to the integration of schools, white flight from public schools to segregation academies and parochial schools in the Deep South after *Brown v. Board of Education* (1954), and very low investment in education.

27   *guaranteed virtual starvation:* Davis, Gardner, and Gardner, *Deep South.*

27   *diets were deficient:* Dorothy Dickens, "A Nutrition Investigation of Negro Tenants in the Yazoo Mississippi Delta," Mississippi Agricultural Experimental Station, A & M College, Mississippi, 1928, 46.

27   *"The consequences":* Johnson, *Shadow of the Plantation,* 187.

28   *"figures for mortality":* Johnson, *Shadow of the Plantation,* 204.

28   *Frank Mandeville Rogers was experimenting:* Eldred E. Prince, *Long Green: The Rise and Fall of Tobacco in South Carolina* (Athens: University of Georgia Press, 2000).

29   *"landscape was literally transformed":* Prince, *Long Green,* 77.

29   *688-fold increase:* Prince, *Long Green,* 75.

29   *"the father of Texas onions":* News item in *Austin-American Statesman* (untitled, no author), June 17, 1910, p. 4: "T.C. Nye of Laredo, father of the onion industry in West Texas, yesterday conferred with the department of agriculture."

30   *"greatest land-colonization schemes":* James Weeks Tiller, *The Texas Winter Garden: Commercial Cool-Season Vegetable Production*, Research Monograph No. 33 (Austin: Bureau of Business Research, University of Texas at Austin, 1971).

31   *subdivided and sold:* David Montejano, *Anglos and Mexicans in the Making of Texas, 1836–1986* (Austin: University of Texas Press, 1987).

31   *amassing large parcels:* Montejano, *Anglos and Mexicans*, 64.

31   *deception or violence:* Joe S. Graham, *El Rancho in South Texas: Continuity and Change from 1750* (Denton: University of North Texas Press, 1994).

31   *Capital from British and eastern US sources:* Montejano, *Anglos and Mexicans*, 62.

31   *"large quantities of foreign money":* Dale Lasater, *Falfurrias: Ed C. Lasater and the Development of South Texas* (College Station: Texas A&M University Press, 1985), 46. In 1882, Mifflin Kenedy sold all his land and livestock for $1.1 million to a syndicate from Dundee, Scotland, called the Texas Land and Cattle Company. Graham, *El Rancho in South Texas*, 39.

31   *"irrigated district":* Paul S. Taylor, *Mexican Labor in the United States: Dimmit County, Winter Garden District, South Texas*, University of California Publications in Economics, vol. 6, no. 5 (Berkeley: University of California Press, 1930), 310.

32   *displaced thousands:* Gilbert Joseph and Jürgen Buchenau, *Mexico's Once and Future Revolution* (Durham, NC: Duke University Press, 2013), 1.

32   *governed by paternalism:* Montejano, *Anglos and Mexicans*, 159. For the local economy, the consequences of relying so heavily on cheap migrant labor were severe. Montejano quotes one farmer interviewed by Paul Taylor in the late 1920s who told him, "We have got about as far as we can with cheap labor. . . . Our merchants have no [customers]. Labor [paid these] wages can't buy [much]. Our lands of about 12,000 acres under cultivation are in the hands of about a dozen [Anglos]. They are not farmers; they are speculators in onions."

32   *typically paid $1 a day:* Taylor, *Mexican Labor*, 349.

32   *control Black labor:* Taylor summarized the "race" relations there as "separation in domicile, separation in politics, and separation in education." Taylor, *Mexican Labor*, 414.

32   *"web of labor controls":* Montejano, *Anglos and Mexicans*, 201.

32   *bigoted beliefs:* Arnoldo De León, *They Called Them Greasers: Anglo Attitudes Toward Mexicans in Texas, 1821–1900* (Austin: University of Texas Press, 1983).

32   *fearful of labor revolts:* Similarly, Black Belt slaveholders were continually on high alert for any show of Black resistance, especially after the bloody (and victorious) Haitian Revolution, which they feared would be replicated in the region. See Walter Johnson, *Rover of Dark Dreams: Slavery and Empire in the Cotton Kingdom* (Cambridge, MA: Belknap Press, 2013).

33   *eschewed sharecropping:* As one farmer interviewed for "Harvest of Shame," a 1960 CBS special report on the plight of migrant farmworkers, told journalist Edward R. Murrow, "We used to own our slaves. Now we just rent them." "Harvest of Shame," *CBS Reports,* directed by Fred W. Friendly, aired November 26, 1960, on CBS.

33   *somewhat higher percentage:* Selden C. Menefee, *Mexican Migratory Workers of South Texas* (Washington, DC: Federal Works Agency, 1941).

33   *denying them the vote:* Because of the virtual one-party political system in the South that existed until the late 1960s, winning the Democratic primary was tantamount to being elected. See "Smith vs. Allwright: White Primaries," *The Texas Political Project,* https://texaspolitics.utexas.edu /archive/html/vce/features/0503_01/smith.html.

33   *deemed ineligible:* Robert Lee Maril, *The Poorest of Americans: The Mexican-Americans of the Lower Rio Grande Valley of Texas* (Notre Dame, IN: University of Notre Dame Press, 1989).

34   *large coal outcroppings:* The biographical information about Hotchkiss is from Jerry B. Thomas, "Jedediah Hotchkiss, Gilded-Age Propagandist of Industrialism," *Virginia Magazine of History and Biography* 84, no. 2 (1976): 189–202.

34   *the Cherokee attacked:* John C. Campbell, *The Southern Highlander and His Homeland* (New York: Russell Sage Foundation, 1921), 29.

35   *half of present-day Kentucky:* Robert F. Collins, *A History of the Daniel Boone National Forest, 1770–1970* (Lexington, KY: US Department of Agriculture Forest Service Southern Region, 1975), chap. 8.

35   *three-quarters of the land:* Dwight B. Billings and Kathleen M. Blee, *The Road to Poverty: The Making of Wealth and Hardship in Appalachia* (New York: Cambridge University Press, 2000), 51.

35   *"largely owned by a few men":* James S. Brown, *Beech Creek: A Study of a Kentucky Mountain Neighborhood* (Berea, KY: Berea College Press, 1988), 3.

35   *"mineral men":* Ronald D. Eller, *Miners, Millhands, and Mountaineers: Industrialization of the Appalachian South, 1880–1930,* 1st ed., Twentieth-Century America Series (Knoxville: University of Tennessee Press, 1982), 54.

35   *"by whatever means":* Caudill, *Night Comes to the Cumberlands,* 307.

36   *"a virtual land monopoly":* Alan J. Banks, "Land and Capital in Eastern Kentucky, 1890–1915," *Appalachian Journal* 8, no. 1 (1980): 8–18.

36   *central Appalachia transitioned:* John Alexander Williams, *Appalachia: A History* (Chapel Hill: University of North Carolina Press, 2002), 249.

36   *"a separate and inferior people":* Billings and Blee, *Road to Poverty,* 28–29.

36   *"Our Contemporary Ancestors":* William Goodell Frost, "Our Contemporary Ancestors in the Southern Mountains," *Atlantic Monthly,* March 1, 1899, www.theatlantic.com/magazine/archive/1899/03/our-contemporary -ancestors-southern-mountains/581332/.

37   *Appalachian subsistence farmers:* Charles Kenneth Sullivan, *Coal Men and Coal Towns: Development of the Smokeless Coalfields of Southern West Virginia,*

1873–1923, Garland Studies in Entrepreneurship (New York: Garland, 1989), 20.

37   *US Coal Commission found:* United States, *What the Coal Commission Found,* Human Relations Series (Baltimore: Williams & Wilkins, 1925).

37   *"constant and grim companion":* United States, *What the Coal Commission Found,* 150.

37   *"maintain their feudal proprietorship'":* Quoted in Sullivan, *Coal Men and Coal Towns,* 152.

37   *"silent instructions":* David C. Andrews, "A Sociological Study of a Coal Mining Town" (thesis, Columbia University, 1916).

37   *"Falls of coal":* Laurel Shackelford and Bill Weinberg, eds., *Our Appalachia: An Oral History* (Lexington: University Press of Kentucky, 1988), 218–19.

37   *lost their lives:* Keith Dix, *Work Relations in the Coal Industry: The Hand-Loading Era, 1880–1930,* West Virginia University *Bulletin,* ser. 78, no. 7-2 (Morgantown: Institute for Labor Studies, Division of Social and Economic Development, Center for Extension and Continuing Education, West Virginia University, 1977), 69, https://catalog.hathitrust.org/Record /100840214.

Chapter 2: Separate, Unequal

40   *local revenue per pupil:* Bill Peterson, "Kentucky Public Schools Ruled Unconstitutional," *Washington Post,* June 9, 1989, www.washington post.com/archive/politics/1989/06/09/kentucky-public-schools-ruled -unconstitutional/18216585-e5a7-487c-9dfb-f5ec7e00d3c8/.

40   *college completion rates:* Cynthia M. Duncan, *Worlds Apart: Poverty and Politics in Rural America,* 2nd ed. (New Haven, CT: Yale University Press, 2015).

41   *"highly profitable to the white schools":* Davis, Gardner, and Gardner, *Deep South,* 248n4. See also Horace M. Bond, *Education of the Negro in the American Social Order* (New York: Prentice-Hall, 1934).

41   *Black children had to walk:* Davis, Gardner, and Gardner, *Deep South,* 249.

42   *"both have the same grade system":* Powdermaker, *After Freedom,* 315–16.

42   *"less amenable to the caste sanctions":* Davis, Gardner, and Gardner, *Deep South,* 249–50.

42   *"potentiality of competition":* Dollard, *Caste and Class,* 202.

42   *"cannot go directly to college":* Dollard, *Caste and Class,* 193.

43   *"Jim Crow in a Sombrero Hat":* "The Other Texans: The Last Angry Americans," *Look,* October 8, 1963, 70.

43   *The report found:* Taylor, *Mexican Labor,* 372.

43   *"we don't enforce the attendance law":* Taylor, *Mexican Labor,* 372.

43   *per-pupil allocation:* Taylor, *Mexican Labor,* 377; Montejano, *Anglos and Mexicans,* 192.

43   *"rather his daughter was dead":* Taylor, *Mexican Labor,* 389.

44   *"want 12 cents a row":* Taylor, *Mexican Labor,* 440.

44   *"the more ignorant they are"*: Taylor, *Mexican Labor,* 378.

44   *migratory cycle:* Refugio I. Rochín, Anne M. Santiago, and Karla S. Dickey, "Migrant and Seasonal Workers in Michigan's Agriculture: A Study of Their Contributions, Characteristics, Needs, and Services," Julian Samora Research Institute Research Report No. 1 (Michigan State University, November 1989), https://jsri.msu.edu/upload/research-reports /rr01.pdf.

44   *average Hispanic eighteen-year-old:* Selden C. Menefee, *Mexican Migratory Workers of South Texas* (Washington, DC: Government Printing Office, 1941), 45.

45   *organization established:* Richard Rubin, "Should the Mississippi Files Have Been Re-opened? No, Because . . ." *New York Times Magazine,* August 30, 1998; "Last Founder of White Citizens' Council Dies," *Clarion-Ledger* (Jackson, MS), September 25, 2017, www.clarionledger.com/story /news/local/journeytojustice/2017/09/25/last-founder-of-white-citizens -council-dies/700344001.

45   *not a single school desegregated:* Michael W. Fuquay, "Civil Rights and the Private School Movement in Mississippi, 1964–1971," *History of Education Quarterly* 42, no. 2 (2002): 159–60.

45   *had not one integrated classroom:* "Three States Maintain Full Segregation," *New York Times,* February 4, 1961.

46   *all-white private schools:* Neil R. McMillen, *The Citizens' Council: Organized Resistance to the Second Reconstruction, 1954–64* (Champaign: University of Illinois Press, 1994); Stephanie R. Rolph, *Resisting Equality: The Citizens' Council, 1954–1989* (Baton Rouge: Louisiana State University Press, 2018).

46   *step-by-step instructions:* "How to Start a Private School," *The Citizen,* September 1964.

46   *Pillow Academy:* Rubin, "Should the Mississippi Files."

46   *"last best hope of segregation":* Rubin, "Should the Mississippi Files."

46   Time *magazine reported:* "Private Schools: The Last Refuge," *Time,* November 14, 1969, http://content.time.com/time/subscriber/article /0,33009,840365,00.html. See also Jeffery Stewart, "Private School Movement. AKA: Segregation Academies," Encyclopedia of Arkansas, last updated October 19, 2022, https://encyclopediaofarkansas.net/entries /private-school-movement-9384.

46   *academy would not survive:* "South's All-White Private Academies Double This Year," *Chicago Tribune,* November 27, 1970, D7.

47   *"evade the requirements of federal law":* Fuquay, "Civil Rights," 159–60.

47   *tuition vouchers:* "Court Rules Out Mississippi Aid: Says Private School Funds Encourage Segregation," *Baltimore Sun,* January 31, 1969.

47   *Woodland Hills Academy:* Hinds County, which includes Jackson, is ranked number 154 on our Index of Deep Disadvantage.

47   *"surplus books we don't need":* Jack Rosenthal, "A White Academy Gets Public Texts," *New York Times,* September 5, 1970, www.nytimes.com

/1970/09/05/archives/a-white-academy-gets-public-texts-jackson-miss
-transfers-800-books.html.

47   *"the shell of the building"*: David Nevin and Robert E. Bills, *The Schools That Fear Built: Segregation Academies in the South* (Longboat Key, FL: Acropolis Books, 1976), 14.

47   *"Our fight song was the same"*: Debbie Hewitt Smith, "As Sesame Street Started So Did Our Seg Academy," The Academy Stories, www.theacademystories.com/post/as-sesame-street-started-so-did-our-seg-academy.

48   *donate the land:* Cobb, *Most Southern Place on Earth*, 194; Nevin and Bills, *Schools That Fear Built.*

48   *all but two:* Frank Parker, "Protest, Politics, and Litigation: Political and Social Change in Mississippi, 1965 to Present," *Mississippi Law Journal* 57 (1987): 677–704.

48   *mass exodus of whites:* "Mass Exodus Hits Schools in Mississippi," *Chicago Tribune*, January 4, 1970.

48   *enrollment in private academies:* Kenneth T. Andrews, "Movement-Countermovement Dynamics and the Emergence of New Institutions: The Case of 'White Flight' Schools in Mississippi," *Social Forces* 80, no. 3 (March 2002): 30, www.jstor.org/stable/3086461.

48   *more than triple:* Authors' calculations.

48   *750,000 white students:* Nevin and Bills, *Schools That Fear Built.*

48   *"Resegregation is virtually complete"*: John C. Walder and Allen D. Cleveland, "The South's New Segregation Academies," *Phi Delta Kappan* 53, no. 4 (December 1971): 234–35, www.jstor.org/stable/20373159?refreqid =excelsior%3A1bac5cd55450cea88e71c29bc545049a&seq=1#metadata _info_tab_contents.

48   *Whites in Lowndes County:* Lowndes County, Alabama, is ranked number 43 on our Index of Deep Disadvantage.

49   *enrolled 335 white students:* Using statistical techniques, sociologist Kenneth T. Andrews confirmed these conclusions, finding that the proportion of Black school-age children in the county had a very strong and statistically significant association with the number of students attending academies. Andrews, "Movement-Countermovement Dynamics," 30. David Campbell, "2 Schools Show Lowndes Way of Life," *Alabama Journal*, May 3, 1968, 15. Some corrections: Black children outnumbered white children six to one; the first day of school at Lowndes, 210 students showed up: "When school bells rang at Hayneville School for the start of the 1967-68 school term, the year that segregation was to be completely ended, there were no white pupils enrolled."

49   *mythic history:* Terry Doyle Carroll, "Mississippi Private Education: An Historical, Descriptive, and Normative Study" (PhD diss., University of Southern Mississippi, 1981).

49   *"segregationist parents"*: Fuquay, "Civil Rights," 161. After the Voting Rights Act, when power was no longer solely vested in the hands of whites, such

schools, "created for the purpose of maintaining segregation, came to be seen as an effective means to reduce the power of interracial local governments while decreasing the tax burden on white citizens [who would reject adequate funding for the public schools]."

49   *"uptown Klan":* Rubin, "Should the Mississippi Files."

50   *legal legitimation:* Ellen Ann Fentress, "White Churches Involved at Every Step," The Academy Stories, www.theacademystories.com/post/white -churches-involved-at-every-step. See also J. Crespino, *In Search of Another Country: Mississippi and the Conservative Counterrevolution* (Princeton, NJ: Princeton University Press, 2009).

50   *Southern Baptist churches:* J. Egerton, "Segregation Academies, with Much Church Aid, Flourish in South, as Other Private Schools Wane," *South Today*, September 1974, 7.

50   *Appealing to "quality":* "Private Schools: The Last Refuge," *Time*, November 14, 1969, http://content.time.com/time/subscriber/article/0,33009 ,840365,00.html.

50   *"five most influential men":* Reese Cleghorn, "The Segs," *Esquire*, January 1, 1964, https://classic.esquire.com/index.php/article/1964/1/1/the-segs.

51   *"and anti-white racism":* William J. Simmons, "The Citizens' Councils and Private Education," *Citizen*, February 1966, 9.

51   *three classes of segregation schools:* "Segregation Academies and State Action," *Yale Law Journal* 82, no. 7 (June 1973): 1436–61.

51   *"curriculums are generally not on a level":* James T. Wooten, "Private Schools Thrive in South, but Finances Restrict Quality," *New York Times*, January 30, 1970.

51   *"insufficient pool of children":* Nevin and Bills, *Schools That Fear Built*, abstract.

52   *"I started fourth grade":* Renee McCraine Taylor, "The Bubble That Never Was," The Academy Stories, www.theacademystories.com/post/the-bubble -that-never-was.

52   *"slurs and racist jokes":* Ellen Ann Fentress, "When Your High School Has a Racist History," *Faith & Leadership*, August 18, 2020, https://faithand leadership.com/when-your-high-school-has-racist-history.

52   *white supremacist ideology:* Donna Ladd, "White Flight in Noxubee County: Why School Integration Never Happened," Mississippi Free Press, October 29, 2021, www.mississippifreepress.org/16642/white-flight -in-noxubee-county-why-school-integration-never-happened/.

52   *"What we learned":* Ellen Ann Fentress, "Are You a Seg Academy Alum, Too? Let's Talk," *The Bitter Southerner*, https://bittersoutherner.com /from-the-southern-perspective/are-you-a-seg-academy-alum-lets-talk.

53   *B grade:* "Pillow Academy," Niche, www.niche.com/k12/pillow-academy -greenwood-ms/.

53   *questionable from the outset:* Fuquay, "Civil Rights," 165.

55   *chose to desegregate:* John Staples Shockley, *Chicano Revolt in a Texas Town* (Notre Dame, IN: University of Notre Dame Press, 1974), 20.

55   *school districts followed suit:* Robert D. Jacobus, *Black Man in the Huddle: Stories from the Integration of Texas Football* (College Station: Texas A&M University Press).

56   *"beating from the Texas Rangers":* C. Brochin, "The History I Never Learned in School: Diana Palacios Recounts Crystal City in 1969," *Lare-DOS*, October 2001.

58   *protests and white flight:* Mark Odintz, "Crystal City, TX," Texas State Historical Association, www.tshaonline.org/handbook/entries/crystal-city-tx.

59   *"Christian principles":* "About Us," Marvell Academy website, www.marvellacademyeagles.com/about-us.html.

59   *"stated as quality education":* "About," DeSoto School website, www.desotothunderbirds.com/.

59   *a single Black student:* Rubin, "Should the Mississippi Files."

59   *90 percent of whom are white:* "Pillow Academy School," Homefacts, www.homefacts.com/schools/Mississippi/Leflore-County/Greenwood/Pillow-Academy.html.

59   *"Diversity is key":* "Statement of Diversity," Pillow Academy website, www.pillowacademy.com/apps/pages/index.jsp?uREC_ID=1807360&type=d&pREC_ID=1973268.

59   *less than a quarter of the students:* "Education Week's Quality Counts: Mississippi Top Five Most Improved State for Chance-for-Success," Mississippi Department of Education, February 3, 2020, www.mdek12.org/news/2020/2/3/Education-Weeks-Quality-Counts-Mississippi-Top-Five-Most-Improved-State-for-Chance-for-Success_20200203.

60   *ACT scores at Greenwood High:* "Greenwood High School," GreatSchools, www.greatschools.org/mississippi/greenwood/279-Greenwood-High-School/.

60   *Quality Counts 2020:* Sterling C. Lloyd and Alex Harwin, "Nation's Schools Get a 'C' Once Again, Even as Pandemic Turns Up the Heat," *Education Week*, September 1, 2020, www.edweek.org/ew/articles/2020/09/02/nations-schools-get-a-c-once-again.html.

60   *National Assessment of Educational Progress:* "Mississippi Ranks No. 1 Nationally for Score Gains on National Assessment of Educational Progress (NAEP)," Mississippi Department of Education, November 12, 2019, www.mdek12.org/news/2019/10/30/Mississippi-Ranks-No-1-in-Nation-for-Score-Gains-on-National-Assessment-of-Educational-Progress-NAEP_20191030.

60   *evenly split:* "Mississippi Succeeds Report Card," Mississippi Department of Education, https://msrc.mdek12.org/.

60   *A grade:* "Ocean Springs School District Math Performance," Mississippi Department of Education, https://msrc.mdek12.org/performance?EntityID=3021-000&Component=MPERF&SchoolYear=2018.

60   *schools labeled failing:* Stephen G. Katsinas, Noel E. Keeney, Emily Jacobs, and Hunter Whann, "School Enrollment in Alabama's Black Belt

Continues to Decline," Issue Brief No. 44 (Education Policy Center, University of Alabama), http://edpolicy.ua.edu/wp-content/uploads/2020 /10/200831_school-enrollment-decline-al-black-belt.pdf.

60   *Georgia Cotton Belt:* Stephen Owens, "Education in Georgia's Black Belt: Policy Solutions to Help Overcome a History of Exclusion," Georgia Budget & Policy Institute, October 10, 2019, https://gbpi.org/education -in-georgias-black-belt/.

61   *"dated" or even "terrible":* "Greenwood Comprehensive Plan, City of Greenwood, Mississippi 2010–2040," Greenwood Comprehensive Plan Steering Committee, October 19, 2010, 51, www.greenwoodms.com /images/uploads/Greenwood_Comprehensive_Plan_FINAL_PLAN _201207180842473831.pdf.

61   *would not support a bond issue:* "Greenwood Comprehensive Plan," 61.

61   *"perceived lack of quality":* "Greenwood Comprehensive Plan," 22.

61   *115 times greater:* Kenny V. Anthony, Dana P. Franz, and Devon Brenner, "Understanding the Nature of the Teacher Shortage in Mississippi," *Mississippi Economic Review* 1 (2017): 24–31.

61   *teacher recruitment and retention:* Aallyah Wright and Kelsey Davis Betz, "After Years of Inaction, Delta Teacher Shortage Reaches 'Crisis' Levels," Mississippi Today, February 18, 2019, https://mississippitoday.org /2019/02/18/after-years-of-inaction-delta-teacher-shortage-reaches-crisis -levels/.

61   *"de facto white public school":* Fuquay, "Civil Rights," 180.

61   *"fresh coat of paint":* https://hechingerreport.org/you-cant-help-but-to -wonder-crumbling-schools-less-money-and-dismal-outcomes-in-the -county-that-was-supposed-to-change-everything-for-black-children -in-the-south/.racey Harris, "Black Students in the Mississippi Delta Still Face Education Inequality," Truthout, February 20, 2020, https:// truthout.org/articles/black-students-in-the-mississippi-delta-still-face -education-inequality/.

62   *struggle for integration in Texas schools:* Aliyya Swaby and Alexa Ura, "It Took This Texas School District 48 Years to Desegregate. Now, Some Fear a Return to the Past," The Texas Tribune, November 29, 2018, www.texas tribune.org/2018/11/29/texas-longview-school-segregation-disintegration/.

64   *the low test scores:* "2018–19 School Report Card," Texas Education Agency, https://rptsvr1.tea.texas.gov/perfreport/src/2019/campus.srch.html; "Zavala Elementary School," The Texas Tribune, https://schools.texastribune .org/districts/crystal-city-isd/zavala-elementary-school/. Texas did not assign school ratings for the 2019–20 academic year due to the COVID-19 pandemic.

65   *at or below level one literacy:* "U.S. Skills Map."

65   *exceed the state average:* It should be noted that the overall Texas average is not high. See "Literacy Facts," Literacy Texas, www.literacytexas.org /impact/literacy-facts/.

66   *more than twice the national average:* "KIDS COUNT Indicators for Counties in Texas," Annie E. Casey Foundation, https://datacenter.kidscount.org/data/customreports/6538,6768/3063,3065.

67   *Rucker Johnson powerfully illustrates:* Reagan administration report quoted in Rucker C. Johnson, *Children of the Dream: Why School Integration Works* (New York: Basic Books, 2019), 13; second quote 17.

Chapter 3: Nothing to Do Here but Drugs

69   *he vividly recounted:* Bill Estep, "Chapter 12: A Drug-Addled City Hits Bottom, Strives to Get Clean," *Lexington (KY) Herald-Leader,* August 24, 2019, www.kentucky.com/news/special-reports/fifty-years-of-night/article44456061.html.

70   *"kids start dying":* Estep, "Chapter 12."

70   *feared turnout would be low:* "Enough: 2003 Drug March Remembered," *Manchester (KY) Enterprise,* May 19, 2019, www.nolangroupmedia.com/manchester_enterprise/2003-drug-march-remembered/article_5289f838-74c0-11e9-b806-cb466e505333.html.

70   *"veiled threats":* Estep, "Chapter 12."

70   *"save our county":* "Enough: 2003 Drug March Remembered."

70   *sickest region of all:* "Stats of the State of Kentucky," National Center for Health Statistics, www.cdc.gov/nchs/pressroom/states/kentucky/kentucky.htm; "Stats of the State of West Virginia," National Center for Health Statistics, www.cdc.gov/nchs/pressroom/states/westvirginia/westvirginia.htm.

70   *Carrie Hodousek's reporting:* Carrie Hodousek, "West Virginia Among Top States with Most Annual Drug Overdose Deaths," MetroNews, November 17, 2021, https://wvmetronews.com/2021/11/17/west-virginia-among-top-states-with-most-annual-drug-overdose-deaths/.

71   *1.3 prescriptions:* "U.S. County Opioid Dispensing Rates, 2019," Centers for Disease Control and Prevention, www.cdc.gov/drugoverdose/rxrate-maps/county2019.html.

71   *start using heroin:* Molly Schnell, "The Opioid Crisis: Tragedy, Treatments and Trade-offs" (policy brief, Stanford Institute for Economic Policy Research, February 2019), https://siepr.stanford.edu/publications/policy-brief/opioid-crisis-tragedy-treatments-and-trade-offs.

72   *"deaths of despair":* Anne Case and Angus Deaton, *Deaths of Despair and the Future of Capitalism* (Princeton, NJ: Princeton University Press, 2020).

72   *epidemic didn't manifest:* Janet Currie and Hannes Schwandt, "The Opioid Epidemic Was Not Caused by Economic Distress but by Factors That Could Be More Rapidly Addressed," *Annals of the American Academy of Political and Social Science* 695, no. 1 (2021): 276–91.

72   *squarely on Big Pharma:* Patrick Radden Keefe, *Empire of Pain: The Secret History of the Sackler Dynasty* (New York: Doubleday, 2021).

72   *"targeted certain regions":* Keefe, *Empire of Pain,* 213.

73   *disability claims:* John Gettens, Pei-Pei Lei, and Alexis D. Henry, "Perspectives: Accounting for Geographic Variation in Social Security Disability Program Participation," *Social Security Bulletin* 78, no. 2 (2018), www.ssa .gov/policy/docs/ssb/v78n2/v78n2p29.html.

73   *"doctors as 'whales'":* Keefe, *Empire of Pain*, 213.

73   *probably overprescribing:* Keefe, *Empire of Pain*, 213. See also Yngvild Olsen, Gail L. Daumit, and Daniel E. Ford, "Opioid Prescriptions by U.S. Primary Care Physicians from 1992 to 2001," *Journal of Pain* 7, no. 4 (2006): 225–35.

73   *"sedatives became commonplace":* Quoted in Estep, "Chapter 12." One mystery Keefe's narrative attempts to solve is why the areas first targeted— places like central Appalachia and Maine—were overwhelmingly rural and white. He speculates that Purdue based its strategy on a form of racial prejudice—the company was loath to market to nonwhites, especially Blacks, because it assumed that they would be more likely to abuse the drugs (despite there being no evidence to support this claim). That abuse would then expose Purdue to greater government oversight. Keefe also raises the possibility that doctors generally might be less likely to take the pain of their Black and Latino patients seriously. Or perhaps Richard Sackler and other decision-makers at Purdue thought it would be easier to hide any early problems if the pills were introduced into isolated, rural, white communities. Keefe, *Empire of Pain*.

73   *nearly three and a half times:* "U.S. County Opioid Dispensing Rates, 2006," Centers for Disease Control and Prevention, www.cdc.gov/drug overdose/rxrate-maps/county2006.html.

74   *"spiral of dependence and addiction":* Keefe, *Empire of Pain*, 226.

74   *"pill mills":* Alene Kennedy-Hendricks, Matthew Richey, Emma E. McGinty, Elizabeth A. Stuart, Colleen L. Barry, and Daniel W. Webster, "Opioid Overdose Deaths and Florida's Crackdown on Pill Mills," *American Journal of Public Health* 106, no. 2 (2016): 291–97.

74   *more opioid prescriptions than people:* "U.S. County Opioid Dispensing Rates, 2020," Centers for Disease Control and Prevention, www.cdc.gov /drugoverdose/rxrate-maps/county2020.html. Prescriptions were new or refill prescriptions dispensed at a retail pharmacy.

75   *degradation of democracy:* Robert Putnam, *Bowling Alone: The Collapse and Revival of American Community* (New York: Simon & Schuster, 2000).

77   *"shared spaces":* Eric Klinenberg, *Palaces for the People: How Social Infrastructure Can Help Fight Inequality, Polarization, and the Decline of Civic Life* (New York: Crown, 2018), inside front cover.

77   *740 more deaths in Chicago than usual:* Klinenberg, *Palaces for the People*, 2.

77   *"key differences":* Klinenberg, *Palaces for the People*, 5.

78   *robust social infrastructure:* Klinenberg, *Palaces for the People*, 7.

78   *"Countless close friendships":* Klinenberg, *Palaces for the People*, 18.

78   *"social infrastructure gets degraded":* Klinenberg, *Palaces for the People*, 21.

79   *coal camp homes:* Coal camp homes were typically board-and-batten houses with thin walls, three or four rooms, and a front stoop or porch. These came to be called "Jenny Lind houses" due to the cheap building method used at the Jenny Lind Mine in Colorado. That mine was so named after the singer Jenny Lind, billed as "the Swedish Nightingale," sang from the back of a train's caboose in a nearby town. Dave Tabler, "What Is a Jenny Lind House?," Appalachian History, www.appalachianhistory .net/2020/05/what-is-a-jenny-lind-house.html.

79   *pricey Air Raid trampoline park:* Air Raid website, https://airraidky.com /pricing/. When we checked the prices in 2022, the cost was $29 per kid for two hours including taxes and socks with necessary traction.

79   *price of an ATV:* Cherise Threewitt, "2021 ATV Segment Buying Guide," *U.S. News & World Report,* October 29, 2020, https://cars.usnews.com /powersports/atvs.

79   *county residents who are Black:* "QuickFacts: Clay County, Kentucky," US Census Bureau, www.census.gov/quickfacts/fact/table/claycountykentucky /PST045221.

80   *Despite its illegality:* Although cockfighting is illegal in Kentucky, residents are allowed to own a fighting cock. They will receive a misdemeanor for a first offense.

81   *the density of nonprofits:* Michael J. Zoorob and Jason L. Salemi, "Bowling Alone, Dying Together: The Role of Social Capital in Mitigating the Drug Overdose Epidemic in the United States," *Drug and Alcohol Dependence* 173 (April 2017): 1–9.

82   *civic safety net:* Alan Latham and Jack Layton, "Social Infrastructure and the Public Life of Cities: Studying Urban Sociality and Public Spaces," *Geography Compass* 13, no. 7 (2019), https://compass.onlinelibrary.wiley .com/doi/full/10.1111/gec3.12444.

82   *"good analog for social connection":* Klinenberg, *Palaces for the People,* 119.

82   *"Opioids mimic":* Maia Szalavitz, "Opioids Feel Like Love: That's Why They're Deadly in Tough Times," *New York Times,* December 6, 2021, www.nytimes.com/2021/12/06/opinion/us-opioid-crisis.html.

83   *kept to themselves:* Fourteen out of twenty-two interviewees explicitly said that they kept to themselves.

85   *"set boundaries":* Klinenberg, *Palaces for the People,* 40.

85   *municipal swimming pools:* Jeff Wiltse, *Contested Waters: A Social History of Swimming Pools in America* (Chapel Hill: University of North Carolina Press, 2007). See also Heather McGhee, *The Sum of Us: What Racism Costs Everyone and How We Can Prosper Together* (New York: One World, 2021).

85   *"Swimming pools":* Klinenberg, *Palaces for the People,* 155–56.

86   *notably low:* Thomas R. Ford, ed., *The Southern Appalachian Region: A Survey* (Lexington: University of Kentucky Press, 1962), 202–3, https://core .ac.uk/download/pdf/232571735.pdf.

86   *"joint participation":* Klinenberg, *Palaces for the People,* 11.

88   *Construction peaked*: When the US Coal Commission completed its study of the industry in 1925, it found that nearly 80 percent of West Virginia's miners and about two-thirds of the miners in the rest of the bituminous coal region were living in company towns. Crandall A. Shifflett, *Coal Towns: Life, Work, and Culture in Company Towns of Southern Appalachia, 1880–1960* (Knoxville: University of Tennessee Press, 1991), 33.

88   *dotted the map*: Shifflett, *Coal Towns*, is the authoritative source on this topic, and we draw heavily on Shifflett's work for this part of the book, with appreciation.

88   *named after the mine owners*: Shifflett, *Coal Towns*, 34.

88   *"gutted it"*: Shackelford and Weinberg, eds., *Our Appalachia*, 152–53.

88   *towns were often planned*: Shifflett, *Coal Towns*, 37.

88   *"contentment sociology"*: Shifflett, *Coal Towns*, 54.

89   *"the town that Jack built"*: George D. Torok, *A Guide to Historic Coal Towns of the Big Sandy River Valley* (Knoxville: University of Tennessee Press, 2004).

89   *"seven to ten [dollars]"*: Shackelford and Weinberg, eds., *Our Appalachia*, 207.

89   *"gone to heaven"*: Shifflett, *Coal Towns*, 147.

89   *Not all amenities:* In 1920, just under 60 percent of miners in the bituminous coal fields were native-born whites, a third were foreign-born—mostly Italians, Poles, Hungarians, and Slavs—and just under 10 percent were Black. Shifflett, *Coal Towns*, 72.

90   *"putting him on"*: Shifflett, *Coal Towns*, 64.

90   *separate facilities:* Shifflett, *Coal Towns*, 64.

90   *"social and economic nexus"*: Shifflett, *Coal Towns*, 176.

90   *"mecca for everyone"*: Quoted in Shifflett, *Coal Towns*, 177.

90   *two of each kind:* In 1930, a survey conducted by the US Department of Agriculture counted 14,423 churches in the 117 Appalachian counties studied—one congregation every 2.3 miles if spread out evenly. That was twice as many per thousand people as in the United States as a whole. Shifflett, *Coal Towns*, 192.

91   *"Gone too"*: Shifflett, *Coal Towns*, 211.

91   *"ended the sport"*: Shifflett, *Coal Towns*, 64.

92   *challenges the region faced:* Sharon Rodriguez, Nathan L. Vanderford, Bin Huang, and Robin Vanderpool, "A Socioecological Review of Cancer Disparities in Kentucky," *Southern Medical Journal* 111, no. 4 (2018): 213–19, www.ncbi.nlm.nih.gov/pmc/articles/PMC5935122/.

Chapter 4: A Tradition of Violence

95   *"surrender immediately"*: F. Uenuma, "The Massacre of Black Sharecroppers That Led the Supreme Court to Curb the Racial Disparities of the Justice System," *Smithsonian*, August 2, 2018, www.smithsonianmag.com /history/death-hundreds-elaine-massacre-led-supreme-court-take-major -step-toward-equal-justice-african-americans-180969863/.

95   *"nothen But dogs"*: Sean Clancy, "Marking a Tragedy: Memorial to Those Who Died in the Elaine Massacre Enmeshed in Controversy," *Arkansas Democrat Gazette*, September 29, 2019, www.arkansasonline.com /news/2019/sep/29/marking-a-tragedy-20190929/. See also Robert Whitaker, *On the Laps of Gods: The Red Summer of 1919 and the Struggle for Justice That Remade a Nation* (New York: Crown, 2008).

95   *"orgy of bloodshed"*: Corporal Leroy Johnston and Ida B. Wells-Barnett, "Twelve Men Condemned by the Court. Drs. D. A. E. and L. H. Johnston Two of the Four Johnston Brothers Killed by the Helena, Ark. Rioters," available at Northern Illinois University Digital Library, https://digital .lib.niu.edu/islandora/object/niu-gildedage%3A24320.

95   *245 Black killings:* Equal Justice Initiative, "Lynching in America," https:// lynchinginamerica.eji.org/explore/arkansas.

96   *nearly three hundred killed:* Oklahoma Commission to Study the Tulsa Race Riot of 1921, *Tulsa Race Riot* (independently published, February 28, 2001), 23–22, www.okhistory.org/research/forms/freport.pdf.

96   *Leflore Massacre:* Willis, *Forgotten Time.*

96   *sense of unease:* Nobody knows what influence the events in Leflore County had on James Z. George, US senator from Mississippi, though John Willis argues for a direct link between the events and Delta planters like George moving to support a constitutional convention to curb the growing political power of Black Mississippians. Willis, *Forgotten Time*, 136. George owned large plots of land in the county at Runnymede, near Itta Bena, though his plantation home, Cotesworth, lay several miles east of Greenwood, in Carroll County. George had opposed a new state constitution but changed his mind in the waning months of 1889—just after the massacre in his backyard. He was a revered figure among white Mississippians and always seemed to be at the forefront of crusading for white racial supremacy in the state. In January 1861, he led the charge for Mississippi's secession from the Union, and while some had argued about the protection of "states' rights" and other motives for the formation of the Confederacy, Mississippi's declaration—which George helped to draft— leaves no room for doubt. "Our position," it reads, "is thoroughly identified with the institution of slavery." Timothy B. Smith, *James Z. George: Mississippi's Great Commoner* (Jackson: University Press of Mississippi, 2012), 41. Fourteen years later, George was key in another landmark effort to establish white dominance. As head of Mississippi's Democratic Party, he was one of two men to wrest the state from Republican rule in 1875, ending Reconstruction. Albert D. Kirwan, *Revolt of the Rednecks: Mississippi Politics, 1876–1925* (Lexington: University Press of Kentucky, 1951), 3.

On October 16, 1889, with events in Leflore still fresh in his mind, George spoke in Greenville on what he called the "Negro voting problem" and the necessity for a new constitution. Appealing to the fears of a white minority inflamed by the recent violence, he predicted that by 1900, the Black population would outnumber whites in the state by two to one. The acknowledged purpose of the 1890 Mississippi convention was to disenfranchise the state's Black citizens while not appearing to violate the Fifteenth Amendment. Tagged as "the central figure" or even "the father" of the convention by contemporaries and historians, George drafted a key section—the notorious "understanding" clause, which allowed registrars great discretion in judging applicants' comprehension of sections of the state constitution. "It was ingenious and vague, but it was constitutional, George believed, and made it possible to eliminate most black voters while keeping white ones." Smith, *James Z. George*, 153.

Like the end of Reconstruction years earlier, the Mississippi convention of 1890 was a severe blow to Black political representation and signaled a resurgence of white domination in the state. As if to underscore this point in the most dramatic way possible, the convention placed the Confederate battle insignia prominently on the Mississippi flag, where it stayed for 130 years until a voter referendum replaced it in November 2020.

96   *Farmers' Alliance cooperative store:* William F. Holmes, "The Leflore County Massacre and the Demise of the Colored Farmers' Alliance," *Phylon* 34, no. 3 (1973): 267–74.

96   *show their support for Cromwell:* Holmes, "Leflore County Massacre."

97   *accompanied by Lowry himself:* Willis, *Forgotten Time*.

98   *counties like Phillips and Leflore:* Stewart Tolnay and E. M. Beck, *A Festival of Violence: An Analysis of Southern Lynchings, 1882–1930* (Champaign: University of Illinois Press, 1995).

99   *devastating impact of Jim Crow:* Charles S. Johnson, *Growing Up in the Black Belt: Negro Youth in the Rural South*, prepared for the American Youth Commission, American Council on Education, Washington, DC, 1941.

100   *Writing about this dynamic:* Davis, Gardner, and Gardner, *Deep South*, 47, 49.

100   *"real and neurotic fear":* Dollard, *Caste and Class*, 320.

100   *"rational and measured tread":* Dollard, *Caste and Class*, 333.

101   *overly familiar terms:* Dollard, *Caste and Class*, 46.

101   *"the little things that prick":* Powdermaker, *After Freedom*, 343.

101   *strongest expression:* Davis, Gardner, and Gardner, *Deep South*, 16.

101   *"challenged if seen":* Davis, Gardner, and Gardner, *Deep South*, 299, 301.

102   *"profound and permanent":* Johnson, *Growing Up in the Black Belt*, 317.

102   *"earliest days":* Dollard, *Caste and Class*, 331.

102   *"sentence of death":* Dollard, *Caste and Class*, 359.

102   *"part of the routine":* Johnson, *Shadow of the Plantation*, 317–18.

102   *"spreading epidemic":* Dollard, *Caste and Class*, 316. See also L. F. Litwack, *Trouble in Mind: Black Southerners in the Age of Jim Crow* (New York: Vintage Books, 1998).

103   *"under the ground":* Davis, Gardner, and Gardner, *Deep South*, 225.

103   *permanently flee:* Paula J. Giddings, *Ida: A Sword Among Lions* (New York: HarperCollins, 2009).

103   *"boiling of aggressive affect":* Dollard, *Caste and Class,* 267, 269.

103   *"fight and shoot":* Dollard, *Caste and Class,* 193. See also John Dollard, Neal E. Miller, Leonard W. Doob, O. H. Mowrer, and Robert R. Sears, *Frustration and Aggression* (New Haven, CT: Yale University Press, 1939).

104   *"'the reformatory'":* Johnson, *Shadow of the Plantation,* 189–90.

104   *health department records:* Johnson, *Shadow of the Plantation,* 187.

104   *"differential application":* Dollard, *Caste and Class,* 274–75, 280.

104   *"one cannot help":* Dollard, *Caste and Class,* 280.

104   *humiliation of poverty:* Jock Young, *The Vertigo of Late Modernity* (London: Sage, 2007).

104   *poor and rural:* Bindu Kalesan and Sandro Galea, "Patterns of Gun Deaths Across US Counties, 1999–2013," *Annals of Epidemiology* 27 (2017): 302–7.

104   *homicides involving guns:* Jeffrey A. Butts, "Gun Violence Is Not an 'Urban' Problem," Research and Evaluation Data Bits, John Jay College of Criminal Justice, May 24, 2018, revised January 2020, https://johnjayrec .nyc/2018/05/24/databit201801.

107   *found a skull:* M. Hoskins, "Human Remains Sent for Identification," *Manchester (KY) Enterprise,* March 10, 2021, 1.

107   *a second skull:* Staff Report, "Two Human Skulls Found," *Manchester (KY) Enterprise,* March 24, 2021, 1.

107   *"Indictments!":* "Indictments!," *Manchester (KY) Enterprise,* April 28, 2021, 1.

107   *semiautomatic rifle:* Staff Report, "Murder at Bullskin," *Manchester (KY) Enterprise,* May 26, 2021, 1.

107   *allegedly stabbing:* Staff Report, "Clay Man Allegedly Attempts to Kill Mother," *Manchester (KY) Enterprise,* May 26, 2021, 1.

108   *public intoxication:* Staff Report, "Woman Tells Police She Shot Boyfriend," *Manchester (KY) Enterprise,* June 2, 2021, 1.

108   *two middle-aged men:* Staff Report, "Hammons Shot, Killed; Grand Jury to Hear Case," *Manchester (KY) Enterprise,* July 21, 2021, 1.

108   *man in his thirties:* C. Myrick, "Two Charged in Murder: Former Clay County Man Stabbed to Death During Altercation in Knox County," *Manchester (KY) Enterprise,* August 4, 2021, 1.

108   *fatally wounded:* Staff Report, "Man Enters Residence, Gunned Down," *Manchester (KY) Enterprise,* August 18, 2021, 1.

108   *spacious lawns:* "The Boulevard," *Greenwood (MS) Enterprise,* April 21, 1910, https://aboutgreenwoodmississippi.com/grand-boulevard.html.

116   *frequency of lynchings:* Steven F. Messner, Robert D. Baller, and Matthew Zevenbergen, "The Legacy of Lynching and Southern Homicide," *American Sociological Review* 70, no. 4 (August 2005): 633–55, www.jstor.org /stable/4145380?seq=1#metadata_info_tab_contents.

116   *elevated homicide rates:* Nick Peterson and Geoff Ward, "The Transmission of Historical Racial Violence: Lynching, Civil Rights–Era Terror, and

Contemporary Interracial Homicide," *Race and Justice* 5, no. 2 (January 2015), https://journals.sagepub.com/doi/abs/10.1177/2153368714567577 ?journalCode=raja.

117   *police officer–involved shootings:* Jhacova Williams and Carl Romer, "Black Deaths at the Hands of Law Enforcement Are Linked to Historical Lynchings," *Working Economics Blog*, Economic Policy Institute, June 5, 2020, www.epi.org/blog/black-deaths-at-the-hands-of-law-enforcement -are-linked-to-historical-lynchings-u-s-counties-where-lynchings-were -more-prevalent-from-1877-to-1950-have-more-officer-involved-killings/.

117   *more mental health challenges:* Jacob Bor, Atheendar S. Venkatara-mani, David R. Williams, and Alexander C. Tsai, "Police Killings and Their Spillover Effects on the Mental Health of Black Americans: A Population-Based, Quasi-Experimental Study," *The Lancet* 392 (June 21, 2018): 302–10, www.thelancet.com/journals/lancet/article/PIIS0140-67 36(18)31130-9/fulltext.

117   *limit the chances:* Patrick Sharkey and Gerard Torrats-Espinosa, "The Ef-fect of Violent Crime on Economic Mobility," *Journal of Urban Economics* 102 (November 2017): 22–33, https://doi.org/10.1016/j.jue.2017.07.001.

119   *Leflore County, Mississippi:* Equal Justice Initiative, "Lynching in America," https://lynchinginamerica.eji.org/explore/mississippi.

119   *"Emmett Till Generation":* Joe Sinsheimer, "The Emmett Till Generation," *Southern Exposure Magazine*, Summer 1987, 40.

120   *317 bullet holes:* Isis Davis-Marks, "Bearing Witness to Racism in Amer-ica Today: The Smithsonian's National Museum of American His-tory Displays a Bullet-Riddled Sign That Documented Emmett Till's Brutal Murder," *Smithsonian*, August 27, 2021, www.smithsonianmag .com/smithsonian-institution/smithsonian-displays-bullet-riddled-sign -documented-site-emmett-tills-horrific-murder-180978334/.

120   *"careful around whites":* Endesha Ida Mae Holland, *From the Mississippi Delta* (New York: Simon & Schuster, 1997), 37.

120   *"could take nothing for granted":* Holland, *From the Mississippi Delta*, 11.

Chapter 5: Little Kingdoms

122   *"Rejecting Nearly All":* Bryce Covert and Josh Israel, "Mississippi Is Re-jecting Nearly All of the Poor People Who Apply for Welfare and the State Won't Explain Why," ThinkProgress, April 13, 2017, https://archive .thinkprogress.org/mississippi-reject-welfare-applicants-57701ca3fb13/.

122   *Of that number:* Anna Wolfe, "Data Dive: Mississippi Is Not the Only State Turning Away Most Welfare Applicants," Mississippi Today, Octo-ber 5, 2022, https://mississippitoday.org/2022/10/05/mississippi-reject -most-welfare-applicants/. In 2022, that figure stood at about 92 percent.

122   *"There are many reasons":* Jimmie E. Gates, "MDHS Confirms Most New Applicants Rejected for Welfare," *Clarion-Ledger* (Jackson, MS), April 20, 2017, updated April 21, 2017, www.clarionledger.com/story

/news/2017/04/20/mdhs-confirms-most-new-applicants-rejected
-welfare/100692926/.

123   *"constant fight"*: "Mississippi Today's Anna Wolfe Explains Sprawling
Welfare Fraud Case," Mississippi Today, December 23, 2021, https://
mississippitoday.org/2021/12/23/anna-wolfe-mississippi-welfare-fraud
-case/.

123   *sprawling public embezzlement scheme:* Anna Wolfe, "Connecting the
Dots: Players in Massive Welfare Embezzlement Case Got Millions
from Taxpayers, but Helped Few," Mississippi Today, February 6, 2020,
https://mississippitoday.org/2020/02/06/connecting-the-dots-players-in
-massive-welfare-embezzlement-case-got-millions-from-taxpayers-but
-helped-few/.

123   *conspired with the director:* Tim Kalich, "The Squeeze on Nancy New,"
Greenwood (MS) Commonwealth, October 16, 2021, www.gwcommon
wealth.com/columns-opinion-top-stories/squeeze-nancy-new#s; Anna
Wolfe, "Accountant Pleads Guilty in Welfare Embezzlement Case, Is
Working with Prosecutors," Mississippi Today, October 11, 2021, https://
mississippitoday.org/2021/10/11/accountant-pleads-guilty-in-welfare
-embezzlement-case-is-working-with-prosecutors/.

123   *$77 million:* The auditor's office issued a demand to Davis for $96.313
million—which includes interest—for his role authorizing more than
$77 million in illegal TANF spending, https://www2.osa.ms.gov/news
/auditor-demands-repayment-of-misspent-welfare-money/.

123   *"equestrian activities":* Anna Wolfe, "Sports Legend's Madison County
Horse Ranch Being Paid by Nonprofit at Center of Welfare Embezzlement Firestorm," Mississippi Today, March 18, 2020, https://
mississippitoday.org/2020/03/18/sports-legends-madison-county-horse
-ranch-being-paid-for-by-nonprofit-at-center-of-welfare-embezzlement
-firestorm/.

123   *actually took place:* Wolfe, "Sports Legend's Madison County Horse Ranch
Being Paid."

123   *with TANF funds:* Wolfe, "Accountant Pleads Guilty"; Anna Wolfe, "Son of
'Million Dollar Man' Admits to Defrauding Mississippi's Welfare Agency,
Turns State's Evidence," Mississippi Today, December 17, 2020, https://
mississippitoday.org/2020/12/17/son-of-million-dollar-man-admits-to
-defrauding-mississippis-welfare-agency-turns-states-evidence/.

124   *reimburse the state:* Michael Levenson, "Brett Favre Repays $600,000 in
Mississippi Welfare Fraud Case," *New York Times*, October 27, 2021, www
.nytimes.com/2021/10/27/us/brett-favre-mississippi-welfare.html#:~:text
=Brett%20Favre%2C%20the%20Hall%20of,to%20the%20state%20
auditor's%20office.

124   *denies the state's claim:* Levenson, "Brett Favre Repays."

124   *Favre's text messages:* Laura Strickler and Ken Dilanian, "'Santa Came
Today': Brett Favre Texts Show His Role in Mississippi Welfare

Scandal," NBC News, September 14, 2022, www.nbcnews.com/politics
/politics-news/brett-favre-texts-show-role-mississippi-welfare-scandal
-rcna47654.

124   *"activities that benefit"*: Anna Wolfe, "Why Did a Welfare Organization
Pay $5 Million to Build a Volleyball Stadium?," Mississippi Today, Febru-
ary 27, 2020, https://mississippitoday.org/2020/02/27/welfare-program
-paid-5-million-for-new-volleyball-center/.

124   *October 2018:* Anna Wolfe, "The Governor, the Quarterback and the
Concussion Discussion," *Gazebo Gazette*, March 8, 2020, https://
thegazebogazette.com/2020/03/the-governor-the-quarterback-and-the
-concussion-discussion/.

125   *a lot of wiggle room:* Edin and Shaefer, *$2.00 a Day.*

125   *ranks among the most corrupt:* The extent of public corruption is notori-
ously hard to measure, for reasons explained in Adriana S. Cordis and Jeffrey Milyo, "Measuring Public Corruption in the United States: Evidence
from Administrative Records of Federal Prosecutions," *Public Integrity* 18,
no. 2 (2016): 127–48.

125   *highest official child poverty rate:* "Mississippi Report 2019," TalkPoverty
.org, https://talkpoverty.org/state-year-report/mississippi-2019-report/;
"QuickFacts: Mississippi," US Census Bureau, www.census.gov/quick
facts/fact/table/MS/IPE120220#IPE120220. See also official TANF
caseload data at Resource Library of the Office of Family Assistance,
US Department of Health and Human Services, www.acf.hhs.gov/ofa
/resource-library?f%5B0%5D=program%3A270&f%5B1%5D=program
_topic%3A634&sort_by=combined_publication_date&sort_order=
DESC&items_per_page=10.

125   *only 5 percent:* "Mississippi TANF Spending," Center on Budget and
Policy and Priorities, www.cbpp.org/sites/default/files/atoms/files/tanf
_spending_ms.pdf.

125   *"multi-generational, collaborative approach":* Wolfe, "Sports Legend's Madison County Horse Ranch."

125   *"increase poverty":* Kalich, "Squeeze on Nancy New."

126   *$5 million in fines:* Julia James, "Feds Add Charges for Nancy and Zach
New in Alleged Education Fraud Scheme," Mississippi Today, July 15,
2021, https://mississippitoday.org/2021/07/15/nancy-new-zach-new-federal
-charges-fraud-scheme/.

126   *barbaric penal institutions:* Anna Wolfe, "Nancy and Zach New Plead
Guilty to Bribery and Fraud in State Welfare Case," Mississippi Today,
April 22, 2022, https://mississippitoday.org/2022/04/22/nancy-new-zach
-new-plead-guilty-welfare-scandal/.

126   *Brett Favre insisted:* Levenson, "Brett Favre Repays."

126   *Anna Wolfe questioned:* "Mississippi Today's Anna Wolfe Explains."

127   *Illegal casinos:* Staff, "Letty Liked the Liners," The Falfurrias News,
June 16, 2016, http://thefalfurriasnews.com/2016/06/16/letty-liked-liners/.

127   *implicated not only the city:* Alan Greenblatt, "Why Is Public Corruption So Common in South Texas?," Governing, April 27, 2016, www.governing .com/archive/gov-public-corruption-crystal-city-texas.html.

127   *"Most Corrupt Little Town":* Matt Zapotosky, "This Might Be the Most Corrupt Little Town in America," *Washington Post,* March 5, 2016, www .washingtonpost.com/world/national-security/this-might-be-the-most -corrupt-little-town-in-america/2016/03/05/341c21d2-dcac-11e5-81ae -7491b9b9e7df_story.html.

127   *"jobs boost":* Staff, "Diaper Company Adding 262 Jobs in Mullins in Next Four Years," *Post and Courier* (Charleston, SC), September 28, 2009.

127   *"Foul Smell":* Rick Brundrett, "Foul Smell for Taxpayers in S.C. Diaper Plant Project," The Nerve, November 11, 2013.

127   *"grossly inflated rates":* Rick Brundrett, "Struggling Diaper Plant President Speaks Out; Public Officials Largely Silent," The Nerve, January 13, 2014, https://thenerve.org/2014/01/struggling-diaper-plant-president-speaks -out-public-officials-largely-silent/.

128   *"six years in prison":* SCNow Staff, "Judge Sentences Ex–Mullins Schools Leader to Six Years in Prison," SCNow, October 19, 2011, https://scnow .com/news/local/judge-sentences-ex-mullins-schools-leader-to-six-years -in-prison/article_90c8bafd-5229-58af-bcf6-123e5840db9c.html.

128   *corrosive effects of corruption:* Bill Estep, "Decades of Poverty and Vote-Buying Led to Widespread Corruption in Clay County," *Lexington (KY) Herald-Leader,* August 24, 2019, www.kentucky.com/news/special-reports /fifty-years-of-night/.

128   *"semi-autonomous state":* Robert Ireland, *Little Kingdoms: The Counties of Kentucky, 1850–1891* (Lexington: University Press of Kentucky, 1977), 1, 142–43.

128   *"hardest place":* Alan Flippan, "Where Are the Hardest Places to Live in the U.S.?," *New York Times,* June 26, 2014, www.nytimes.com/2014/06/26 /upshot/where-are-the-hardest-places-to-live-in-the-us.html.

129   *akin to that of cotton:* Billings and Blee, *Road to Poverty.*

129   *salt was in constant demand:* Frederick J. Turner, "The Significance of the Frontier in American History," *Proceedings of the State Historical Society of Wisconsin* 41 (1893): 18.

129   *"readily converted into cash":* John A. Jakle, "Salt on the Ohio Valley Frontier, 1770–1820," *Annals of the Association of American Geographers* 59, no. 4 (December 1968): 701. See also Mark Kurlansky, *Salt: A World History* (New York: Penguin Books, 2003).

129   *quarter of a million bushels:* Alan Banks, "Class Formation in the Southeastern Kentucky Coalfields: 1890–1920," in *Appalachia in the Making,* ed. Mary Beth Pudup, Dwight B. Billings, and Altina L. Waller (Chapel Hill: University of North Carolina Press, 1995), 323.

129   *enabled the rise:* Billings and Blee, *Road to Poverty,* 48.

129   *highly stratified social order:* Billings and Blee, *Road to Poverty,* 53–55.

130   *vastly unequal:* Billings and Blee, *Road to Poverty,* 23; Steven A. Channing, *Kentucky: A Bicentennial History* (New York: Oxford University Books, 1977), 43.

130   *"feudal fashion":* John C. Campbell, *The Southern Highlander and His Homeland* (New York: Russell Sage Foundation, 1921), 42.

130   *most powerful men:* Dwight Billings and Kathleen Blee, "Agriculture and Poverty in the Kentucky Mountains: Beech Creek, 1850–1910," in Pudup, Billings, and Waller, eds., *Appalachia in the Making,* 237; Billings and Blee, *Road to Poverty,* 57.

130   *20,000 acres by 1860:* Billings and Blee, "Agriculture and Poverty," 237.

131   *"economic and political dynasties":* Pudup, Billings, and Waller, eds., *Appalachia in the Making,* 237; Billings and Blee, *Road to Poverty,* 237.

131   *remove children:* Billings and Blee, *Road to Poverty.*

131   *"within the compass":* Billings and Blee, *Road to Poverty,* 252.

132   *"feuds or vendettas":* Altina L. Waller, "Feuding in Appalachia: Evolution of a Stereotype," in Pudup, Billings, and Waller, eds., *Appalachia in the Making,* 351–52.

132   *reflect the rivalries:* Waller, "Feuding in Appalachia," 237, 364.

132   *began to collapse:* Billings and Blee, "Agriculture and Poverty," 238.

132   *"deepening economic and geographical isolation":* Billings and Blee, *Road to Poverty,* 243.

132   *"grubbing hoe and plow":* Quoted in Billings and Blee, *Road to Poverty,* 199.

132   *"for later industrial exploitation":* Paul Salstrom, *Appalachia's Path to Dependency: Rethinking a Region's Economic History, 1730–1940* (Lexington: University Press of Kentucky, 2015), 11, www.jstor.org/stable/10.2307/j.cttl30hmt7.

132   *Billings and Blee recount:* Billings and Blee, *Road to Poverty,* 281. Note that the Oneida Baptist Institute in Oneida, Kentucky, was founded in 1899 to solve violence and feuding. See https://www.oneidaschool.org/about/history.cfm.

133   *twin collapse:* Billings and Blee, "Agriculture and Poverty," 256.

133   *"pathetic remnants":* Williams, *Appalachia: A History,* 250.

133   *absentee capitalists:* Mary Beth Pudup, "The Boundaries of Class in Preindustrial Appalachia," *Journal of Historical Geography* 15, no. 2 (1989): 139–62.

133   *positioned to benefit:* For example: "Edward G. and William T. Garrard signed an agreement with a New York City timber magnate to protect his Clay County lands from trespassers, to aid in securing tenants to occupy the land, and to procure the rights of way for the removal of timber in exchange for half of the net timber proceeds." Billings and Blee, *Road to Poverty,* 275.

133   *potential mineral wealth:* Williams, *Appalachia: A History,* 195.

133   *selling rights-of-way:* Historian John Alexander Williams writes, "The transforming effect that even a modest feeder line could have is illus-

trated by the L&N branch that reached Manchester, the county seat of Clay County, Kentucky, in 1917. . . . Within a few weeks of its completion, Clay County coal mines—confined to local markets since the antebellum saltworks had finally closed down—were shipping coal to urban and industrial markets." Williams, *Appalachia: A History*, 233.

134   *"equity positions"*: Pudup, "Boundaries of Class," 159.

134   *"the development of underdevelopment"*: Richard Mark Simon, "The Development of Underdevelopment: The Coal Industry and Its Effects on the West Virginia Economy, 1880–1920" (PhD diss., University of Pittsburgh, 1978), quoted in Pudup, "Boundaries of Class," 4.

134   *"economic colony"*: Eller, *Miners, Millhands, and Mountaineers*, 85.

134   *Political patronage:* Billings and Blee, *Road to Poverty*, 328.

134   *"threaten the social structure"*: Billings and Blee, *Road to Poverty*, 330.

134   *"control over patronage"*: Billings and Blee, *Road to Poverty*, 330.

135   *Community Action Program (CAP):* Douglas O. Arnett, "Eastern Kentucky: The Politics of Dependency and Underdevelopment" (PhD diss., Duke University, 1978), 232.

135   *failure to achieve:* Comptroller General of the United States, "Financial and Management Activities of the Jackson-Clay Community Action Group, Incorporated Manchester, Kentucky" (Washington, DC, Office of Economic Opportunity; Department of Health, Education, and Welfare; and Department of Labor, January 19, 1972), www.gao.gov/assets/b-171949.pdf.

135   *denial of suffrage:* For a discussion of elite capture and vote buying in another Appalachian county, see Duncan, *Worlds Apart*.

135   *use of bribes:* Billings and Blee, *Road to Poverty*, 159.

135   *records show:* Karen Samples, "Oversight of Community Action Lax: Antipoverty Groups Raised Questions over Priorities," *Lexington (KY) Herald-Leader*, February 16, 1997, 1. See also Karen Samples, "Material Didn't All Go to Poor, Poverty Agency's Workers Say," *Lexington (KY) Herald-Leader*, January 30, 1997, 1.

136   *nearly absolute:* Cynthia Duncan also points to the fact that in her research from field sites in central Appalachia and the Mississippi Delta, she finds a few families hold local control, although she focuses less on corruption. Duncan, *Worlds Apart*.

136   *"closely guarded patronage preserves"*: Pudup, "Boundaries of Class," 155.

137   *pawnshop owner:* Estep, "Sentence Cut."

137   *illicit sale:* Estep, "Chapter 12."

137   *"In one of the bloodiest"*: Francis X. Cline, "In Eastern Kentucky, Politics Extends a Bloody Legacy," *New York Times*, June 2, 2002, www.nytimes.com/2002/06/02/us/in-eastern-kentucky-politics-extends-a-bloody-legacy.html.

138   *gain the sympathy:* Bill Estep, "Mayor Says She Was Told to Buy Votes," *Lexington (KY) Herald-Leader*, November 10, 2015, www.kentucky.com/news/state/kentucky/article44024610.html.

138   *gotten some dirt:* Cline, "In Eastern Kentucky."

138   *lesser sentences:* United States v. Adams (July 17, 2013), https://caselaw
.findlaw.com/us-6th-circuit/1639076.html. Those testifying against Maricle and Adams included Jennings White's crony Vernon Hacker, who used
his position as director of the 911 system to tip off drug dealers, including Kenneth Day, when complaints or tips came through 911. Denver
Sizemore, who was serving as county clerk despite a felony conviction
for dealing drugs, also testified. Jennings White himself testified that he
witnessed the competition's cronies buying votes while he was out doing
the same. Bill Estep, "Former Clay Clerk Describes $100,000 Worth of
Vote-Buying in 2002 Primary," *Lexington (KY) Herald-Leader,* November 10, 2015, www.kentucky.com/latest-news/article44025060.html.

139   *all convicted:* Bill Estep, "Jury Convicts All 8 Defendants in Clay Vote-
Buying Case," *Lexington (KY) Herald-Leader,* November 10, 2015, www
.kentucky.com/news/state/kentucky/article44027145.html.

139   *"mountain politics":* Janet Paiton and Valerie Honeycutt Spears, "Vote
Buying Reports Come In from 11 Counties: Perry Man Allegedly Gave
Out Ballot Sheets, $20," *Lexington (KY) Herald-Leader,* May 19, 2010, 2.
We found that residents often voted in local elections but were more
disconnected from state and national elections.

140   *state of mind:* Duncan, *Worlds Apart,* see chapter 1. See also Jennifer Sherman, *Those Who Work, Those Who Don't: Poverty, Morality, and Family in
Rural America* (Minneapolis: University of Minnesota Press, 2009).

141   *one central distinction:* For more on this, see Sherman, *Those Who Work;*
Emily E. N. Miller and Kathryn Edin, "Coming of Age in Appalachia,
Emerging or Expedited Adulthood?," *RSF: The Russell Sage Foundation
Journal of the Social Sciences* 8, no. 4 (May 2022); Robert Wuthnow, *The
Left Behind: Decline and Rage in Small-Town America* (Princeton, NJ:
Princeton University Press, 2018), 108.

141   *"pauper idiots":* Arthur Estabrook, "The Pauper Idiot in Kentucky," *Social Forces* 7, no. 1 (September 1928): 68–72. In Clay, the proportion has
historically been unusually high, according to Estabrook, who quotes a
state auditor's report from 1881, which reads, "I am fully satisfied, that this
charity is greatly abused. . . . A very large portion of these beneficiaries
are mere children, less than ten years old. . . . I am creditably informed
that in some counties people go around and hunt up children, who do
not manifest the ordinary degree of sprightliness, take them before the
county court, and obtain a verdict of idiocy with the understanding that
the person [bringing the child forward] shall . . . receive a portion of the
annual allowance." Receipt of government benefits was also high in 1935,
during the New Deal, when twenty-one of the twenty-nine US counties
with the highest rates of receipt were in Appalachia, eleven of them in
Kentucky. Williams, *Appalachia: A History,* 315.

141   *draw government assistance for life:* Nicholas Kristof, "Profiting from a Child's Illiteracy," *New York Times,* December 7, 2012, www.nytimes .com/2012/12/09/opinion/sunday/kristof-profiting-from-a-childs -illiteracy.html.

141   *only 213:* "Kentucky: Table 3. Number of Recipients [of SSI] in State . . . and Amount of Payments, by County, December 2020," www.ssa.gov /policy/docs/statcomps/ssi_sc/2020/ky.pdf.

142   *Only 185 kids:* "Kentucky: Table 3. Number of Recipients [of SSI] in State . . . and Amount of Payments, by County, December 2019," www .ssa.gov/policy/docs/statcomps/ssi_sc/2019/ky.pdf.

142   *"political battles":* Jason Bailey, "Speak Your Piece: Why Regions Fail," The Daily Yonder, January 14, 2013, https://dailyyonder.com/speak-your -piece-why-regions-fail/2013/01/14/.

142   *official labor force participation rate:* Authors' analysis of US Census Bureau, American Community Survey data.

143   *some form of disability:* Authors' analysis of data from the Social Security Administration.

143   *$600,000 in kickbacks:* John Cheves, "Social Security Lawyer Conn Charged with Fraud, Money Laundering," *Lexington (KY) Herald-Leader,* April 6, 2016, www.kentucky.com/news/local/watchdog/article70011212 .html. See also WSAZ News Staff, "Former Administrative Law Judge Daugherty Dies While Serving Prison Sentence in SSA Fraud Case," WSAZ News Channel 3, April 7, 2016, www.wsaz.com/content/news /Third-Suspect-Accused-in-SSA-Fraud-Case-Arrested-in-South -Carolina-374959721.html.

143   *cutting off his disability:* Bill Estep and Karla Ward, "As Apple TV+ Series Premieres, Eric Conn's Chaos Isn't over for His Former Clients," *Lexington (KY) Herald-Leader,* May 6, 2022, www.kentucky.com/news/local /crime/article261077927.html.

144   *A report examining:* "20 Years in the Making: Kentucky's Workforce Crisis" (report, Kentucky Chamber Foundation, September 2021), www .kychamber.com/sites/default/files/pdfs/20%20Years%20in%20the%20 Making%20-%20Kentucky%27s%20Workforce%20Crisis_2.pdf.

145   *physically demanding work:* Case and Deaton, *Deaths of Despair.*

145   *"has deep historical roots":* Luis Angeles and Kyriakos Neanidis, "The Persistent Effect of Colonialism on Corruption," *Economica* 82, no. 326 (April 2015): 319–49.

145   Lexington Herald-Leader *editorialized:* J. Carfagno, "Corruption No Way to Attract Business to State," *Lexington (KY) Herald-Leader,* March 13, 2011, www.kentucky.com/opinion/op-ed/article44083989.html.

146   *"small-time political machines":* "Who Will Lead E. Ky. out of Economy-Crushing Corruption?," *Lexington (KY) Herald-Leader,* www.kentucky .com/opinion/editorials/article97240397.html.

Chapter 6: The Invisible Hand

147   *The Invisible Hand:* Special thanks to our research colleagues Jasmine Simington and Meg Duffy, whose work was central in the development of this chapter. See Meg Duffy and H. Luke Shaefer, "In the Aftermath of the Storm: Administrative Burden in Disaster Recovery," *Social Service Review* 96, no. 3 (2022): 507–33; Jasmine Simington, "Displaced Trust: Disrupting Legal Estrangement During Racialized Disaster Recovery" (University of Michigan working paper, 2022).

147   *"Everything is gone":* Bo Petersen, "Nichols, Other SC River Towns Face Flood 2 years After Hurricane Matthew Disaster," *Post and Courier* (Charleston, SC), September 14, 2018.

148   *told the local news:* Matthew Edwards, "Two Years Later, S.C. Town Still Recovering from Back-to-Back Hurricane Losses," Carolina News & Reporter, October 20, 2022, https://carolinanewsandreporter.cic.sc.edu /two-years-later-s-c-town-still-recovering-from-back-to-back-hurricane -losses/.

148   *"It was pitch-black":* Edwards, "Two Years Later."

148   *Pace's Pharmacy:* Chloe Johnson and Stephen Hobbs, "After 2 Major Floods in 3 Years, Half of the Residents of This SC Town Never Came Home," *Post and Courier* (Charleston, SC), October 5, 2019, www.postandcourier .com/news/after-2-major-floods-in-3-years-half-of-the-residents-of-this -sc-town/article_6924111c-c823-11e9-b098-1bc79ec41762.html.

149   *"raise our house":* Tonya Brown, "Some Marion County Residents Strug- gle to Recover from Hurricanes, Say County Isn't Helping," WPDE ABC News, March 27, 2019, https://wpde.com/news/local/some-marion -county-residents-struggle-to-recover-from-hurricanes-say-county-isnt -helping.

149   *structural racism:* Some of the themes described in this chapter are in line with the arguments of critical race theory. See Kimberlé Crenshaw, Neil T. Gotanda, Gary Peller, and Kendall Thomas, eds., *Critical Race Theory: The Key Writings That Formed the Movement* (New York: New Press, 1996).

150   *The Gini Index is a metric:* "Gini Index," US Census Bureau, www.census .gov/topics/income-poverty/income-inequality/about/metrics/gini-index .html#:~:text=The%20Gini%20Index%20is%20a,across%20the%20 entire%20income%20distribution; "Gini Index," World Bank, https:// data.worldbank.org/indicator/SI.POV.GINI.

151   *a viable path:* Noam Scheiber, "Building Solar Farms May Not Build the Middle Class," *New York Times*, July 16, 2021, www.nytimes.com /2021/07/16/business/economy/green-energy-jobs-economy.html.

152   *$1.5 billion in damages:* Duffy and Shaefer, "In the Aftermath."

152   *"most impacted and distressed area":* Duffy and Shaefer, "In the Aftermath."

152   *increasingly violent weather events:* The EPA has reported that climate

change "is causing increases in temperature across the Southeast." "Climate Impacts in the Southeast," US Environmental Protection Agency, January 19, 2017, https://19january2017snapshot.epa.gov/climate-impacts/climate-impacts-southeast_.html.

152 *hit the hardest:* Increasing hurricane activity and intense wet periods are expected to be accompanied by increasing spells of extreme heat and drought in the Southeast, which appears to be in for both more severe wet and more severe dry weather. "Climate Impacts in the Southeast."

154 *"serious needs":* "FEMA Fact Sheet: Individuals and Households Program," US Department of Homeland Security, updated May 2018, https://colfaxne.com/pdfs/emergency_manager/Individuals%20and%20Households%20Programs%20Fact%20Sheet.pdf.

154 *"heir's property":* To learn more about heir's property, see Thomas W. Mitchell, "Reforming Property Law to Address Devastating Land Loss," *Alabama Law Review* 66, no. 1 (2014).

156 *millions of acres:* "Amount of Land Owned as Heirs' Property," Heirs' Property, Farmland Access Legal Toolkit, Center for Agriculture & Food Systems, https://farmlandaccess.org/heirs-property/#amountoflandowned.

156 *held claim to land:* B. James Deaton, "Land 'in Heirs': Building a Hypothesis Concerning Tenancy in Common and the Persistence of Poverty in Central Appalachia," *Journal of Appalachian Studies* 11, nos. 1/2 (2005): 83–94.

156 *a beginning reader:* "U.S. Skills Map."

157 *shaped by cultural traditions:* Deaton, "Land 'in Heirs'"; Janice F. Dyer and Conner Bailey, "A Place to Call Home: Cultural Understandings of Heir Property Among Rural African Americans," *Rural Sociology* 73, no. 3 (2008): 317–38.

158 *"ensure legal title":* Barton Myers, "Sherman's Field Order No. 15," New Georgia Encyclopedia, updated September 30, 2020, www.georgiaencyclopedia.org/articles/history-archaeology/shermans-field-order-no-15.

158 *"to have land":* Henry Louis Gates Jr., *100 Amazing Facts About the Negro* (New York: Pantheon, 2017). See PBS.org site for quote.

158 *acquired homesteads:* Warren Hoffnagle, "The Southern Homestead Act: Its Origins and Operation," *The Historian* 32, no. 4 (1970): 612–29.

159 *Black landholdings:* John Francis Ficara and Jaun Williams, "Black Farmers in America," NPR, February 22, 2005, https://www.npr.org/2005/02/22/5228987/black-farmers-in-america.

159 *eventually became owners:* W. E. B. Du Bois, "The Negro Landholder of Georgia," *Bulletin of the United States Bureau of Labor* 35, no. 6 (July 1901): 89–219.

159 *Black farm ownership:* Ficara and Williams, "Black Farmers in America."

159 *Vann Newkirk reported:* Vann R. Newkirk II, "The Great Land Robbery: The Shameful Story of How 1 Million Black Families Have Been Ripped from Their Farms," *The Atlantic,* September 2019, www.theatlantic.com/magazine/archive/2019/09/this-land-was-our-land/594742/.

160   *completed an application:* Duffy and Shaefer, "In the Aftermath."

162   *incomes below $15,000:* "Low-Income Households Disproportionately Denied by FEMA Is a Sign of a System That Is Failing the Most Vulnerable," Harvey Recovery, Texas Housers, November 30, 2018, https://texashousers .net/2018/11/30/low-income-households-disproportionately-denied-by -fema-is-a-sign-of-a-system-that-is-failing-the-most-vulnerable/.

163   *any such loophole:* Duffy and Shaefer, "In the Aftermath."

163   *policy feedback loop:* Duffy and Shaefer, "In the Aftermath."

164   *"a growing body of research":* Christopher Flavelle, "Why Does Disaster Aid Often Favor White People?," *New York Times*, June 7, 2021, www .nytimes.com/2021/06/07/climate/FEMA-race-climate.html.

165   *In one study:* Junia Howell and James R. Elliott, "Damages Done: The Longitudinal Impacts of Natural Hazards on Wealth Inequality in the United States," *Social Problems* 66, no. 3 (2018): 448–67, https://academic .oup.com/socpro/article/66/3/448/5074453?login=true.

165   *analysis conducted for us:* Analysis by Meg Duffy and John Laycock of Texas Appleseed based on OpenFEMA Individuals and Households Program Housing Assistance Data.

166   *higher rates of mortality:* Melba Newsome, "Unchecked Growth of Industrial Animal Farms Spurs Long Fight for Environmental Justice in Eastern NC," NC Health News, October 20, 2021, www.northcarolinahealth news.org/2021/10/20/environmental-justice-and-industrial-farming-in -eastern-nc/; Julia Kravchenko, Sung Han Rhew, Igor Akushevich, Pankaj Agarwal, and H. Kim Lyerly, "Mortality and Health Outcomes in North Carolina Communities Located in Close Proximity to Hog Concentrated Animal Feeding Operations," *North Carolina Medical Journal* 79, no. 5 (2018): 278–88, www.ncmedicaljournal.com/content/79/5/278.full.

166   *further polluting:* Cameron Oglesby, "Hurricane Season Spurs Hog Waste Worries in North Carolina," *Environmental Health News*, May 17, 2021, www.ehn.org/north-carolina-hurricanes-hog-farms-2652972415/hog -death-during-storms.

166   *"early life exposure":* Council on Environmental Health, American Academy of Pediatrics, "Pesticide Exposure in Children," *Pediatrics* 130, no. 6 (2012): e1757–63.

167   *waterways and nearby soil:* Nicole Kehoe, "How Dangerous Is Pesticide Drift?," *Scientific American*, September 17, 2012, https://www.scientific american.com/article/pesticide-drift/

167   *He has found:* Michael Hendryx and Benjamin Holland, "Unintended Consequences of the Clean Air Act: Mortality Rates in Appalachian Coal Mining Communities," *Environmental Science & Policy* 63 (September 2016): 1–6.

Chapter 7: Revolt and Retribution

169   *periodic revolt:* For a deeper discussion of some of the themes in this chapter, see Christian Davenport, *How Social Movements Die: Repression and*

Demobilization of the Republic of New Africa, Cambridge Studies in Contentious Politics (New York: Cambridge University Press, 2015); Michael Hechter, *Internal Colonialism: The Celtic Fringe in British National Development* (Berkeley: University of California Press, 1975).

169   *demand for coal plummeted:* John Gaventa, *Power and Powerlessness: Quiescence and Rebellion in an Appalachian Valley* (Champaign: University of Illinois Press, 1980).

169   *bituminous coal:* John C. Hennen, "Introduction to the New Edition," in *Harlan Miners Speak: Report on Terrorism in the Kentucky Coal Fields*, new ed., National Committee for the Defense of Political Prisoners (Lexington: University Press of Kentucky, 2008).

170   *average per capita earnings:* Eller, *Miners, Millhands, and Mountaineers*, 239.

170   *"dumping coal":* Jim Garland, *Welcome the Traveler Home: Jim Garland's Story of the Kentucky Mountains* (Lexington: University Press of Kentucky, 1983), 136.

170   *cotton also staggered:* For example, by 1931 the price of cotton lint (less desirable than cotton, but still critical in manufacturing) had plummeted to 6 cents a pound, compared to 17 cents in 1920.

170   *terrible drought:* John Solomon Otto, *The Final Frontiers, 1880–1930: Settling the Southern Bottomlands*, Contributions in American History, no. 183 (Westport, CT: Greenwood Press, 1999), 83.

170   *hungry families marching:* "England Food Riot of 1931," Encyclopedia of Arkansas, https://encyclopediaofarkansas.net/entries/england-food -riot-of-1931-1308/.

170   *reestablish the union:* John W. Hevener, *Which Side Are You On? The Harlan County Coal Miners, 1931–39* (Champaign: University of Illinois Press, 1978), 33.

171   *"to enter the mine":* Garland, *Welcome the Traveler Home*, 139–40.

171   *"all suffered":* Shaunna L. Scott, *Two Sides to Everything: The Cultural Construction of Class Consciousness in Harlan County, Kentucky*, SUNY Series in Oral and Public History (Albany: State University of New York Press, 1995), 26.

172   *"mine wars":* For a comprehensive account of these wars, see James R. Green, *The Devil Is Here in These Hills: West Virginia's Coal Miners and Their Battle for Freedom* (New York: Atlantic Monthly Press, 2015).

172   *Only 913 remained:* Hevener, *Which Side Are You On?*, 46.

172   *"The effort to break the strike":* Adelaide Walker, "Living Conditions in the Coal Fields," in *Harlan Miners Speak: Report on Terrorism in the Kentucky Coal Fields*, 1st ed., National Committee for the Defense of Political Prisoners (New York: Harcourt, Brace, 1932), 90.

172   *enduring militant ballad:* Hevener, *Which Side Are You On?*, 61.

173   *children were dying:* National Committee for the Defense of Political Prisoners, *Harlan Miners Speak*, 1st ed., 279.

173   *performed her composition:* Several years later, Aunt Molly and part of her

clan would move to New York City to join Woody Guthrie and Pete Seeger in activism through folk music.

173   *extraditable charge:* Kentucky's 1919 statute was passed after World War I
to quell unions and was not deemed in violation of the First Amendment
until 1966.

173   *three-fourths of the Cotton Belt's Black workers:* Arthur Franklin Raper, *Pref-
ace to Peasantry: A Tale of Two Black Belt Counties,* Southern Classics Series
(Columbia: University of South Carolina Press, 2005), 237.

174   *organized 92 percent:* Hevener, *Which Side Are You On?,* 97.

174   *colleagues estimated:* Charles S. Johnson, Edwin R. Embree, and Will Win-
ton Alexander, *The Collapse of Cotton Tenancy: Summary of Field Studies &
Statistical Surveys, 1933–35* (Chapel Hill: University of North Carolina
Press, 1935), 4.

174   *largest cotton plantation:* Otto, *The Final Frontiers,* 94.

174   *Charles S. Johnson and coauthors:* Johnson, Embree, and Alexander, *Collapse
of Cotton Tenancy,* 49–51.

175   *"plough-up" money:* James D. Ross, *The Rise and Fall of the Southern Tenant
Farmers Union in Arkansas* (Knoxville: University of Tennessee Press,
2018), 71.

175   *"On a sultry":* Jerold S. Auerbach, "Southern Tenant Farmers: Socialist
Critics of the New Deal," *Labor History* 7, no. 1 (Winter 1966): 7, https://
doi.org/10.1080/00236566608583975.

175   *"tillers of the soil":* Bulletin of the United States Bureau of Labor Statistics,
Issues 822–836, 307.

176   *potent threat:* Auerbach, "Southern Tenant Farmers," 7.

176   *His book:* Howard Kester, *Revolt Among the Sharecroppers* (New York:
Covici, Friede, 1936).

176   *"incitement of litigation":* Merriam-Webster.com, s.v. "barratry," www
.merriam-webster.com/dictionary/barratry.

176   *without stopping:* H. L. Mitchell, *Mean Things Happening in This Land: The
Life and Times of H. L. Mitchell, Co-founder of the Southern Tenant Farmers
Union* (Montclair, NJ: Allanheld, Osmun, 1979), 55.

176   *"wanted investigated":* Mitchell, *Mean Things Happening,* 60.

176   *kept secret:* Mitchell, *Mean Things Happening.*

177   *convicted and fined:* Van Hawkins, *Plowing New Ground: The Southern
Tenant Farmers Union and Its Place in Delta History* (Virginia Beach: The
Donning Company Publishers, 2007).

177   *"forlorn faces":* Hawkins, *Plowing New Ground,* 131.

177   *violating public health codes:* Hawkins, *Plowing New Ground,* 134. The union
continued to exist for many years. It was renamed the National Farm
Labor Union in 1944, and in 1948 it moved to Washington, DC, only officially closing up shop with the death of Harry Mitchell in 1989. During its
existence, it was continually beset by internal strife. One major problem

was the interracial nature of the union, which was so at odds with southern social codes of the times.

177 *"pressure was generated"*: Michael Harrington, foreword to Mitchell, *Mean
   Things Happening, ix.

178 *"interracial solidarity"*: Jason Manthorne, "The View from the Cotton: Re-
   considering the Southern Tenant Farmers' Union," *Agricultural History*
   84, no. 1 (2010): 21.

178 *Block replied, without hesitation:* Joe Sinsheimer, "Never Turn Back: An Interview with Sam Block," *Southern Exposure Magazine* 25, no. 2 (Summer
   1987): 40.

179 *"militant campaign"*: John Dittmer, *Local People: The Struggle for Civil
   Rights in Mississippi (Champaign: University of Illinois Press, 1994), 128,
   http://hdl.handle.net/2027/mdp.39015066055859.

179 *just over 47,000 residents:* Dittmer, *Local People,* 129.

179 *received the surplus commodities:* Dittmer, *Local People,* 148.

179 *"the largest single registration effort"*: Dittmer, *Local People,* 147.

180 *"answer this kind of violence"*: Charles M. Payne, *I've Got the Light of Free-
   dom: The Organizing Tradition and the Mississippi Freedom Struggle (Berkeley: University of California Press, 2007), 163.

180 *"testing ground"*: Dittmer, *Local People,* 148.

180 *"doubled the size"*: Dittmer, *Local People,* 150.

180 *interceded to protect:* Dittmer, *Local People,* 153.

181 *"The Justice Department retreat"*: Dittmer, *Local People,* 155.

181 *"building a solid movement"*: Payne, *I've Got the Light of Freedom,* 175.

181 *Mississippi Summer Project:* Doug McAdam, *Freedom Summer* (New York:
   Oxford University Press, 1990). There are several firsthand accounts by
   Freedom Summer workers in Greenwood, including Sally Belfrage, *Freedom Summer* (University of Virginia Press, 1965); Holland, *From the Mississippi Delta,* 1997; Sinsheimer, "Never Turn Back," 37–50. The Library
   of Congress has videos and transcripts of civil rights workers recalling
   their experiences in Greenwood and other places through its Civil Rights
   History Project, www.loc.gov/collections/civil-rights-history-project
   /about-this-collection/.

181 *deep resistance from whites:* Payne, *I've Got the Light of Freedom.*

182 *tried to register:* McAdam, *Freedom Summer,* https://kinginstitute.stanford
   .edu/encyclopedia/freedom-summer.

183 *"consistently refused service"*: Payne, *I've Got the Light of Freedom,* 319–20.

183 *charged its Black customers:* Payne, *I've Got the Light of Freedom,* 320.

183 *important ally:* Payne, *I've Got the Light of Freedom,* 324.

184 *"raw white supremacy"*: Payne, *I've Got the Light of Freedom,* 327–28.

184 *"There is one Texas"*: "The Other Texans," 68.

184 *Armando Navarro details:* Armando Navarro, *The Cristal Experiment: A
   Chicano Struggle for Community Control (Madison: University of Wisconsin

Press, 1998). This section draws heavily on this work, with thanks. He also uses the concept of internal colony to discuss the Crystal City case.

185 *One historical account:* Marc Simon Rodriguez, *The Tejano Diaspora* (Chapel Hill: University of North Carolina Press, 2011), 50.

185 *the face of the electorate:* Navarro, *Cristal Experiment.*

186 *"against tactics":* Rodriguez, *Tejano Diaspora,* 52.

186 *"fifth-grade educations":* Rodriguez, *Tejano Diaspora,* 51–52.

186 *"afraid to participate":* Julian Samora, Joe Bernal, and Albert Pena, *Gunpowder Justice: A Reassessment of the Texas Rangers* (Notre Dame, IN: University of Notre Dame Press, 1979), 103, quoted in Navarro, *Cristal Experiment.*

186 *"Los Cinco":* Teresa Palomo Acosta, "Crystal City Revolts," Handbook of Tejano History, Texas State Historical Association, December 1, 1994, www.tshaonline.org/handbook/entries/crystal-city-revolts#:~:text=The%20Hispanics%20selected%20a%20slate,intimidation%20by%20the%20political%20establishment.

186 *the needed paperwork:* Navarro, *Cristal Experiment.*

186 *wearing campaign buttons:* Acosta, "Crystal City Revolts."

186 *"outside agitators":* Rodriguez, *Tejano Diaspora,* 52.

187 *double wages:* Navarro, *Cristal Experiment;* Acosta, "Crystal City Revolts."

187 *"Mexicans crossed the square":* "Races: Revolt of the Mexicans," *Time,* April 12, 1963, https://content.time.com/time/subscriber/article/0,33009,828075,00.html.

187 *"there was pandemonium":* Larry Goodwyn, "Los Cinco Candidatos," *Texas Observer,* April 18, 1963, quoted in Navarro, *Cristal Experiment,* 35

187 *informal victory party:* Navarro, *Cristal Experiment,* 35

187 *took the top post:* Goodwyn, "Los Cinco Candidatos."

187 *"keep my mouth shut":* As quoted in Navarro, *Cristal Experiment,* 38.

188 *"came back to haunt":* Shockley, *Chicano Revolt,* 42

188 *defeated the incumbents:* Acosta, "Crystal City Revolts." See also "Nation: CASA, not PASO," *Time,* April 16, 1965, http://content.time.com/time/subscriber/article/0,33009,841824,00.html.

188 *"100 per day":* Navarro, *Cristal Experiment.*

189 *Mexican Americans in other states:* "A Brief History."

189 *offered bilingual and bicultural instruction:* J. Barbour, "'Yo Soy Chicano!' Chrystal City Awakens to New Reality," *El Paso Times,* June 16, 1974.

189 *more federal funds:* R. Beene, "A Look at Crystal City—Two Years Later," *San Antonio Express,* August 6, 1972.

189 *"racial hatred":* Beene, "A Look at Crystal City."

189 *"Chicano dominance":* Barbour, "'Yo Soy Chicano!'"

189 *"state of Communism":* Beene, "A Look at Crystal City."

189 *boycott the school system:* Beene, "A Look at Crystal City."

190 *nuns left in protest:* R. Beene, "Echeverria Interested in Crystal City," *Marshall (TX) News Messenger,* July 20, 1972.

190   *eminent domain:* Navarro, *Cristal Experiment.*

190   *"had shunned Crystal":* Navarro, *Cristal Experiment.*

190   *"this stuff blew over":* Navarro, *Cristal Experiment.*

190   *tax strike:* Navarro, *Cristal Experiment.*

190   *block federal grants:* "Crystal City in Uproar over 'Little Cuba' Barb," *Fort Worth Star-Telegram,* October 22, 1976.

191   *new ways to establish industry there:* Beene, "Echeverria Interested."

191   *Gutiérrez did not deny:* Navarro, *Cristal Experiment,* 141–42.

191   *raise rates significantly:* R. Ochoa, "Crystal, Lo-Vaca Fail to Settle Dispute," *San Antonio Express,* August 10, 1977.

191   *lost their case:* G. Garvin, "Gas Cutoff Stings Like a Cold Bath," *Austin American-Statesman,* September 25, 1977.

191   *terminated service:* J. Yemma, "When the Gas Was Cut Off, a Texas Town Began Thinking," *Washington Post,* January 3, 1980.

191   *leaders' radicalism:* R. Scott, "Crystal City Gas Supply Stations Under Police Guard," *Brownwood (TX) Bulletin,* July 31, 1977.

191   *laid the blame:* Garvin, "Gas Cutoff Stings."

191   *dragged into January:* L. Lomax, "Crystal City Struggling to Overcome Decade of Misfortune," *Austin American-Statesman,* June 10, 1979.

192   *indictments were politically motivated:* B. Boesch, "Party Is (Pick One) 1. Sitting This Election Out 2. Dying," *Corpus Christi Caller-Times,* September 5, 1976.

192   *misappropriating funds:* Boesch, "Party Is (Pick One)."

192   *He fled across the border:* Diana A. Terry-Axios, "Ramsey Muniz: The First Hispanic Texan to Appear on a General Election Ballot Is Still Fighting the System—from Behind Bars," *Texas Monthly,* November 2002, www .texasmonthly.com/articles/ramsey-muniz/.

192   *"put the cap on":* J. Curtis, "Chicano Party Falls Apart in Texas," *Fort Worth Star-Telegram,* December 8, 1980.

192   *loss of state funding:* Teresa Palomo Acosta, "Raza Unida Party," Handbook of Tejano History, Texas State Historical Association, originally published 1976, updated May 1, 2019, www.tshaonline.org/handbook/entries/raza -unida-party.

195   *"because we won":* For some of the other positive benefits that La Raza Unida Party had on the political voice of Mexican Americans, Latinos, and Black Americans in Texas and across the nation, see Benjamin Márquez and Rodolfo Espino, "Mexican American Support for Third Parties: The Case of La Raza Unida," *Ethnic and Racial Studies* 33, no. 2 (2010): 290–312.

195   *Revolt and retribution:* See, for example, Maureen A. Craig and Jennifer A. Richeson, "On the Precipice of a 'Majority-Minority' America: Perceived Status Threat from the Racial Demographic Shift Affects White Americans' Political Ideology," *Psychological Science* 25, no. 6 (2014): 1189–97. See also Mara C. Ostfeld, "The New White Flight? The Effects of

Political Appeals to Latinos on White Democrats," *Political Behavior* 41, no. 3 (2019): 561–82, which offers evidence that even appeals to Latinos in political outreach produce a backlash among white voters (mostly white Democrats).

196   *Those leaders fought for:* Trevon D. Logan, "Do Black Politicians Matter?," *Journal of Economic History* 80, no. 1 (2020): 181–206.

196   *"organizing the labor":* Megan Stewart and Karin Kitchens, "Explaining Variation in Political Leadership by Marginalized Groups: Black Office-holding and 'Contraband Camps'" (paper, posted September 4, 2021, last revised March 2, 2022), https://ssrn.com/abstract=3902116. For contrast, see Luna Bellani, Anselm Hager, and Stephan E. Maurer, "The Long Shadow of Slavery: The Persistence of Slave Owners in Southern Law-making," *Journal of Economic History* 82, no. 1 (2022): 250–83.

Chapter 8: The Sins of Our Fathers

198   *went for Joe Biden:* "Mississippi Presidential Election Results," *New York Times,* November 3, 2020, www.nytimes.com/interactive/2020/11/03/us/elections/results-mississippi-president.html.

198   *Congressman Bennie Thompson:* "Black-American Members by Congress," History, Art & Archives, US House of Representatives, https://history.house.gov/Exhibitions-and-Publications/BAIC/Historical-Data/Black-American-Representatives-and-Senators-by-Congress/.

199   *first significant manufacturing concern:* "The Baldwin Story," Baldwin Piano, www.baldwinpiano.com/history.html; "First Expansion of Production by Baldwin Piano Plant Here," *Greenwood (MS) Commonwealth,* May 16, 1961, 1.

199   *numerous newspaper ads:* "Your Child Deserves the Best," advertisement, Baldwin Piano, *Greenwood (MS) Commonwealth,* January 21, 1982, 12; "This Christmas Make It a Musical One," advertisement, Baldwin Piano, *Greenwood (MS) Commonwealth,* December 5, 1982, 21.

199   *demand for pianos began to drop:* US International Trade Commission, *Pianos: Economic and Competitive Conditions Affecting the U.S. Industry* (publication no. 3196, Washington, DC, May 1999), www.usitc.gov/publications/docs/pubs/332/pub3196.pdf.

199   *he told the* Union Appeal: "Smith Hoping Pianos Will Spur Educational Benefits in Greenwood Schools," *Union Appeal,* October 10, 1990, 2.

199   *closed in 2001:* Bob Darden, "Baldwin Piano to Close," *Greenwood (MS) Commonwealth,* January 30, 2001, www.gwcommonwealth.com/archives/baldwin-piano-close#sthash.4mYBWt7r.dpbs.

199   *two factories in China:* "The Baldwin Story."

199   *first catfish pond:* Karen Senaga, "Tasteless, Cheap, and Southern? The Rise and Decline of the Farm-Raised Catfish Industry" (PhD diss., Mississippi State University, 2016). See also Adrian Miller, *Soul Food: The Surprising*

Story of an American Cuisine One Plate at a Time (Chapel Hill: University of North Carolina Press, 2013).

200 *"moved the catfish"*: Senaga, "Tasteless, Cheap, and Southern?," 5.

200 *first Leflore County catfish pond:* M. Dean, "Catfish Industry Prospers in County," *Greenwood (MS) Commonwealth*, May 2, 1990, 11.

200 *"invade[d] the land of cotton":* M. D. Allen, "Catfish Invade the Land of Cotton," *Greenwood (MS) Commonwealth*, June 14, 1989, 5.

200 *top producers in the state:* Dean, "Catfish Industry Prospers." See also D. Johnson, "New Processing Plant Gives Town Ray of Hope," *Greenwood (MS) Commonwealth*, February 21, 1988, 1; D. Johnson, "America's Catch Sees Growth in '88," *Greenwood (MS) Commonwealth*, January 18, 1989, 1; D. Johnson, "New Catfish Plant Off to Booming Start," *Greenwood (MS) Commonwealth*, June 26, 1988, 1.

200 *A second Itta Bena plant:* R. Williams, "Tacketts Try Hand at Processing," *Greenwood (MS) Commonwealth*, March 28, 1996, 2A; "Heartland Catfish Company—Our Story and Values," www.heartlandcatfish.com/heartland-catfish-company.

200 *"The goal of catfish farmers":* J. Emmerich, "Catfish on Every Table Is Farm Goal," *Greenwood (MS) Commonwealth*, August 9, 1982, 1.

200 *"domestic piscine delicacies":* J. J. Kilpatrick, "Catfish Doesn't Need P.R.," *Clarion-Ledger* (Jackson, MS), November 7, 1986, 17A.

200 *Cooking magazines: Southern Living 1989 Annual Recipes* (Birmingham, AL: Oxmoor House, 1989), 52.

200 *"haute cuisine":* Berkeley Rice, "A Lowly Fish Goes Upscale," *New York Times Magazine*, December 4, 1988, www.nytimes.com/1988/12/04/magazine/a-lowly-fish-goes-upscale.html.

200 *"world's largest catfish processor":* J. J. Kilpatrick, "Cheers for the Lowly Catfish!," *Greenwood (MS) Commonwealth*, November 7, 1986, 4.

200 *catfish-loving celebrities:* "Celebrities Celebrate National Catfish Month," *Greenwood (MS) Commonwealth*, August 13, 1995, 6B.

201 *"one of the fastest growing":* "Mississippi Still King of Catfish Production," *Greenwood (MS) Commonwealth*, November 28, 1993, 5B. See also W. F. West, "Leading the Catfish Industry: Catching the Future," *Greenwood (MS) Commonwealth*, March 26, 1998, 5B.

201 *undercut by foreign competition:* M. Means, "A Catfish by Any Other Name," *Greenwood (MS) Commonwealth*, February 17, 2002, 4A; Andrew Soergel, "The Catfishing of America: Swamped by Imports, U.S. Catfish Production Has Fallen Dramatically from a Decade Ago—but the Industry's Presence Is Still Vital Down South," *U.S. News & World Report*, April 17, 2018, www.usnews.com/news/healthiest-communities/articles/2018-04-17/mississippi-catfish-industry-swamped-by-imports-regulations.

201 *fallen to about half:* Soergel, "Catfishing of America." The catfish industry continues to employ nearly 7,600 people across the United States.

See also Matt Krupnick, "How the Catfish Capital of the World Was Hit by an Asian Fish Flood," *The Guardian*, April 12, 2019, www.theguardian .com/environment/2019/apr/10/belzoni-mississippi-catfish-capital-world -asian-fish-flood.

201   *on-site inspections:* S. Salter, "Cochran Wins Catfish Fight," *Greenwood (MS) Commonwealth*, December 3, 2015, 5A; R. Wicker, "A Win for U.S. Catfish," *Greenwood (MS) Commonwealth*, December 16, 2015, 5.

201   *alleged racism:* Julian Rankin, *Catfish Dream: Ed Scott's Fight for His Family Farm and Racial Justice in the Mississippi Delta* (Athens: University of Georgia Press, 2018).

201   *remaining farms:* Senaga, "Tasteless, Cheap, and Southern?," 216. At Delta Pride, the Delta's largest catfish processing plant, workers went on strike to protest job conditions. Though the concessions they won were modest, the threat of another strike in 2010 staved off management's efforts to make changes to worker contracts that would have significantly curtailed their rights. J. Atkins, "Strike Talk Defused," *Clarion-Ledger* (Jackson, MS), October 3, 2010, 11B; Senaga, "Tasteless, Cheap, and Southern?," 228.

202   *less competitive:* "Baldwin Piano Closing in Greenwood," *Enterprise-Journal* (McComb, MS), February 1, 2001, 6.

203   *graced by the brand:* "Greenwood Can Be Proud of Viking," *Greenwood (MS) Commonwealth*, November 20, 1992, 4.

203   *Viking laid off:* Tim Kalich, "Shakeup at Viking," *Greenwood (MS) Commonwealth*, February 1, 2013, www.gwcommonwealth.com/news-top-stories /shakeup-viking?e_term_id=15921#sthash.rCEQ23hI.dpbs. In 2013, in a middle-of-the-night surprise, Fred Carl Jr. sold Viking to the Middleby Corporation for $388 million, promising that the sale would be "good for Viking, good for its employees, and good for Greenwood." Despite assurances by the new owners that they would retain much of the workforce, employment shrank markedly after the sale. Tim Kalich, "Viking Sold for $380M," *Greenwood (MS) Commonwealth*, January 2, 2013, www .gwcommonwealth.com/news-top-stories/viking-sold-380m?e_term _id=15921#sthash.INB8BUbb.dpbs.

203   *moved some operations:* "The History of Milwaukee Tools," Cable Organizer.com, www.cableorganizer.com/learning-center/articles/history -of-milwaukee-tools.html.

203   *chasing cheaper labor:* John Martin, "Milwaukee Tool Expanding Operation," *Greenwood (MS) Commonwealth*, September 19, 2002, www.gwcom monwealth.com/archives/milwaukee-tool-expanding-operation#sthash .TYUdEpga.dpbs; "Milwaukee Tool Opens New Facility in Greenwood," http://da.mdah.ms.gov/musgrove/pdfs/3875.pdf.

204   Mississippi Business Journal *reported:* Lynne Willbanks Jeter, "International Tool Maker Moving to Greenwood," *Mississippi Business Journal*, December 24, 2001, www.djournal.com/mbj/news/international-tool

-maker-moving-to-greenwood/article_eec4d8eb-71b7-5fd4-a92f-d692b
88e34a9.html.

204 *huge operation:* Tom Held, "Milwaukee Tool Plans $16.8M Expansion in
Mississippi, Adding 126 Jobs," *Milwaukee Business Journal,* June 23, 2015,
www.bizjournals.com/milwaukee/news/2015/06/23/milwaukee-tool
-plans-16-8m-expansion-in.html. See also "Milwaukee Tool to Hire 75 in
$3.2M Greenwood Expansion," MS State Wire, AP News, June 8, 2016;
"Milwaukee Tool Keeps on Growing," *Greenwood (MS) Commonwealth,*
December 7, 2017.

204 *"Thank God":* Gavin Maliska, "Marketing as a Team: Regional Approach,
Work Readiness Stressed," *Greenwood (MS) Commonwealth,* February 21,
2019. The article also notes that the area had found a "sweet spot" in distribution, given the several dozen employees hired to staff PepsiCo and
Coburn Supply distribution centers in the area.

204 *"only [decent job]":* Geoff Pender, "Milwaukee Tool Expands in Mississippi,
Says It Will Create 1,200 Jobs," Mississippi Today, April 20, 2021, https://
mississippitoday.org/2021/04/20/milwaukee-tool-mississippi-grenada
-expansion-jobs/. Many of these were temporary positions managed by a
staffing agency and thus offered low pay and fewer benefits.

205 *even modest amounts:* Anna Wolfe and Michelle Liu, "Think Debtors Prisons Are a Thing of the Past? Not in Mississippi," The Marshall Project,
January 9, 2020, www.themarshallproject.org/2020/01/09/think-debtors
-prisons-are-a-thing-of-the-past-not-in-mississippi.

205 *notorious penal farm:* William B. Taylor, *Down on Parchman Farm: The Great
Prison in the Mississippi Delta* (Columbus: Ohio State University Press,
1999).

206 *twice the national average:* US Bureau of Labor Statistics, "Unemployment
Rate in Leflore County, MS," FRED Economic Data, https://fred.stlouis
fed.org/series/MSLFURN.

206 *not in the labor market:* Authors' analysis of American Community Survey
data.

207 *myth of the "welfare queen":* Edin and Shaefer, *$2.00 a Day,* chap. 1.

207 *rare feat:* "TANF Cash Assistance Should Reach Many More Families in
Mississippi and Lessen Hardship," Center on Budget and Policy Priorities, www.cbpp.org/sites/default/files/atoms/files/tanf_trends_ms.pdf.

207 *$586 per month in SNAP:* "A Quick Guide to SNAP Eligibility Benefits,"
Center on Budget and Policy Priorities, updated October 4, 2022, www
.cbpp.org/research/food-assistance/a-quick-guide-to-snap-eligibility
-and-benefits. Cash-strapped householders who sell their SNAP benefits on the black market receive only about 50 cents on the dollar in the
Delta, by one report, and families who do so usually run out of food only
a week or so into the month, leading to severe hunger. Edin and Shaefer,
$2.00 a Day. The disabled are not included in the labor force participa-
tion rate. Yet it is interesting to note that in 2017, 1,604 Leflore County

non-elderly adults received some form of federal disability payment, a relatively high rate for a county with a population of roughly 28,000 that year. "SSI Recipients by State and County, 2017," Office of Retirement and Disability Policy, Social Security Administration, www.ssa.gov/policy /docs/statcomps/ssi_sc/2017/ms.html; "QuickFacts: Leflore County, Mississippi," US Census Bureau, www.census.gov/quickfacts/fact/table /leflorecountymississippi/AGE775219#AGE775219.

208   *work requirements:* "Able-Bodied Adults Without Dependents (ABAWD): Supplemental Nutrition Assistance Program," Mississippi Department of Human Services, August 1, 2015, www.mdhs.ms.gov/wp-content /uploads/2018/03/SNAP-ABAWD.pdf.

208   *CD players and audiobooks:* Vincent C. Buchanan, "Reading on the Job Turns Catfish Farm Workers into Bookworms," *Greenwood (MS) Commonwealth*, July 25, 2004, www.gwcommonwealth.com/archives/reading -job-turns-catfish-farm-workers-book-worms?e_term_id=18761#sthash .xpIDrMH2.dpbs.

209   *soil had been used up:* See Frederick Law Olmsted, *The Cotton Kingdom: A Traveller's Observations on Cotton and Slavery in the American Slave States, 1853–1861* (New York: Da Capo Press, 1996).

209   *unemployment rate:* "South Africa Unemployment Rate 1991–2022," Macrotrends, www.macrotrends.net/countries/ZAF/south-africa/unemployment -rate.

210   *train guest workers:* Miriam Jordan, "Black Farmworkers Say They Lost Jobs to Foreigners Who Were Paid More," *New York Times*, November 12, 2021,   www.nytimes.com/2021/11/12/us/black-farmworkers-mississippi -lawsuit.html.

210   *initially unpopular:* Though only a small percentage of the total—5,508 workers in 2020—hailed from South Africa, South Africans were the second most numerous visa claimants that year (following Mexicans), their numbers rising 441 percent between 2011 and 2020. Jordan, "Black Farmworkers."

210   *"disastrous pattern":* Mississippi Center for Justice, "Black Farmworkers Sue Mississippi Farm for Racial Discrimination, Lost Wages, and Abuse of Immigration System to Deny U.S. Workers of Jobs," press release, September 8, 2021, https://mscenterforjustice.org/black-farmworkers-sue/.

211   *work ethic:* Jordan, "Black Farmworkers."

211   *sued Kyle Mills:* Will Stribling, "Immigrant Agricultural Workers Sue Mississippi Farm Owner for Visa Fraud, Unpaid Wages," Mississippi Today, March 25, 2021, www.mississippitoday.org/2021/03/25 /immigrant-agricultural-workers-sue-mississippi-farm-owner-for-visa -fraud-unpaid-wages/.

211   *brutal global competition:* Llewellyn Jones, "Mississippi Is Losing the Catfish Wars," Mississippi Today, June 21, 2001, https://mississippitoday .org/2021/06/21/mississippi-is-losing-the-catfish-wars/.

211   *losing their jobs:* "Black Farmworkers Sue Mississippi Farm." Mostly, though, agriculture has largely given way to industry across the Cotton Belt, yet without the diversification necessary to build a stable economy with decent wages or advancement opportunities. According to rural sociologist Conner Bailey and colleagues, in the Alabama Cotton Belt, more than 60 percent of the land is held by absentee owners who continue to profit from highly mechanized agriculture but contribute little in taxes. Meanwhile, fully a quarter of the residents live in poverty. Due to these social and economic conditions, these writers describe rural Alabama as a place where, even today, "key decisions are made by powerful outside forces supported by local elites." This holds true for the rest of the vast internal colony stretching from the coastal Carolinas through the Mississippi Delta. Conner Bailey, Abhimanyu Gopaul, Ryan Thompson, and Andrew Gunnoe, "Taking Goldschmidt to the Woods: Timberland Ownership and Quality of Life in Alabama," *Rural Sociology* 86, no. 1 (2020): 50–80. See also Robin Kaiser-Schatzlein, "Alabama Takes from the Poor and Gives to the Rich," *New York Times*, July 27, 2022, www.nytimes.com/2022/07/27/opinion/alabama-fines-fees.html.

213   *"a cold peace":* Rubin, "Should the Mississippi Files."

215   *catastrophic drop:* Hilary Hylton, "Frackers Guzzle Water as Texas Goes Thirsty," *Time*, September 29, 2013, https://nation.time.com/2013/09/29/frackers-guzzle-water-as-texas-goes-thirsty/print.

215   *new brand of economic venture:* Mark Odintz, "Winter Garden Region," Handbook of Texas, Texas State Historical Association, March 26, 2019, www.tshaonline.org/handbook/entries/winter-garden-region.

215   *At Four Seasons Ranch:* "Four Seasons Ranch: A World-Class Hunting Experience," Four Seasons website, www.fourseasonsranch.com/.

216   *Ox Ranch offers:* Ox Ranch website, www.oxhuntingranch.com/. The ranch is in Uvalde, which in 2022 was the scene of one of the most horrific school shootings in American history. The school had a largely Mexican American student population.

216   *the experience is pricey:* Similar experiences can be found in the Alabama Cotton Belt. See John N. Felsher, "The Black Belt's Rich Soil Creates a Special Place for Sporting Adventures," *Alabama Living*, October 31, 2019, https://alabamaliving.coop/articles/the-black-belts-rich-soil-creates-a-special-place-for-sporting-adventures/.

217   *more migrant deaths:* Carlos Sanchez, "The Texas Checkpoint That Forces Migrants into Dangerous Terrain—and Death," *The Guardian*, September 20, 2021, www.theguardian.com/us-news/2021/sep/20/us-immigration-checkpoint-falfurrias-station-texas-documentary.

217   *"a brighter future":* "Congressman Rogers Secures $2.2 Million Earmark for Market Place in Downtown Manchester, KY," ClayCoNews, March 15, 2022, www.clayconews.com/news/19741-congressman-rogers-secures-2-2-million-earmark-for-downtown-manchester-kentucky-market-place.

217   *"provide fun activities":* "Gov. Beshear, Congressman Rogers Host Virtual Ribbon-Cutting Ceremony for Abandoned Mine Lands Pilot Projects," Office of the Governor, August 13, 2020, https://kentucky.gov/Pages /Activity-stream.aspx?n=GovernorBeshear&prId=305.

218   *"how we're going to do it":* Graham Shelby, "Promoting Tourism in Clay County," *Kentucky Living*, January 7, 2022, www.kentuckyliving.com /explore/promoting-tourism-in-clay-county.

218   *social support systems:* John W. Morris, "The Potential of Tourism," in *The Southern Appalachian Region: A Survey*, ed. Thomas R. Ford (Lexington: University of Kentucky Press, 1962), 136–48, https://core.ac.uk/download /pdf/232571735.pdf.

219   *rendered meaningless:* Billy Corriher, "Fighting Gerrymandering in the South's Black Belt," *Facing South*, December 16, 2021, www.facingsouth .org/2021/12/fighting-gerrymandering-souths-black-belt.

221   *proven anti-violence programs:* "Crime Lab: Becoming a Man," UChicago Urban Labs, https://urbanlabs.uchicago.edu/projects/becoming-a-man.

221   *In a move:* Associated Press, "Mississippi County Chooses New Site for Confederate Monument," September 29, 2021, WLBT Channel 3, www .wlbt.com/2021/09/29/mississippi-county-chooses-new-site-confederate -monument/.

221   *sculpture of Emmett Till:* Kevin Edwards, "Emmett Till Statue to Be Installed Friday," *Greenwood (MS) Commonwealth*, October 19, 2022.

Chapter 9: Healing America's Internal Colonies

224   *vast uninterrupted fields:* Increasingly, however, farmers are renting out their land rather than working it themselves and taking jobs in nearby towns and cities. Robert Wuthnow, *Remaking the Heartland: Middle America Since the 1950s* (Princeton, NJ: Princeton University Press, 2011).

225   *In 2015, Christopher Ingraham:* Christopher Ingraham, "Every County in America, Ranked by Scenery and Climate," *Washington Post*, August 17, 2015, www.washingtonpost.com/news/wonk/wp/2015/08/17/every-county -in-america-ranked-by-natural-beauty/.

225   *called the Natural Amenities Scale:* "Natural Amenities Scale," USDA Economic Research Service, last updated August 20, 2019, www.ers.usda.gov /data-products/natural-amenities-scale.aspx.

225   *If You Lived Here:* Christopher Ingraham, *If You Lived Here You'd Be Home by Now: Why We Traded the Commuting Life for a Little House on the Prairie* (New York: HarperCollins, 2019).

226   *remain economically vibrant:* Wuthnow, *Remaking the Heartland*. Note, however, that the soil here, too, has been overused, and some of the Midwest's topsoil has been lost to erosion due to a century of plowing. Dan Charles, "New Evidence Shows Fertile Soil Gone from Midwestern Farms," *Morning Edition*, NPR, February 24, 2021, www.npr

.org/2021/02/24/967376880/new-evidence-shows-fertile-soil-gone
-from-midwestern-farms.

227 *single location in the world:* "About," Blue Bunny website, https://www.blue
bunny.com/about.

227 *"hollowing out":* Patrick J. Carr and Maria J. Kefalas, *Hollowing Out the
Middle: The Rural Brain Drain and What It Means for America* (Boston:
Beacon Press, 2009).

227 *Local job opportunities:* Wuthnow, *Remaking the Heartland.*

228 *20,000 to 30,000 migrant workers:* Sandra M. Gonzales, "Aztlán in the Midwest and Other Counternarratives Revealed," in *Latinos in the Midwest,*
ed. Rubén O. Martinez (East Lansing: Michigan State University Press,
2011), 17–31. See also Jim Norris, *North for the Harvest: Mexican Workers,
Growers, and the Sugar Beet Industry* (St. Paul: Minnesota Historical Society Press, 2009); Dionicio Nodín Valdés, *Al Norte: Agricultural Workers in
the Great Lakes Region, 1917–1970* (Austin: University of Texas Press, 1991);
Dionicio Nodín Valdés, *Barrios Norteños: St. Paul and Midwestern Mexican
Communities in the Twentieth Century* (Austin: University of Texas Press,
2000).

229 *forcibly relocated:* John Biewen, "Part 10: Payback for the Dakota—
Banishment," MPR News, December 11, 2012, www.mprnews.org/story
/2012/12/11/dakota-war-part10.

229 *must be reckoned with:* Some of these stories are invisible to our index,
because the Native lands in question are spread across several counties
with more prosperous, white populations. One such place is the Red Lake
reservation, right next door to Red Lake County. In 2013–2017, poverty
among the reservation's Native American population was 37 percent,
while the average household income was less than $35,000. "Red Lake
Reservation: Demographics," Center for Indian County Development,
Federal Reserve Bank of Indianapolis, www.minneapolisfed.org/indian
country/resources/reservation-profiles/red-lake-reservation.

231 *threatening to secede:* Linda Jacobson, "Wealthy Neighborhood Seeks
Split from Atlanta, Leaving Parents in Limbo," Yahoo News, February 8, 2022, https://news.yahoo.com/wealthy-neighborhood-seeks-split
-atlanta-180100278.html; Kendra Taylor, Erika Frankenberg, and Gen-
evieve Siegel-Hawley, "Racial Segregation in the Southern Schools,
School Districts, and Counties Where Districts Have Seceded," *AERA
Open* 5, no. 3 (2019), https://journals.sagepub.com/doi/full/10.1177/23
32858419860152?utm_source=newsletter&utm_medium=email&utm_
campaign=cb_bureau_national.

232 *less attention paid:* Andrew Isserman and Terance Rephann, "The Eco-
nomic Effects of the Appalachian Regional Commission: An Empirical
Assessment of 26 Years of Regional Development Planning," *Journal of the
American Planning Association* 61, no. 3 (1995): 345–64.

232   *communities it serves:* John Pender and Richard Reeder, "Impact of Regional Approaches to Rural Development: Initial Evidence on the Delta Regional Authority," Economic Research Service Economic Research Report No. 119 (US Department of Agriculture, June 2011).

232   *tools to cope:* Combine that with the fact that Americans own 393 million guns, more than one for every man, woman, and child in the country and more than twice the rate of any other nation. Research has found that places with fewer guns have fewer gun deaths and fewer police-involved deaths. Thomas Black, "Americans Have More Guns Than Anywhere Else in the World and They Keep Buying More," Bloomberg, May 25, 2022, www.bloomberg.com/news/articles/2022-05-25/how-many-guns -in-the-us-buying-spree-bolsters-lead-as-most-armed-country. See also Michael Siegel, Craig S. Ross, and Charles King III, "The Relationship Between Gun Ownership and Firearm Homicide Rates in the United States, 1981–2012," *American Journal of Public Health* 103, no. 11 (2013): 2098–2105; David Hemenway, Deborah Azrael, Andrew Conner, and Matthew Miller, "Variation in Rates of Fatal Police Shootings Across US States: The Role of Firearm Availability," *Journal of Urban Health* 96, no. 1 (2019): 63–73.

232   *"interrupters" who can mediate conflicts:* Daniel Webster, "Public Health Approaches to Reducing Community Gun Violence," *Daedalus* 151, no. 1 (2022): 38–48; Editorial Board, "READI Anti-violence Program Is Proof That Crime Prevention Can Work," *Chicago Sun-Times*, April 23, 2022, https://chicago.suntimes.com/2022/4/23/23037263/anti-violence -program-readi-university-of-chicago-crime-lab-editorial.

233   *Becoming a Man:* "Crime Lab: Becoming a Man."

233   *Choose to Change:* "Choose to Change," UChicago Urban Labs, https:// urbanlabs.uchicago.edu/programs/choose-to-change.

233   *prosocial identities:* Stefanie Deluca, Susan Clampet-Lundquist, and Kathryn Edin, *Coming of Age in the Other America* (New York: Russell Sage Foundation, 2015).

235   *other libraries' teams:* Klinenberg, *Palaces for the People*, 26–29.

235   *sociologist Mario Small:* Teresa Eckrich Sommer, Terri J. Sabol, P. Lindsay Chase-Lansdale, Mario Small, Henry Wilde, Sean Brown, and Zong Yang Huang, "Promoting Parents' Social Capital to Increase Children's Attendance in Head Start: Evidence from an Experimental Intervention," *Journal of Research on Educational Effectiveness* 10, no. 4 (2017): 732–66.

236   *memoir by Richard Rubin:* Richard Ruben, *Confederacy of Silence: A True Tale of the New Old South* (New York: Atria Books, 2003).

236   *run for local office:* For a detailed examination of some of these leaders, see C. Alter, *The Ones We've Been Waiting For: How a New Generation of Leaders Will Transform America* (New York: Viking Press, 2020).

237   *historian Douglas Arnett:* Arnett, "Eastern Kentucky."

238   *write grant applications:* See Shoshana Shapiro, "Inequality of the Safety

Net: The Rural-Urban Continuum, County-Level Poverty, and Non-profit Human Services Expenditures," *Social Service Review* 95, no. 4 (2021): 652–92.

238   *Sociologist Laura Tach:* Laura Tach, Alexandra Cooperstock, Sam Dodini, and Emily Parker, "Federal Place-Based Policy and the Geography of Inequality, 1990–2015," Working Paper, 2023.

239   *prepare local leaders:* "Investing in a Safer, Stronger Baltimore: Final Report of the White House Taskforce for Baltimore City" (Executive Office of the President, December 14, 2016), https://obamawhitehouse.archives .gov/sites/whitehouse.gov/files/images/Blog/White%20House%20 Taskforce%20for%20Baltimore%20City.pdf.

240   *charged more:* Kristen Broady, Mac McComas, and Amine Ouazad, "An Analysis of Financial Institutions in Black-Majority Communities: Black Borrowers and Depositors Face Considerable Challenges in Accessing Banking Services," Brookings, November 2, 2021, www.brookings .edu/research/an-analysis-of-financial-institutions-in-black-majority -communities-black-borrowers-and-depositors-face-considerable-challenges -in-accessing-banking-services/.

240   *more in property taxes:* Michelle Aronowitz, Edward L. Golding, and Jung Hyun, "The Unequal Costs of Black Homeownership," October 1, 2020, https://gcfp.mit.edu/wp-content/uploads/2020/10/Mortgage-Cost-for -Black-Homeowners-10.1.pdf.

240   *A recent study:* Michael A. Gara, Shula Minsky, Steven M. Silverstein, Theresa Miskimen, and Stephen M. Strakowski, "A Naturalistic Study of Racial Disparities in Diagnoses at an Outpatient Behavioral Health Clinic," *Psychiatric Services* 70, no. 2 (February 1, 2019), 130–35.

240   *worse in Detroit:* Patrick Cooney, Elizabeth Phillips, and Joshua Rivera, "Auto Insurance and Economic Mobility in Michigan: A Cycle of Poverty" (policy brief, Poverty Solutions, University of Michigan, March 2019), http://sites.fordschool.umich.edu/poverty2021/files/2021/03/auto _insurance_and_economic_mobility_in_michigan_2.pdf.

240   *best predictor:* Amanda Nothaft and Patrick Cooney, "Building on Michigan's Auto Insurance Law" (policy brief, Poverty Solutions, University of Michigan, December 2021), http://sites.fordschool.umich.edu /poverty2021/files/2021/12/PovertySolutions-Auto-Insurance-Reform -PolicyBrief-December2021.pdf.

242   *Huge numbers of jobs:* Jiwon Choi, Ilyana Kuziemko, Ebonya L. Washington, and Gavin Wright, "Local Economic and Political Effects of Trade Deals: Evidence from NAFTA," National Bureau of Economic Research Working Paper No. 29525 (November 2021), www.nber.org/papers /w29525.

242   *major political shift:* Choi et al., "Local Economic and Political Effects."

243   *shifting of manufacturing:* David Autor, David Dorn, Gordon Hanson, and Kaveh Majlesi, "Importing Political Polarization? The Electoral

Consequences of Rising Trade Exposure," *American Economic Review* 110, no. 10 (2020): 3139–83.

243   *only camp built expressly:* Robyn Ross, "The Legacy of Crystal City's Internment Camps," *Texas Observer*, January 14, 2014, www.texasobserver.org/otherness-among-us/.

243   *strict oversight:* "Crystal City (Family) Internment Camp," Texas Historical Commission, www.thc.texas.gov/crystalcity.

243   *"Fence sickness":* Jane Jarboe Russell, *The Train to Crystal City: FDR's Secret Prisoner Exchange Program and America's Only Family Internment Camp During World War II* (New York: Scribner, 2015).

244   *modest reparations:* Sonni Efron, "German-American Challenges Reparations for War Internees; Courts: Man Claims Law Giving Japanese-Americans Compensation Discriminates on Basis of National Origin," *Los Angeles Times*, November 22, 1991, www.latimes.com/archives/la-xpm-1991-11-22-mn-54-story.html.

244   *"'not repeat it again'":* Bilal Qureshi, "From Wrong to Right: A U.S. Apology for Japanese Internment," *All Things Considered*, NPR, August 9, 2013, www.npr.org/sections/codeswitch/2013/08/09/210138278/japanese-internment-redress.

Appendix A: The History and Theory of Internal Colonies

251   *Charles Pinderhughes locates it:* Charles Pinderhughes, "21st Century Chains: The Continuing Relevance of Internal Colonialism Theory" (PhD diss., Boston College, 2009), chap. 1.

251   *subjugation of southern Italy:* Robert J. Hind, "The Internal Colonial Concept," *Comparative Studies in Society and History* 26, no. 3 (1984): 544.

251   *"subjugated nation":* Harry Haywood, *Black Bolshevik: Autobiography of an Afro-American Communist* (Chicago: Liberator Press, 1978), 233.

252   *"economic exploitation":* Jonathan Judaken, "The Heresies of Albert Memmi," *Tablet*, June 24, 2020, www.tabletmag.com/sections/arts-letters/articles/albert-memmi-obituary.

252   *far-ranging influence:* Homi K. Bhabha, "Foreword: Framing Fanon," in *The Wretched of the Earth*, by Frantz Fanon (New York: Grove Press, 2004), xxviii.

252   *own minority groups:* Mario Barrera, *Race and Class in the Southwest: A Theory of Racial Inequality* (Notre Dame, IN: University of Notre Dame Press, 1979).

253   *his 1967 book*, Black Power: Kwame Ture and Charles V. Hamilton, *Black Power: The Politics of Liberation* (New York: Vintage Books, 1992).

253   *Mexican Indigenous peoples:* Pablo Gonzalez Casanova, "Internal Colonialism and National Development," *Studies in Comparative International Development* 1, no. 4 (April 1965): 27, https://doi.org/10.1007/BF02800542.

253   *co-opt the Black Power movement:* Robert L. Allen, *Black Awakening in Capitalist America: An Analytic History* (New York: Doubleday, 1969).

253   Social Problems *article:* Robert Blauner, "Internal Colonialism and Ghetto Revolt," *Social Problems* 16, no. 4 (1969): 393–408, https://doi .org/10.2307/799949.

253   Racial Oppression in America: Robert Blauner, *Racial Oppression in America* (New York: Harper & Row, 1972).

254   *comparative look:* Joan W. Moore, "Colonialism: The Case of the Mexican Americans," *Social Problems* 17, no. 4 (1970): 463–72, https://doi.org /10.2307/799679.

254   Colonialism in Modern America: Helen M. Lewis and Edward E. Knipe, "The Colonialism Model: The Appalachian Case," in *Colonialism in Modern America: The Appalachian Case,* ed. Helen Matthews Lewis, Linda Johnson, and Donald Askins (Boone, NC: Appalachian Consortium Press, 1978), 9–31, https://doi.org/10.2307/j.ctt1xp3n1t.28.

254   *racial subjugation:* Barrera, *Race and Class in the Southwest.* There have been more-recent attempts to use what is now called "settler colonialism" to understand racial subjugation in the United States. See, for example, Evelyn Nakano Glenn, "Settler Colonialism as Structure: A Framework for Comparative Studies of U.S. Race and Gender Formation," *Sociology of Race and Ethnicity* 1, no. 1 (2015): 52–72.

254   *1975 book* Internal Colonialism: Michael Hechter, *Internal Colonialism: The Celtic Fringe in British National Development* (Berkeley: University of California Press, 1975).

254   *individual studies:* For an assessment of these and other uses of the concept during this time, see Hind, "Internal Colonial Concept."

255   *"essential defining features":* Michael Hechter, "Towards a Theory of Ethnic Change," *Politics & Society* 2, no. 1 (December 1, 1971): 36, https://doi .org/10.1177/003232927100200102.

255   *"loses in rigor":* Hind, "Internal Colonial Concept," 53.

255   *virtually disappeared:* Within the field of Appalachian studies, the concept's demise was due more to a deliberate attack by scholars preferring a stricter Marxian class analysis than the emphasis on external corporate control highlighted by the internal colony perspective. David S. Walls, "Internal Colony or Internal Periphery? A Critique of Current Models and an Alternative Formulation," in Lewis, Johnson, and Askins, eds., *Colonialism in Modern America,* 319–50; Billings and Blee, *Road to Poverty.*

255   *including Robert Blauner:* Bob Blauner, *Still the Big News: Racial Oppression in America,* rev. and expanded ed. (Philadelphia: Temple University Press, 2001).

255   *Pinderhughes's 2009 dissertation:* Pinderhughes, "21st Century Chains." See also Pinderhughes, "Toward a New Theory of Internal Colonialism."

255   *more recent article:* Tim Bowman, "Negotiating Conquest: Internal Colonialism and Shared Histories in the South Texas Borderlands," *Western Historical Quarterly* 46, no. 3 (2015): 19. See also Navarro, *Cristal*

Experiment, which refers to internal colonialism in describing Crystal (Cristal) City, Texas.

256 *"American capitalism":* C. Matthew Snipp, "The Changing Political and Economic Status of the American Indians: From Captive Nations to Internal Colonies," *American Journal of Economics and Sociology* 45, no. 2 (1986): 151.

257 *new Utah Territory:* Reséndez, *The Other Slavery.*

257 *complementary yet distinctive:* We owe a great debt of gratitude to David Grusky for his insights, which are reflected in this section.

257 *fewer natural resources:* Benjamin Smith and David Waldner, *Rethinking the Resource Curse* (New York: Cambridge University Press, 2021).

257 *lively debate:* See Anthony J. Venables, "Using Natural Resources for Development: Why Has It Proven So Difficult?," *Journal of Economic Perspectives* 30, no. 1 (February 2016): 161–84; Michael L. Ross, "What Have We Learned About the Resource Curse?," *Annual Review of Political Science* 18 (May 2015): 239–59.

257 *exploitative conditions:* Beckert, *Empire of Cotton.*

257 *family farms:* Gavin Wright, *Old South, New South: Revolutions in the Southern Economy Since the Civil War* (New York: Basic Books, 1986).

258 *passed down:* See N. A. Youssef, L. Lockwood, S. Su, G. Hao, and B. P. F. Rutten, "The Effects of Trauma, with or Without PTSD, on the Transgenerational DNA Methylation Alterations in Human Offsprings," *Brain Science* 8, no. 5 (May 2018): 83; Dora Costa, Noelle Yetter, and Heather DeSomer, "Intergenerational Transmission of Paternal Trauma Among US Civil War Ex-POWs," *Proceedings of the National Academy of Sciences* 115, no. 44 (2018): 11215–20.

258 *South is more prone:* Howard W. Odum and Vicky Wells, *Race and Rumors of Race: The American South in the Early Forties* (Baltimore, MD: Johns Hopkins University Press, 1997); Rupert B. Vance, *Human Factors in Cotton Culture: A Study in the Social Geography of the American South* (Chapel Hill: University of North Carolina Press, 1929). More recent literature in this vein comes from criminological research on violence, known as the "culture of honor thesis." For a definitive statement on this thesis, see Richard E. Nisbett and Dov Cohen, *Culture of Honor: The Psychology of Violence in the South* (Boulder, CO: Westview, 1996).

258 *"America's No. 1 economic problem":* David L. Carlton and Peter A. Coclanis, eds., *Confronting Southern Poverty in the Great Depression: The Report on Economic Conditions of the South with Related Documents* (New York: Bedford/St. Martin's, 1996).

259 *enduring legacies:* Robert J. Sampson, *Great American City: Chicago and the Enduring Neighborhood Effect* (Chicago: University of Chicago Press, 2012).

259 *"underappreciated causes":* Sampson, *Great American City,* ix.

259 *becomes counterproductive:* Federico Cingano, "Trends in Income Inequal-

ity and Its Impact on Economic Growth," OECD Social, Employment and Migration Working Paper No. 163 (Organisation for Economic Co-operation and Development, 2014), https://doi.org/10.1787/5jxrjncwx v6j-en.

259 *"bad inequality"*: Clifton B. Parker, "'Bad' Inequality on the Rise, Stanford Scholar Says," Stanford News, December 26, 2015, https://news.stanford .edu/2015/12/26/inequality-grusky-qna-121915/.

Appendix B: The Index of Deep Disadvantage

261 *multidimensional index of disadvantage:* Silvia Robles, Jasmine Simington, and Samiul Jubaed were instrumental to this work, and all contributed to the writing of this technical appendix.

262 *sociologist James Coleman:* James S. Coleman, *The Foundations of Social Theory* (Cambridge MA: Belknap Press of Harvard University, 1990), 20.

263 *does a bit better:* Kathryn Edin and H. Luke Shaefer, "Response to Moffitt and Fitzgerald," *Brookings Papers on Economic Activity Spring Conference—* Day 2 Pt. 2 The Supplemental Expenditure Poverty Measure (May 6, 2022), https://www.brookings.edu/wp-content/uploads/2022/03/16265 -BPEA-Sp22_FitzgeraldMoffitt_Comment_EdinShaefer_WEB.pdf.

263 *beyond poverty:* National Academies of Sciences, Engineering, and Medicine, *A Roadmap to Reducing Child Poverty* (Washington, DC: National Academies Press, 2019), https://doi.org/10.17226/25246; Edin and Shaefer, *$2.00 a Day.*

264 *Low birth weight is known:* N. S. Paneth, "The Problem of Low Birth Weight," *Future Child* 5, no. 1 (Spring 1995): 19–34, https://pubmed.ncbi .nlm.nih.gov/7633862/.

264 *predictor of future disadvantage:* Richard A. Polin, Steven H. Abman, David Rowitch, and William E. Benitz, *Fetal and Neonatal Physiology E-Book*, 5th ed. (Philadelphia: Elsevier Health Sciences, 2016), https://books.google .com/books/about/Fetal_and_Neonatal_Physiology_E_Book.html?id =JootDAAAQBAJ.

264 *Shorter than average life expectancy:* Max Roser, "Why Is Life Expectancy in the US Lower Than in Other Rich Countries?," *Our World in Data*, October 29, 2020, https://ourworldindata.org/us-life-expectancy-low.

264 *US Department of Agriculture:* "Rural Poverty & Well-Being."

265 *multidimensional method of poverty measurement:* Sen, *Development as Freedom.*

268 *Feeding America:* Feeding America, "Map the Meal Gap: An Analysis of County and Congressional District Food Insecurity and County Food Cost in the United States in 2020," Technical Brief, 2022, https:// www.feedingamerica.org/sites/default/files/2022-08/Map%20the%20 Meal%20Gap%202022%20Technical%20Brief.pdf.

269 *SAIPE methodology:* "SAIPE Methodology," US Census Bureau, last revised October 8, 2021, www.census.gov/programs-surveys/saipe/technical -documentation/methodology.html.

270   *publicly available data:* "County Health Rankings & Roadmaps," University of Wisconsin Population Health Institute, www.countyhealthrankings .org/; "City Health Dashboard," NYU Langone Health, www.cityhealth dashboard.com/.

271   *measure of social mobility:* Chetty and Hendren, "Impacts of Neighborhoods."

Credits

Index

$2.00 a Day: Living on Almost Nothing in America (Edin and Shaefer), 2, 261

77 Ranch, 30–31

Abandoned Mine Land Fund, 217
Abner, Doug, 69–70, 81, 236
Adams, Debra, 220, 233
Adams, Doug, 137, 138, 139
Adams, Ernest, 220, 233
After Freedom (Powdermaker), 42, 99, 101
after-school programs, 233–34
Agricultural Adjustment Act (AAA) of 1933, 174–76
agriculture
  Black Americans and farm ownership, 157–59, 174–78
  Black Americans and tenancy farming, 26–28, 98, 174
  health impacts of industrial, 166–67
  mechanization in, 209–10
  in Mississippi Delta, 209–11
  in Winter Garden of South Texas, 29–33
Agriculture, US Department of (USDA), 160, 181, 264
  Cooperative Extension System, 237
  Natural Amenities Scale, 225
Aguilera, Serna, 57–58
Alexander v. Holmes County Board of Education, 48
Allee, Alfred Young, 187
Allen, Robert L., 253
All God's Dangers (Rosengarten), 11
Alma, Arkansas, 21

Amanda Elzy High School, 63
American Dream, 232
Anderson, Sherwood, 172–73
anti-nepotism laws, 230
anti-poverty policies. *See* principles for action
Appalachia, 6, 13, 20–21, 218
  author's driving tour of, 15–16
  collapse of Big Coal, 87–92, 169
  corruption in, 128–46
  cultural stereotypes of, 36, 72
  drug epidemic in, 69–87, 137–38
    causes, 74–81
    lack of social infrastructure, 10, 75–79, 81–87, 91–92
    role of churches, 69–70, 73, 80–81, 85–87, 90–91
  drug epidemic in, 106–8
  health disparities in, 91–92, 166–68
  high school completion rates in, 39–40
  history of Big Coal in, 33–37, 169–74
  investing in social infrastructure in, 232–34
  revolts and strikes (Coal Wars), 169–74
  tradition of violence in, 106–8, 232–34
Appalachian Regional Commission (ARC), 232
Arkansas Food Riot of 1931, 170
Arnett, Douglas, 134–35, 237
Auerbach, Jerold, 175
Axis Coffee Shop & Gathering Place, 142

Bailey, Jason, 142
Baker, Abner, 129
Baker, Abner, Jr., 131–33
Baker, Frazier, 103
Baldwin Piano and Organ Company, 199, 202
Barrera, Mario, 254
Barwick Coal Camp, 39, 88
Bates, Daniel, 131
Battle, Lawson, 148
Battle of Evarts, 171–72
Baudette, Minnesota, 227
Baugh, Labrandon, 113
Beckert, Sven, 24, 257
Beckley, West Virginia, 21
Belafonte, Harry, 120, 179
Bell County, 36, 170, 173
Benham, Kentucky, 15–16, 20–21
Beshear, Andy, 218
Bevel, James, 178
Beverly, Valdemir, 113
Bezos, Jeff, 150
Biden, Joe, 198
Big Coal, 9, 33–37, 71–72, 87–92, 134
Big Lick, Virginia, 34
Big Pharma, 71, 72–73
Big Timber, 9, 71–72, 87, 133–34
Billings, Dwight, 129–30, 132–33, 134–35
Bills, Robert, 47, 48
birth defects, 167
Black Americans
  civil rights activism of, 178–84, 196–97
  coal mining and segregation, 89–90
  education inequality, 59–64, 66–68
    before Brown, 41–44
    rise of segregation academies, 44–54
  farm ownership, 157–59, 174–78
  Index of Deep Disadvantage, 6
  invisible hand of structural racism
    (see government programs and structural racism)
  making structural racism visible and confronting it, 239–41
  race and tradition of violence, 94–121
  slavery and (see slavery)

Black Awakening in Capitalist America (Allen), 253
Black Convention Movement, 251
Blackfoot Indians, 226
Black Metropolis (Drake), 100
Black Mountain Coal Camp, 172
Black Panthers, 252
Black Power, 182–83, 253
Black Power (Ture and Hamilton), 253
Black Skin, White Masks (Fanon), 252
Blauner, Robert, 253–54, 255
Blee, Kathleen, 129–30, 132–33, 134–35
Block, Sam, 178–79
Blue, Michael, 162–63, 164
Blue Diamond Mining Camp, 37
Bolivar County, 15, 99, 174
bookstores, 235–36
Boone, Daniel, 34–35
Boothe, Mary, 183
Bowling, Paul, 140
bowling alleys, 9, 75–76, 82, 88, 93, 235
Boyd Shaw, Tamala, 62–64
Boys & Girls Clubs, 233
brain drain, 227
Branton, Wiley, 180
Breathitt County, 141–42
Briscoe, Dolph, 190, 193
Brooks County, 7–8, 9, 214–17
  corruption in, 127
  education inequality in, 44, 62, 65
  intergenerational mobility rates, 118–19
Brough, Charles Hillman, 95
Brown, Anjuan, 204
Brown, James S., 35
Brownsville, Texas, 55, 65
Brown v. Board of Education, 40–41, 45–46, 54–55, 67, 178, 183, 213
Bryant, Deborah, 123
Bryant, Phil, 123
Buffalo County, 228–29
Bunyan, Paul, 226

Cadle, Tillman, 170
Caldwell, Jeremy "Ta-Ta," 107
Campbell, John, 130
Camp Pike, 95

Capitol insurrection of 2021, 198
Capone, Al, 176
Cardenas, Antonio, 186, 187
Carl, Fred, Jr., 202
Carmichael, Stokely, 9, 182–83, 253
Carnegie, Andrew, 234
Carolina Eastern, 148
Carpenter, C. T., 176
Carr, Patrick, 227
Carrizo Springs High School, 58
Casanova, Pablo Gonzalez, 253
Casas, Maria, 65
Case, Anne, 72, 144–45
Caste and Class in a Southern Town
        (Dollard), 42, 99–104, 117, 118
Catfish Farmers of America, 200
catfish farming, 199–202, 211
Caudill, Harry M., 16, 73, 132
Chad's Hope, 80–81
Cherokee Indians, 34–35
Chicago
    heat wave of 1995, 77–78
    race riot of 1919, 99
    violence in, 99, 100, 106, 232–33
Chicago Commission on Race
        Relations, 99
Chicago Tribune, 46
Chickasaw Nation, 24
Children of the Dream (Johnson), 66–68
Child Tax Credit, 237
Chippewa Indians, 226
Choctaw Nation, 24
Citizens' Council, 45, 213
Citizens' Councils, 40, 45–46, 49–51
"citizenship schools," 178–79
Civil Rights Act of 1964, 45–46, 182,
        183
civil rights movement, 49, 116, 178–97
    in Mississippi, 178–84
    in South Texas, 184–96
Civil War, 11, 25, 30, 33–34, 132,
        157–58, 196
Clark, Kenneth, 9
Clay, Bill, 233–34
Clay County, 7–8, 9
    author's driving tour of, 15–16,
        74–75
    collapse of Big Coal, 87–92

corruption in, 128–46
    rooting out, 236–38
drug epidemic in, 69–87, 106–8,
        137–38
    causes of, 74–81
    role of churches, 69–70, 73,
        80–81, 85–87, 90–91
education inequality in, 230
history of, 35–37
new employment opportunities in,
        217–19
revolts and strikes (Coal Wars),
        170–71
tradition of violence in, 106–8
welfare and labor force
        participation rates, 207
Clay County Development Association,
        134
Clay County High School, 141
Clay County Historical Society, 217,
        218
Cleveland, Allen, 48
climate change, 152
Coal Country, 8, 20–21
    author's driving tour of, 15–16
    collapse of Big Coal, 87–92
    drug epidemic in, 69–87
        causes, 74–81
        role of churches, 69–70, 73,
            80–81, 85–87, 90–91
        social infrastructure, 10, 75–79,
            81–87, 91–92
    high school completion rates in,
        39–40
    history of Big Coal, 33–37
    revolts and strikes in, 169–74
coal mining
    collapse of, 87–92, 169
    health effects of, 91–92, 166–68
    history of, 33–37, 169–74
    mountaintop mining removal,
        35–36, 167
    revolts and strikes, 169–74
Coal Towns (Shifflett), 89–90, 91
Coal Wars, 170–73
Cobb, James C., 11, 24
Cobb, Ned, 11
Cochran, Thad, 201

cockfights, 80
Cohn, David, 25
Coleman, James, 262–63
Collins, Robert, 114
Colonialism in Modern America (Lewis), 254
Colored Farmers' Alliance, 96–97
Community Action Program (CAP), 135, 237
Community Kitchen, 205
community-level trauma, 258
community schools, 51
Conn, Eric, 143
contentment sociology, 88–89
Contested Waters (Wiltse), 85
continuing legacies of place, 259
Corkran, Harold, 46
Cornejo, Juan, 185, 186, 187, 192, 195, 237
corruption, 9–10, 122–46
    in Clay County, 128–46
    Mississippi welfare funds scandal, 122–26
    rooting out, 236–39
Cotton Belt, 6, 8, 13, 19–20, 224
    author's driving tour of, 15, 92–93
    Black farm ownership, 157–59, 174–78
    civil rights activism in, 92, 173–84, 196–97, 198, 221
    education inequality in, 39–54, 60–61, 68
        Black children, 41–42, 44
        high school completion rates, 39–40
        health impacts of industrial agriculture, 166–67
    history of, 22–28, 170, 198–214
    new employment opportunities in, 198–214, 221, 242
    research and histories of, 11, 96
    tradition of violence in, 10, 94–104, 106, 108–16, 118, 119–21, 231
Cotton Belt Communist Party, 251
cotton gins, 23, 26
Council of Federated Organizations (COFO), 181

COVID-19 pandemic, 7, 13, 60, 63, 70–71, 81, 241
critical race theory, 231
Cromwell, Oliver, 96–97
cronyism, 136, 239
Cross-S Ranch, 30–31
Crow Creek Reservation, 228–29
Crystal City, Texas, 8, 19–20, 21 30, 226, 243
    civil rights activism in, 184–96
    corruption in, 127
    education inequality in, 39–41, 44, 65–66
        Chicano resistance and white flight, 54–58
    new employment opportunities in, 215–16, 222
Crystal City Development Corporation, 190
Crystal City High School, 44, 55, 61–62, 64–65, 194
    cheerleader revolt, 55–59, 62, 65
Crystal City Internment Camp, 243
Crystal City Spinach Festival, 19
cultural stereotypes, 36, 72
"culture of poverty," 36
Culver, Jeff, 138, 139, 142–43
Cumberland Valley District Health Department, 238
cumulative measures of disadvantage, 262, 264
Curry, Angela, 60–61, 204–5, 221
cyclical measures of disadvantage, 262, 263

Dakota War of 1862, 228–29
Daniel Boone Development Council, 135
Darwin, Minnesota, 227
Davis, Elizabeth, 100
Davis, John, 123, 125–26
Davis, William Boyd "Allison," 11, 41, 42, 100–103
Davis Elementary School, 199
Day, Kenneth, 137
day schools, 51
"deaths of despair," 72
Deaton, Angus, 72, 144–45

decolonization, 252
"deep disadvantage"
    Index of Deep Disadvantage (*see*
        Index of Deep Disadvantage)
    map of enslavement from 1860
        compared with, 11, *12*
    use of term, 4
Deep South (Davis), 41, 100–103
deforestation, 167
Del Monte, 54, 185, 186–87
Delta Catfish, 200, 208
Delta & Pine Land Company, 174
Delta Regional Authority (DRA), 232
Delta Streets Academy, 63
Democratic National Convention
    (1964), 121
Desmond, Matthew, 2
DeSoto School, 46, 59, 94
Detroit, 240–41
DiBiase, Brett, 123–24
DiBiase, Ted, 123–24
disability benefits, 73, 110, 141–45, 208
Dittmer, John, 179, 181
Doar, John, 180–81
Dollard, John, 11, 26, 42, 45, 99–104,
    117, 118
Door of Hope Christian Church, 162
Dos Passos, John, 172–73
Douglass, Frederick, 9, 251
Downtown Manchester Market Place,
    217, 236
Drake, St. Clair, 100
Dreiser, Theodore, 172–73
drought, 152, 170, 215
drug epidemic, 9, 69–87
    causes of, 74–81
    corruption and, 123–24, 136, 137, 139
    lack of social infrastructure, 10,
        75–79, 81–87, 91–92
    role of churches, 69–70, 73, 80–81,
        85–87, 90–91
    violence and, 106–8, 110, 116
Du Bois, W. E. B., 159, 251
Ducas, Andrea, 2–3
Duffy, Meg, 6–7, 151, 160, 161
Duggan, Mike, 240
Duncan, Cynthia, 140
Dupree, Marcus, 123

East, Clay, 175
Eastland, Jim, 180
Echeverría, Luis, 191
Economic Policy Institute, 116–17
Edmund Pettus Bridge, 93
education inequality, 9, 39–68
    before *Brown* in Cotton Belt, 41–44
    Chicano resistance and white flight,
        54–58
    ending separate and unequal
        schooling, 230–31
    improving quality, 59–66
    rise of segregation academies,
        44–54
Elaine Massacre of 1919, 94–96, 97
election of 1932, 173, 175
election of 2020, 198
elite capture, 134, 138–39, 237
Elkhorn Coal Company, 88
Eller, Ronald, 134
Emmett Till Antilynching Act
    of 2022, 98
"Emmett Till Generation," 119–20
Emmett Till Square, 221
Empire of Pain (Keefe), 72–74
endorphins, 83
England Food Riot of 1931, 170
enkephalins, 83
environmental degradation, 166–68
Equal Justice Initiative, 15, 95, 97, 119
Espy, Mike, 198
Estep, Bill, 69
eugenics, 36
Evangelist, Michael, 82
Every Man Has His Price (DiBiase),
    123–24
extreme weather, 151, 152

Fairview Plantation, 175
Falfurrias, Texas, 62, 127, 216–17
Fanon, Frantz, 252
Farmer, Joe, 142
Farm Security Administration (FSA),
    178
Favre, Brett, 124, 126
Federal Emergency Management
    Agency (FEMA), 148–49, 154–57,
    168

Fentress, Ellen Ann, 52–53
Fisk University, 11, 27, 99
Flavelle, Christopher, 164–65
Floyd County, 88–89
Forgotten Time (Willis), 96
Forman, North Dakota, 225
Fort Thompson, 229
"forty acres and a mule," 157–58, 226
Four Seasons Ranch, 215
Fox, John, Jr., 36
fracking, 214–16
Frazier, Garrison, 158, 159
Freedmen's Bureau, 158
Freedom Rides, 178
Freedom Schools, 181–82
Freedom Summer, 121, 181–84
From the Mississippi Delta (Holland),
    120–21
Frost, William Goodell, 36
Fuquay, Michael, 46–47, 49, 53, 61
"furnish system," 27

Garcia, Juan Martin, 186
Gardner, Burleigh, 100
Gardner, Mary, 100
Garland, Jim, 171
Garrand-White feud, 130–34
Garrard, Daniel, 130–31
Garrard, James, 130–31
Garrett, Hilton, 89–90, 91
Garza, Letty, 127
Garza, Rochelle, 54
Gates, Bill, 150
Gates, Henry Louis, Jr., 158
Gates, Jimmie E., 122–23
geology and destiny, 21–22
Gini Index, 150–51, 262
glyphosate, 166–67
God's Closet, 76, 81, 233
Goose Creek, 128–29, 132
government benefits, 122, 141–45
    See also welfare
government corruption. *See* corruption
government programs and structural
    racism, 10, 147–67
    Black farm ownership, 157–59
    health disparities, 166–68
    history of, 157–59

making racism visible and
    confronting it, 239–41
property ownership claims, 154–57,
    159–60, 161–62
Sellers vs. Nichols, 10, 151–57,
    160–66
Gramsci, Antonio, 251
Gray, Freddie, 239
Great Depression, 20, 159, 169, 226
Great Migration, 159
Great Pee Dee River, 20, 152
Great Recession of 2008, 203, 204
Green, Christie, 238
Greene, Catherine, 22–23
Greene, Nathanael, 22–23
Greenwood, Mississippi, 19–20, 25–26
    civil rights activism in, 178–84, 253
    corruption in, 122–26, 139–40
    education inequality in, 59–64
    ending violence and sparking
        mobility, 234–35
    investing in social infrastructure in,
        234–35
    new employment opportunities in,
        198–214, 219–21
    tradition of violence in, 10, 108–16,
        232–34
Greenwood Commonwealth, 10, 20, 112,
    113–14, 125, 201, 204, 236
Greenwood Community Center, 220
Greenwood Comprehensive Plan, 61
Greenwood Cotton Ball, 20, 220
Greenwood County Jail, 205
Greenwood High School, 60, 63, 236
Greenwood-Leflore-Carroll Economic
    Development Foundation, 61,
    203–4, 221
Greenwood Leflore Civic Center, 220
Greenwood Mentoring Group, 233
Gregory, Dick, 179
Grisham, John, 200
Growing Up in the Black Belt (Johnson),
    99, 101–2
Guerrero, Andi, 66, 222
gun violence, 104–16, 232–33
Gutiérrez, Jose, 55–56, 57, 185,
    188–92
Guzman, Maricela, 62, 64, 194–95

H2-A visas, 210–11, 240
Hacker, Vernon, 137
Hamer, Fannie Lou, 120
Hamilton, Charles V., 253
Hand County, 229
Harlan County, 15–16
Harlan County War, 170–73
Harlan Miners Speak (report), 173
Harris, Clint, 136
Harris, Jack, 136
Harrison, Eliza, 160, 161
Harris Russell Farms, 211
Hawkins, Van, 177
Hayneville School, 49
Haywood, Harry, 251
Head Start, 235
health, 270–71
health disparities, 3–4, 5, 27–28,
    166–68, 262
    Index of Deep Disadvantage, 4–6, 5,
        11, 14, 270–71
Heart of David Ministry, 124
Hechter, Michael, 254, 255
"heir's property," 154–57, 161–62
Helena, Arkansas, 94–95
Help, The (movie), 203
Hendryx, Michael, 167
Hernandez, Mario, 186, 187
Highlander Folk School, 179
high school graduation rates, 9,
    39–40, 42
"hillbillies," 36, 72
Hillbilly Elegy (Vance), 72
Hodousek, Carrie, 70–71
Holland, Ida Mae, 120–21
Homestead Acts, 158–59, 226
Hoover, Herbert, 170, 171
Hoovervilles, 170
Hopkins, Barbara, 151–57, 162–64,
    220
Horse Creek, 88
Hotchkiss, Jedediah, 33–34
housing affordability, 267
Housing and Urban Development
    (HUD), 160
Howard University, 119, 182
"hunger hypothesis," 118–19, 241
hunting resorts, 215–16

Hurricane Florence, 147–48, 152, 160,
    162, 164, 165
Hurricane Harvey, 162
Hurricane Matthew, 147–48, 152, 165
Hyde-Smith, Cindy, 198

If You Lived Here You'd Be Home by Now
    (Ingraham), 225–26
immigration (immigrants), 37, 216–17,
    226, 254
Impact Outdoor Adventures, 217
income inequality. See inequality
Index of Deep Disadvantage, 4–6, 5, 11,
    14, 223, 255–56, 261–74
    author's driving tour of places,
        13–16
    geographic unit of analysis, 271–74
    selected outcomes for communities
        by index rank, 266
    sources of data for, 268–71
Index of Greatest Advantage, 223–29
Indianola, Mississippi, 45, 99
Individuals and Households Program
    (IHP), 154, 165
industrial agriculture, health impacts of,
    166–67
inequality, 9, 35, 140–41, 149–51,
    223–24, 228
infant mortality rate, 3, 4, 166–67
Ingraham, Christopher, 225–26
Inland Steel, 88–89
Institute for Health Metrics and
    Evaluation (IHME), 105
intergenerational mobility, 4, 5, 209,
    271
    ending violence and sparking,
        231–34
    violence and, 117–19
Internal Colonialism (Hechter), 254
internal colonies
    as distinctive perspective, 257–60
    history of a concept, 251–57
    Index of Deep Disadvantage, 4–6,
        5, 11, 14
    living legacy of, 38
    See also specific places
International Harvester Company, 15,
    16, 21

interpersonal violence, 104–8, *105*
invisible hand of structural racism.
     See government programs and
     structural racism
Ireland, Robert, 128

Jackson, Mary "Aunt Molly," 173
Jackson, William, 50
Jakle, John, 129
Jang-Trettien, Christine, 7, 53–54
Japanese Americans, internment of,
     190, 243–44
Jefferson, Thomas, 23
Jennings, Johnny, 202, 214
Jenny Lind houses, 79
Jim Crow laws, 15, 43, 67, 89–90, 98,
     99, 197, 207, 211
Johnson, Andrew, 158, 226
Johnson, Charles S., 11, 27–28, 49, 99,
     101–2, 103–4, 117, 174–75
Johnson, Kenton, 113
Johnson, Lanora, 7, 83, 151–52
Johnson, Lyndon B., 3, 17
Johnson, Rucker, 66–68, 230
Johnston, Oscar, 174
Jones, Billy, 147–48
Jordan, David, 221
Jordan, Edd, 137
Justice Department, 180–81

Kalich, Tim, 125
Keefe, Patrick, 72–74
Kefalas, Maria, 227
Keillor, Garrison, 229
Kennedy, Edward "Ted," 57–58,
     191–92
Kennedy, Robert F., 39, 88, 180
"Kentucky Miners' Wives' Ragged
     Hungry Blues" (song), 173
Kenyatta, Jomo, 252
Kerry, John, 146
Kiffmeyer, Thomas, 135
King, Martin Luther, Jr., 120, 253
King Ranch, 31
Kitchens, Karin, 196–97
Kizzire, Melba, 89
Klinenberg, Eric, 77–78, 82, 85, 86,
     234–35

Kling, Karen, 7
Knipe, Edward E., 254
Kristof, Nicholas, 141
Ku Klux Klan (KKK), 132, 175
Kyle Mills Trucking & Custom
     Harvesting, 211

labor force participation rate, 206–9
labor strikes, 170–78
Ladner, Joyce, 119–20
land titles, 154–57
La Raza Unida Party, 188–96, 237
Lary, Curtis, 180
Lasater, Dale, 31
Lasater, Ed, 31
Layton, R. B., 47
Lee, Robert E., 33–34
LeFlore, Greenwood, 24
Leflore County, 6, 8, 10, 15
     civil rights activism in, 178–80
     education inequality in, 59–63
     income inequality in, 150–51
     new employment opportunities in,
          198–214, 219–21
     tradition of violence in, 10, 96–100,
          114, 116, 118, 119–21
Leflore County Board of Supervisors,
     114, 179, 221
Leflore County Massacre, 96–97
Leflore Legacy Academy, 62–63, 220
Left Behind, The (Wuthnow), 140, 226
Legacy Museum (Montgomery), 15
Leland High School, 47–48
Le Mars, Iowa, 227
Lenin, Vladimir, 251
Letcher County, 156
Lewis, Carmen, 128, 138, 139, 142, 217,
     236–37
Lewis, Helen Matthews, 254
Lewis, John, 172, 182
Lexington Herald-Leader, 69, 70, 135,
     145–46
libraries, 234–35
life expectancy, 3–4, 5, 151, 267
Lincoln, Abraham, 158
literacy rates, 9, 38, 48, 65, 156, 211
"little kingdoms," 128
     See also corruption

Little Pee Dee River, 148
logging, 71–72, 87, 133–34
Lonoke County Food Riot of 1931, 170
Louisiana Purchase, 23
Lo-Vaca Gathering Company, 191–92
Lowndes Academy, 45, 48–49
Lowry, Robert, 97
Lumber River, 148, 152
Lynch, Kentucky, 15–16, 21
lynchings, 15, 53, 95–97, 98, 101–3, 116–17, 119–21, 176, 178–79

Machesky, Nathaniel, 182, 183–84
macro-level costs of inequality, 259–60
Main Street Greenwood, 212
Malcolm X, 9
Maldonado, Manuel, 186, 187
Manchester, Kentucky
    church march of 2004, 69–70, 73, 81
    collapse of Big Coal, 87–92
    corruption in, 128, 134–43
        rooting out, 236–37
    drug epidemic in, 69–72, 75, 86–87
    new employment opportunities in, 217–19, 221–22
Manchester Baptist Church, 69–70, 73, 81, 86–87, 141
Mandle, Jay, 25
Mann, Liv, 7, 83, 118–19
Manthorne, Jason, 177–78
March Against Fear (1966), 182
Maricle, Cletus, 137, 138, 139
Marion County, 6–8, 156, 220
    corruption in, 127–28
    education inequality in, 44–45
    government programs and structural racism, 10, 147–66
    history of, 157–59
    making it visible and confronting it, 239–41
    property ownership claims, 154–57, 159–60, 161–62
    Sellers vs. Nichols, 10, 151–57, 160–66
    history of tobacco farming in, 28–29
    income inequality in, 150–51
    investing in social infrastructure in, 234–35

Marion County Long Term Recovery Group, 162
Marvell Academy, 46, 48, 49, 59, 94
McAdams, Carolyn, 108–9, 114
McCormick, Maureen, 200
McCown, Bryan, 143
McKinley, William, 103
McWhorter, Charlie, 81
Medicaid, 71, 73
Medicare, 154
Memmi, Albert, 252
Mendoza, Reynaldo, 186
Meredith, James, 182
Messner, Steven, 116
Mexican American Chamber of Commerce, 186
Mexican Americans, 32–33
    civil rights activism of, 184–96
    education inequality of, 42–44
        Chicano resistance and white flight, 54–58
Mexican Revolution, 32
migrant workers, 30, 33, 54, 210–11, 216–17, 228, 240
Miller, Emily, 7, 83
Miller, Nathaniel, 128
Miller, Phineas, 23
Mills, Kyle, 211
Milwaukee Tool Company, 203–6, 208, 219
"mineral men," 35
Miners, Millhands, and Mountaineers (Eller), 134
Mingo County, 174
Minnesota, 225–28
Mississippi Business Journal, 204
Mississippi Community Education Center, 123
Mississippi Delta, 6–7
    author's driving tour of, 15
    civil rights activism in, 178–84
    corruption in, 122–26
    education inequality, 45–54, 59–60, 59–64
        high school completion rates, 39–40
    history of, 22–28

Mississippi Delta (*cont.*)
  investing in social infrastructure
    in, 235
  new employment opportunities in,
    198–214
  tradition of violence in, 94–99, 102,
    106, 120–21, 232
  See also Cotton Belt
Mississippi Department of Corrections,
  205
Mississippi Department of Education,
  60, 126
Mississippi Department of Human
  Services (MDHS), 122–23
Mississippi Freedom Democratic Party
  (MFDP), 121, 181–82, 183
Mississippi Freedom Trail, 182–83
Mississippi River, 94, 96
Mississippi Summer Project, 181–84
Mississippi welfare funds scandal,
  122–26
Missouri Sharecropper Roadside
  Demonstration of 1939, 177
Mitchell, Harry, 176
Mitchell, Harry Leland, 175, 177
Montejano, David, 32
Montgomery, Alabama, 15
Moore, Joan Willard, 254
Moses, Bob, 120, 178–79, 180
Most Southern Place on Earth, The
  (Cobb), 11, 24
mountaintop mining removal, 35–36,
  167
Moya, Maricruz, 7
Mulberry Grove, Georgia, 22–23
Mullins, South Carolina, 7–8, 20, 29
Mullins Golden Leaf Festival, 20
Myers, Connor, 176
Myrtle Beach, 150

NAACP, 50, 183
National Assessment of Educational
  Progress, 60
National Guard, 97, 148, 171, 172
National Industrial Recovery Act
  (NRA), 173–74
National Miners Union (NMU), 172–73
Nation at Risk (report), 66, 207

"nation within a nation," 9
Native Americans, 6, 11, 13, 34–35,
  226, 228–29, 256–57
Natural Amenities Scale, 225
Navarro, Armando, 184
Nelson, Paul, 122
Nelson, Willie, 203
Nevin, David, 47, 48
New, Nancy, 123, 124, 125–26, 139
New, Zach, 125–26
New Deal, 159, 173–75, 237
Newkirk, Vann, 159, 168
New Lots Library, 235
New Summit Academy, 139
New York City, 5, 150–51, 223, 235, 272
Nichols, South Carolina, 10, 147–48,
  151, 153, 161–63, 165–66
Niebuhr, Reinhold, 176
Night Comes to the Cumberlands
  (Caudill), 73
Nkrumah, Kwame, 252, 253
Noem, Kristi, 13
Norcross, Hiram, 175
Norfolk and Western Railway, 34
North American Free Trade Agreement
  (NAFTA), 202, 241–43
North New Summit School, 63
"nothing to do," 74–81
nuclear family and addiction, 84
Nye, Thomas Carter, 29–30, 31

Obama, Barack, 239
Odum, Howard W., 258
Office of Economic Opportunity
  (OEO), 135
Oglala Lakota County, 13
Olmsted, Frederick Law, 209, 258
Operation Peace Treaty, 114–16, 232,
  241
opioid epidemic, 9, 69–87
  See also drug epidemic
Our Town (Wilder), 14
Ox Ranch, 216
OxyContin, 72–73, 137–38, 145, 219

Palaces for the People (Klinenberg),
  77–78, 82, 85, 86, 234, 235
Palacios, Diana, 55, 56–57

Pan-Africanism, 253
Parchman Farm, 126, 205
Park, Robert E., 99
Parsons, Ryan, 6–7, 11, 111, 113
Patterson, Robert "Tut," 45–46
Payne, Charles, 181, 183
Pearson, Shun, 115, 232
Pee Dee Academy, 44–45
Pee Dee region, 6–8, 20, 21
    author's driving tour of, 10, 44–45
    corruption in, 127–28
    drug epidemic in, 69–87
    education inequality in, 44–45
    government programs and
        structural racism, 10, 147–67
        Black farm ownership, 157–59
        history of, 157–59
        property ownership claims,
            154–57, 159–60, 161–62
        Sellers vs. Nichols, 10, 151–57,
            160–66
    health impacts of industrial
        agriculture, 166–67
    history of, 28–29
People's Grocery (Memphis), 103
pesticides, 166–67
Peterson, Nick, 116
Phillips, Ulrich, 25
Phillips County
    education inequality in, 46, 59
    tradition of violence in, 94–104
Pillar of Salt, The (Memmi), 252
"pill mills," 74
Pillow Academy, 46, 49, 52–53
Pinderhughes, Charles, 251, 255
Pine Ridge Indian Reservation, 13
Pinkins, Ty, 210–11
Pinson, Jonathan, 127
Pitt Farms, 210–11
place-based disadvantage, 2–13
    Index of Deep Disadvantage, 4–6,
        5, 11, 14
police shootings, 117
Political Association of Spanish-
    Speaking Organizations (PASSO),
    185–88
political corruption. See corruption
political patronage, 134, 230

poll taxes, 33, 38, 185–87
Popeye, 19, 21, 66, 187, 219, 226
poverty, 2–3, 140–41
    anti-poverty policies (see principles
        for action)
    education inequality and, 64–68
    Index of Deep Disadvantage, 4–6,
        5, 11, 14
    intergenerational mobility rates,
        117–19
    structural racism and, 150–51, 167
    violence and, 104, 118–19
    War on Poverty, 3, 17, 128, 134–35,
        142, 237
poverty rates, 65, 125, 223, 263, 268–70
Powdermaker, Hortense, 11, 41–42, 45,
    99, 101
Price, E. R. "Jack," 88–89
principal component analysis (PCA),
    5, 262
principles for action, 230–44
    bringing supply chains home, 241–43
    ending separate and unequal
        schooling, 230–31
    ending violence and sparking
        mobility, 231–34
    investing in social infrastructure in,
        234–36
    making structural racism visible and
        confronting it, 239–41
    rooting out corruption, 236–39
Proffit, Melvin, 89
Pryor, Ike T., 30
public libraries, 234–35
Pudup, Mary Beth, 131, 133–34
Purdue Pharma, 72–73, 145
Putnam, Robert, 75–76

quitclaim deeds, 154–57
Qureshi, Bilal, 244

race
    education inequality, 41–44, 66–68
    health disparities, 3–4, 27–28
    tradition of violence, 10, 94–121
    See also Black Americans
Race and Class in the Southwest (Barrera),
    254

"race mixing," 43
racism, 89–90, 212–14, 231
    See also government programs and
        structural racism
Radford, Virginia, 14
Ramsey, Alexander, 228–29
Raper, Arthur, 173
Raza Unida Party, 188–96, 237
READI Chicago, 232–33
Reagan, Ronald, 66, 207
"rebel yell" academies, 51
Reconstruction, 20, 49, 98, 158–59,
    179–80, 196, 198
Red Bird, Kentucky, 107
Red Cross, 170, 171, 243
Red Lake County, 225–27
Reece, Florence, 172
reparations, 157–58, 226, 243–44
Reséndez, Andrés, 256–57
resource curse, 257
Revolt Among the Sharecroppers
    (Niebuhr), 176
Revolutionary War, 22–23, 130
Rice, Christy, 141
Rice, Roy, 217
RICO (Racketeer Influenced and
    Corrupt Organizations Act), 73
Road to Poverty, The (Billings and Blee),
    129–30, 132–33, 134–35
Robert Wood Johnson Foundation, 2
Rogers, Frank Mandeville, 28–29
Rogers, Harold "Hal," 217, 218
Romer, Carl, 116–17
Roosevelt, Franklin D., 173–74, 258
Roosevelt, Theodore, 15
Rosengarten, Theodore, 11
Rubin, Richard, 46, 236
rural
    Index of Deep Disadvantage, 5, 5–6,
        11, 14
    use of term, 6
Russell Stover, 151

Sackler, Richard, 73
Saint Francis Center, 183–84, 220
Salemi, Jason, 81–82
Salstrom, Paul, 132
salt mining, 8, 9, 35, 36, 128–32

Samples, Karen, 135
Sampson, Robert, 259
San Antonio Express, 187
Sanborn Fire Insurance Company,
    25–26
Sanders, Sarah Huckabee, 231
Sandy Run Academy, 50
school desegregation, 45, 46, 48, 50, 51,
    53, 55, 67–68, 178, 230
school inequality. See education
    inequality
Schools That Fear Built, The (Nevin and
    Bills), 47, 48
Scott, Ed, 201
Scott, Shaunna, 171–72
Seattle, 6, 150, 223
segregation, 40–41, 43, 45–54, 89–90,
    92–93, 212–14
segregation academies, 40, 44–54, 231
Sellers, South Carolina, 10, 151–57,
    160–66
Selma to Montgomery Marches (1965),
    92–93
Sen, Amartya, 265
Shadow of the Plantation (Johnson), 99
sharecropping, 174–78
Sharkey, Patrick, 117–18, 119
Shaw, Boyd, 220
Shaw, Tamala Boyd, 220
Sherman, William Tecumseh, 157–58,
    226
Shifflett, Crandall, 89–90, 91
Shockley, John, 188–92
Shows, Ronnie, 126
Simington, Jasmine, 6–7, 151–52, 155,
    160
Simmons, W. J., 50–51
Sioux County Livestock Company, 225
Sioux Indians, 226, 228–29
Sizemore, Denver, 137–38
slavery (enslavement), 13, 24–27, 129,
    157–58, 196–97
    map of deep disadvantage compared
        to a map of enslavement from
        1860, 11, 12
Small, Mario, 235
Smith, Debbie Hewitt, 47
Smith, Harold, 199

SNAP (Supplemental Nutrition
    Assistance Program), 207–8
Snipp, C. Matthew, 256
social bonds, 10, 75–76
social infrastructure, 10, 149, 225
    drug epidemic and lack of, 75–79,
        81–87, 91–92
    investing in, 234–36
    use of term, 77–78
social isolation, 77, 83–84
Socialist Party, 175
social mobility, 271
    See also intergenerational mobility
social vulnerability index (SVI), 265
Softee Supreme Diaper Corporation,
    127
SOPAKCO, 151
South Africa, 252, 254
South African workers, 210–11, 240
South Carolina Tobacco Museum, 20
Southern Christian Leadership
    Conference (SCLC), 178
Southern Homestead Act of 1866,
    158–59
Southern Tenant Farmers Union
    (STFU), 175–78
South Texas, 6–9, 13, 19, 21, 222
    civil rights activism in, 184–96
    corruption in, 127
    education inequality, 39–41, 42–44,
        60–62, 64–66
        Chicano resistance and white
            flight, 54–58
        high school completion rates,
            39–40
    fracking, 214–16
    health impacts of industrial
        agriculture, 166–67
    history of, 29–33
    illegal immigration in, 216–17
    new employment opportunities in,
        214–17
    tradition of violence in, 106, 118–19
    See also Crystal City, Texas
Special Field Order No. 15, 157–58,
    226
SSDI (Social Security Disability
    Insurance), 73, 143

SSI (Supplemental Security Income),
    73, 141–42, 143
standardized testing, 53, 59–60, 64
Stanton, Edwin, 158
Staunton, Virginia, 33–34
Stennis, John, 180
Stewart, Megan, 196–97
Stivers, Robert, 218
Stockholm syndrome, 139
Stonega Coke and Coal, 88
Strong, Richard, 210–11
structural measures of disadvantage,
    262, 264
structural racism. See government
    programs and structural racism
Student Nonviolent Coordinating
    Committee (SNCC), 120–21,
    178–84, 253
suffrage, 38, 135, 182
Superstorm Sandy, 77
supply chains, 241–43
swimming pools, 77, 85–86
Szalavitz, Maia, 82–83

Tach, Laura, 238–39
Tallahatchie River, 119–20
Tally-Ho (Selma), 92–93, 236
TANF (Temporary Assistance for
    Needy Families), 122–26
Tateishi, John, 244
Taylor, Paul S., 31, 43–44
Taylor, Renee McCraine, 52
teacher shortages, 61
tenancy (tenant farming), 26–28, 98,
    174
Teres, Diana, 56
Testle, Jerry, 153–57, 168
Texas. See South Texas
Texas Appleseed, 165
Texas Classroom Teachers Association,
    189–90
Texas Rangers, 56, 186, 187, 192, 195
The, Evers., 181
Thomas, Norman, 175
Thompson, Bennie, 198
Till, Emmett, 53, 98, 119–20, 178–79,
    221
Tiller, James, 30

timber industry, 9, 71–72, 87, 133–34
tobacco, 7–8, 20–21, 28–29, 149
Tobacco Belt, 7–9, 20–21, 28–29, 220
Tocqueville, Alexis de, 75
Tolstoy, Leo, 224–25
Torrats-Espinosa, Gerard, 117–18, 119
Touré, Sékou, 253
"toxic South" perspectives, 258–59
Trans-Nueces, 31, 62, 214–17
Transylvania Company, 34–35
trauma theory, 258
Treaty of Dancing Rabbit Creek, 24
Treaty of Guadalupe Hidalgo, 30–31
Truly Disadvantaged, The (Wilson), 2
Trump, Donald, 198
Tulsa Race Massacre of 1921, 95–96
Tunica County, 94, 238–39
Turnblazer, William, 170–71
Turner, Ted, 203
Turnrow Book Co., 236

undocumented aliens (UDAs), 216–17
unemployment, 82, 127, 169–70, 184, 203, 204, 206, 209, 228, 239
unequal schooling, 10, 38, 230–31
    See also education inequality
United Mine Workers of America (UMWA), 91, 170–74
university extension programs, 237
US Border Patrol, 216–17
US Coal and Coke Company, 15–16
US Steel, 15–16, 88

Vance, J. D., 72
Vance, Rupert B., 258
Veteran's Land Board Scandal, 184–85
Vietnam War, 252–53
Viking Range, 202–3
violence, tradition of, 10, 94–121
    deaths by interpersonal violence, 104–8, 105
    ending, and sparking mobility, 231–34
    history in present day, 116–19
    intergenerational social mobility and, 117–19
Volunteers of America, 218

Voter Education Project, 180
voting rights, 38, 45–46, 135, 179–82, 182, 185–87, 198, 253
Voting Rights Act of 1965, 45–46, 182

Walder, John, 48
Wallace, Henry, 176
Waller, Altina, 131–32
Wall Street Crash of 1929, 169–70
Ward, Geoff, 116
Warner, W. Lloyd, 99–100
War on Poverty, 3, 17, 128, 134–35, 142, 237
Washington, Booker T., 15
Weathers, Lavoris, 114–15, 118, 119, 206, 232, 241
Welch, Isaiah, 34
welfare, 81, 140, 143–44, 207–8
    Mississippi welfare funds scandal, 122–26
"welfare queen," 207
Wells, Ida B., 11, 95, 103, 117
Wesley Chapel, 180
Wheelwright, Kentucky, 88–91
White-Garrand feud, 130–34
White, Daugh, 135–36, 137
White, Hugh, 130, 136
White, James, 130, 131
White, Jennings, 137, 138
White, John, 130
White, Kennon, 136
White, Michael, 217, 218
White, Shad, 123, 124
White, Susan, 131
"white flight," 48
white supremacy, 49, 52
Whitfield, Owen, 177
Whitney, Eli, 23, 33
Wilder, Thornton, 14
Williams, Cedric, 220–21, 233
Williams, Jhacova, 116–17
Williams, Mary, 220–21, 233
Willis, John, 24, 96
Wilson, William Julius, 2
Wiltse, Jeff, 85
Winfrey, Oprah, 203
Winter Garden, 19, 30–31, 214–17
    See also South Texas

Wolfe, Anna, 122–23, 126
Woodland Hills Academy, 47
Woofter, Thomas J., 26, 42, 45, 99–104,
      117, 118
workers' compensation, 73
Works Progress Administration, 26
World War I, 89
World War II, 190, 243
Wretched of the Earth, The (Fanon),
      252
Wright, Gavin, 257
Wright, Warren, 88
Wuthnow, Robert, 140, 226

Young, Jock, 104

Zavala County, 7–8, 9
      civil rights activism in, 184–96
      corruption in, 127
      education inequality in, 44, 56, 64,
            65, 66
      history of, 30–33
      intergenerational mobility rates,
            118–19
      new employment opportunities in,
            216–17
Zoorob, Michael, 81–82

About the Authors

KATHRYN J. EDIN is the William Church Osborn Professor of Sociology and Public Affairs at Princeton University. The author of nine books, Edin is widely recognized for using both quantitative research and direct, in-depth observation to illuminate key mysteries about poverty. "In a field of poverty experts who rarely meet the poor, Edin usefully defies convention" (*New York Times*).

H. LUKE SHAEFER is the Hermann and Amalie Kohn Professor and associate dean at the Ford School of Public Policy at the University of Michigan, where he directs Poverty Solutions, a presidential initiative that partners with communities to find new ways to prevent and alleviate poverty. The *New York Times* and *Time* magazine have credited Edin and Shaefer's research as one of the driving forces behind the expanded Child Tax Credit of 2021 that led to a historic decline in child poverty.

TIMOTHY J. NELSON is the director of undergraduate studies in sociology and lecturer of public affairs at the School of Public and International Affairs at Princeton University. He is the author of numerous articles on low-income fathers and is the coauthor, with Edin, of the award-winning *Doing the Best I Can: Fatherhood in the Inner City*.